# Praise for THE LAST SULTAN

"Ahmet Ertegun was a man who loved his music and wanted others to hear what may otherwise have gone unheard. . . . We first met when the Stones signed up with Atlantic. The stories began to flow, and a lot of them are in these pages. Robert Greenfield has done a masterful job of relating them. . . . I shall miss Ahmet. He was a great man and a great friend!"

—Keith Richards

"Ahmet Ertegun was a man of passion, loyalty, generosity, and fun, both sacred and profane, who could target like a laser what was authentic and worthwhile in the many worlds he bestrode so seamlessly and successfully. Greenfield's fascinating biography, *The Last Sultan,* gets it right, and I envy readers their opportunity to experience the life and times of this extraordinary man."

—Henry Kissinger

"In many ways, this book is the Bible of rock 'n' roll. A sacred tale rooted in the incredible life journey of my friend Ahmet Ertegun who touched not only me, but also so many other people in so many ways."

—Kid Rock

"Robert Greenfield has written a loving, vividly detailed, and utterly compelling history of one of the most fascinating lives of the twentieth century. . . . *The Last Sultan* is the remarkable odyssey of a truly remarkable man."

—Jann Wenner, Editor, Publisher, and Founder of *Rolling Stone*

"Ahmet Ertegun is not an easy subject—he was both indelible and opaque—but Greenfield has dug deeper than anyone ever has, to reveal one of the most complex Americans of the last half century."

—Taylor Hackford, Director/Producer of *Ray*

"Mesmerizing, entertaining, informative. . . . There are a great many delicious stories in this page-turning work. . . . A vivid portrait of Ertegun but also a colorful panorama of the indie record-business during and after its rough-and-tumble years, when bootleggers sold as many singles as the real labels, gangsters were always angling to squeeze in on the action, and payola was just part of the cost of doing business."

—Tom Nolan, *San Francisco Chronicle*

"Greenfield's book, the first posthumous biography of Ertegun, is also the first to bring Ertegun's story up to date and put it in perspective. . . . This is not your run-of-the-mill music-biz hagiography."

—Alex Abramovich, *The New York Times Book Review*

"Greenfield's portrait of Ertegun is an incisive and compelling account of the sometimes convoluted story of how Atlantic Records became possibly the most respected label in the business."

—Steven Daly, *Businessweek*

"An excellent biography of a titan in the music industry."
—*Booklist* (starred review)

"More than anything, *The Last Sultan* invites yet another round of applause for a man with golden ears, a wicked sense of humor, and a taste for living second to none."

—Jim Farber, *New York Daily News*

"Thoroughly researched and revealing, *The Last Sultan* likely will stand as the definitive work on one of the music industry's most memorable characters."

—Rege Behe, *Pittsburgh Tribune-Review*

"Ertegun was more than just management: He was music executive as rock star, a man who lived as large as the musicians, and presided over what could be called rock's greatest era."

—*Men's Journal*

"Robert Greenfield conjures an era in which music was a progressive cultural and economic force, twining the extraordinary story of Ahmet Ertegun's life with the evolution of pop. . . . The book bubbles with fashion, fame, money, name dropping—and insight into a man above all loyal to himself."

—Carlo Wolff, *Pittsburgh Post-Gazette*

"A compulsively readable, evenhanded biography of Atlantic Records' founder. . . . A flavorful, balanced piece of music-biz history."

—*Kirkus Reviews*

"This enchanting book captures the life and work of a seminal figure without whom the business of making records would not have had its lasting impact."

—*Library Journal*

Ahmet at Atlantic Records in the 1970s.

ALSO BY ROBERT GREENFIELD

*A Day in the Life: One Family, the Beautiful People,
and the End of the Sixties*

*Exile on Main Street: A Season in Hell with the Rolling Stones*

*Timothy Leary: A Biography*

*Dark Star: An Oral Biography of Jerry Garcia*

*Bill Graham Presents: My Life Inside Rock and Out*
(with Bill Graham)

*Temple*

*Haymon's Crowd*

*The Spiritual Supermarket: An Account of Gurus
Gone Public in America*

*S.T.P.: A Journey Through America with the Rolling Stones*

# THE LIFE AND TIMES OF AHMET ERTEGUN

# ROBERT GREENFIELD

# THE
# LAST
# SULTAN

SIMON & SCHUSTER PAPERBACKS

NEW YORK   LONDON   TORONTO   SYDNEY   NEW DELHI

Simon & Schuster Paperbacks
A Division of Simon & Schuster, Inc.
1230 Avenue of the Americas
New York, NY 10020

First Simon & Schuster paperback edition November 2012

SIMON & SCHUSTER PAPERBACKS and colophon are registered trademarks
of Simon & Schuster, Inc.

For information about special discounts for bulk purchases,
please contact Simon & Schuster Special Sales at
1-866-506-1949 or business@simonandschuster.com.

The Simon & Schuster Speakers Bureau can bring authors
to your live event. For more information or to book an event,
contact the Simon & Schuster Speakers Bureau at 1-866-248-3049
or visit our website at www.simonspeakers.com.

Designed by Akasha Archer

Manufactured in the United States of America

10   9   8   7   6   5   4   3   2   1

The Library of Congress has cataloged the hardcover edition as follows:
Greenfield, Robert.
    The last sultan : the life and times of Ahmet Ertegun / Robert Greenfield.
      p.   cm.
    Includes bibliographical references and index.
    1. Ertegun, Ahmet M.   2. Sound recording executives and producers—
United States—Biography.   I. Title.
    ML429.E72G74   2011
    781.64092—dc23
    [B]                    2011028507
    ISBN 978-1-4165-5838-5
    ISBN 978-1-4165-5840-8 (pbk)
    ISBN 978-1-4391-9862-9 (ebook)

Photo Credits
Armen Khachaturian/courtesy of Atlantic Records Archive: p. ii; Courtesy of the Ertegun
family: 1–4; Delia Potofsky Gottlieb/courtesy of the Library of Congress: 5; PoPsie
Randolph: 6, 7, 9–13; Atlantic Records Archive: 8, 17; Ivan Nagy/courtesy of Atlantic
Records Archive: 14; Joel Bernstein/courtesy of Atlantic Records Archive: 15; Courtesy of
Jean Pigozzi: 16, 18–23; Courtesy of Mica Ertegun: 24; Courtesy of Kid Rock: 25; Norma
Jean Roy/courtesy of Atlantic Records Archive: p. 355.

*for mica ertegun and selma goksel, ahmet's better angels*

# Contents

"He was hip. He was hip to the tip, as we say. He was not a square. He was someone who understood the idiom."

> —Herb Abramson, founding partner of
> Atlantic Records, on Ahmet Ertegun

"Ahmet had eyes to make records. He also had ears and tremendous taste."

> —Jerry Wexler, who succeeded Abramson as
> Ahmet Ertegun's partner at Atlantic Records

"Ahmet was sui generis. And then he made himself up as he went along."

> —Henry Kissinger, Ahmet Ertegun's friend

# A Day of Tribute in New York

April 17, 2007. In the tiny village New York can sometimes become when it honors one of its own who has fulfilled the dream of hope on which the city was built, the all-star tribute to Ahmet Ertegun scheduled to begin at six P.M. in the Rose Theater at the Time Warner Center on Columbus Circle was the talk of the town. Those who had labored long and hard to bring about what promised to be the event of the season as well as one of those once-in-a-lifetime evenings that could never happen anywhere else, literally could not think about anything else.

In his office at *Rolling Stone* magazine, Jann Wenner, who along with film director Taylor Hackford was producing the event, nervously wondered whether his old friend Mick Jagger was going to perform this evening. Ensconced in a suite at the Carlyle Hotel, Jagger, who had lost his ninety-three-year-old father only a few months earlier, was incommunicado. Making matters worse, Wenner had just learned that Keith Richards, who had been scheduled to do "Sixty Minute Man" by Billy Ward and the Dominoes at the tribute, had gone to England to be with his ailing mother and so would not be able to perform.

The invitation-only tribute was still the hottest ticket in town. Entry to the private party following the event at The Boat House in Central Park was so tightly controlled that those who feared they would not be allowed to attend either function were frantically doing all they could to wangle their way on to the guest list even at the very last minute.

Faced with the daunting task of doling out twelve hundred free tickets to an event that could have easily filled a much larger venue, Ahmet's assistant Frances Chantly had unwittingly turned up the pressure by insisting there be no reserved seating. To her way of thinking, those who truly loved Ahmet would be there early.

Showing no respect for the dead, a reporter from the *New York Post*'s always scurrilous "Page Six" gossip column, which had previously run a blind item about an aging record executive with a cane engaging in scandalous behavior with two women, called Ahmet's grieving widow at home that afternoon to ask if it was true that other women who were involved with her late husband would be at the tribute. As always, Mica Ertegun patiently explained that Americans did not understand how European women viewed such matters.

While she had not yet been able to bring herself to watch PBS's *American Masters* documentary about Ahmet, the film had been shown the night before at the Anthology Film Archives in the East Village. On the afternoon of the tribute, the documentary was shown again in a plush screening room at the Time Warner Center where cellophane-wrapped cookies bearing Ahmet's likeness from Eleni's Bakery were given to invited guests along with a 60th Anniversary Atlantic Records commemorative CD distributed by Starbucks featuring seventeen songs Ahmet had selected before his death.

Many of those who attended the screening decided the wisest course of action was to just wait there until the tribute began. Patiently, they then stood in line before a brace of secretaries who checked their names off lists before allowing them to board elevators to the fifth-floor theater. Leaving no doubt the stars had come out tonight for Ahmet and it was only in New York that such an event could have taken place, Tom Wolfe strolled through the lobby as Helen Mirren stepped from the elevator to join the crowd waiting to enter the theater. Standing in a long line of well-coiffed women in elegant dresses carrying little handbags suspended from gold chains and silver-haired captains of industry in expensive suits and dark blue blazers, the punk singer and poet Patti Smith looked incongruous yet somehow also at home.

Wearing black, Mica Ertegun sat in the front row of the theater with Ahmet's family and many of the artists who were scheduled to perform. As people filled the seats, there was a good deal of air-kissing, embracing, and handshaking across the rows. A large photograph of Ahmet stood on a bare stage framed by small trees. Befitting the course of his career, the program began with jazz.

Followed by horn players and two drummers, Wynton Marsalis, the artistic director of Jazz at Lincoln Center and a member of the selection committee of the Jazz Hall of Fame Ahmet had founded in his brother Nesuhi's name in 2004, walked through a side door playing trumpet like the second coming of Louis Armstrong on "Oh, Didn't He Ramble," a number often performed by New Orleans brass bands on their way back from a funeral.

Larger than life and sitting on a gilded throne in a three-piece suit, the great soul singer Solomon Burke spoke of "the little Turkish prince, our beloved brother Ahmet." Eric Clapton, whom Ahmet had first heard play forty years earlier at the Scotch of St. James in London, then took the stage. Wearing glasses with his hair closely cropped, Clapton said, "I loved Ahmet. He was like a father to me. In the old days, we'd have a drink and do some other things and any time that happened, he would start singing songs to me . . . We're going to do two of the songs he always sang—'Send Me Someone to Love' and the other by Sticks McGhee called 'Drinkin' Wine Spo-dee-O-Dee.' "

Backed by Dr. John on piano, a drummer, and a bass player, Clapton performed masterful versions of both songs. He then gave way to New York City's billionaire mayor Michael Bloomberg, who concluded his remarks by declaring, "And let us say, Ah-met!" The mayor was followed by Henry Kissinger, Bette Midler, Ben E. King, Kid Rock, and Sam Moore of Sam and Dave. After describing Ahmet as "a ducker and diver" who gave up his student visa to remain in America so he could make his life in music, Taylor Hackford introduced a videotaped statement by an ailing Jerry Wexler in Florida.

Looking old and gaunt in a soft brown sailor's cap, glasses, and a green shirt without a collar, Wexler talked about Ahmet's sense of "irony and tomfoolery" and how he could be speaking in French to the French ambassador only to hang up the phone to greet a black musician by saying, "Hey, homes, what you know good?" Saying he did not know if he had ever specifically thanked Ahmet for giving him a life by making him a partner at Atlantic when he "had no qualifications whatsoever and no experience," Wexler stared directly into the camera and, with the New York street accent he had never lost, said, "Ahmet, thank you for opening the door for me. Thank you."

On a completely black stage, Phil Collins sat down at the piano to perform a stunning version of "In the Air Tonight," the song Ahmet had helped make a hit. After David Geffen told his classic and oft-repeated "bumping-into-geniuses" story about Ahmet, Stevie Nicks sang "Stand Back" and her version of Led Zeppelin's "Rock 'n' Roll."

Jann Wenner read a letter from Keith Richards in which the Stones' guitarist said he had looked up to Ahmet as he did to Muddy Waters. Then Wenner talked about Ahmet's formative role in the creation of the Rock and Roll Hall of Fame. He also recalled that when he asked Mica why Ahmet had looked so well while he was lying in a coma in the hospital, she told him, "Well, he hasn't been drinking." Bette Midler then returned to do her version of Bobby Darin's "Beyond the Sea."

More than two hours into the proceedings, Mick Jagger stepped to the podium. In a suit, a white shirt, and no tie, with his long hair trailing over his ears, a relaxed Jagger delivered what most people agreed was the best speech of the evening. Obviously enjoying himself, he began his remarks by saying, "Ahmet was a father figure, this is true. But to me, he was more like the wicked uncle with the wicked chuckle."

Addressing what he called "a diverse and fascinating group of people like ourselves," Jagger noted how only Ahmet could talk about geopolitics and medieval Islamic history and then pick the next Vanilla Fudge single. Jagger ended his remarks by reminiscing about a party during the 1970s when Ahmet had volunteered to hire strippers to entertain the Rolling Stones and then contacted an agency called the Widows Club who provided "rotund women of a certain age who stripped for free on the weekends."

Crosby, Stills, and Nash then took the stage. With Graham Nash on mouth harp and Stephen Stills on guitar, they did their version of the Beatles' "In My Life." Nash then said, "Here's our friend Neil." Hulking and stoop-shouldered with long hair and gray sideburns, Neil Young played acoustic guitar on "Helplessly Hoping." After the song ended, Nash said, "Here's something you don't see every day. I'm looking forward to this myself. This is Neil and Stephen doing a Buffalo Springfield song." He and Crosby then left the stage.

Leaning into the microphone, Young said, "Ahmet was our man. I just hope that today's musicians have someone like Ahmet taking care of them. Mica, thank you so much for taking care of him." Without having rehearsed it, Stills and Young then began playing "Mr. Soul," the classic Buffalo Springfield song Young had written in 1966 but the two men had not performed together in forty years.

Playing rhythm with so much intensity that he became a one-man band, Young sang in a haunting voice as Stills picked out the leads on his white Washburn electric guitar. Together, they created the kind of musical magic for which Ahmet had lived. When they were done, Young put his hands together and looked up at the heavens as though to give thanks the performance had all come out right in the end.

Ending the tribute nearly three hours after it began, Wynton Marsalis walked down the aisle playing "Down by the Riverside." As though they were now in a church, the crowd got to their feet and began clapping their hands in time. At the party that followed, Kid Rock and Dave Mason of Traffic, backed by Paul Shaffer's band, performed "Feelin' Alright" and Solomon Burke sang "Cry to Me."

While the evening was, as Eric Clapton wrote in his autobiography, both "entertaining and emotionally stirring," the guitarist also noted, "I still felt that had Ahmet been there in the flesh, he would have said something like, 'Let's get out of here and find the real shit.' "

Once he had found it, Ahmet would have drained every glass set before him and tapped his foot in time to the beat while telling the stories he loved best. Staying until the last note of music had been played, he would not have made his way home until the sun was rising. And then, just as he had always done while running Atlantic Records for seven decades, Ahmet would have checked in to see how his business was doing.

Like the subject of the song Wynton Marsalis had played to begin the tribute, Ahmet Ertegun had rambled in and out of town. He had rambled through the city and the street. Throughout the course of his long and astonishing life, Ahmet had rambled all around.

# ONE

# *Coming to America*

*"The older I get, the more I realize how Turkish I am. I display the prime characteristics of Turkish vices: indolence and excess."*
— Ahmet Ertegun

**1**

As much as any man who ever lived, Ahmet Ertegun loved to tell stories. That many of them happened to be about himself was never the point. In his unmistakable nasal hipster's voice tinged with the black inflections of the street and the syncopated rhythms of the jazz music he had loved since childhood, Ahmet always knew how to find the groove when he talked. With the smoke from a cigarette curling into his eyes and a drink in his hand, he was a born raconteur who could command an audience of any size. Taking just as much time as he needed to build to the punch line, Ahmet would tell his favorite stories over and over again, carefully polishing each one like a jeweler.

In a business where everyone loved to gossip and those who ran the world's leading record companies were constantly on the phone talking about one another in the most vulgar way imaginable, no one ever refused to take a call from the man whom they always referred to by only his first name. But then long before most of his colleagues had made their bones in an industry where the ordinary rules of conduct did not apply and the only way to stay on top was to continue putting out one hit after another, Ahmet was already a legend. On any given day during even a casual conversation, there was no knowing what might come out of his mouth. It was just one of the reasons people liked being around him.

Over the years, one story Ahmet loved to tell about himself was repeated constantly by those who would have never dared to criticize him in their own words. God only knows who told it to Steve Ross but David Geffen first heard the story from him. Mo Ostin and Joe Smith in Los Angeles knew it as did Robert Stigwood in London. Outliving the man it was about, the story was posted on a well-read music blog after Ahmet was no longer around to tell it. In its simplest form, the story goes like this.

During the early 1970s, Kit Lambert and Bill Curbishley, the current and future managers of The Who, found themselves locked in a particularly difficult and contentious negotiation with Ahmet in his second-floor office at Atlantic Records in New York City. Although Atlantic had made a ton of money distributing "Fire," a huge but very unlikely worldwide hit by the Crazy World of Arthur Brown that Lambert had produced on his own label, their discussion soon reached a sticking point.

No matter what Lambert or Curbishley said, Ahmet simply would not budge. Knowing he had nothing to lose, Lambert, who in Curbishley's words could sometimes be "a bit Barnum and Bailey," suddenly leaped to his feet and stormed out of the office in a rage. Returning a few seconds later, he threw open the door and shouted at Ahmet, "Do you know why there's so much anti-Semitism in the world?"

Always unflappable, most especially in situations where money was on the line and he was the one who would have to pay it, Ahmet said, "No, Kit. Why is that?" "Because," Lambert replied, "Turks don't travel." Slamming the door behind him, Lambert then made his final exit as Ahmet collapsed with laughter behind his desk.

More than most people in the music business, Kit Lambert would have understood the historical basis of his remark. Like his father, a well-known classical composer, he had been educated at Trinity College, Cambridge. He was also the grandson of the painter who had been commissioned by the Australian government to document that nation's crushing defeat by Turkish forces commanded by Mustafa Kemal at the Battle of Gallipoli during World War I.

Whether any of this was actually on Kit Lambert's mind that day, no one can say for sure. However, the man who was the butt of his joke did not need anyone to explain it to him. In a business dominated by hard-driving Jewish businessmen, Ahmet was the ultimate outsider. On some level, this was also always his role in the world.

Although Ahmet loved to mingle in the most rarefied circles of high society, he never truly belonged there either. In the most famous piece ever written about him, an unnamed woman who seemed comfortable in this world noted there was no one Ahmet did not "feel snubbed by." Whenever another of his socialite friends sensed he was about to say or do something inappropriate, she would caution him by saying, "Ahmet, don't go Turkish on me. Don't go Turk." In order to warn the Rolling Stones that Ahmet was about to appear backstage before a show, their tour manager would tell them, "Boys, Ataturk's coming."

Although he left his native land at the age of two and was shocked to see what Turkey was like when he returned there for the first time six years later, everything Ahmet was and all that he became was shaped by the place of his birth. Had it not been for the fall of the Ottoman Empire and the subsequent creation of the modern Turkish republic, his own life would have followed an entirely different and far more predictable path. And yet to the very core of his being, he could not have been more Turkish.

For countless generations, "the Turk," in the words of Stephen Kinzer, the author of *Crescent and Star: Turkey Between Two Worlds,* had always been viewed in the West as the "scourge of civilization. His chief characteristics were thought to include mendacity, unbridled lust, sudden violence and a passion for gratuitous cruelty." Beginning in 1095 when Pope Urban II sent the Crusaders to reclaim the holy city of Jerusalem from the Ottoman Empire, "Europeans came to perceive Turks as the epitome of evil. They were presumed to be not only bent on destroying Christianity but also determined to kill or enslave every man, woman, and child in Christendom." Five centuries later, Martin Luther, who began the Protestant Reformation, declared, "The Turks are the people of the wrath of God." In a letter to King Fredrick II of Prussia during the eighteenth century, the famed French essayist Voltaire wrote, "I shall always hate the Turks. What wretched barbarians!"

After the Allies defeated the Ottoman Empire in World War I, the onerous conditions imposed by the Treaty of Sèvres were specifically designed to reduce a once great power to ruins. In large part, Mustafa Kemal's nationalist movement blossomed because of his refusal to abide by the provisions of the agreement, which soon proved impossible to enforce. His subsequent rise to power eventually forced all parties to the treaty to return to the negotiating table in Lausanne, Switzerland, in 1922.

Mehmet Munir, who served as chief legal adviser and translator for the delegation from the Ottoman Empire during talks that went on for months, was present when the Treaty of Lausanne was signed on July 24, 1923, thereby bringing the modern Turkish republic into being. Seven days later, Ahmet was born, as he would later recall, "in a house on the rocky hills of Sultantepe in Uskudar on the Asiatic side of Istanbul, that grand old decaying city which had once been Byzantium and Constantinople."

A child of privilege like his older brother Nesuhi, Ahmet spent the first two years of his life in a truly primitive land where nearly everyone was illiterate, life expectancy was short, epidemics commonplace, and medical care virtually nonexistent. In a territory stretching for more than a thousand miles where most men eked out a living as subsistence farmers, there were only a few short stretches of paved road and the most common means of travel was by horse-drawn cart. Most villages did not have a central square or plaza, reinforcing the widely held belief that life was meant to be lived within the family or clan.

While those like Ahmet's father who had been born and raised in Istanbul enjoyed a far more cosmopolitan existence, nothing in his background could have prepared him for the rapid succession of sweeping social changes that transformed the remnants of the Ottoman Empire into the modern Turkish republic in a relatively short period of time. Born into a family from Uzbekistan in central Asia, Mehmet Munir was the grandson of a Sufi sheik who presided over the Ösbekler Tekkesi, a dervish lodge in Istanbul. His father was a career bureaucrat who spent his life working in the Ministry of Monuments and Antiquities. His mother was one of the first Turkish women to make the pilgrimage to Mecca by camel.

Exempt from military service by imperial decree because he had been born in the city where the Sultan held court, Mehmet Munir graduated from Istanbul University with a degree in law in 1908. He then began working in the imperial chancery, rising to the rank of chief legal adviser eight years later.

After his short-lived first marriage ended when he was in his twenties, his parents, in accordance with the custom at the time, arranged for him to wed Hayrunnisa Rustem. Fourteen years younger than he, she could play any keyboard or stringed instrument by ear, loved to dance and sing, and, as Ahmet would later say, "probably would have become a singing star or musician or performer if she had lived in a time when well-born girls were allowed on the stage. She was an outgoing, fun loving, good looking young girl who had been quite disappointed to find that the husband picked for her was a quiet, scholarly young law and philosophy student who did not share her love of music and dancing."

Three years after they were married, Mehmet Munir embarked on the journey that would change his life as well as the future of his homeland. On December 5, 1920, as part of a high-powered delegation headed by Salih Pasha and Ahmet Izzet Pasha, two of the Sultan's most trusted ministers, he traveled about two hundred and fifty kilometers by train from Istanbul to the railway station at Bilicek to help negotiate an agreement to end the civil conflict between the Sultan and the new nationalist government in Ankara headed by Mustafa Kemal.

Unlike the leaders of the delegation and the great war hero they had come to meet, Mehmet Munir had never seen combat on any of the battlefields where the fate of the empire had been contested during the past two decades. Bespectacled, with a thick mustache and a receding hairline, he was then thirty-seven years old, the father of a three-year-old son, and a devout Muslim who prayed five times a day.

After making the delegation wait for an entire day at the railway station, Mustafa Kemal finally arrived. Thirty-nine years old, with piercing blue eyes and high Oriental cheekbones, he had the commanding look of a fearless soldier who had already proven himself in battle. Introducing himself as the prime minister of the government in Ankara, Kemal shocked Salih Pasha and Ahmet Izzet Pasha by asking them who they were.

Explaining he could not possibly speak to them as cabinet ministers because he did not recognize the government in Istanbul, Kemal said he was perfectly willing to talk with them as fellow patriots. After a discussion that lasted for hours, Kemal told both men he could not let them return to Istanbul. Instead, they would now accompany him to Ankara so they could get a sense of what life was like under the nationalist government. Knowing they had no choice in the matter, the entire delegation boarded a train heading in the opposite direction from which they had come the day before. Although the word was never used, they were now being held as hostages.

Because the nationalists controlled the army and no one in Istanbul could mount an expedition to free them, the delegation remained in Ankara for the next three months. When Salih Pasha and Ahmet Izzet Pasha realized Kemal's movement was directed not just against the foreigners occupying their homeland but the Sultan as well, they both made it plain they could never become part of it.

Not so Mehmet Munir. After a period of intensive soul searching, he decided only Kemal and his followers could preserve what little was left of his beloved homeland. Switching sides, he threw in his lot with them. Born with the personality of a true diplomat, Mehmet Munir had a set of unique personal credentials that made him an immediate asset of great value to the new nationalist government.

Having served two years earlier as the chief legal adviser to the Ottoman delegation at the signing of the Treaty of Brest-Litovsk that forced Russia to return all the territory it had seized from the empire during World War I, he had already dealt with foreign powers across the bargaining table. Fluent in French, then the language of diplomacy all over the world, he also spoke English.

On February 6, 1921, Salih Pasha and Ahmet Izzet Pasha signed a handwritten document giving Mehmet Munir official permission to attend the international Peace Conference that would begin in London six days later. To ensure his safety as well as their own, the signers made it plain they were being kept in Ankara against their will and that Mehmet Munir had been repeatedly and insistently pressured to attend the conference because of his personal ability and professional knowledge. Serving as an adviser and a translator, he then represented the Ankara government at peace talks in England to which the Sultan also sent his own set of representatives.

In March 1921, Kemal finally decided to allow the rest of the delegation to return to Istanbul on the condition that Salih Pasha and Ahmet Izzet Pasha would not resume their government positions—which they both soon did. When Mehmet Munir's wife read the morning newspaper only to learn that everyone but her husband had returned safely to Istanbul, she was furious. In every sense, he had now become the odd man out.

Unlike those who had chosen to continue supporting the Sultan, Mehmet Munir had aligned himself with a movement that in time would change the modern world. For him, it had all begun with the decision he made after that fateful meeting in the railway station at Bilicek on December 5, 1920. And while Mustafa Kemal himself once proclaimed, "I have no religion, and at times I wish all religions to the bottom of the sea," Mehmet Munir steadfastly continued to roll out his carpet to pray five times a day even after he had become one of Kemal's most trusted aides. In Ahmet's words, "Although my father was basically a timid man, he had great stubbornness in living out his convictions and defending his beliefs. His sense of morality somehow governed all his actions."

In 1925, Kemal rewarded Mehmet Munir for his service to the new republic by appointing him the ambassador to Switzerland. As Ahmet would later write, his father "left behind the teeming hodgepodge of the Istanbul that he loved, the shoeless porters, the grimy street kids, the blind beggars, the black-shawled peasant women, the hawking vendors, all of whom hovered below the countless majestic mosques and minarets that formed the skyline of this mysterious city, crossroads of many civilizations; the last stop of the Orient Express, the last capital of the fallen Ottoman Empire, 'the sublime port,' the city of my father's dreams."

Accompanied by his wife, his two sons, and their newborn daughter, Selma, Mehmet Munir set off to represent his fledgling nation's diplomatic interests in Bern. Beginning what would become a life of constant travel, Ahmet embarked on the long and highly improbable journey that eventually brought him to the land where he would make his fame and fortune.

## 2

In "the clean quiet serenity of the capital city of Bern, with many green gardens, parks, churches, clocks, and chimes," Ahmet's first real childhood memory of himself was as a two-and-a-half-year-old boy playing in the immense gardens of the Turkish legation. Befitting his status as the Turkish ambassador to "this bland beautiful sterile country," Mehmet Munir and his family were now able to live in a manner that would not have been possible in their still impoverished and chaotic homeland.

Their large house at 18 Kalcheggweg was staffed by several servants the family had brought with them from Turkey. A young Swiss governess who spoke French took care of Ahmet, who was soon communicating with his brother and sister in "a mixture of Turkish and French with a sprinkling of the French-German patois that we picked up on the street and in kindergarten."

Charged with more responsibility than ever before, Ahmet's father was always busy working. In addition to his diplomatic duties in Bern, he made regular visits to Geneva, where in two years' time he became the Turkish observer to the League of Nations while also traveling to Paris to meet with other Turkish diplomats and statesmen. Unlike his wife, he had little difficulty adjusting to their new life.

During the early years of their marriage, Ahmet's mother had been able to avail herself of the loving support of both her own and her husband's extended families. She had also spent a good deal of time traveling back and forth from Istanbul to Ankara by train and horse-drawn carriage, a journey that in 1921 had taken eight days. In Bern, where her primary job was to run a household where she was addressed in Turkish by those who served her as "Hanimefendi" or "Madame," the fissures in her prearranged marriage grew wider.

A short, stout woman with a broad face and straight brown hair she tinted auburn, Ahmet's mother felt isolated in this strange new culture and sought solace in music. Over and over on the family's hand-wound phonograph, she would play her favorite Turkish records until "the sad haunting Oriental music of Istanbul" brought tears to her eyes. In Ahmet's words, "When she could no longer hold back her sobs, she would retire to her room so as not to upset the children. I could not tell whether it was because of her homesickness or her unhappiness with my father or her missing some unknown lover of the past, or whether it was just the music that evoked in her this deep melancholy."

The scene around the family dinner table when all the guests were Turkish was far happier. Once the meal was over, Ahmet's mother would sing and play the piano or the oud and people would dance. Although Ahmet's father "would never participate in these carryings-on," he would "regale all those present with funny anecdotes about the anomalies between the Near Eastern and Western cultures and some of the ridiculous situations that resulted."

Still too young to go to school, Ahmet and Selma spent their days being looked after by "nurses, governesses, and maids." Foremost among them was Madame Yenge (*yenge* being the Turkish word for aunt) whom Ahmet's sister would later describe as "a beloved distant relative who was like a doting grandmother to us." One day as she was walking with Ahmet, who was then four years old, "a miserable-looking beggar" approached them. Yenge was about to walk away when Ahmet grabbed her hand, "started crying furiously, and refused to budge until she had given him a few pennies."

In later years, Yenge would tell this story with tears in her eyes to show how compassionate Ahmet had been as a young boy. However, he could also be quite headstrong and, in his sister's words, "perhaps a bit spoiled." After Yenge had left Ahmet alone for a few minutes to fetch something from the top floor of the house, he began to scream, "Why didn't you take me with you?" When Yenge came back to get him, Ahmet refused to go with her. Insisting she should have taken him with her in the first place, he continued crying while repeating she had "wronged him."

During this period, Ahmet's only real companion was eight-year-old Nesuhi. "He was like a hero to my sister and me," Ahmet wrote. "At seven or eight, he seemed to be a big grown-up man who had much more in common with the adults than with us." In a photograph from this period, Ahmet sits on his brother's knee peering at the camera with a shy, inquisitive look on his face. Enacting the role he would play for many years in Ahmet's life, a broadly smiling Nesuhi has both his arms wrapped protectively around his younger brother.

In the afternoon, the brothers often played soccer together on the large lawn behind their house. Some days, the two sons of the Swiss president, who were roughly the same age, would come to join them. Placing two caps at each end of the field to serve as goal markers, they would pretend Turkey was playing Switzerland in a match that "was always a bloody battle."

The most significant moment of Ahmet's life in Bern occurred when his father brought home a motion picture projector. Ahmet would later remember watching silent films starring Charlie Chaplin.

No matter how many times Ahmet's father showed these films, his children never wanted them to stop. As a special treat, Ahmet and his sister would occasionally be taken to the cinema, which they adored.

In 1931, Mehmet Munir was posted to Paris as ambassador. His family moved with him into a house at 33 rue de Villejust in the 18th Arrondissement, the bohemian district of Montmartre. Soon after moving to Paris, Ahmet's mother began looking for a new governess to care for her two younger children. Ahmet and Selma were sitting on the floor of their playroom when their mother entered with the woman she was considering for the job.

As Ahmet's mother talked to her, Ahmet leaned over to his sister and whispered in her ear, "I don't like this woman. See what I'm going to do." Taking the scissors he and Selma had been using to cut up pictures, Ahmet crawled over to the woman and began cutting her skirt. She screamed, "I can't take care of savages like these!" Ahmet's mother, who had to pay for the skirt, was horrified and punished her son.

A very imaginative child, Ahmet also invented elaborate fantasy games to play with his sister. Using a broomstick as a mast, he would pretend the sofa was a small boat in which they were sailing around the world and being tossed about by huge waves only to be marooned on an island where they were then attacked by natives.

Along with his brother, Nesuhi, who attended the upper school, Ahmet was sent to the exclusive Petit Lycée Janson de Sailly on the rue de la Pompe in the 16th Arrondissement, where the poet and critic Stephan Mallarmé, the actor Jean Gabin, and the filmmaker Jean Renoir had been before them. Always a far better student than his older brother, Ahmet regularly achieved perfect scores in French and calculus and began studying English. Now listening to records by Josephine Baker, the Mills Brothers, Bing Crosby, Paul Whiteman, and Louis Armstrong, Ahmet would travel with his mother each year to Deauville for the Concours d'Elegance, where the most fashionable cars of the day were on display.

In 1931 at the age of eight, Ahmet was taken back to Turkey by his mother so he could be circumcised in accordance with Islamic law. While the family was living in Switzerland and France, Ahmet would sometimes say how beautiful his physical surroundings were only to be told by others in the household, "It's nothing. Turkey is so much more beautiful." He soon came to believe the land of his birth was "an incredible, wonderful paradise."

As Ahmet walked with his mother from the central railway station in Istanbul down a street full of holes with lights that did not work, he turned to her and said, "Mother, what happened here? Did a bomb fall? I mean, it's so dirty." As Ahmet would later say, "And then I noticed all the people walking around without shoes on. Instead of shoes, they had pieces of cloth that were tied together with strings and I said, 'How could you talk—why did everybody lie to me about how fantastic this country is?' It took me a few weeks to look beyond the poverty and to see an inner beauty which exists in a country."

At his own request in 1932, Mehmet Munir was transferred to England, where he assumed his new post as the Turkish ambassador to the Court of St. James's. In London, he and his wife were presented to the king and queen. Although Ahmet did not accompany them, Nesuhi did take him to see a duke who changed the course of both their lives.

## 3

Nine years old and barely able to speak English, Ahmet was wearing a beret as he stepped off the train from Paris with his family in London and immediately got into a fight with "a couple of ruffians who were hanging around the railway station." Swept up into a rarefied life of luxury and privilege in a country where the class system was still in place, he would have no further contact with anyone from the street in England. In a city where the fog was often still so thick his mother panicked one day when she let go of his hand for a moment only to lose sight of him, Ahmet's childhood soon became far more structured than before. In no small part this was due to the heightened nature of his mother's social life.

After Mehmet Munir presented his credentials to the Court of St. James's on July 23, 1932, he and his wife were invited to dine with King George V and Queen Mary. Fearing she might lose her balance as she was introduced to the queen, Ahmet's mother, who was overweight at the time, carefully practiced her curtsy before going out that night. When she called upon the Duchess of York, the mother of the future Queen Elizabeth II, the two women discussed their daughters, both of whom were about the same age.

Ahmet and Nesuhi were sent to school at the French Lycée in Cromwell Gardens in South Kensington. In the Turkish ambassador's residence at 69 Portland Place in Marylebone, Ahmet and his sister ate their meals separately from their parents, whom "they hardly ever saw." Their new governess, Miss Whittingham, who "was very British and very strict," had previously looked after the Duke and Duchess of York's daughters, Princesses Elizabeth and Margaret, and so made Ahmet and Selma dress each night for dinner.

"We wore our party clothes and Miss Whittingham wore evening gowns, rose or yellow chiffon dresses with matching satin shoes," Ahmet's sister would later say. "We had dinner in the dining room but at a much earlier time than our parents. In accordance with Miss Whittingham's rules of etiquette, I led the procession into the dining room with Miss Whittingham behind me and Ahmet third and last. I don't know how we did it but we were even taught how to eat grapes with a knife and fork."

In London, Selma first realized her brother "was interested in women from an early age." When their new governess wanted to undress both children so she could put them to bed, six-year-old Selma refused to let her do so but "Ahmet just sort of left himself in her hands and threw himself at her. He wanted her to undress him."

Ahmet was ten years old when Edward Kennedy "Duke" Ellington, "the King of Jazz," came to London for the first time on June 12, 1933, to perform with "His Famous Orchestra" at the London Palladium. The grandson of a former slave, Ellington was then thirty-four years old. Raised in Washington, D.C., he had begun taking piano lessons when he was seven years old, written his first composition at the age of fourteen, and begun his career as a professional musician four years later.

Duke Ellington's two-week engagement at the Palladium was a cultural event of major proportions, changing not only how he performed but also the way in which his music was perceived. Long before Ellington's genius was fully appreciated in America, British audiences demanded he play his more serious extended compositions as well as the dance music "typically expected of black artists in the jazz world." English critics compared Ellington's work to Arnold Schönberg's twelve tone system, while also noting its relationship to "the primitive, discordant, rule-breaking" rhythms of sixteenth-century Elizabethan madrigals.

On Ellington's opening night in the Palladium, the curtain opened to reveal an expansive stage decorated with three huge cardboard cutouts of cartoonlike black musicians, all of which would now be considered racist. In a pearl gray suit, white shirt, and tie, the impossibly elegant and regal-looking Duke sat behind a concert grand piano. Before he could play a single note, the audience of nearly four thousand, who had paid from 9 pence (about 20 cents) to 5 shillings (about a dollar and a quarter) to see the show, greeted him with the kind of extended ovation that had before been given only to well-known classical performers in England.

Facing an orchestra composed of three trumpet players, three saxophone players, a banjo player, three trombone players, three clarinet players, and a drummer, Ellington kicked off the show with "Ring Dem Bells." During what was a full-fledged variety show, he played "Bugle Call Rag" and "Black and Tan Fantasy" and brought out Ivie Anderson who sang "Stormy Weather" while leaning against a marble pillar. The dancers Bill Bailey and Derby Wilson gave "a display of neat and fast footwork," Bessie Dudley, "the original snake hips girl," did "an impressive rhythmic dancing turn," and trumpeter Freddy Jenkins sang the Sophie Tucker favorite "Some of These Days." Ellington brought "the program to a happy conclusion" with "the somber strains of 'Mood Indigo.' "

The "scores of smartly dressed young English people" in the expensive seats, among them the Duke of Kent, the third son of King George V, stomped their feet, shouted, whistled, and applauded in approval as did the "hundreds in the hinterlands of the Palladium." After the show, "a small army of autograph seekers," sixty women among them, "besieged the Duke and his musicians" outside the stage door.

In what one English jazz scholar would later call "a precursor to Beatlemania," fans clung to Ellington's limousine as he was driven from the hall. After paying Ellington the highest broadcast fee in its history so he would repeat his stunning performance on the radio, the

BBC extended the program for five minutes so Ellington could play "Mood Indigo" in its entirety.

For Ahmet, who was taken to the show by his brother, the evening was an ear-shattering, life-changing experience he would never forget. "It was nothing like hearing the records," Ahmet would later say. "The engineers at the time were afraid that too much bass or too much drums would crack the grooves on the 78s so they recorded them very low. And when you heard these bands in person, it was explosive. This boom-boom-boom incredible rhythm. It went through your body. I went, 'Oh my God, *this* is jazz. This is not this bullshit thing we hear on a record player. This is *real* jazz.' . . . The very loudness of the sound, the reverberation of the bass and drum in the theater frightened me, it was so powerful . . . I'd never heard music with that kind of strength . . . For the first time, I saw these beautiful black men wearing shining white tuxedos and these brass instruments gleaming. It was an incredible sight."

A year later, Nesuhi took Ahmet to see Cab Calloway at the Palladium. Although Ahmet would later often confuse the dates of these two shows as well as what the musicians had been wearing, the transformative effect of those magical nights at the London Palladium made him want to make records as powerful as the live performances he had experienced as a boy.

When in June 1934 Mehmet Munir was posted to Washington, D.C., as the ambassador to the United States from the Republic of Turkey, Ahmet was very excited. In his words, "I was twelve when I got to America so my impressions were that I knew about cowboys and Indians but the most important thing for me was jazz. And I was dying to see Louis Armstrong and I thought, 'Well, that's where we're going.' "

## 4

Leaving his family behind, Mehmet Munir went by himself to Washington so he could begin representing his country's interests in America as soon as possible. Ahmet's mother then returned with her children to Turkey for a summer visit that extended for months as she prepared for the long journey to a land where no one she knew had ever gone.

In the very formal, stilted English he had learned at school in London, Ahmet regularly wrote letters to his father in which he expressed his desire to come to America because he thought "there were very many cowboys there." Although he had already received one from someone else, he also thanked his father for the gift of a new Kodak camera. Repeatedly, Ahmet asked for soccer journals, which did not then exist in America. He concluded one of his letters by writing, "I kiss you a hundred of times, Your dear son, A. Munir."

During the last week in December 1934, Ahmet, his mother, and his sister traveled to Genoa on the Orient Express and then boarded the ship that would take them to America. At a time when, as Ahmet would say, "making the trip from Europe to America was a major event," his family did so in the grand manner to which they had all become accustomed. In first-class, they embarked on the SS *Rex,* the luxurious Italian ocean liner that in August 1933 had won the Blue Riband for the fastest westward crossing of the Atlantic by completing the journey from Gibraltar to New York in the astonishing time of four days, thirteen hours, and fifty-eight minutes.

As they journeyed to a country gripped by the Great Depression, Ahmet, his mother, and sister occupied a suite that was "a rung above the first-class cabins and certainly the most luxurious accommodation the ship had to offer." In an era when the average salary in America was less than $1,400, their passage cost more than most people in the United States earned in an entire year. Because it was the custom for ambassadors and their families to be sent abroad in the best possible circumstances, all their expenses were paid for by the Turkish government.

With them from Turkey, his mother had brought two Armenian families who were in third-class on the *Rex.* "But when the sea got rough," Ahmet recalled, "she went down to get them. We had this huge suite and we had all these poor people sleeping with us. Because down there, it was much worse. Where we were, at least you could look out the window. It had air." Ahmet and his family spent New Year's Eve on the ship but, in Selma's words, because the passage was so stormy, "There were only a few passengers well enough to take part in the festivities, which consisted of dinner and a dance orchestra with nobody dancing. It was hard enough to keep one's balance just standing up."

The crossing became so rough at one point that Ahmet's mother, who blamed herself for having postponed their trip until midwinter, tearfully embraced her two children while telling them she was the cause of their impending deaths. Neither Ahmet nor Selma, both of whom "enjoyed roaming around the empty corridors of the ship, trying to keep our balance as we superiorly belittled those who were throwing up in their cabins," took her seriously. To keep her children busy, she gave them "thousands of dollars" to bet on a "fake horse race with dummy horses" and a dice game that was held each afternoon on the ship. "My sister and I won every day," Ahmet would later say. "We used to go back and give her all these huge sums of money."

After the *Rex* landed in New York, the family was greeted by the consul general of Turkey and two people from his staff. As Ahmet recalled, "We arrived in the evening and the first thing I said was, 'I want to see 42nd Street.' Because I'd seen the movie, right? We drove down 42nd Street, Times Square. It was incredible. It was America the way I expected it."

After staying in a hotel that night, the family took a train to Washington, on which Ahmet would later remember seeing "the black Pullman porters who would say, 'Yes sir, I'll give you a shine.' " At Union Station, the family was met by the Turkish embassy limousine, a navy blue Packard. Eleven and a half years old, Ahmet had finally arrived in the land he had only read about in comic books. His initial expectations of America had also been formed by Miss Whittingham, his "very strict" and "difficult" English governess in London, who had told him "Americans were savages. . . . They spoke like peasants and were not upper-class people at all. They were just ruffians."

## 5

By the time Ahmet arrived in Washington, his father had already become embroiled in a heated controversy for which none of his previous diplomatic service could have prepared him. In the fall of 1934, a novel entitled *The Forty Days of Musa Dagh* by Franz Werfel, an Austrian Jew who had served as an Austro-Hungarian artillery corporal during World War I, was published in America to uniformly positive reviews.

Written in a very grand, florid style, the novel recounts the heroic stand taken by its hero, Gabriel Bagradian, to defend his fellow Armenians against deportations, mass murder, and rape at the hands of the "Young Turks" who had led the Ottoman Empire in 1915. While as many as a million and a half Armenians of the Christian faith were killed during this period, the Republic of Turkey steadfastly denied that such acts had ever occurred. Any reference to the Armenian massacre as genocide was considered a grievous insult to Turkish pride.

Although Mustafa Kemal had denounced the massacres as "a shameful act" in 1919, he wanted to distance his new nation from the actions of the Young Turks as well as the legacy of the Ottoman Empire. To bind his people into a single nation, he also "outlawed ethnic and minority identity" and removed all public references to Armenians within Turkey.

When Irving Thalberg, "The Boy Wonder" who was then the head of production at Metro-Goldwyn-Mayer began implementing the studio's plan to film *The Forty Days of Musa Dagh,* the government of Turkey reacted swiftly to the news by sending its new ambassador to America to meet with Wallace Murray, the State Department's chief of Near Eastern Affairs. During their meeting, Mehmet Munir told Murray he "earnestly hoped" the studio "would desist from presenting any such picture, which would almost certainly stir up anti-Turkish feelings in the country."

Pursuing the matter as though this was now his top priority, Mehmet Munir continued corresponding with Murray. He also visited the Hays Office in New York where the Motion Picture Production Code was enforced to insist the film be terminated and informed MGM's legal counsel that all of the studio's films would be banned in Turkey if the company insisted on making this movie. In June 1935, he agreed to accept two copies of the script so he could read one himself while sending the other to the Foreign Affairs Office in Ankara.

In Turkey, the story had become headline news. On a daily basis, newspapers published anti-American and anti-Jewish harangues protesting the project. The issue soon became so inflamed that a group of Armenian intellectuals gathered in a churchyard in Istanbul where they set the book and a photograph of its author on fire as they sang the Turkish national anthem to prove their loyalty to the government.

In September 1935, Mehmet Munir contacted Secretary of State Cordell Hull to inform him the Turkish government considered the script "utterly negative. Kindly exert your high influence with a view to precluding the carrying out of the project." He then told an official at Loew's, the company that owned MGM, "If the movie is made, Turkey will launch a worldwide campaign against it. It rekindles the Armenian question. The Armenian question is settled. How else would you explain the presence of Armenians in the Turkish Parliament? The movie will only stir up troubles about a situation that has been smoothed out."

Due in great part to Mehmet Munir's unrelenting efforts, MGM eventually scrapped its plan to film *The Forty Days of Musa Dagh*. Forty-seven years after the studio first purchased the rights to the book, what was generally considered an atrocious version of the novel finally made its way to the screen.

As Peter Balakian, the author of *The Burning Tigris: The Armenian Genocide and America's Response,* would later say, "Munir Ertegun became a pit bull on this with the State Department. He was clearly a very successful political animal. Nevertheless, he was an absolute purveyor of the Turkish denialist narrative on the Armenians and the Armenian genocide, and it is really a dark and twisted immoral story of huge proportions."

"My personal view," Ahmet's sister Selma would later write, "is that my father did this because it was his duty to try to stop anti-Turkish propaganda in whatever form it appeared. He was certainly instructed by the government to do whatever he could to stop the film. This does not mean he condoned the actions of the Ottoman government. I was too young then to know what his personal thoughts were. All I can recall is that it was a very difficult and stressful time. I am still amazed he was able to succeed in his efforts to stop the making of a film in a democratic country like the U.S."

In 1994, Ahmet, who by then had become a very wealthy man, donated $3.5 million to create the M. Munir Ertegun Turkish Studies Foundation in the Department of Near Eastern Studies at Princeton University. Four years later, Ahmet publicly conceded that deaths had in fact taken place in Armenia in 1915. Stating they were casualties of war and not part of a planned genocide, he added, "There are different interpretations of what happened."

In 1998, Ahmet also contacted Harut Sassounian, the publisher of *The California Courier,* the oldest independent English-language Armenian newspaper in the United States, to discuss the issue with him. After Ahmet's death in December 2006, Sassounian wrote that as a precondition to their meeting Ahmet needed to acknowledge the Armenian genocide. Over a lunch that lasted for more than two hours at the Peninsula Hotel in Beverly Hills, Ahmet "made it clear that he was not acknowledging the Genocide in order to appease the Armenians. He believed that it was, first of all, in Turkey's interest to acknowledge the Genocide, because doing so would help Ankara's application for membership in the European Union and get rid of the stigma that had haunted his native land for so many years."

Although Sassounian wrote it was "a shame that the public statement we had discussed regarding the Armenian Genocide never materialized," he noted Ahmet had contacted him not because "he was pro-Armenian, but because he sincerely wanted to help erase the stigma of the Genocide from Turkey's name." Sassounian added, "I could not write this column while he was alive since I did not want to make him the target of hate mail and threats from Turkish extremists by alerting them that he was considering the possibility of issuing a public statement on the Armenian Genocide. Alas, he passed away without being able to do so, which is a loss for both Armenians and Turks."

# TWO

# The Nation's Capital

*"When I was just a record collector, a jazz fan hanging around the Howard Theatre, I got to know a lot of the sharp guys and there was this guy I called, 'My Man Harvey.' Everybody called him 'My Man Harvey.' He called himself 'My Man Harvey.' He was very, very well dressed and a big numbers man and everything was shiny and just perfect. There was going to be a party around midnight. 'Come up. There'll be a lot of girls.' I said, 'Fine. Yeah.' He gave me the address and I had to walk up two flights and knock on the door. When I knocked on the door, a black lady opened it halfway and looked out and said, 'What do you want?' I said, 'Well, I was invited to come here.' She said, 'Who invited you?' I said, 'Harvey. My Man Harvey.' 'Just a minute.' She closed the door and said, 'Hey, man, there's an ofay out here.' So I hear Harvey's voice inside saying, 'What's his name?' She opens it and says, 'What's your name?' I said, 'Ahmet.' She said, 'Ahmet.' He says, 'Ahmet! Let that nigger in!' "*

—Ahmet Ertegun

## 1

In the nation's capital, Ahmet's life soon became as divided as the city itself. Although one fourth of its population was black, the District of Columbia in 1935 was still a Southern city where complete segregation was the rule. In great numbers after World War I, African Americans had migrated to the former "seat and center of domestic slave traffic" only to discover that because there was no industry in the city, jobs were scarce.

In tiny wooden shacks that would not have looked out of place on some great Southern plantation before the Civil War, seven thousand African Americans still lived below the poverty line in more than a hundred ramshackle alleys littered with refuse. In the alleys, the crime rate was high, people drank heavily, knives and pistols were often used to settle domestic and gambling disputes, and few white faces were ever seen. Those who dwelled there considered "John Law" to be "the natural enemy."

As Selma Ertegun would later recall, one such collection of "rows of small squalid houses totally inhabited by 'colored people' " was located just a few hundred yards from the palatial Turkish embassy on Sheridan Circle where she and Ahmet lived with their parents. The huge gray stone mansion had originally been built for Edward Hamlin Everett, the very wealthy industrialist who had invented the modern screw top bottle cap. Hamlin's only instructions to George Totten Jr., the architect who had designed the American embassy in Istanbul and Izzet Pasha's official residence while he was grand vizier of the Ottoman Empire, were "to spend and to dream."

Totten then spent two years building a mansion at 23rd Street and Massachusetts Avenue that combined the "architectural elements of 18th century Europe with Romanesque and 15th century Italianate details." Considered one of the most "remarkable structures" on Embassy Row, the mansion featured a huge ballroom with a parquet floor, a conservatory with stained glass windows and a mosaic ceiling, and a formal dining room in which heads of state could be entertained in style. Overlooking Rock Creek Park, the building's rounded portico and impressive facade of fluted columns made it look much like a smaller version of the White House.

In 1936, Kemal Ataturk decided the house should be purchased as the permanent residence of the ambassador of the Republic of Turkey to the United States. Fully furnished, the mansion cost $400,000. The modern-day equivalent of the purchase price would be more than $6 million. At a time when the president of the United States earned $75,000 a year, gasoline cost 10 cents a gallon, and the average price of a new house was less than $4,000, it was an astonishing sum.

"So we wound up in Washington, which was nothing like 42nd Street or Times Square," Ahmet would later say. "Suddenly, we were in this very staid, quiet, dull kind of place but the embassy was beautiful." Even though his father was then already at war with the motion picture industry, one of the first things Ahmet did after arriving in the nation's capital was to go with his sister to see Bing Crosby in the 1934 Paramount musical comedy *Here Is My Heart*. By doing so, he immediately made it plain that his life in America would be different from the one his father had envisioned for him.

In Ahmet's words, "I first found myself in a school called St. Albans and my sister went to National Cathedral. Very staid, conservative schools and there were no cowboys, no gangsters, no Indians, no Negroes, no nothing. No Jews. Also, no sophistication." Ahmet liked St. Albans but "unfortunately mentioned" to his father one day that all St. Albans students were required to attend chapel each morning.

On April 13, 1935, the Reverend Albert Hawley Lucas, the headmaster at St. Albans, wrote Ahmet's father on school stationery in response to the ambassador's request that his son be "excused from both chapel and religious education." Stating he would have been "glad indeed to accede to this request if by doing so a precedent was not established," Lucas explained that because St. Albans was a church school, attendance at both chapel and weekly religious education was compulsory.

Although in the past quarter century the school had admitted many non-Christian students, the Reverend Lucas wanted "Your Excellency" to understand that at St. Albans such students had "learned to regard Christianity in a more tolerant and sympathetic light." Lucas closed his letter by writing he hoped Mehmet Munir would express his "sympathy with St. Albans' position."

Three days later, Ahmet's father replied to "Mr. Headmaster" by writing, "I am sorry to realize that you insist for my son who is a Mohammedan to attend your chapel and to have religious education. Such attendance and training being against our principles, I regret to inform you that I am obliged to send him to a school in which he will not have such obligations."

Ahmet was then sent to the independent, nonsectarian Landon School in Bethesda, Maryland, just outside Washington. As he would later say, "My father took me out of that school and put me in another school where they didn't have religion. Except they did have a religion which was American football. However, my father did not allow me to play American football because Europeans think it is a brutal sport. So most of the year when everyone was doing American football practice, I was let out and I spent that time unbeknownst to my family going to the skid row section of town looking things up and seeing what was what."

Never very athletic as a boy, Ahmet also broke his arm "at least three times and his shoulder once" during his childhood, thereby giving his father good reason not to allow him to play football. With his prominent forehead, thick glasses, and protruding teeth, Ahmet also looked far more like a skinny studious bookworm than someone who could compete for his school on the gridiron.

At the Landon School, where the English accent he had acquired in London immediately set him apart from his classmates, Ahmet quickly learned how to imitate the way they spoke while also occasionally lapsing into "imitation black speech . . . like 'What say, man?' " that he had picked up from Cleo Payne, an ex-fighter who worked as a janitor at the embassy. Payne, who also gave Ahmet boxing lessons, became the boy's guide to the city's black neighborhoods.

Seeking refuge in music just as his mother had done in Switzerland, Ahmet set off to find the kind of jazz he had seen Duke Ellington play at the Palladium in London. "Washington was like a Southern city," Ahmet would later say. "Totally Jim Crow. I wanted to buy jazz records. So I got in the car and the chauffeur took me to the biggest record shop in Washington, which was on G Street. They had only RCA and Brunswick records. I asked for Louis Armstrong. They said, 'Oh, we don't have those.' I mean, they'd never heard Bessie Smith. This very nice woman took me aside and said, 'Listen, if you want to buy those kind of records, you have to go to the nigger part of town . . .' So then eventually I found the record shops in the black section, in the ghetto."

Telling his parents he was going to the movies, Ahmet would head straight for stores like the Quality Radio Repair Shop on Seventh and T Streets owned by Max Silverman, later known as "Waxie Maxie," where old jazz 78s could be bought for as little as "a dime apiece or three for a quarter." Living a dual life that would provide him with a rigorous classical education as well as an encyclopedic knowledge of jazz that was second to none, Ahmet began learning "things that others my age did not know. I learned that at Brooks Brothers you could have ties made to your specifications from very good material for not very much more money than off-the-rack ties and I learned things about black America."

Demonstrating a taste for the low life he would never lose, Ahmet became "a habitué of the Gaiety Burlesque Theater," where the skits were "like commedia dell'arte." He also befriended a street corner medicine man for whom he "shilled for a while" by purchasing a bottle of hair tonic that "was really just colored water for 50 cents which was a lot of money because you could eat lunch for 40 cents." After Ahmet had given the hair tonic back in return for his 50 cents, the medicine man would treat Ahmet to a sandwich or a cup of coffee in some "greasy place" and then take him backstage at the Gaiety, where he introduced him to "all the strippers and the chorus girls and the comedians," who were "a tough crew of people."

Left to his own devices, Ahmet also spent time with an "Eastern European Gypsy who ran a sideshow freak show. They'd hook you in by saying, 'Well, if you want to go in and see a hermaphrodite without any clothes on, it costs another dollar.' " He also frequented "beer joints where they had black jug bands. Some of these black bands played very funky blues and there was very rough dancing. I mean coming close to the sex act kind of dancing."

By the time he was fourteen years old, Ahmet was also a regular at the Howard Theatre on U Street, then known in Washington as the "Black Broadway" or the "Colored Man's Connecticut Avenue." At the Howard, which Ahmet would later describe as "the Washington equivalent of the Apollo where all the same shows that played the Apollo would go down and play the following week in Washington," he "got to hear everyone but I used to be the only white person and I was just fourteen. The black people were very nice to white people because they were really scared of them."

Even as he was getting an education on the streets, Ahmet excelled at his studies in school. At Landon, where "everything clicked" for him, "I was good in math. I was good in history. Of course I was precocious in a sense because of my brother, who had made me start to read things like D. H. Lawrence which other kids had never heard of but the teacher knew and he would say, 'Oh, you're not supposed to bring that up yet. That's two years from now.' In French and Latin, I was superior to everybody because Latin is very rigorous in European schools." After his second year at Landon, Ahmet was elected class president. In a school where "a lot of the teachers were politically very conservative" and there were often heated arguments about the Spanish Civil War, he often found himself at odds with the "school's more traditionalist attitude."

As Ahmet would later say of his family, "We were always considered to be part of the upper classes but intellectually, we were friends with Woody Guthrie and I knew John Steinbeck and his wife and 'The Ballad of Tom Joad.' All that was very close to our hearts. We were leftist intellectually but we lived in an embassy with sixteen servants, with limousines. It never seemed like a contradiction. I also had a great love of high living. We belonged to the Chevy Chase Club, which is the most exclusive country club in Washington. It had no Jews . . . but I think we were members only because my father was an ambassador."

In 1936, the somewhat confusing matter of the family's last name was finally resolved. On June 21, 1934, in accordance with the law requiring all Turkish citizens to adopt surnames of their own choosing, Mustafa Kemal had officially become Kemal Ataturk, the "father of all Turks." From "a long list of names that were acceptable because they were 'pure' Turkish words that contained no foreign elements," Mehmet Munir chose "Eren," which in Turkish means "he who has arrived at the divine truth," as his new surname.

Two years later, he was informed by the Turkish government that the quota for this name in the district where he had been born had already been filled. Mehmet Munir then chose the name "Ertegun," which, as his daughter Selma would later explain, "is a made-up word having two components: 'erte' meaning 'following,' 'next,' or 'coming'; and 'gun' (with umlaut) meaning 'day.' My father probably chose it for its religious connotation."

During that same year, Ahmet persuaded his father to let him accompany a visiting Turkish air force commander to New York. After asking permission to go to the movies by himself, Ahmet bought a ticket, "waited till the coast was clear, hailed a cab, and said, 'Take me to Harlem.'" In the Plantation Club on 126th Street and Lenox

Avenue, Count Basie's former trumpet player Oran "Hot Lips" Page was blowing the Kansas City blues. When Ahmet, then still a skinny kid in short pants, boldly asked Page to play "Satchelmouth Swing," a song recorded and made famous by Louis Armstrong, Page laughed and turned him down but said he would instead play "Lips Page's special message to a young ofay!"

At four in the morning, Ahmet was still in the club enjoying the music with a chorus girl Page had sent to his table. She then took him to a rent party in Harlem, where he saw James P. Johnson, the man who had taught Fats Waller how to play piano. Sidney Bechet, the famed New Orleans clarinetist, sax player, and composer, asked Ahmet what he was drinking. When Ahmet told him scotch and soda, Bechet took the drink from his hand and gave him a joint. That night, Ahmet smoked what he always called "ma-ree-wanna" for the first time.

When Ahmet returned to the Turkish consulate in Midtown at eight A.M., he learned the police had already been alerted and a full-scale search for him was underway. Escorted back to Washington under the strict personal supervision of the Turkish consul, Ahmet was confronted by his understandably furious father. Hitting his son for the first and only time, he slapped Ahmet across the face. For Ahmet it must have seemed like a small price to pay for what had been his first thrilling taste of nightlife in New York City.

In 1939, Ahmet's family decided it was no longer safe for Nesuhi to remain in Paris. Twenty-two years old, he abandoned his studies at the Sorbonne and joined his family in America. With him, Nesuhi brought a copy of *Ulysses* by James Joyce, a novel that had been banned in America for years and was still not widely available. By this point, Ahmet had already amassed a fairly large record collection but after Nesuhi arrived in Washington, the two brothers "started collecting very seriously and soon we had over twenty thousand 78 RPM jazz and blues records."

In an article entitled "Collecting Hot" in *Esquire* magazine, the brothers were mentioned by name as prominent jazz record collectors. After the piece appeared, the headmaster at the Landon School counseled Ahmet's father that his son should not be mentioned in the press as this would give him "a big head." He added that he was not sure Ahmet "didn't have Communist tendencies." However, when the first Jewish boy ever to be admitted to Landon School was about to begin attending classes, the headmaster chose Ahmet to look after him because as a "European," he "would be closer to the Jews than our other boys are."

In 1939, when Ahmet was fifteen, the Daughters of the American Revolution, a group open only to women whose ancestors had helped the United States win its independence, refused to allow the great black contralto Marian Anderson to perform before an integrated audience in Constitution Hall. President Franklin D. Roosevelt then authorized Secretary of the Interior Harold L. Ickes to arrange for Anderson to give a free concert on Easter Sunday on the steps of the Lincoln Memorial.

Along with his sister, Ahmet listened to the radio broadcast that was heard by millions from coast to coast. As Selma would later recall, the entire family, "including my parents, were shocked and angry" about this "disgraceful episode." Inspired in part by the controversy, Ahmet and Nesuhi soon began putting on jazz shows for integrated audiences in the nation's capital.

By the time he was sixteen, Ahmet had become what can only be described as a creature of his own creation. An astonishingly detailed account of what he was then like can be found on two pieces of typewritten paper in the Ahmet Ertegun Archive at the Rock and Roll Hall of Fame. Although the author is unknown, the monograph may have been written by George Frazier, the Harvard-educated jazz fanatic and columnist for *The Boston Globe* who became the ultimate arbiter of style in America.

In handwriting at the top of the first page are the words "My first meeting with Ahmet at a very small cocktail party in Washington." Describing Ahmet's appearance in 1939 as "bizarre," the author writes, "The little hair that he had was plastered down and combed in the middle of his flat head; his eyes were watery and, through his rimless glasses, I detected a look that inspired me with compassion . . . Over his upper lip he wore a very thin moustache that looked like the identification of a minor railroad line in a school map."

Perhaps to compensate for his physical appearance that night, Ahmet was wearing a pale blue shiny silk shirt, a blue tie held in place by "a gold pin that represented, either a fox or a wolf's head, with encrusted rubies in its eye sockets," a loosely fitted waistcoat over leather braces with "heavy regulator-buckles" as well as a large cobra-skin belt and a "key chain which must have been contrived out of thin wire covered also by cobra-skin . . . His suit was, more or less the color of brown chocolate with a trace of liver in it. When he got up to offer me a cigarette, I noticed that the broad shoulders that he seemed to have when sitting down were the result of an amazing amount of padding. His double breasted jacket was very much taken in at the waistline and the side pockets had buttons in its flaps, the whole accentuating the frailty of his constitution. Standing up, it was difficult to see his shoes, his feet and shoes being large enough—because the length and width of his trousers all but covered them. However cobra-skin shoes do not go unnoticed very often."

After the author lit the Melachrino cigarette Ahmet had offered him "out of his mother of pearl cigarette case," Ahmet sat back down to reveal a pair of "light blue socks that matched his tie even to the clocks on their sides ending with a red fox or wolf's head." Asked what time it was, Ahmet withdrew "a large round watch from his front jacket pocket where he also carried two fountain pens and one automatic pencil and pressed a button on the lid. Presently I heard the first few notes of Auld Lang Syne; he pressed shut the watch—the music stopped— and told me it was nine o'clock. We were then in mid-August and I asked him about his plans for the summer."

And there the account abruptly ends. The only hint of the life Ahmet would lead was the outfit he had chosen to wear that night to a small cocktail party in the nation's capital. It was a zoot suit, a look then much favored by black jazz musicians as well as "hep cats" who, just like Ahmet, worshipped this music.

## 2

In September 1940 when he was seventeen years old, Ahmet entered St. John's College in Annapolis, Maryland. Founded in 1696 as King William's School, St. John's was a small, all-male school that was "not well known except in the most rarefied of pedagogy circles." The program of studies, which was based on the University of Chicago's one hundred Great Books program, was rigorous and consisted entirely of tutorials that met for two hours twice a week.

Each year, students were expected to master a different language. As a freshman, Ahmet would have studied Attic Greek before going on to Latin, German, and French. There were also math tutorials. In the words of Jac Holzman, the founder of Elektra Records, who attended St. John's eight years later, "You started out with Euclid's elements in Attic Greek. You then went to Apollonius, conic sections, algebra in the second year, Cartesian math, and Nikolai Lobachevsky's theory of parallels in the fourth year. There would be philosophical discussions around the math. The whole idea was to stimulate you into rigors of thinking without being rigid. My guess is Ahmet was stimulated by the Socratic discussion and the seminars and the egality of tutors and students."

The "jewel of the program" was a tutorial in which students were expected to read *The Iliad* in a single week before moving to *The Odyssey*. Tutors began each seminar by posing a question that often led to fierce intellectual arguments. "My first question," Holzman would recall, "was, 'Did Agamemnon want to achieve immortality?' You'd argue about all this stuff and then at the end of the two hours, you'd go down to the coffee shop and argue until three in the morning. That was the heart of the program and Ahmet would have loved that. Because he would have loved the argument."

During his years at St. John's, Ahmet wrote papers on Ralph Waldo Emerson and Walt Whitman, Oscar Wilde, Samuel Butler, G. K. Chesterton, Joseph Conrad, and D. H. Lawrence. Throughout this period, Ahmet continued to look to his older brother for guidance and advice.

In every way, the two brothers could not have been more different. Slight of stature but blessed with a full head of thick black wavy hair, large expressive eyes, and a ready smile, Nesuhi had the exotic good looks of a Latin playboy. Women were always attracted to him and over the course of his life he would marry four times, once to his own cousin. Far more athletic than Ahmet, Nesuhi was also an excellent tennis player. Even though he had no degree of any kind, Nesuhi was so knowledgeable about jazz that he taught the first accredited course in the subject ever offered at the university level in America at UCLA.

Unlike Ahmet, who always gravitated to his father, Nesuhi adored his mother. Because she had cared for him herself when he was a child,

Nesuhi was her favorite as well. As adults Ahmet and Nesuhi would often argue about anything and everything in Turkish, but the bond between them was incredibly strong. Growing up in the shadow of an overwhelmingly accomplished older brother who seemed to excel at everything he did was a major factor in shaping Ahmet's own complex personality.

Soon after arriving in America, Nesuhi began giving lectures on jazz at what Ahmet later called "an intellectual bookshop" in Washington that some people "said was a communist front." The lectures were attended by "a mixed crowd" of blacks and whites, which was then "very unusual in Washington." After one of Nesuhi's lectures, as Ahmet would later say, "a young guy came up to him from the audience and engaged him in such informed and absorbing conversation that they came back to the embassy to continue their discussions and listen to some more music. That was the first time that I met my business-partner-to-be and good friend, Herb Abramson."

The coterie of white jazz fanatics in the nation's capital was then still small. After a brilliant Lehigh graduate named Bill Gottlieb began writing "Swing Session," the first jazz column in *The Washington Post,* his wife, Delia, read about the sons of the Turkish ambassador being record collectors and suggested that her husband interview them. Before Gottlieb could do so, Nesuhi called him to say, "We've been reading your column and we'd like to meet you." The only white people who regularly found themselves backstage at the Howard Theatre, the four soon became fast friends.

In 1940, Ahmet and Nesuhi took the extraordinary step of inviting musicians they had seen perform at the Howard on Saturday night to come to Sunday lunch at the embassy. After being served by waiters in white jackets, the musicians would gather together for a jam session in the embassy ballroom.

In a series of black and white photographs taken by Gottlieb, great jazz luminaries like Teddy Wilson, Mezz Mezzrow, Lester Young, Sidney DeParis, and Red Allen can be seen standing in a relaxed and casual manner with Ahmet and Nesuhi in front of a huge bust of Kemal Ataturk that had been displayed at the 1939 New York World's Fair. Wearing impeccably tailored double-breasted suits with neatly folded white handkerchiefs tucked into the front pocket of their jackets, perfectly knotted ties, and expensive leather shoes polished to perfection, the musicians look more like delegates at some high-powered international diplomatic conference than men who made their living playing jazz night after night in smoky clubs.

In an era when blatant racism was the order of the day, the elegant-looking men who came to jam at the Turkish embassy on Sunday afternoons were black royalty in America. Despite the esteem in which they were held by those who loved jazz, the only restaurant in the nation's capital where they could eat at the same table with a white person was in Union Station. Forced to deal with segregation and prejudice on a daily basis even as they were being lionized for their talent, they lived such schizophrenic lives that many developed personalities as unique and distinctive as their musical abilities.

Dubbed "The President" by Billie Holiday, Lester Young would later be called by a writer for *Rolling Stone* magazine "quite possibly the hippest dude who ever lived." "Prez," as he was known to his friends, even spoke in a language that was all his own. Perhaps the first man to call money "bread," he coined the phrases "That's cool" and "You dig?" Whenever he sensed racial prejudice, Young would say, "I feel a draft." When he saw something he liked, his only comment would be "bells" as in "I hear bells." Young's trademark crushed black porkpie hat inspired bassist Charles Mingus, who recorded for Nesuhi at Atlantic, to write "Goodbye Pork Pie Hat" after the great sax player drank himself to death at the age of forty-nine in 1959.

No less a character in his own right, Milton Mesirow had been born into a middle-class Jewish family in Chicago but decided at an early age, in his own words, "to be a Negro musician, hipping the world about the blues as only Negroes can." Renaming himself Mezz Mezzrow, he played clarinet and sax but became as renowned in the jazz world for smoking and selling marijuana as for his musical ability. For years in Harlem, a joint was known as a "Mezz roll." His autobiography, *Really the Blues*, written with Bernard Wolfe in 1946, remains one of the essential hipster texts.

Coming into such close contact with musicians he idolized at a young age, Ahmet appropriated not only the way they talked and dressed but also how they viewed the "squares" who comprised mainstream society. In the jazz world, the first commandment was always to be cool. On this principle, Ahmet founded his own personality.

At some point after the Sunday lunch and jam session had become a regular weekly event at the embassy, Ahmet's father received a letter from an "outraged Southern senator" who wrote, "It has been brought to my attention, Sir, that a person of color was seen entering your house by the front door. I have to inform you that in our country, this is not a practice to be encouraged." As Mehmet Ertegun had often expressed the view "that God had created all human beings as equals and that it was a sin to look down on anyone because of his or her race," his response consisted of what Ahmet would later call "a terse one-sentence reply. 'In my home, friends enter by the front door—however we can arrange for you to enter from the back.' "

In 1942, Nesuhi decided to begin presenting jazz concerts featuring black musicians to a mixed race audience in the nation's capital. As Ahmet, who was then still functioning as his older brother's "errand boy," would later say, "When we gave our first concert, we couldn't find a venue that would allow us to have a mixed audience as well as mixed players. The only place that would let us put on this concert was the Jewish Community Center and that's where we gave our first concert. Not very big." The first show, which had been "advertised in the white paper" as well as through "little flyers in the record shops in the black area" put up by Ahmet and Nesuhi, featured Sidney Bechet, Joe Turner, Pete Johnson, and Pee Wee Russell. In Ahmet's words, those who attended the performance "didn't know it would be integrated."

By threatening to "make a big scene out of it if they didn't let us rent it," Ahmet and Nesuhi then persuaded the National Press Club at 14th and F Streets to let them use its auditorium for their second show. On Monday, May 25, 1942, Teddy Wilson, Joe Marsala, J. C. Higginbotham, Zutty Singleton, Max Kaminsky, and Lead Belly (as he was billed and also called himself) appeared at a concert entitled "Swingtime in the Capital—A Jam Session of Jazz Giants."

When Huddie William Ledbetter (aka Lead Belly), who had spent much of his life in prison for violent crimes, saw the size of the crowd that night, he said, "Man, you gotta give me twice the price, otherwise I'm not going on." As Ahmet would later say, "So of course we did— we gave him everything we could, and, you know, we certainly weren't pretending to be experienced promoters, we were just doing it for the love of the music."

## 3

Nine weeks before Paris fell to the Nazis in the spring of 1940, Mehmet Ertegun was called into the State Department by Assistant Secretary of State Adolph Berle Jr. for a frank discussion about the war in Europe. In the official memorandum summarizing the meeting Berle sent to President Franklin D. Roosevelt, he wrote, "The Turkish Ambassador came in at my request. I asked for definite suggestions he might have by which we could improve Russian relations. I don't really know that he has any. . . . He thought that the German drive would begin to blow up the Balkans, possibly within a week's time, yet devout Mohammedan that he is, he expressed faith in ultimate victory: the kind of thing going on in Europe simply could not succeed."

Berle, who had graduated from Harvard Law School at the age of twenty-one and was now serving as the State Department's intelligence liaison with the White House, also noted, "There is a great gulf fixed between the devoutness of this wise old Mohammedan imam and the devoutness of my mother's New England Puritanism; but somehow the two merged in a fantastic moment of realization that a great faith and a kindly God produces characters that are much alike. Even the voice and face for half a second seemed the same."

As always where matters of state were concerned, Mehmet Ertegun's unwavering faith in God was not the only reason he was held in such high regard by Roosevelt's administration. Even as the Turkish ambassador was meeting with Berle at the State Department, Franz von Papen, the former chancellor of Germany who now represented the Third Reich's interests in Ankara, was doing all he could to persuade the Turkish republic to align itself with the Axis powers. On June 26, 1940, Turkey declared it would remain neutral. In Ahmet's words, "My father was the main strength in the government against Turkey going into the war unless we went in on the Allied side."

After Pearl Harbor was attacked on December 7, 1941, and the United States went to war against Japan and Germany, uniformed soldiers filled the streets of Washington. However, life in the nation's capital went on much as it had before. As the sons of the official representative of a neutral power, Ahmet and Nesuhi could not enlist or become part of the American war effort without compromising their father's diplomatic position. Nor had either of them ever been raised to bear arms. At the embassy, Ahmet and his family continued to live just as they always had. With servants to attend to their every need, they entertained a succession of famous and successful visitors while enjoying the endless round of formal lunches and dinners that comprised a diplomat's social life.

Always starstruck, Ahmet's mother had driven with her children and a female Turkish journalist who was a family friend to California before America entered the war. Given, in Selma Goksel's words, "the star treatment in Hollywood because of my father, we were able to visit several studios. We saw Fred Astaire and Rita Hayworth and Ahmet loved it." They also met and had their photograph taken with Clark Gable, who along with Spencer Tracy and Claudette Colbert, was then filming *Boom Town*. That Gable had once been slated to portray Gabriel Bagradian in MGM's ill-fated production of *The Forty Days of Musa Dagh* was not discussed.

A year later in July 1942, Cary Grant and his new wife, Woolworth heiress Barbara Hutton, spent ten days at the Turkish embassy in Washington. Attracted to the tall, handsome butler who while serving dinner had retrieved the jewel-encrusted evening bag she had dropped on the floor, Hutton gave it to him as a gift. When the butler asked nineteen-year-old "Monsieur Ahmet" whether he should not give it back to her, Ahmet told him to keep the bag but that if Hutton summoned him to her room while her husband was out and asked him to do something for her, he could decide whether or not to return the favor. When the butler asked again if he should return the gift, Ahmet replied, "Listen, you return that to a pawn shop is where you return that to."

As Ahmet would recall, "I don't know if they ever consummated anything but Cary Grant used to go sightseeing and my mother gave him our second car and second chauffeur to take him around. There was a big scandal because Cary Grant had stopped somewhere for lunch and asked the chauffeur to sit and have lunch with him at the same table and somehow this got back to my mother and she said to my father, 'You see, you can't really trust these Americans. They always do something wrong.' " By this point, her own social standing in the nation's capital had reached such an elevated level that Ahmet's "heart used to sink" whenever his mother would bawl out servants of whom he was very fond after making them all "stand at attention like soldiers" as she ate her breakfast each day.

At another dinner at the embassy, Ahmet's father told a joke in Turkish that caused everyone at the table to begin laughing hysterically. Unable to control himself, the German butler the family had hired because help was so difficult to find during the war began laughing as well. "At which point," Ahmet said, "we realized he was a German spy. Because he spoke Turkish. He understood the Turkish joke." The butler, who did not deny the charge, was immediately let go.

Because it was so "difficult, if not impossible to travel during the war," Mehmet Ertegun continued to serve as the ambassador to the United States long after he might have been transferred to another post under ordinary circumstances. By 1944, he had spent more time in the nation's capital than any other foreign ambassador and so became the dean of the diplomatic corps.

On March 14, 1944, Ahmet graduated with honors from St. John's College. He then began taking graduate courses in medieval philosophy at Georgetown University while his sister, Selma, went off to college at Bryn Mawr. On the morning of October 29, 1944, as the "whole embassy was astir preparing for the reception that was to take place that afternoon to celebrate the twenty-first anniversary of the founding of the Turkish Republic," Mehmet Ertegun "suddenly complained of pain just under his left shoulder."

Although the doctor who was called to the embassy "prescribed some medicine and complete rest, this happened to be a time when Turkey was being wooed by both the Allies and the Germans to enter the war on their side. My father thought his absence from the reception might be construed as a sign Turkey was on the verge of a decision. So in spite of his pain and the doctor's advice, he got up and stood in the receiving line for at least two hours." The ambassador then returned to bed.

In a photograph taken two days later, Mehmet Ertegun sits in a plush velvet armchair wearing a thick herringbone tweed jacket, a white shirt, a neatly buttoned vest, and a tie. In his hands are two tiger-striped kittens. Completely bald with his thick mustache having gone entirely gray, he looks much older than his years and not at all well as he stares into the camera through the thick lenses of his rimless glasses. Early in the morning on Armistice Day, November 11, 1944, Mehmet Munir Ertegun died of a coronary thrombosis at the age of sixty-one. Along with their mother, both Ahmet and his sister were with him.

"I am deeply grieved by the news of the sudden death of my personal friend the Turkish Ambassador Mehmet Munir Ertegun," President Roosevelt said in a press release issued that day. "Turkish interests in this country have been ably represented by him for more than ten years and during this period I, along with hundreds of others both in and out of the Government have come to esteem him as a diplomat of the highest type—kindly, sincere and accomplished. His personal integrity was outstanding."

On January 25, 1946, President Harry S. Truman gave permission for Mehmet Ertegun's body, which had been kept at Arlington National Cemetery for the duration of the war, to be taken back in state to Turkey on a naval cruiser. In April, the ambassador's remains were transported to Istanbul on the USS *Missouri*. In Ahmet's words, this was "the battleship on which the official Japanese surrender had been signed. The day the ship arrived, the docks were festooned with flowers and thousands of people were there holding banners in support of the Allies and the new leadership of Turkey."

As Ahmet's sister would later write, "Although we felt this was a great honor for us, we knew that the U.S. was using this as a show of strength to the Soviet Union, which had been making demands on Turkey for two provinces adjoining Russia. In a way, we were happy that even in death, Father was able to serve his country." In the family graveyard in Sultantepe, Uskudar, in Istanbul, Mehmet Munir Ertegun was laid to rest alongside his Sufi grandfather.

No longer bound to follow in his father's footsteps by pursuing a career in the Turkish diplomatic service, Ahmet was now free to do whatever he liked in a country where the postwar economy was booming and jobs were available in every field. For someone who had never worked a day in his life, it was neither an easy nor an enviable choice. With no visible means of support, no marketable skills, and no real idea what he wanted to do with his life, Ahmet was now for the first time truly on his own.

# THREE

# Making Records

*"After the Second World War when there was a shortage of shellac, the major companies only pressed records by their biggest stars and the first area to suffer was what they called 'race music.' Which opened an area for anybody who could find a pressing facility. You didn't have to have artists. You didn't have to have songs. You had to have availability of pressing. A man named Al Green started National Records. The reason he went into the record business was that he was a tough guy from Chicago, a friend of all the famous Chicago racketeers. He was a very colorful personage with long hair who used to quote Schopenhauer and was always drunk all day long. Here was this Jewish tough guy from Chicago who had somehow acquired a couple of blocks in Philipsburg, Pennsylvania, and discovered that on one of them was a derelict record plant and so he reactivated it. Because with the advent of the Second World War, the Depression was suddenly over. Black people had work. Women had work. Everybody had work and people had money. And there was a sudden boom for records and there wasn't enough supply of records and there weren't enough pressing plants. So when Al Green found he had a pressing plant, the next thing he had was a record company. Because he said, 'Why should I press for these other people? When I can press something?'"*

—Ahmet Ertegun

1

Unlike the classical heroes Ahmet had studied in college, the sudden reversal of fortune brought about by the death of his father did not cause him to take dramatic action of any kind. With the kind of unflappable cool that would become the bedrock of his personality as an adult, he continued living much as he had before as the rest of his family did their best to cope with the harsh reality of trying to survive in America without the endless largesse of the Turkish government to sustain them.

After spending weeks in bed grieving for her husband while being "visited by close friends who tried to console her," Ahmet's mother auctioned off some of her personal belongings to help settle the family's debts. She then moved into an apartment at 2500 Q Street in George-town that was far too small to accommodate the huge record collection her sons had amassed while living at the embassy.

In order to supplement the $100 monthly student allowance the Turkish government had agreed to provide both Ahmet and his sister from their father's pension, Ahmet decided to sell what may have been as many as fifteen thousand 78 records. Originally purchased for a nickel or a dime apiece, each record was now worth from $5 to $25.

Although the money he realized from the sale did not last long, Ahmet was not yet ready to accept help from his father's powerful friends. When Eugene Meyer, the publisher of *The Washington Post*, offered Ahmet a job as a cub reporter that paid $20 a week, he replied, "I get more than that as my allowance." He also turned down offers of employment from Wall Street bankers who were family friends.

When his mother and sister returned to Turkey in July 1947, Ahmet did not accompany them because he was "working hard" on his master's thesis in medieval philosophy at Georgetown University. He also "didn't feel like going back to Turkey because that meant military service. So I wanted to put that off." In a nation where military service was compulsory for all males between the ages of twenty and forty and the army was such an integral part of the social fabric that even to speak out against the draft was a criminal offense, such behavior would have been completely unacceptable.

After Orhan Eralp, a good friend who had served as a secretary at the Turkish embassy and in time would become his nation's perma-nent representative to the United Nations, took over the lease on the apartment on Q Street, he allowed Ahmet to continue living there for free. Ahmet also sometimes stayed with his steady girlfriend, a very attractive young woman from Nashville who worked as a secretary for the government, and with Dr. Tom Williston and his wife, Carol, a black couple whom he had first met through his brother.

After moving to Los Angeles, Nesuhi had married a woman named Marili Mordern in 1945. Now running the Jazzman Record Shop she had founded on Melrose Avenue, Nesuhi somehow managed to send Ahmet $30 a month during this period. As their sister would later write, "Ahmet had some pretty hard times. He told me he had had to subsist on a cheap brand of canned fish and bread. He said he chose fish because it was the best nourishment he could afford."

Still looking for a way to support himself, Ahmet wrote her, "I have not found a really desirable job yet. They all pay so little except jobs like painter, butler, chauffeur, salesman and so on which no one thinks I should like." Intent on finding a job that would pay him more than $25 a week, Ahmet noted he was also trying to put together a jam session with Bunk Johnson, Sidney Bechet, Teddy Wilson, Meade Lux Lewis, Pee Wee Russell, Max Kaminsky, and Ben Webster that he hoped would bring him "about five hundred bucks."

By looking through the want ads, Ahmet found the only job he would ever hold before going into the record business. His term of service at U.S. Insurance, a fly-by-night company that tried to pass itself off as part of the government, did not last long. After Ahmet had signed up all the members of the local musicians' union, his boss offered him a raise rather than the large commission he was due. By the time his boss reconsidered, Ahmet had scuttled the sale by telling the president of the musicians' local the insurance company was run by "a bunch of crooks." As Ahmet would later say, "After that, I said I was going to be in the record business."

Why it had taken Ahmet so long to reach this decision seems difficult to understand. Born with such a good ear for music that "he could memorize a tune he heard only once," Ahmet would often sing the songs he and his sister had just heard at the movies on their way home. For his fourteenth birthday, Ahmet's mother had given him a recording machine, which he loved.

When he was nineteen years old, Ahmet had gone into "a cheap recording studio" in Washington to cut some sides with Mildred Cummings, a twenty-year-old singer known as Little Miss Cornshucks who performed with a bandanna around her head and a basket in her hand and "could sing the blues better than anybody I've ever heard to this day." Having paid for the session out of his own pocket, Ahmet made the record strictly for himself and never considered its possible commercial value.

Ahmet's social standing was also a major factor in forestalling his decision to make his career in music. Able to mix comfortably with other ardent record collectors and passionate jazz fans in the nation's capital, he had virtually nothing in common with those who then earned their living in the record business. While hanging out in what had now become known as Waxie Maxie's Quality Music Shop, Ahmet had already met "all these guys who had these independent record companies and they were all a bunch of third-rate crooks. They were jukebox operators or they had nightclubs in black sections or whatever. Anyway, they were all like very rough-and-tumble guys who didn't know much about music. I figured, 'If they could make it, I certainly can. I know much more than they do.' I knew much more about what black people bought in record shops than any of these people. I knew who the musicians were. I knew the singers. And I knew who was buying what and what to make."

Ahmet also felt he "knew what black life was like in America. I felt I knew what black music was in America. I felt I knew what black roots were—gospel music and blues from the Delta that went to Chicago and Texas blues that went to the West Coast. In loving America, I felt I knew more about America than the average American knew about it."

What Ahmet did not know about actually running a record company was equally staggering. Even after he finally came "around to thinking about running a record label myself, I figured I could do it by working on it one day a week putting out just a few records. I thought that if one of ten shops in America were to buy just one of my records, I could make some money. That was my projection, right? I had no idea about how records were pressed or who distributed them. It just never occurred to me how a record came to be in a shop."

Ahmet happened to be in a record shop one day when nineteen-year-old Bob Clark "breezed in" and said, "I'd like one of everything." After reassuring the astonished clerk that he did in fact want a copy of every record in the store, Clark, whose father had "made a lot of money" as the owner of "a string of cheap hotels," invited Ahmet to inspect his massive record collection. After Ahmet told Clark he wanted to go into the record business but did not have any money, Clark said, "Oh, I've got money. Don't worry about that."

On August 22, 1947, Ahmet wrote Selma that Clark was "a rich friend whom I knew during my first year at St. John's. He wants to form a record company with me and has deposited $8,000, of which we are half-and-half partners. He is also paying for all my expenses (around $200–$300 a month). I have been staying at the Ritz-Carlton [in New York] for the last 15 days. Last week we recorded our first records. They are not jazz but popular music. My friend is very rich. He is ready to give more if necessary. It's such a good offer that I couldn't help but accept. I am living like a lord."

After cutting four sides with Boyd Raeburn, "who had an avant-garde Stan Kenton-type band" fronted by his wife, a beautiful singer named Ginnie Powell, Ahmet took the masters to John Hammond, who was then working for Mitch Miller at Mercury Records. After praising the work Ahmet had done, Miller offered him a job. "I'm not interested in a job," Ahmet replied. I want to have my own record company. I'm looking for a distributor." When Miller told him Mercury did not distribute records it did not own, Ahmet decided not to sell him the masters.

By then, Bob Clark had become friendly with Raeburn. Down on his luck and living with Ginnie Powell "in the Forest Hotel, this dumpy little place in Times Square," Raeburn told Clark, "What do you need this Ahmet character for? You put up the money and we'll do this together." Telling Clark and Raeburn it was fine with him if they wanted to go into business together, Ahmet gave them back the masters. After Raeburn and Ginnie Powell were divorced, Bob Clark began dating her but nothing ever came of his partnership with the band leader. The four sides Ahmet had produced were eventually released on Atlantic.

Having failed at his first attempt to start a record label, Ahmet then persuaded Lionel Hampton, the great jazz vibraphone player and band leader, to come up with $15,000 for a company they planned to call Hamp-Tone Records. To finalize the deal, Ahmet went with Hampton one night to the theater in New York where Hampton was performing.

Because Hampton was managed by his wife, Gladys, "a very tough lady" who "held all of Lionel's money," she was what Ahmet would later call "the equivalent of the bank."

Along with the white sax player in Hampton's band who was her boyfriend, Gladys occupied "the star dressing room while Hampton would be in the small room next door." After knocking on the dressing room door "with the big star," Hampton went inside to talk to his wife as Ahmet waited in the corridor. As Ahmet would later say, "It quickly became apparent that the walls in this particular theater must have been extremely thin, because I soon began to hear raised voices, mainly Lionel's wife screaming, 'You're what? You're going to give this kid how much? You're going to give our money to this little jerk who's never worked a day in his life?' So that was the end of that."

Ahmet then approached Herb Abramson, with whom he had been "best friends for a long time." They agreed to become partners but, in Ahmet's words, "We didn't have the finances so we approached Waxie Maxie. We had one label, Quality, and another, Jubilee, that was supposed to be only for gospel music. We made one record, Sister Ernestine Washington accompanied by Bunk Johnson and His Orchestra. Then we made a couple of records on Quality. None of them sold. Max Silverman said he didn't want to put up any more money so that was the end of the Quality deal. Then I started Atlantic with Herb."

The false starts were now over. With his good friend Herb Abramson, Ahmet was about to found what would become the most prestigious record label in a business about which Ahmet then knew woefully little.

## 2

Ever since he had first caught sight of the brilliant lights of 42nd Street at night as a boy and then spent a thrilling night on his own in Harlem as a teenager, Ahmet had known that New York City was where he belonged. The record company he was about to found would reflect not only his unique personality but also that of his new partner.

Born in Brooklyn on November 16, 1916, Herbert Charles Abramson was a multitalented real-life golden boy who had also chosen to make his life in music simply because he loved it so much. His father, an amateur songwriter who at one point published a small newspaper in Oswego, New York, had died when Herb was twelve. Born in Russia, his mother had emigrated to the United States when she was two. His uncle was a state senator from Queens and his first cousin was Stanley Kramer, the noted film director and producer.

After graduating from Erasmus Hall High School in 1934, Abramson attended the City College of New York. In an era when admission quotas for Jewish undergraduates were actively enforced by Ivy League colleges, CCNY was known as "the poor man's Harvard," or more accurately "the Jewish man's Harvard." Wanting to become a doctor so "he could find a cure for cancer," Abramson transferred to New York University, where he pursued a premed program. He was not admitted to medical school because, in the words of his third wife Barbara, "he was a Jew and the quota was filled."

Abramson was working in Washington when he became part of Ahmet and Nesuhi's social circle. He then helped them put on their early concerts in the nation's capital. Knowing he was about to be drafted into the army, Abramson left his job and returned to New York to live with his mother until he was called up for service. It was there he met and began keeping company with Miriam Kahan, another ardent jazz fan from Brooklyn. Seven years younger than Abramson, she had also graduated from Erasmus Hall High School in Brooklyn and had worked as a proofreader for G. P. Putnam's Sons and advertising agencies before being employed as a bookkeeper at Hearn's, a large department store on 14th Street between Fifth and Sixth Avenues where "a lot of very prominent people worked part-time for a while."

Drafted into the army in 1944, Abramson, who much like Ahmet had no desire whatsoever to serve in the military, "tried desperately to get out." After being ordered to climb an eighteen-foot-high pole to install a telephone wire one day, Abramson fell to the bottom only to be ordered to climb it again so he would not lose his nerve. Replying, "I already lost my nerve," Abramson "ran five miles without stopping because the place where you signed up for medical education in the army was closing at five o'clock, and he put his foot in the door."

Selected for the Army Specialized Training Program because of his premed background, Abramson was sent back to NYU, where he enrolled in an accelerated dentistry program. To avail himself of the extra $50 a week granted by the army to wedded students in the program, Abramson married Miriam in the fall of 1945. The couple went to Washington, D.C., on their honeymoon to see some of Abramson's old friends but when Abramson called Ahmet, he was, in Miriam's words, "very late in calling us back because his father was ill. That was the illness that became fatal."

Discharged from the army in 1946, Abramson, who "did a lot of things part-time," continued his dental studies while working as a talent scout for Al Green, the long-haired, hard-drinking character who ran National Records. After becoming head of A&R (artists and repertoire) at the label, Abramson recorded Billy Eckstine, Joe Turner, the Ames Brothers, the Ravens, Pete Johnson, and Charlie Ventura. Abramson's two biggest hits on National were Dusty Fletcher's version of "Open the Door, Richard" and "Sioux City Sue" by Dick Thomas.

In 1947, Abramson graduated from NYU with a doctor of dental science degree as an endodontist, but as Barbara Abramson would later say, "He didn't like dentistry. I asked him why and he said, 'Because I never saw a hip filling.' " In the words of his first wife, Miriam, Abramson had "a different kind of mind. He could cook. He could build. Herb could do anything. He really could."

Before the year was out, however, Abramson decided he could no longer work for Green. "The reason Herb left National," Barbara Abramson explained, "was because Al Green did not want to deal with female artists if he could avoid it. He said they were too much trouble. When Billy Eckstine brought in Sarah Vaughan, he said, 'No broads. No broads.' At that point, Herb felt he had to move on."

Abramson then founded the Jubilee label, on which he released two gospel recordings. Because "his heart was in jazz and blues," Abramson sold his interest in the label to his partner, Jerry Blaine, in return for his original $2,500 investment. While Ahmet never failed to praise Herb Abramson for the role he played in the creation of their new record label, his new partner also brought more than just a shared interest in black roots music and hands-on experience in actually making records to the venture.

By the middle of 1947 when the two men were actively working to start their new company, the American Federation of Musicians had already announced plans to go out on strike on January 1, 1948, and so had ceased granting any new recording licenses. "Atlantic was formed on Herb's charter from Jubilee," Barbara Abramson would later say. "It could not have been established without the charter because they weren't issuing any more. Herb was the only experienced founding partner."

By then, Abramson, in Ahmet's words, already "knew all the aspects of the music business which I didn't know: how to get a lawyer, how to write a contract, what the going rate of pay was, how to sell records . . . he knew where to get pressings and we didn't press at National because Herb knew it wasn't a very clean operation. They used to press one for you, one for me."

While the license was essential, the new company could not have been created if Ahmet had not managed to find the money to bankroll the label. The way in which he did so has since become a cornerstone of the Atlantic Records story as well as an essential part of Ahmet's legend. As rock critic Ellen Sander would later write, "Ahmet was such a bullshitter that his dentist couldn't get him to shut up long enough to drill his teeth. At one point he was telling stories of his success in picking and reselling those rare old 78s and the dentist got talked into lending him some money to start Atlantic Records."

Now perfectly willing to accept help from his father's friends, Ahmet had approached some of them for financial backing but, "They all knew my background and refused to show any confidence whatsoever in my ever being able to run any kind of business. Finally, in desperation, I turned to my dentist, Dr. Vahdi Sabit, who actually fell for the line I was peddling at the time, which was something like, 'If we could only sell one record to each record shop . . .' He turned out to be a gambler and mortgaged his house in order to put up the $10,000 that we needed, became a partner with Herb and myself, and we started recording in 1947."

Related by marriage to the previous Turkish ambassador, Dr. Vahdi Sabit had been part of Ahmet's social circle and regularly came to Sunday lunch at the embassy. As Ahmet's sister would later say, "We all went to him for our teeth and he wouldn't ask for any money. My parents would say, 'No, let us pay you,' and he wouldn't accept it. And then after my father died, he suddenly presented us with a huge bill."

Although the family liked Dr. Sabit, they also "thought he was a little nuts. But he was fun and he was funny. I don't think he understood music. He was a gambler. If he hadn't been a gambler, he never would have given Ahmet that money."

Nor did Sabit come up with his entire investment before the label began operating. As Barbara Abramson recalled, "Over a two-and-a-half-year period, Dr. Sabit paid bills when they couldn't be met like rent and light bills, electricity bills. He did not extend the money in a lump sum. The reason he invested at all was that he had been apprised of Herb's prior track record. Like Sabit, Herb was also an educated man, a dentist. So Dr. Sabit came in as a limited partner and there was a time period during which he could be bought out."

In a letter to his sister during the spring of 1948, Ahmet wrote, "Dr. Sabit hasn't been able to sell his house yet, and therefore is in a bad situation financially. That is why I was unable to pay off some of our debts with the $300 you sent me but had to use it for our own expenses. We put a lot of money into this business and should be able to get returns on it soon. Originally Dr. Sabit said he would put in $12,000, but due to the house not being sold, he is in a difficult position. We will repay you the $300 as soon as possible."

On December 31, 1947, Sabit, Abramson, and Ahmet signed a contract consisting of three typewritten pages with five line-outs and two addendums that each partner initialed six separate times. All three parties, with Sabit in first position as the major investor, agreed to form a stock corporation pursuant to the laws of the state of New York known as Horizon Records, Inc. Crossed out by hand, this name was replaced by the Atlantic Recording Corporation.

As Ahmet would later say, "The name Atlantic was probably about our eightieth choice, because every name we came up with—Horizon, Blue Moods, all kind of names like that—had already been taken. We'd call the union and the union would say, 'We already have a record company registered by that name.' I'd heard of a label that called themselves Pacific Jazz at that time. So in desperation, I said, 'Look, they call themselves Pacific; let's call ourselves Atlantic.' That's how that happened. It wasn't a name we were crazy about—it was so generic. There are so many Atlantics, A&P and all of that, but finally we said, who cares what we call it?"

The contract also stipulated that fifty of the company's one hundred shares would be given to Sabit in return for his payment of $12,500. Ten shares of stock were issued to Herb Abramson for his payment of $2,500. In return for services rendered to the corporation, Herb Abramson received an additional twenty shares. Ahmet was given nineteen shares with the remaining share going to Sabit. Because they would be "active in promotional and other endeavors on behalf of the corporation," Abramson and Ahmet would each receive $40 a week for expenses in return for expending thirty (the word "forty" having been crossed out) hours a week in such endeavors.

At the end of each year, all parties would receive an equal bonus from one half of the company's net profits with the other half to be distributed in accordance to the shares they owned. Abramson was named as the president of the company with Ahmet as vice president and secretary, and Dr. Sabit as treasurer as well as chairman of a board of directors, which consisted of the three men and two other members they would elect.

The first incarnation of the company's record label was a red and black circle with the long, red, skinny legs of the "A" in Atlantic stretching down the left side as the remaining letters appeared beside it on an extended red horizontal line on a black background with the name of the title and the artist in black below on a field of red. Depending on who told the story, the "A" itself, which was the label's most prominent graphic feature, stood either for "Ahmet" or "Abramson."

On November 21, 1947, more than a month before the partners signed the agreement, Ahmet and Herb Abramson cut their first track on Atlantic with a group called the Harlemaires, who performed "The Rose of the Rio Grande." Working constantly over the next five weeks in studios like WOR, Beltone, and Apex, Ahmet and Abramson cut sixty-five sides. Even for an established company, this would have been an astonishing number of tracks to record in such a short period of time. As partners in a fledgling label without a name, Abramson and Ahmet were motivated by a sense of utter panic. As Ahmet would later say, "We were grabbing at straws because of the coming strike and we recorded lots of semi-names, unknown artists. . . . We must have spent three or four thousand dollars just making recordings in 1947 without ever releasing anything."

After the strike began, Ahmet learned to his great chagrin that although he had thought "the major companies would be doing a lot of recording in Europe and we couldn't afford to do that, 'Europe' turned out to be New Jersey because you could go there and record anybody you wanted because the local wasn't sending anybody to check up. The guys who were used to making scale would come up and say, 'Hey, listen, we're willing to record nonunion. . . . Don't let anybody know and we'll do it for $25 a session.' Suddenly, with the strike on, the price went down. All the musicians were scuffling for work."

Many of the sessions Ahmet and Abramson cut in 1947 were then "just thrown in the garbage because I should have known better and certainly Herb Abramson should have known better. You can't record a lot of stuff in advance hoping to release it later because later it doesn't sound so good." After what proved to be but the first of many decisions by the partners that did not turn out as planned, the real miracle was that Atlantic Records itself managed to survive.

## 3

To house his new company, Ahmet rented a tiny two-room suite on the ground floor of the Hotel Jefferson, a derelict, broken-down old building at 208 West 56th Street between Seventh Avenue and Broadway that would soon be condemned. Using the living room as the Atlantic Records office, he shared the bedroom with his cousin, a Turkish poet named Sadi Koylan who had upgraded his own living situation by moving from the flophouse where he had formerly resided. The rent on Suite 102 was $60 a week but since the hotel switchboard operator answered all incoming calls, Ahmet did not need to hire a secretary. Songwriters like Doc Pomus and Rudy Toombs soon began dropping by to audition songs.

On January 22, 1948, Nesuhi congratulated his younger brother on having finally launched his own record company by writing, "The name sounds good, label nice. Some of the recordings you made strike me as terribly exciting." Now running his own small jazz label called Crescent Records from his record shop in Los Angeles that featured New Orleans musicians like the legendary trombonist Kid Ory, Nesuhi counseled Ahmet not to bring out his records too fast so they would have "time to be properly exploited" and added, "Received press release from your publicity man. This, to me, seems to be an unnecessary luxury: I mean the hiring of a PA. I would think that between you and Herb, you could take care of that angle yourselves. Why increase your overhead?"

Far more organized than his younger brother and obsessed with detail, Nesuhi would throughout this period continue sending Ahmet long letters from Los Angeles without ever getting a timely reply or managing to persuade him to heed his advice. Even as Ahmet was sharing a bedroom with his cousin while trying to draw attention to Atlantic's first releases by having Waxie Maxie play them on his radio show in Washington, he conducted his business exactly like someone who had grown up in incredibly privileged circumstances.

Despite how doggedly Ahmet had worked to find the money to start Atlantic, he was still caught between two worlds, a point reinforced by Nesuhi when he asked, "By the way what happened to your studies? When are you getting your degree, and are you? You are being very foolish to reject your studies; you will bitterly regret it the rest of your life."

While in many ways Ahmet was still the pampered rich boy he had been brought up to be, he had learned to rely on the kindness of friends to survive. Before starting Atlantic, Ahmet would often come to New York and spend the night on the couch in the living room of the furnished three-room apartment Herb and Miriam Abramson rented for $45 a month at 106 West 13th Street. "Nobody believes this story," she would later say, "but when I used to go to work in the morning, Ahmet would still be asleep because he had been going to clubs all night and when I came home in the evening, all the sheets and pillow cases were neatly folded on the couch. If you know Ahmet, he was from a privileged background and he had never done any of that. In a way, he was coddled all his life."

In the words of his old friend Delia Gottlieb, "Ahmet was still very naive. He would say, 'I don't have any shirts. I don't know what to do.' When I got into the hotel, he had a pile of shirts in the closet he had worn. I said, 'You know, you're supposed to take them to the laundry and they wash them for you.' The servants or his aunt had always taken care of them for him."

When it came to his own appearance, however, Ahmet was never frugal. "He didn't have a nickel," Gottlieb recalled, "and he would say, 'I need a pair of alligator shoes. I have to order them from Lobb's.' Back then, who knew what they cost? He didn't pay his bills because the gentry don't do that. But Ahmet was having the time of his life. He liked the music and he knew the music and he understood the people and he had this enormous gift—he could talk to musicians and he could talk to dukes."

In Miriam Abramson's words, "Ahmet had been cosseted at the embassy where they had taken care of everything. He didn't know anything about the practicalities of life. He had all these personal bills and I said, 'Why don't you pay these?' He said, 'If I pay them, they'll think I'm closing the account.' That was what would happen at the embassy because they would keep credit going forever for those people."

In 1948, Atlantic had some success with two jazz instrumentals, "Old Black Magic" by Tiny Grimes and "The Spider" by Joe Morris, who also recorded "Lowe Groovin'," which then became the theme song for Washington R&B radio deejay Jack Lowe Endler, known to his listeners as Jackson Lowe. In November, Ahmet produced "Midnight Special" by Morris and the song went to number twelve on what was then known as *The Billboard* Juke Box chart. The money on which Ahmet was living however did not come from record sales but regular payments his mother sent him from Turkey.

Although an American dollar then cost nearly four times as much on the black market in Turkey than it was worth in the United States, Ahmet's mother continued raising money to settle family debts in America by "selling most of the things" she had brought with her from Washington. "I only hope," Selma wrote, "you haven't been annoyed by angry creditors too much. It is some comfort to think that sort of thing never bothered you so much as it does me." Ignoring the bills, Ahmet was in fact using the money to keep Atlantic going.

He was also keeping company with Mynell Allen, a black vocalist with the Sam Donahue Orchestra, who, in Miriam Abramson's words, was "very sweet and not very pretty. A lovely woman. I think he was more interested in Ginnie Powell with the Boyd Raeburn band. What was interesting considering Ahmet's background and education was that I don't think he'd had much success with girls. He was beautifully educated with wonderful manners but rather shy and when he first came from Washington, he had an inferiority complex about girls. But that faded fast."

With the Hotel Jefferson about to be knocked down so the Mutual of New York building could be built on the site, Ahmet and Herb Abramson were forced to move the Atlantic office to a tenement building at 301 West 54th Street just around the corner from Stillman's Gym, the center of the boxing universe in the city. Located above a storefront, the office had no desks so Herb and Miriam Abramson bought a used partner's desk, which Abramson then refinished because, in her words, "He could do everything, and that was our furniture."

"We were very short on help," Ahmet would later remember. "There was just Herb, Miriam, and me. Occasionally, if we had a particularly heavy box of records to send out, we would give one of the less successful heavyweight fighters a dollar to come and carry our shipment to the local post office." In the words of Francine Wakschal, who began working at Atlantic in February 1949, "It was a funky neighborhood. When I went to work, there was a shipping clerk who used to come in early in the morning and wait for me so I could go into the lobby because there were always bums sleeping around. It was not a great building and the area was not good."

In time, the West Side of Manhattan from 42nd to 56th Streets between Broadway and Tenth Avenue would become the home of the independent record business in Manhattan with "dozens of small independent record labels and distributors eking out an unsteady existence in the burgeoning rhythm and blues field." Tenth Avenue, which boasted the largest concentration of independents, most of which were located in storefronts, came to be known as "the Street of Hope."

By the time Ahmet and Herb Abramson set up shop not far from Madison Square Garden, then located at 50th Street and Eighth Avenue, Ike and Bess Berman were already doing business at Apollo Records. Herman Lubinsky, who knew nothing about music, had started Savoy Records from his electrical parts store in Newark. Syd Nathan had founded King Records in Cincinnati. In Los Angeles, Art Rupe, whose real name was Arthur Goldberg, was doing business at Speciality Records. Jules, Saul, Joe, and Lester Bihari, four brothers who had grown up in a large Hungarian Jewish family in Tulsa, Oklahoma, were running Modern Records. Eddie and Leo Mesner were putting out hits on Aladdin. In Chicago, another set of brothers named Leonard and Phil Chess were converting the Aristocrat label into Chess Records. In an industry that was still relatively small, Ahmet and Herb Abramson had gotten in on the ground floor.

Which did not mean Atlantic was yet doing all that well. In a fourteen-page letter on January 28, 1949, to his sister, "Dearest sweetest darling Selma," Ahmet noted he was "working harder than I ever have. There is a lot at stake and I just have to make good. We started this record company at a time when business on the whole was on a downgrade and have done remarkably well, considering that fact. Of course, at first we were making no money at all, so I had to borrow quite a bit from Dr. Sabit in order to live in New York."

Hedging his bets in case the record business did not work out for him, Ahmet was also running a "patent development" company called Industrial Improvements for Dr. Sabit, who in return for a $6,000 investment had acquired a half-interest in some "sixty odd inventions" by a fellow Turk named Sukru Fenari. Although Fenari and Sabit would eventually be granted a patent for an automobile carburetor on which Ahmet had been "working very hard," none of Fenari's inventions had yet been sold and "getting the patents is a long tedious process, and of course all one does is spend money at first and that's all we have been doing."

Each morning at about nine-thirty or ten, Ahmet would go to the Industrial Improvements office at 104 West 40th Street and then report to the new Atlantic office where he "usually had quite a few appointments." Staying there until about seven at night, he would "return home, wash up and go out to dinner. After dinner, I often have to go to the opening night of one of our artists, or have to go hear some new talent. Sometimes we have recording sessions at night. Or else I have to go see some disc jockey." After "paying for my laundry, food, and other necessities," Ahmet didn't "have a hell of a lot left to go out" and usually went "to bed by one o'clock so that I still get plenty of sleep."

In Ahmet's estimation, "The record company is now worth about $25,000 and growing every day. We had some tough luck at first but we're doing extremely well now, that is, we're not getting rich yet but the company is now one of the top 25, and to do this in one year when there are some 500 companies is pretty good." Ahmet, Herb, and

Miriam Abramson were all drawing salaries "and we make a profit every month, and this increases solidly every month. But we keep investing all the money in order to let Atlantic grow healthily so that we may build something worthwhile for the future." Within a year, Ahmet believed they could all "become quite well-to-do."

Although Atlantic had been unable to make any new records during the past year because of the musicians' strike, it was now selling forty thousand records a month "and this figure is increasing. When we hit 75,000, then we'll be able to take some sizeable profits out of the Atlantic Corporation, without it hurting the company." As Ahmet noted, Atlantic already had "26 distributors in all parts of the U.S.A. and sell[s] more records in a month than a company like Nesuhi's sells in a year. Our records are in almost all the shops." Because his accountant and his lawyers had advised him not to declare any dividends, "This is why I don't have any extra money now in large enough quantity to repay you the money I owe you, even though my share of Atlantic is worth quite a lot, but I would have to sell out to get it."

By running both companies for Dr. Sabit, Ahmet was taking home "$90.00 to $100.00 a week, on which I just manage to get along, as New York is tremendously expensive" but was now settled in a large four-room furnished apartment in a building with a doorman at 150 West 55th Street. Still living with his cousin Sadi Koylan, Ahmet had a "tremendous master bedroom with two double beds and a nice living room" in an apartment he shared with the "elderly couple" from whom he was subletting his two rooms. They were "extremely nice, well-bred Southern people and they like me very much, so that I'm really very happy and so are they to have me."

Just a week before he wrote the letter, Ahmet told his sister he and Herb Abramson had completed recording background music composed by Vernon Duke for *This Is My Beloved*, a collection of poems by Walter Benton. Although Miriam Abramson, who had first brought the project to Ahmet's attention, thought the poetry itself was "absolutely schmaltz," she believed it would "make a great record" because the book was so popular she had found it in a drugstore lending library where usually only romance novels and mysteries could be borrowed for 10 cents a day.

Although Ahmet could not persuade "either Montgomery Clift, a new Hollywood star, or Tyrone Power" to participate in the project, he proceeded with it nonetheless. As he would later recall, "We made a recording of a book of poetry called *This Is My Beloved* by Walter Benton which was slightly erotic and the number one book that all the soldiers in the American army took with them when they went to war. We got this second-rate movie actor John Dall to read this poetry and I got Vernon Duke, who wrote 'April in Paris,' 'Autumn in New York,' 'I Can't Get Started with You,' to write this semiclassical score, and that sold fairly well."

Released in March 1949, *This Is My Beloved* was the first 33⅓ RPM album on Atlantic. Miriam Abramson would later recall that the record "did not sell particularly well" and this would seem to be confirmed by a letter written to Ahmet from Paris by Vernon Duke, a very elegant and eccentric character who had been born Vladimir Alexandrovitch Dukelsky in Russia. Addressing Ahmet as "Dear Ahmedakis," Duke wondered why there had been no publicity for the record "in *Variety, Newsweek, Life, Time,* etc. . . . I am frankly astounded at the total lack of a *single* detail of the propaganda campaign in your letter. Not one clipping!"

Whatever level of success Ahmet may have achieved with *This Is My Beloved*, he continued recording material no other independent record label would have even considered. Thinking that if Atlantic issued "a series of Shakespeare's plays on record that hadn't been done, every university would buy at least one copy," Ahmet enlisted the well-known Shakespearean actors Eva Le Gallienne and Richard Waring to record *Romeo and Juliet* accompanied by "the music of Mendelssohn." Ahmet's belief that universities all across the country would snap up this release was "of course a mistake. They were not interested in buying any. We were very dismayed that this album of Shakespeare's most famous play did not sell."

Ahmet and Herb Abramson then released a series of children's records that also did not sell. In order to survive, Atlantic needed a hit record. Establishing what would become the pattern of his career, Ahmet soon found one.

# 4

Once a week from his office, Ahmet would call his distributors to take orders for Atlantic's records. After William B. Allen, his New Orleans distributor, had placed an order for thirty singles that retailed for 79 cents each, Ahmet plaintively asked him, "Can't you push these a little more?" Telling Ahmet those were all he needed because no one in New Orleans was looking for anything on Atlantic, Allen said there was a record selling like crazy down there on both the Harlem and Cincinnati labels that no one could find. If he could locate some copies for him, Allen offered to take what Ahmet would later recall as either five or thirty thousand of them. Stunned by the size of the prospective order, Ahmet asked Allen to send him a copy of the record, "Drinkin' Wine Spo-Dee-O-Dee" by Stick McGhee.

Born in Knoxville, Tennessee, on March 23, 1917, Granville "Stick" McGhee had acquired his nickname as a boy while pushing around his older brother, who suffered from polio as a child, in a wagon with a stick. In a photograph taken when both brothers were in their early thirties, they sit across from one another holding guitars before an ancient microphone. A handsome light-skinned man with a wispy mustache and a shiny lustrous conk, Stick peers down at his left hand as he fingers a G-seventh chord on his guitar. In an open-necked white shirt, a pair of boldly pinstriped dark suit pants held up by skinny black suspenders, white socks, and leather sandals, he looks like a gentleman who had little trouble attracting the ladies.

Drafted into the army in 1942, McGhee first heard what was then a drinking song popular with black soldiers. In the song's original chorus, the phrase "Drinkin' wine motherfucker" was repeated numerous times. After he was discharged in 1947, McGhee cleaned up the lyrics, added some verses, and recorded the song with his guitar and a slap bass on the Harlem label for J. Mayo Williams, a pioneering black record producer who had been an outstanding athlete at Brown University, played in the National Football League, and then spent a decade running the "race music" department at Decca Records. Although Williams attached his name to the song as cowriter, he did little to promote the record, which nonetheless became a runaway hit in New Orleans.

With no idea how to find thousands of copies of a record on a label he had never heard of, Ahmet decided to remake the song and then ship the Atlantic version to New Orleans and so began looking for someone to record it. As he would later say, "The only blues singers we knew were Sonny Terry and Brownie McGhee, but they were doing Carnegie Hall-type blues—more like folk singers, doing hollers and that sort of thing." When Ahmet called Brownie McGhee to say he was looking for someone to cover "Drinkin' Wine Spo-Dee-O-Dee," McGhee replied, "That's my brother's record!" After Ahmet asked if he knew how to get hold of him, McGhee said, "He's right here."

When Stick McGhee came on the line, Ahmet asked him if he had ever signed anything when he had recorded the song. In an era when the independent record business was still so fly-by-night that such arrangements were common practice, Stick McGhee replied, "No man, I never signed anything. They gave me $75 and a couple of hot dogs." Ahmet promptly offered him $500 to cut the song for Atlantic.

Ahmet and Herb Abramson then spent twelve hours in the studio trying to get Stick McGhee to do an exact copy of the original record. Unable to get it right, they sent him home. When McGhee returned the next day, they cut the song in an hour. At the session on February 14, 1949, Ahmet and Abramson added Wilbert "Big Chief" Ellis on piano and Gene Ramey on bass and had Brownie McGhee sing backup vocals. Credited to "Stick McGhee & His Buddies," the Atlantic track was far superior to the original version.

Although the song was a twelve bar blues, Stick McGhee would, in Ahmet's words, "sometimes sing 13 bars, sometimes eleven and a half, so it took us a long time but finally we got it right—and that was the first big hit we ever had. We sold at the time, I would say, 700,000 copies of 'Drinkin' Wine Spo-Dee-O-Dee,' and the bootleggers sold a million."

Released in April 1949, the record went to number two on the Juke Box chart and number twenty-six on the Pop chart. Entering the Best Sellers chart on April 16, it remained there for twenty-three weeks. Even though Decca Records then bought the original from Mayo Williams and released it as well, the Atlantic version outsold the Decca side by far, which "gave us confidence in our production techniques and marketing."

A month after he had released the song on Atlantic, Ahmet went to Houston, Texas, to find a local distributor only to walk into a record store where he saw "a stack of about 300 copies of our record, 'Drinkin' Wine Spo-Dee-O-Dee,' which lots of people were coming in and buying! I picked up a copy and it had the Atlantic logo and label, but it wasn't our pressing." In an era when "the police couldn't have cared less," it was also common practice for bootleggers to issue their own pressings of a hit record they would then sell for cash to anyone who would buy them.

Determined to personally confront whoever had been stealing money from him and his company, Ahmet learned the men who had pressed the bootleg record were holed up in the mountains outside Paris, Texas, where they also made their own rye whiskey and bathtub gin. After being informed they kept five or six armed men on guard twenty-four hours a day, Ahmet decided his life was worth more than the money and did nothing to stop their operation.

Despite how many illegal copies of Stick McGhee's record may have been sold, Atlantic had its first hit. For independent record men like Ahmet and Herb Abramson, a hit was the high tide that floated all boats. Above all else, a hit allowed a record man to stay in business so he could produce more hits. The only problem was that once a record man made a hit, he had to make another, if only to get the distributors to pay what they owed for the first one. The need to generate hits would soon become Ahmet's lifelong addiction.

Along with the money "Drinkin' Wine Spo-Dee-O-Dee" brought Atlantic, the success gave Ahmet credibility. No longer just a rich boy dabbling in a business in which he had learned there were no rules, everyone stole, cheated, and lied, and making hits was all that really mattered, Ahmet had himself now become an authentic record man.

# FOUR

# The House That Ruth Built

*"Ahmet was eyeing up good musicians all the time, and they could see he knew a lot about the blues. So the only way he was able to sign artists was by becoming friendly with them, 'cause he sure couldn't give them more money or even as much as most of the other companies because he didn't have it in those days. So it was due to personal contact and through friendship . . . It was really through a personal relationship. Ahmet's 'personal touch' extended to some artists he'd never met. For instance, one night he was in Washington, this would be in the late 40's, forty nine or so, he went to a club and there was an unknown girl singing, it was Ruth Brown. Immediately he said, 'Look I just started a company called Atlantic and I'd like to record you.' She'd never received a recording offer before, she was very young, she said fine, great, and they made a deal right there and then in a small club in Washington. Anyway, she was involved in a bad car accident on her way to New York to record, and Ahmet took care of her, made sure she was okay before she eventually recorded in New York, and she became very big."*

—Nesuhi Ertegun

## 1

Both Ahmet and Herb Abramson knew the next step in building Atlantic was to find, sign, and then develop an artist who would give the label staying power in the marketplace. Much like the motion picture industry in Hollywood, the record business had always been all about stars and the best way to ensure a label's enduring success was to have as many of them under contract as possible. Atlantic's first great star was Ruth Brown. Although even she never seems to have known who created the phrase, the label became known in its early days as "The House That Ruth Built," a play on the well-known nickname for Yankee Stadium.

Between 1949 and 1961, Brown cut nearly one hundred sides for the label. Five of her records went to number one on the rhythm and blues charts. Eight more made it to the Top Ten. Onstage at the Apollo Theater in Harlem in 1955, Ahmet and Abramson presented the singer with a plaque to commemorate the sale of five million of her records. When Ruth Brown joined the label in 1948, Atlantic was ranked twenty-fifth in the R&B field. By 1951, in her words, "and from then on, Atlantic was the undisputed number one."

Ahmet would later describe the relationship between a record label and an artist as being very much like marriage. While there was always a great deal of excitement at the beginning and that went on for a while, it did not last forever. Eventually, the artist would leave to record for a richer company or the label would find someone younger and the two would part company, often not on the best of terms. In every sense, this was the nature of the relationship between Ruth Brown and Atlantic.

The daughter of a dockhand who directed the local church choir, Ruth Brown was born Ruth Weston on January 30, 1928, in Portsmouth, Virginia. Inspired by Sarah Vaughan, Billie Holiday, and Dinah Washington, she began singing at USO shows and in local nightclubs. At the age of seventeen, she ran away from home with trumpeter Jimmy Brown, whom she then married.

By the time Ruth Brown joined the Lucky Millinder Orchestra as their second female vocalist in 1948, the band was playing hard-driving rhythm and blues powered by saxophonists Clarence "Bull Moose" Jackson and Eddie "Lockjaw" Davis. After spending a month on the road with the band, Brown performed for the first time on July 4 at Turner's Arena, a two-thousand-seat venue in Washington, D.C.

As the singer was signing autographs after the opening set, one of the saxophone players asked her to bring the band some sodas. After she handed them to her fellow musicians, Millinder came to the edge of the stage and told her, "I hired a singer, not a waitress. You're fired! And besides, you don't sing too good anyway." Twenty years old, Brown found herself stranded without any money in the nation's capital. She then, in her words, "got a job at a little club called the Crystal Cavern on 11th and U Street."

Founded in 1926 in a drugstore basement, the Club Caverns, also known as the Crystal Caverns and later as the Bohemian Caverns, was where "Washington's elite would come in droves dressed in the most formal attire, to be entertained by the likes of Duke Ellington and Cab Calloway." A curving replica of a black and white piano keyboard ran along the building's facade above the club's front door. Inside, elegantly dressed guests sat at tables beneath a low ceiling made of swirling concrete designed to look like the roof of a cave replete with stalactites.

In 1948, the Club Crystal Caverns, which still billed itself as the "Rendezvous of the Socially Elite," was owned by Blanche Calloway. The older sister of Cab Calloway, whom Ahmet had first seen perform at the Palladium in London in 1934, she was "a gorgeous lady, tall, graceful, and statuesque" who as a singer shared her famous brother's "high energy performance style." Calloway let Brown audition for her and then offered the singer a one-week engagement for $30 so she could earn enough money to go back home.

Brown was performing at the club one night when Duke Ellington walked in with Sonny Til, the lead singer of the Orioles, and Willis Conover, the bespectacled, professorial-looking white jazz disc jockey whose nightly broadcasts on the Voice of America radio network would make him a cult figure throughout Eastern Europe and the Soviet Union during the Cold War. After dedicating the song to Sonny Til, Brown began singing "It's Too Soon to Know," a hit the Orioles had just recorded for Jerry Blaine on Jubilee that was rising on both the R&B and pop charts.

Getting up from his seat as Brown was singing, Conover went to a pay phone in the coat check room, called Western Union, and sent a telegram to Atlantic Records in New York telling the partners, in Miriam Abramson's words, "There is a girl in Washington who is a cross between Ella Fitzgerald and Sarah Vaughan. You must come and hear her."

According to Brown, a promotion man and talent scout named Blacky Sales who worked for Atlantic went to see her perform, followed by Abramson and finally Ahmet himself. As Abramson would later say of Brown, "She was, at that time, as good as she ever was.

I mean, she was a finished performer, one of the best we had ever seen. . . . Ahmet and I not only wanted to sign her up, which we did, but also have control of her career and try to build her. We had great faith in her because she was great."

Nearly sixty years later, after Ruth Brown had gone toe-to-toe with Ahmet in a very public controversy over royalties owed her by Atlantic, he would say, "Ruth Brown was kind of a shitty singer but she had good rhythm and she thought of herself as a pop singer. The reason I signed her up was that she sang this song 'So Long' imitating the way Little Miss Cornshucks used to sing it. I couldn't find Miss Cornshucks, who had sort of disappeared, but Ruth Brown must have heard her singing that song and she would imitate her."

Although the partners clearly had differing views of her talent right from the start, Brown was then a pop singer whose repertoire included hits by mainstream white artists like Vaughn Monroe, Bing Crosby, and the Andrews Sisters. Her biggest number at the time was "A-You're Adorable," a song that had been a hit for both Perry Como and the Fontane Sisters. In Ahmet's words, "Ruth Brown wanted to sing like Doris Day and I wanted her to sing like Little Miss Cornshucks." Believing no other label was interested in signing her, Brown made a verbal agreement with Abramson to record for Atlantic.

In *Miss Rhythm*, the autobiography she wrote with Andrew Yule that was published in 1996, Ruth Brown said Blanche Calloway had never told her Capitol Records, a major label for whom Nat "King" Cole was then a star, also wanted to sign her to a recording contract. In 1973, Ahmet told rock writer Charlie Gillett, "Capitol also wanted her. Blanche was her manager and they had to choose—Capitol had Nat King Cole—but all our friends were there to persuade her to take a chance with us and she did." Ahmet would also later say Calloway had gone to Waxie Maxie Silverman for advice and he persuaded her it would be better for Brown to be on Atlantic.

In her autobiography, Brown insisted she had learned for the first time in the spring of 1994 that "The well-established Capitol Records . . . had come talent-scouting at the Crystal Caverns at the same time as Atlantic. They had offered a contract and been turned down, completely without my knowledge, in favor of Atlantic, a company with no track record to speak of. Why would Blanche have come to that decision? You tell me. All I can say is that I was nineteen years old, trusting and just glad to be getting signed by anyone at all."

Calloway, who in Abramson's words was now Brown's " 'manager'— in quotes," extended the singer's one-week engagement at the club into a four-month run. On the strength of the Atlantic contract Brown had not yet signed, Calloway persuaded Frank Schiffman, the owner of Harlem's Apollo Theater, to book Brown on a show with Billie Holiday. Because Lady Day did not want another female singer on the bill, Schiffman delayed Brown's debut a week and she was scheduled to appear there on October 29, 1948, with Dizzy Gillespie and His Orchestra as the headliners.

After Brown's husband showed up in Washington and announced his intention to accompany his wife to New York, Calloway changed her plan to make the trip by bus and decided instead to go "in her powder-blue convertible" with her barman and his girlfriend sharing the driving as she navigated in the front seat with Brown and her husband sitting in back. After Brown's last show at the club, they set off at three in the morning only to run into a tree outside Chester, Pennsylvania. Suffering two broken legs and a back injury that put her in traction, Brown spent the next eleven months recuperating.

On January 12, 1949, Brown's twenty-first birthday, Ahmet and Abramson came to visit her in the hospital. With them, they brought an Atlantic Records contract, which she signed. Because Brown had told them she wanted to learn how to read music, they also gave her a book on how to sight-read, a pitch pipe, and a large tablet "on which to scribble lyrics." Less the $1,000 provided by an insurance company to cover her extensive medical costs, the partners also paid Brown's hospital bill. Although her "love of Ahmet Ertegun and Herb Abramson began right there in that hospital," Brown would later say that by the time she joined the label, she was "already in their debt."

In an era when nearly all independent record company owners treated their artists like hired help who could be easily replaced, only Herb Abramson and Ahmet (as well as John Hammond and Goddard Lieberson, both of whom were then working at major labels) would have extended themselves in such a manner for a singer they had not yet recorded. In Brown's words, neither partner then even knew "what I would sound like in the studio."

Still on crutches, Ruth Brown cut her first side for Atlantic on April 6 at the end of a John "Texas Johnny" Brown session. "Ruth Brown wanted to sing like Sarah Vaughan," Ahmet would later say, "but did not have the range and so we recorded her doing bluesier things. . . . I said, 'Let's sing some blues.' And she told me she didn't like the blues. So I had artists like her sing one blues song for me as a favor."

On May 25, Brown returned to the studio for her first real session. The way in which she came to be there demonstrates just how clever Ahmet had already become in drawing attention to his new label. Eddie Condon, a white Dixieland guitar player and band leader who had his own jazz club in Manhattan, had just hired Ernie Anderson as his publicist. Formerly Louis Armstrong's promoter, Anderson had persuaded *Time* magazine, which was then producing a documentary newsreel series known as *The March of Time* that was shown in movie theaters all over America, to do a segment during which the theme song for the series would be recorded by Atlantic.

"For us," Ahmet said, "this was a huge thing." After Ahmet had expressed surprise his label had been selected for this great opportunity, Anderson hit him with the catch. "He said, 'Yeah. But you've got to record Eddie Condon's band. We want him on the thing.' So I got Eddie Condon's band to back up Ruth Brown on her first single. They were totally unrelated." Killing more than two birds with a single stone, Ahmet came out of the session with Brown's version of "So Long," a moody ballad he had first heard Little Miss Cornshucks sing that had been composed by band leader Russ Morgan, who used it as his closing theme. Backed with "It's Raining," the record became Atlantic's second hit of the year, going to number four in the R&B charts and remaining there for nine weeks. Brown's next four releases, in her words, "went nowhere."

For Brown, the initial period of excitement that characterized an artist's early days with a label lasted for quite a while. Ahmet and Herb and Miriam Abramson took her with them to all the leading clubs in Harlem as well as to a new restaurant each week to eat foreign food until she felt as though "I had tasted the world." Whenever she liked, Brown could pick up the phone and call Ahmet and be put straight through to him. To teach her about the blues, he played her records by Bessie Smith and Ma Rainey.

Although Brown "loved and respected" Ahmet, whom she considered "the more forceful" of the partners, she felt closer to Herb Abramson. During this period, he was in the studio producing her while Ahmet and Jessie Stone, who later wrote "Shake, Rattle and Roll," "made many of the decisions regarding" the material she was given to record.

Brown would later remember songwriter Rudy Toombs coming into Atlantic one day with "Teardrops from My Eyes," a song he had composed "especially" for her. Recorded in September 1950, it went to the top of the charts and stayed there for eleven weeks. The side also became the first Atlantic record released on seven-inch 45 RPM vinyl as well as the standard ten-inch 78 shellac.

Two years later, Brown would have her second number one record on Atlantic with "5–10–15 Hours." Also written by Rudy Toombs, the song featured sax player Willis "Gator Tail" Jackson, with whom Brown was then keeping company and would later marry. In 1953, "Mama, He Treats Your Daughter Mean," a song Brown did not like until it became a hit, became her third number one record on the R&B charts.

Paid about $70 to record a side, the highest fee Ruth Brown ever received for a session at Atlantic was $250. As she would also later say concerning what was then standard practice in the industry, "They were charging you for everything. The studio, the musicians, the charts, all records given out for PR purposes, you paid for everything. If you needed something, you could always go to the record company and get a couple of hundred bucks."

Like all musicians during this era, Brown made her real money by performing, earning as much as $750 a night on the road, which even she conceded was a lot of money at the time. But what Ruth Brown did not know was that Ahmet and Herb Abramson were also her managers.

Nearly forty years later, rock critic and writer Dave Marsh, who became one of the founding members of the Rhythm and Blues Foundation, came across a one-paragraph article in the July 30, 1949, issue of *The Billboard,* as the weekly bible of the record business was then known. Beneath the headline "Calloway Assoc. Formed," the article, dated July 23, read, "Herb Abramson, president, and Ahmed [*sic*] Ertegun, vice-president of Atlantic Records, have joined with Blanche

Calloway in forming Blanche Calloway Associates, an artists management organization. The first artist pacted is Ruth Brown, vocalist, currently appearing at Cafe Society. Miss Brown records for Atlantic." In Marsh's words, "I actually called Ruth and told her about it myself and she didn't know about it until then. Absolutely not. Because for Ruth at that moment, a lot of things fell into place. She talks about it in her book."

"What did it mean?" Brown wrote in her autobiography. "Only that every time I had sung my heart out on the back of a tobacco truck, suffering slings and arrows while making far from outrageous fortune, the boss men in New York, not content with giving handouts instead of proper royalty accounting on my records, had systematically been collecting their pound of flesh from the road as well. Who do I blame? Blanche, for surrendering two-thirds to Herb and Ahmet of the ten per cent I paid her? Certainly she could and should have told me, for the association raises all sorts of questions of conflict of interest. I tell myself she had to play along, for who would voluntarily accept one-third of her due? Let me put it this way: I think we can be fairly sure the suggestion of the 'Associates' did not come from Blanche. As for Ahmet and Herb, well, at least with the likes of Morris Levy [the owner of Roulette Records] you knew going in to expect statutory rape. With Atlantic it was a case of date rape."

That Blanche Calloway might have welcomed an infusion of cash from the record label to which she had signed her only client seems never to have occurred to Brown. Nor did the fact that neither Ahmet nor Herb Abramson would have allowed the announcement to appear in *Billboard* if they had intended to make money under the table by paying themselves from both ends of the deal.

Before Brown's autobiography was published, Abramson, who by then had long since ended his association with Atlantic, told Chip Deffaa, the author of *Blue Rhythms: Six Lives in Rhythm and Blues*, "Blanche Calloway diplomatically agreed to become co-manager—we were the co-managers. So Ahmet and I were managers of Ruth Brown for a period of time. However, before the hits started to come in, I would say that our function as managers really consisted of laying out money for gowns, arrangements, and transportation—everything to try to build her. But we never took a cent in commission."

"I was Ruth's manager for a while," Miriam Abramson would later say, "and I used to get these calls from her in the middle of the night. 'You know, it's five hundred miles to the next gig,' and that kind of stuff. Ruth Brown's manager was Blanche Calloway and I don't remember why it was I got involved in it but it was not for long. Ruth Brown got a lot of attention from us. She really did and I don't think she was ever grateful at all. I can't tell you how many people thought they built Atlantic Records. Everybody built Atlantic Records."

In truth, the house that Ruth Brown built at Atlantic had a foundation so shaky that sixty years after it had been laid, the principal architects still could not agree about how it had been put together. As Miriam Abramson would later put it, "The whole thing is *Rashomon*."

## 2

If you really loved the music in those days, you had to go out on the road to find it being played in its original form in crowded, smoke-filled juke joints and roadside honky-tonks in the Deep South where the smell of spilled whiskey and beer and the overwhelming funk of sweating bodies on the dance floor made it hard even to breathe. For any record man worth his salt, this was the pilgrimage. It was the haj—the holy journey first undertaken in July 1933 by John Lomax, who after installing a 315-pound acetate phonograph disc recorder in the trunk of his Ford sedan went to the Louisiana State Penitentiary in Angola, where he recorded Huddie Ledbetter playing twelve-string guitar.

As the curator of the Archive of American Folk Song of the Library of Congress, Lomax spent much of the next nine years on the road with his son Alan, recording hundreds of singers, some of whom no one but friends and immediate family had ever before heard perform. As music scholars, Ahmet and Herb Abramson knew Lomax's work very well. As record men, they had yet to make the journey themselves.

In May 1949, the partners decided to set out on their first field trip down South. They went because they could not find, in Ahmet's words, "any real funky blues singers or players in New York because that was not where they were." Ahmet, who was also looking for distributors in the South to improve Atlantic's sales, intended to end the journey by visiting his brother for the first time in Los Angeles.

"Unfortunately," as Ahmet would later say, "neither of us owned a car back then. As luck would have it, a girl I used to date was given a Ford convertible by her parents for her graduation from Sarah Lawrence. She had no idea how to get the car back to Texas where she lived. So I volunteered to drive it to Fort Worth for her and she thought this was very kind of me and she invited us to stay with her and her parents on their ranch. Herb and I did eventually make it to Texas, but only after criss-crossing the south in that convertible, covering some ten thousand miles—looking for new music and making business contacts. To this day, I'm not sure she knows how important that car was to the beginning of Atlantic Records."

In what Ahmet considered "the most incredible story of my whole career," he was walking down a main street in the black section of Atlanta when he came upon a blind man sitting on a street corner with his back against a building singing gospel songs and "playing incredible slide guitar" as passers-by dropped coins into a hat. After handing the blind singer some money so he "could tell it was bills, not coins," Ahmet asked, "Have you ever heard of Blind Willie McTell?" To Ahmet's astonishment, the singer replied, "Man, I am Blind Willie McTell."

Unable to believe he had actually stumbled on to the blues man with whom John Lomax had recorded more than two dozen songs in an Atlanta hotel room in November 1940, Ahmet asked McTell if he would cut some sides for his company in New York. When McTell asked how everyone at RCA-Victor was doing, Ahmet told him he was from another record company. "No man," McTell replied, "if you're from the New York record company, that's Victor-RCA-you."

Although Ahmet was convinced he had found a completely authentic backwoods bluesman, historian Sean Wilentz would later write that by then Blind Willie McTell had already "made himself into a successful, consummately professional entertainer, and something of an urban sophisticate" whose "everyday wardrobe" consisted of "a suit and tie and a fashionable billed cap."

Later that day, Ahmet took McTell into a local studio only to have the singer tell him he would record only gospel songs. To get him to play the blues, Ahmet offered to release his material under the name

"Barrelhouse Sammy." Six months after he had recorded McTell in Atlanta, Ahmet released a single under the name Barrelhouse Sammy that did not sell. The rest of the session did not appear on Atlantic until 1992 when it was released under McTell's real name. Still relatively unknown when he died at the age of fifty-six in 1959, Blind Willie McTell had by then become famous. The Holy Modal Rounders, Tom Rush, Dave Van Ronk, Taj Mahal, and the Allman Brothers had all covered his "Statesboro Blues," and Bob Dylan had immortalized the singer by writing and recording the song that bears his name.

Leaving Atlanta, Ahmet and Herb Abramson drove to New Orleans, where they heard about "a musical magician who played in a style all his own" known as Professor Longhair. After taking a ferry across the Mississippi to the Algiers section of the city at eleven at night, the partners found a white taxi driver who would take them only as far as an open field. Stopping his cab by the side of a road, the driver pointed to the lights of a distant village and said, "I ain't going to that nigger town."

By the light of the moon, Ahmet and Abramson trudged across a muddy field toward the distant lights. With each step they took, the sound of a big rocking band grew louder, "the rhythm exciting us and pushing us on." At last, they reached a nightclub "or rather a shack" that looked to Ahmet "like an animated cartoon" that kept expanding and contracting in time to the pulsing beat.

The joint was packed to the rafters, with people literally hanging out the windows as music blared loudly from within. Because "there had never been any white people there," the big man guarding the door told Ahmet and Abramson they could not come inside. Ahmet was about to tell him they were from Atlantic Records when he remembered one of the reasons he had set off on this trip was because no one in the South knew the label. Making the story up on the spot, Ahmet said, "We're from *Life* magazine . . . and we've come to hear Professor Longhair."

Unimpressed by Ahmet's imaginary press credentials, the man at the door still refused to let them in. "Just put us in a corner," Ahmet pleaded. "Hide us, we want to hear the music." When the man finally relented and began walking Ahmet and Abramson inside, people scattered in all directions "because they figured the law had arrived."

From his seat in a corner of the room, Ahmet realized to his amazement that all the music he had been hearing was coming from a single musician. With an upright bass drum attached to his piano, Professor Longhair was pounding a kick plate with his right foot to keep time while playing his own idiosyncratic rhythms on piano against the beat. In Ahmet's words, Longhair was "creating these weird, wide harmonies" while "singing in the open-throated style of the blues shouters of old."

Insofar as Ahmet could tell, he and Herb Abramson had just hit the mother lode. Going where no white men had ever been before, they had found an unknown artist who could play the kind of authentic gutbucket blues for which Ahmet had been searching ever since he had first begun listening to music. Sounding like a cross between Jelly Roll Morton and Jimmy Yancey, Longhair was mixing the blues with jazz, ragtime, and Cajun music. "My God!" Ahmet told his partner. "We've discovered a primitive genius!"

When Longhair came over to talk to them after his set, Ahmet shook his hand and proudly informed the man born Henry Roeland Byrd, who had acquired his stage name for his long shaggy hair, that he was now going to be recording for Atlantic. "I'm terribly sorry," Longhair replied, "but I signed with Mercury last week." He then added, "But I signed with them as Roeland Byrd. With you, I can be Professor Longhair."

Polished to perfection as Ahmet told the story again and again over the years, the saga of finding Professor Longhair became one of the set pieces of his repertoire. As funny as the punch line always seemed when he delivered it, the true import of the tale was that when it came to finding undiscovered talent in the hinterlands of America in the spring of 1949, Ahmet and Herb Abramson were already late. Sixteen years after John Lomax had recorded Huddie Ledbetter in the state penitentiary in Angola, this particular musical frontier had closed. The sweeping social and economic changes brought about by the Second World War had transformed the South, and it was no longer the isolated backwater it had been during the Great Depression.

Nonetheless, Ahmet and Abramson took Professor Longhair into the same studio in Atlanta where they had recorded Blind Willie McTell and cut three sides with him that were never issued. In October, they recorded him again at Cosimo Matassa's J&M studio on Rampart Street in New Orleans and cut ten tracks, among them "Mardi Gras in New Orleans," which along with "Tipitina" would become one of the artist's signature songs.

Longhair, who had originally recorded "Mardi Gras in New Orleans" for Star Records in Dallas, Texas, as Professor Longhair and the Shuffling Hungarians, was billed on Atlantic as Professor Longhair and His New Orleans Boys. For an artist who at various times in his career was also known as Roy Byrd and his Blues Jumpers, Roy "Bald Head" Byrd, Roland Byrd, Professor Longhair and His Blues Scholars, and Professor Longhair and the Clippers, the name on the record never mattered as much as the music.

While none of the sides Longhair cut for Atlantic sold very well, his unique sound influenced seminal New Orleans musicians like Fats Domino, Allen Toussaint, and Dr. John. After suffering a heart attack and dying in his sleep in 1980 at the age of sixty-two, "Fess" was inducted into the Blues Hall of Fame and the Rock and Roll Hall of Fame.

Although Ahmet and Herb Abramson had not been able to find an artist in the South who had not yet been approached to record by someone else, they had given it their best shot. As they drove from one city to the next in the new Ford convertible they did not own, they also had one hell of a time together. For Ahmet even then, this was always a good reason for doing anything.

## 3

Having managed to avoid compulsory military service in the land of his birth, Ahmet was forced to register for the draft in America after Congress passed the Selective Service Act in June 1948 decreeing that all men between the ages of nineteen and twenty-six would now be required to spend twenty-one months in the army. Busy running a record company that was not yet providing him with enough income to live as he would have liked, Ahmet had no desire to be subjected to the draft and so dealt with the problem in his usual manner.

Blithely, he ignored a written request from Lieutenant Colonel

Walter S. Welsh, chief of the Manpower Division of the Judge Advocate General Division in Washington, to appear in Welsh's office with his passport and visa so it could be determined if he would be exempt from registering as a "male alien who has not declared his intention to become a citizen of the United States." If Ahmet could prove he had entered the country as a student, he would also not have to register.

Over the course of the next three months, Welsh sent Ahmet three more letters to which he also did not respond. When Ahmet finally appeared in Welsh's office, he explained he had come to America under a diplomatic visa and remained in the United States to pursue his graduate studies at Georgetown University. Rather than solve his problems, this explanation served only to complicate them.

On March 29, 1949, Welsh wrote Ahmet that if he was "not now entitled to remain in the United States under a diplomatic visa or because of diplomatic connections," his status would be reported to the Bureau of Immigration. Until the bureau reached its decision, Ahmet would be subject to Selective Service procedures like any other registrant, pending further clarification of his current status, "that is, your attendance at school or your employment, if employed."

Although Ahmet was still writing his mother and sister in Turkey that he planned to return home at some point, the diplomatic visa on which he had entered the United States was no longer valid. Technically an illegal alien, Ahmet could not leave the country even if he had wanted to and was now subject not only to conscription but possible deportation as well.

Ahmet's first problem was solved by the kind of good fortune he would enjoy throughout his life. During the same month Welsh informed Ahmet he was still subject to military service in America, the army declared an unofficial "draft holiday." Due to the high rate of voluntary enlistments, just thirty thousand of the nine million young men who had registered had been inducted.

Ahmet however still needed to find a way to stay in America. In a handwritten letter to Welsh, he explained that he had remained in America after his diplomatic visa had expired to "continue my studies, and did so until recently when I finished my courses and began to write a thesis. I hope to be able to finish my thesis in a few months. Meanwhile, however, I have been spending much of my time with the

Atlantic Recording Corporation . . . a company I started with some associates, in which I am a stockholder. It is my plan to return to Turkey in about a year, when I hope to have fulfilled all my business."

Quite possibly to maintain the fiction that he was still a student in America, Ahmet did enroll two years later in a graduate course in economic theory at the New School for Social Research taught by Dr. Eduard Heimann, a well-known socialist who had emigrated from Germany to America in 1933 because of his political views. On January 30, 1951, Ahmet appended the following explanation in an examination booklet on the unlikely subject of Crops and Labor—"Dr. E. Heimann, I was unavoidably detained and arrived at the examination half an hour late so that I was unable to complete my answers. My excuses." He still managed to receive a B on the exam.

Ahmet was far more successful in solving his immigration problem than his brother. Facing deportation charges with an actual warrant for his arrest having been issued, Nesuhi wrote a frantic letter to his brother in November 1953 telling him he had hired a very expensive immigration lawyer to represent him at an upcoming hearing. Nesuhi implored Ahmet to persuade the Turkish consul to issue him a new passport to replace the outdated document he had been carrying since 1946. "Please explain to him," Nesuhi wrote, "that this is a question of life and death for me. . . . I hope to God it will not be impossible for him to issue a passport."

Ahmet finally solved his own visa problem by hiring a lawyer who advised him to apply for permission from the Immigration and Naturalization Service to leave America so he could return as a "preference immigrant." Following his lawyer's instructions, Ahmet went to Montreal, where the American consul issued him the visa. On June 8, 1953, Ahmet was granted official status as a permanent resident alien.

In time, both brothers became American citizens. Having come to the United States under privileged circumstances, they had fulfilled the first task of every immigrant, which was to stay at all costs in the land where they had chosen to make their lives.

## FIVE

# *Mess Around*

*"Although Ray, I'm sure, knew about boogie woogie piano playing, he had not at that time heard of Cow Cow Davenport, one of the pioneers of that style. So in explaining 'Mess Around,' I was trying to put across to Ray the very precise phrasing of Cow Cow Davenport, when he suddenly started to play the most incredible style of that playing I've ever heard. It was like witnessing Jung's theory of the collective unconscious in action—as if this great artist had somehow plugged in and become a channel for a whole culture that just came pouring through him."*

—Ahmet Ertegun

## 1

Long after he had become a wealthy man, Ahmet would say, "I remember when my dream was to make a hundred dollars a week. My God, if I could ever make a hundred dollars a week, I'd be a rich man." By 1950, his third year at Atlantic, he had yet to achieve this goal, earning just $4,880, a scant $500 more than the average income for an American family. Nonetheless, it was enough to persuade him to sign away his interest in the patent company to his partners, Dr. Vahdi Sabit and Sukru Fenari, in return for "one dollar and other valuable consideration," thereby freeing him to devote all his time and energy to the record business.

Two years later, Ahmet and Herb Abramson signed the greatest artist who ever recorded for Atlantic. Born Ray Charles Robinson in Albany, Georgia, on September 23, 1930, Ray Charles would come to be known at various times throughout his long and illustrious career as "Brother Ray," "The Genius," "The Father of Soul," and "The High Priest." None of these nicknames adequately describe the astonishing talent of a man whose impassioned singing, piano playing, and unique ability to write songs in several genres would change popular music in America.

The son of a sharecropper and a railroad repair man who grew up in Tallahassee, Florida, Ray Charles began losing his sight when he was five years old and was completely blind by the age of seven. He attended the Florida School for the Deaf and the Blind in St. Augustine, where he began playing piano and singing. After both of his parents died before he was sixteen years old, Charles began his career as a professional musician. Spending most of his life on the road, he was married twice, fathered twelve children by nine different women, and first began using heroin while playing in a jazz band in Seattle in 1948.

An artist who always lived according to his own rules, Ray Charles brought the chord changes, structure, and deeply felt emotion of black gospel music to an audience who had never before experienced its power. That he did so while recording for Atlantic was due in great part to the way in which Ahmet influenced him during the early days of his career.

Ahmet first heard Ray Charles in 1951 when Herb and Miriam Abramson played him "Baby Let Me Hold Your Hand" on Swing Time Records, a Los Angeles-based label owned by Jack Lauderdale, a black record business entrepreneur. Although Charles then still played piano "in a style modeled closely on Charles Brown" and sounded very much like Nat King Cole when he sang, Ahmet, who as a boy had regularly seen the King Cole Trio perform at a Chinese restaurant in Washington called the Lotus Club, said, "I want a piano player like that on our label."

When Billy Shaw, who was then booking Ray Charles, learned that Jack Lauderdale was looking to let Charles go, he put the word out to Chess Records in Chicago, King Records in Cincinnati, and Atlantic. Leonard Chess and Syd Nathan were both interested in signing Charles but after Shaw told Ahmet that if he made hit records with the artist, Shaw could book him as a headliner, Ahmet said, "I guarantee we'll make great records with him—how do I get him?" When

Shaw told Ahmet he could buy Charles's contract from Lauderdale for $2,500, Ahmet said, "Done deal."

Billed as "Ray Charles, Blind Pianist," Charles came to New York on February 29, 1952, to perform for the first time at the Apollo Theater on a bill headlined by the Orioles and Lowell Fulsom and his band. Charles was staying at the Braddock Hotel on 126th Street and Eighth Avenue adjoining the backstage door of the Apollo when Ahmet and Herb Abramson came to meet him for the first time. After they exchanged handshakes, the partners welcomed Charles to the label but said they were in no hurry and would wait until he returned to New York to do their first session with him.

Ahmet would later remember first meeting Ray Charles in the Atlantic office. After Charles had sat down at the piano and played, Ahmet said, "Ray Charles! You're home here. You are home, man. We're gonna make some hits. We're gonna make beautiful music, 'cause you're the greatest!" Charles replied, "Oh man, I'm gonna try to live up to this, to what you say about me." He then gave Ahmet a hug. In Ahmet's words, "We became brothers right away."

Ahmet and Abramson first recorded Charles on September 11, 1952, but the session "produced four jazz-influenced sides which were barely noticed when they were issued." Abramson wanted Charles to emulate what blues singer Big Joe Turner had already done at Atlantic by recording songs that rocked harder but Ahmet believed the problem was that New York musicians tended to look down on illiterate blues-men from the South. In truth, Charles had not yet found what would become his characteristic sound.

Unlike Ruth Brown, who did not write her own material and let Ahmet help shape her career by recording songs that became hits, Ray Charles was, in the words of songwriter and arranger Jesse Stone, who was then working on the staff at Atlantic, "very temperamental and hard to get along with, it was hard to persuade him to do the rock type things. But finally after we'd done a few sessions the way he wanted to do them, he came into the studio and said, 'Okay, I'm not saying any-thing, you guys tell me what to do and I'll do it.' "

In May 1953, Charles spent a week in New York with Ahmet play-ing piano and exploring new musical ideas. Although Ahmet could not read music or play an instrument and his voice left a good deal to be desired, he had by then begun writing songs because Atlantic was "such a small company that publishers didn't want to give us their good songs."

With Abramson, Ahmet had already formed a publishing company called Progressive Music, thereby ensuring that the partners would earn 50 percent of the net proceeds for all piano copies and 5 cents a copy for all orchestrated versions of the original material they generated at Atlantic. When Ahmet cowrote "I Know" with Rudy Toombs and Abramson in 1950, the songwriting royalties were split among the three men according to the contribution each had made to the song with Ahmet being allotted 45 percent of the royalties for the lyrics. The partners profited from the record as the owners of the label, the songwriters, and the publisher as well.

Although many independent record company executives regularly attached their names to music they had done nothing to create, Ahmet would write out his lyrics in capital letters across music staffs on sheet music paper with Roman numerals above each verse. He would then go to one of the recording booths in the Times Square arcade where for a quarter or 50 cents he would make "a flimsy vinyl demo" of a song by singing it to the melody in his head. In the studio, where time was precious because he was paying for it by the hour, Ahmet would then present the song in the most efficient manner possible.

In 1951, Ahmet came up with a slow, mournful blues entitled "Chains of Love." Arranged by Jesse Stone, it became a hit for Joe Turner. The song featured the incredible piano playing of Harry "Piano Man" Van Walls, "an eccentric who dressed like a black Sherlock Holmes," and so Ahmet gave him co-songwriting credit. Some years later, Van Walls asked Ahmet for $500 for his half of the song. Ahmet did not want to make the deal but when Van Walls said he would sell it to someone else because he needed the money, Ahmet bought the song back. As he would later say, "Some people still go around saying that I stole the song from him."

Ahmet had first realized he could write songs by watching Rudy Toombs come up with his own material. A tap dancer who had performed at the Apollo and so "had a great sense of rhythm," Toombs would start snapping his fingers to a beat only he could hear and then begin singing lyrics he had come up with on the spot. "We'd get an arranger to transcribe what he was singing," Ahmet recalled. "When I saw him do that, I knew I could do that. I must have written a *hundred* songs . . . I'd write these songs the day before a session and try to get one rehearsal in before we recorded."

While none of Ahmet's songs was particularly original, his goal was to come up with material that would sell. In his words, "I wrote teenage records, not songs." Still thinking he would at some point return to Turkey to serve in the diplomatic corps as his father had done before him, Ahmet hid his true identity by reversing the letters of his last name and using "A. Nugetre" as his songwriting nom de plume.

When Ray Charles came into the studio in May 1953, Ahmet took a far more active role in the recording process than he had during their previous session by setting the tempo for one track and asking Jesse Stone to come up with a new verse for a song that was too short. When Stone suggested a tenor sax solo for one song, Charles rejected the notion by saying it would not help sell the record and he could not stand that sort of thing. Late in the session, Ahmet sat down beside Charles on the piano bench and began singing "Mess Around."

His inspiration for the song had come from "Pinetop's Boogie Woogie," a well-known blues number first recorded in December 1928 by Pinetop Smith, who died three months later at the age of twenty-four from a gunshot wound. Having first come up with the song at a rent party in St. Louis, Smith talked as he played piano, instructing those listening to the song not to move until he told them to mess around.

Ahmet set his own version of the song at a barbecue pit where both the band and the people were jumping and everyone was juiced as they did the mess around. With Charles on the piano, Ahmet can be heard performing the song in the studio in a flat, wavering voice. Since he never sings the line about the girl with the diamond ring who knows how to shake that thing, Charles must have come up with it on his own while he was recording the song. With Ray Charles ripping up the vocal in his own gut-wrenching manner and the horns blaring in a jump version of the song, "Mess Around" became a minor hit.

One of the many maxims associated with the music that would come to be called rock 'n' roll was that the form came about because white singers and musicians began imitating black singers and musicians, who then turned around and began imitating them. In May

1953, when the races in America were still essentially separate, Ahmet and Ray Charles had already begun the process of cross-pollination that would transform both the independent record business and popular culture in America.

Because the nature of true genius can never be really understood, it is impossible to say how Ray Charles was able to take what Ahmet wanted him to do in the studio and make it sound as good as he did. But then as Ahmet himself would later say, "Whereas we thought we were producing Ray Charles, I realized by the third session that he was not only teaching me about music but also showing me how to make records."

## 2

During a visit to New York in 1952, Nesuhi called his old friends Bill and Delia Gottlieb to say he was coming to Queens to see them only to be told Ahmet was also expected that evening. When Nesuhi told Delia Gottlieb he had a couple of women with him, she told him to bring them along. It was in her house that Ahmet met the woman who became his first wife.

Jan Holm was, in Ahmet's words, "a very attractive Swedish-American girl from California who looked like Greta Garbo." The daughter of Carl Enstam, a minister, and Antoinette Holmes, Holm used a shortened version of her mother's maiden name as her stage name when she began her acting career as a teenager in Hollywood. In 1938 at the age of seventeen, she appeared in eight different movies in a variety of roles so small that she received screen credit for just two of them. A year later, her image appeared as part of a series of "glamour girls" cards distributed inside packs of cigarettes by the Ardath Tobacco Company in the United Kingdom.

Two years older than Ahmet, Jan Holm had been married once before to Walter "Bunny" Rathbun. After studying drama at Yale, he had served as an army lieutenant who put on USO shows in the South Pacific during World War II and then produced the first professional summer stock theater in Laguna Beach, California. In 1947, the two were divorced on grounds of mental cruelty. Rathbun, who then remarried and went to work for Universal Studios, died of Hodgkin's disease in 1952.

Moving to New York, Jan Holm became a model. Her Hartford Agency composite listed her as standing five feet seven inches with blond hair and green eyes, weighing 112 pounds, measuring 35-23-35, with a dress size of 10–12. Smiling broadly with her hair pulled back from her face in a photograph taken on the beach during the summer of 1951, she wears a good deal of lipstick and a fashionable floral print two-piece bathing suit in which she looks both stylish and thin. In New York, Jan Holm became involved with theater and, in Ahmet's words, "did stage sets and stage management and directed certain things. She was involved in many different plays and thought of herself as a theater person."

Now making what seemed to him like the astronomical salary of $250 a week because Atlantic had released a succession of hits by the Clovers and Ruth Brown, Ahmet had moved to "a nice apartment" at 14 East 60th Street when he began double-dating with Jan Holm and her roommate, an aspiring actress who was seeing director Arthur Penn. The roommate then began dating someone who proposed to her. "When they got married," Ahmet would later say, "Jan suddenly no longer had a roommate and we no longer had anybody to double-date with and I felt sorry for her. So I thought, 'Well, the gallant thing to do is propose to her.' She was a very nice girl but I was not madly in love with her and I don't think she was in love with me. But anyway, I proposed to her and she accepted it because it seemed to be the only thing to do."

As curious as his explanation seems, Ahmet and Holm, who listed her occupation on their marriage license as "artist" while he referred to himself as a "Phonograph Record Manufacturer," were wed on February 6, 1953, by a New York justice in the Tweed Courthouse on Chambers Street in lower Manhattan. The ceremony was officially witnessed by Sadi Koylan and Jacqueline Donnet, but Ahmet would later say *New Yorker* cartoonist Charles Addams was also there.

After Ahmet and his new wife "finally found an apartment that she thought was all right," her friend the actor "James Dean came and stayed with us for a while." In Ahmet's words, "She then became ill. She had psychological problems and she started going to an analyst two or three times a week and she slept most of the day and was up all night. So that really wasn't working out. I had a lot of friends who liked her and she was a very nice person, a good person, but she had a lot of personal problems."

"They got married," Miriam Abramson would later say, "and she had what was called a nervous breakdown and she was so attached to her psychiatrist that because they all used to stop practicing in the summer at that time and go to Maine, she went to Maine with the shrink." On July 23, 1954, Jan Holm wrote Ahmet, who was then in Los Angeles, from the Lookout Club in Ogunquit, Maine, to say her doctor was in fact up there with her and she was "getting very tan and slowly gaining weight."

Noting that everyone was waiting for the arrival of Vice President Richard Nixon in August with his wife, Pat, and their daughters, Tricia and Julie, who were then eight and six years old, she asked Ahmet if his mother could possibly bring a coffee table, a brass tray, or a rug with her from Turkey when she came to visit him in America. She also asked if Ahmet had yet seen designer Rudy Gernreich, her mother in nearby Manhattan Beach, "Jim Dean," who was then living at 1667 South Bundy Drive, or the actress Barbara Reed. Closing her letter, she wrote, "Have a good time, dear, I miss you. Love, Jan."

That the gulf between Ahmet and Holm may have always been insurmountable would seem to be supported by a story Ahmet told Jenni Trent Hughes, who worked for him many years later at Atlantic. "He used to be notoriously, pathologically late all the time. To the point where his first wife said, 'Look, I can't live like this. You've got to go see a shrink. I can't deal with this.' He went to see the guy two or three times and he was so late that the guy said, 'Look, don't come back. I can't help you.'"

Having grown up with servants who had catered to his every need, Ahmet, who could be fussy about not only his clothing but his surroundings as well, also had problems adjusting to the way Holm took care of their apartment. "When I was married to Jan, who had no feeling of any kind of formality in the household, we were kind of living a nomadic life. Just throw things around and nobody picks them up and eventually the dishes pile up which are not washed."

When Ahmet's sister, Selma, who was then working in the Foreign

Ministry in Turkey, came to New York in 1954 on a state visit with a group of officials accompanying the Turkish president, she sent Ahmet a telegram from the boat notifying him of her arrival. "He told me then she wasn't well," Selma would later say. "She couldn't come out and be in crowds of people and he said she wouldn't be able to meet me when the boat landed. He had been married about a year. She came to see us later and I liked her a lot actually. She was a very sweet, very nice girl."

"It was difficult," Ahmet would later say. "To be married to somebody is not easy and to be married to somebody when neither person loves the other is even more difficult." After two years, Ahmet and Holm "decided to separate and then we got a divorce. It was painful only in the sense that I was so anxious to get a divorce that when it came to a settlement, I agreed to give her everything. We had two cars so she got both cars. We had an apartment. She got the apartment."

What bothered Ahmet most about the divorce was that when he tried to claim the Picasso drawing Nesuhi had given him for his birthday, "She said, 'Oh no, it says in the agreement that I get the furnishings of the house and that's part of the furnishings.' So she wouldn't let me take it. And I thought to myself, 'Well, I'm so happy to get out of this that I'm willing to give up everything. And I gave her 50 percent of what I made. At the time of the divorce, I was making fifty thousand a year. So I gave her twenty-five thousand. Plus, I gave her all my possessions. She didn't want my records."

Miriam Abramson, who considered Holm "a good friend of mine," would later say, "It was a mistake, that marriage." In Ahmet's words, "I was very sorry I had gone through that whole wedding thing with her but it was at a time when it seemed the natural thing to do and there were some good things about the marriage but I'm not angry or upset. Although she behaved rather badly at the end but I guess she was angry because I took it so lightly."

While another man might have taken the failure of his first marriage to heart, Ahmet used his divorce as a launching pad for the nonstop social life that soon became his trademark. Spending virtually every night out on the town, he became a fixture in Manhattan's most exclusive nightspots, usually with a stunning young model on his arm. "After Jan and I started to get our divorce, I had a whole new group of friends because I was more set up. I didn't have a lot of money but

I spent a lot of money. And I always did that. I never spent more than I was earning but I would spend what I was earning. And it looked to a lot of people like I was spending much more than I did."

While Ahmet viewed the collapse of his first marriage with the kind of esthetic distance that would later enable him to survive the loss of many of his greatest artists at Atlantic, only he could have explained his reaction when a woman "who had put on a lot of weight and was wearing something like a muu-muu" came up to say hello to him one night many years later in a theater in New York. "I'm sorry," he told her politely. "I don't know who you are."

"Well," Jan Holm said, "I'm your ex-wife."

# 3

Using some of the profits from the constant stream of hits they had been generating at Atlantic, Ahmet and Herb Abramson decided in 1952 to look for new offices where they could also record so they could stop paying studio fees. The space they found would in time also become a cornerstone of the Atlantic legend. Leasing the top two floors of a five-story wood-framed brownstone at 234 West 56th Street that had once been a speakeasy known as the 23456 Club, the partners converted the fifth floor into their offices while using the floor below for shipping and storage.

In a cramped nineteen- by twenty-eight-foot room with a floor that sagged and creaked, a sloping ceiling with a skylight that had never been cleaned, and a tiny bathroom to which Ray Charles would repair to get high during a session, Ahmet and Herb and Miriam Abramson sat at desks they shoved aside at night to create a recording studio. Adding to the atmosphere, Patsy's Restaurant, where reputed Mafia figures and celebrities like Frank Sinatra often came to dine, was next door.

Able to recognize talent in those with whom he worked as well as the artists he recorded, Ahmet had by now surrounded himself with a cast of characters who fit perfectly with the mise-en-scène. Nominally the office manager, Miriam Abramson had during the label's earliest days done the books, hired musicians for sessions, which she regularly attended, and made certain everyone was paid on time. The fierce lioness who guarded entry to the gates of the inner sanctum at Atlantic, she could pin anyone to the wall with a cutting look or a sharp remark. She once asked songwriter Doc Pomus, "Are you coming in to beg for money again?" Because she understood the bottom line better than Ahmet or her husband, she constantly challenged both partners by asking, in Ahmet's words, "What are these expenses? Why are we paying for this lunch?"

Born with the kind of personality without which no woman could have survived for long in the male-dominated independent record business, Miriam was also in charge of chasing down distributors who owed Atlantic money. "Tokyo Rose was the kindest name some people had for her," Tom Dowd, Atlantic's resident genius in the studio, would later say. "At some companies, they would take it in turns to answer the phone if they knew that she was calling." In her words, "If the distributors didn't pay their bills, I was very nasty."

Ahmet had first met Tom Dowd back when Atlantic was using the Apex studios on 57th Street between Sixth and Seventh Avenues to record as many sides as possible before the musicians' union strike in 1947. The studio was run by Dr. Fredrick Oetegen, who wore a monocle and a white coat and liked his recordings to be "as coldly neutral as a laboratory photograph." When Ahmet made the great mistake of asking "Herr Doktor" if he could have more drums on a cut, Oetegen replied, "Nein, nein. We cannot have more drums."

The second time Ahmet recorded at Apex, Oetegen was busy doing a session for a major label. Angered because he expected "Dr. Schweinfoot" to be there, Ahmet asked who would do the session only to be told, " 'Oh, this young fellow. He'll be your engineer. He's very good.' I turned around and looked at this kid and he literally looked to me like he was fourteen or fifteen years old." With the musicians already there and precious studio time on the line, Ahmet had no choice but to go along. At one point during the session, he asked for more drums. The kid promptly gave him more drums. Ahmet then asked for more bass. Although he had been specifically instructed by Oetegen to watch the dials so the arrows would never go in the red, the kid gave Ahmet more bass.

When Ahmet asked if this would not damage the record, the kid replied, "Don't worry. It won't break anything." As Ahmet would later say, "This kid was Tommy Dowd and he was just much brighter and very imaginative and a terrific engineer and he had the training and the degrees and all that. After that, we always insisted that he be our engineer."

Twenty-two years old when he first Ahmet, Thomas John Dowd was the son of an opera singer and a concert master who had grown up in Manhattan playing piano, violin, tuba, and string bass. After graduating from Stuyvesant High School in 1942, he attended the City College of New York while working in a physics laboratory at Columbia University. Drafted into the army in 1944, Dowd was part of the Manhattan Project, which led to the development of the atomic bomb. He intended to become a nuclear physicist until he took a job engineering at a recording studio.

"He was a very, very bright guy," Miriam Abramson would recall, "but he did not invent the atomic bomb. No question he was a genius in the studio. An absolute genius. If a musician didn't show up, he would play the bass. Tommy Dowd was someone Herb had worked with at National. I had known him since he was a kid and I knew his parents. When Herb and I moved, Tommy Dowd used to install our sound system."

After Herb Abramson persuaded Ahmet to hire Dowd as a full-time employee at Atlantic, he began cutting records in both mono and stereo at the same time long before anyone else was doing so. Because of Dowd, who would become one of the great producers in the history of popular music, Atlantic's records always sounded better than those made by its competitors.

During 1951 and 1952, Atlantic released jazz sides by Billy Taylor, Mabel Mercer, Meade "Lux" Lewis, Dizzy Gillespie, Sylvia Syms, Wilbur De Paris, and Dave Brubeck. However it was the label's rhythm and blues hits that kept it in business while also firmly establishing what soon became known as the Atlantic sound.

"In those days, we were desperate for hits," Ahmet would later say, "but we didn't have the money to tour the South and the Midwest looking for blues singers so we signed up people in New York, Baltimore, and Washington. Most of these singers were very sophisticated and didn't want to record what I knew our audience—the black audience—wanted to hear. The lead singer of the Clovers wanted to do the syrupy ballads Billy Eckstine was recording. While we wouldn't have had a chance against Eckstine, we needed records that were halfway soulful. And that's what we got, with songs that were and artists that weren't and that something in between caught on with the white kids. They wouldn't buy Sonny Boy Williamson, B. B. King, or Muddy Waters but they would buy Ruth Brown, the Clovers, the Coasters, the Drifters, and Clyde McPhatter. Our music was soulful but it was also urban. It was in fact the music that grew into rock and roll."

The man who did the most to create the early Atlantic sound was Jesse Stone. Astonishingly good-looking, with large deep-set eyes, elflike ears, and hair cut close to the skull and parted in the middle, Stone's grandfather was a slave who became the first black man in Kansas to own a Cadillac. Beginning his musical career as a piano player and an arranger, Stone had cut his first record for Okeh in 1927. A good friend of Duke Ellington, with whom he stayed for four months after coming to New York, Stone worked as the bandleader at the Apollo while also writing and arranging material for big bands led by Chick Webb and Jimmie Lunceford. Stone's song "Idaho" was a big hit for both Benny Goodman and Guy Lombardo.

Although they came from entirely different worlds, Cole Porter was a major influence on Stone's songwriting. When they met, Porter asked Stone, "What tools do you use?" Having never heard of a rhyming dictionary, Stone replied, "Hell, if you're gonna dig a ditch, you use a shovel, don't you?" After Porter hipped him to homonyms, assonance, and alliteration, Stone "began to approach songwriting more professionally."

Like Tom Dowd, Stone had worked with Herb Abramson at National. The two men wanted to form their own record label but neither had the money and so their plans went nowhere. Through his connection with Abramson, Stone brought the Harlemaires to Atlantic in 1947. Sax player Frank "Floor Show" Culley then had a hit with an instrumental version of Stone's "Cole Slaw," which had been originally recorded as "Sorghum Switch" by Jimmy Dorsey and then by Louis Jordan, who gave the song its new title.

"Jesse Stone," Ahmet would later say, "did more to develop the basic rock 'n' roll sound than anybody else, although you hear a lot about Bill Haley and Elvis Presley. He was a great, reliable, loose arranger, who could update a five-year-old arrangement with a couple of chord changes. Those arrangements were very important, because although the record never came out exactly as the arrangement had been written, they gave something for everybody to hang on to."

When Ahmet and Herb Abramson made their second visit to New Orleans in October 1949, Stone, who had become the first black person on the Atlantic payroll, accompanied them. Stone put up a sign in the back of a black record shop saying that anyone who had a song should bring it to Cosimo Matassa's studio when the Atlantic Record Company would be there. Songwriters lined up outside the door, as Stone described, "like people going to a movie." With a six-piece band in place, Stone auditioned each applicant, found out which key their song should be played in, and then worked out an arrangement. "In half an hour we cut the song. We got a lot of material that way."

When Stone returned from New Orleans, he began trying to write the kind of music he had heard there. "I listened to the stuff that was being done by those thrown-together bands in the joints down there, and I concluded that the only thing that was missin' from the stuff we were recording was the rhythm. All we needed was a bass line. So I designed a bass pattern, and it sort of became identified with rock 'n' roll . . . I'm the guilty person that started that. . . . When we started puttin' that sound out on Atlantic, we started sellin' like hotcakes."

Because Jerry Blaine was having a run of success with Sonny Til and the Orioles at Jubilee Records, Ahmet and Herb Abramson went looking for vocal groups with the kind of four-part harmony that was a forerunner of the doo-wop sound. After Waxie Maxie Silverman told Ahmet about four high school friends from Washington who called themselves the Clovers and were managed by Lou Krefetz, a record store owner in Baltimore, Ahmet signed them to the label. He then made it plain he did not want them to sound like their idols, the Ink Spots, or to record anything Billy Eckstine had already cut.

Instead, he wrote "Don't You Know I Love You" for them and assigned Jesse Stone to work with them as well as the Cardinals, a vocal group from Baltimore Herb Abramson had signed. Stone did his best to show both groups how to play music "based on the sound I had picked up in the south but they were northern boys and didn't feel it." In the studio, Ahmet got the kind of boogie sound on piano he had first heard Albert Ammons, Meade "Lux" Lewis, and Pete Johnson play and hired Frank "Floor Show" Culley to play a saxophone break. In Ahmet's words, the way the Clovers sang "Don't You Know I Love You" "was all wrong. I wrote it in a much blacker idiom than the way they sang it, which was more pop." Nonetheless, the song went to number one on the R&B charts in 1951.

By 1952 the team was in place at Atlantic Records. On the fifth floor at 234 West 56th Street at night, Tom Dowd would help push back the desks so he could get a clean, crisp sound as he recorded in a room where the walls had been covered with plywood. Jesse Stone was writing hit songs while also arranging other people's compositions so they would become hits. Miriam Abramson was answering the phone, cutting the checks, watching the money, and hounding distributors so Atlantic could stay in business. Ahmet was signing talent, writing songs, and taking an increasing role in producing. By 1953, the label would also have the best session men in New York on call, among them Sam "The Man" Taylor, Budd Johnson, and Willis Jackson on sax, Connie Kay on drums, and Henry Van Walls on piano.

The president of Atlantic Records was still Herb Abramson, who had guided the label through its early years by showing Ahmet the ropes in the studio and teaching him how to get records pressed and distributed. At Atlantic, Abramson was the steady and reliable figure on whom everyone could always depend. And then in the most unlikely way imaginable, the team was torn apart.

# SIX

# Shake, Rattle and Roll

*"With Jerry, things got better."*

—Ahmet Ertegun

## 1

Although Herb Abramson was no longer a practicing dentist, the United States Army had paid for him to become one in return for a commitment to serve two years of active military duty. In February 1953, six years after he had completed his dental studies at New York University and just six months after his wife, Miriam, had given birth to a son, Abramson was ordered to report for service as a lieutenant in the Army Dental Corps in Germany. "When I left for the Army," Abramson would later say, "Ahmet said to me, 'I don't know what we are going to do—after all, you used to supervise most of the sessions.' I said, 'Ahmet, you make three or four recording sessions entirely on your own, and even if each one bombs, by that time you will have learned enough to be confident in yourself.' "

By then, Ahmet had already spent enough time in the studio to know what he was doing. His real problem was to find someone who could function as Abramson had done on a daily basis at Atlantic for the past six years. Out late every night, Ahmet regularly showed up for work long after everyone else. As he would later recall, "Everyone was worried when Herb Abramson went in the army because I was not really a person who would come in the office at eight o'clock in the morning and start calling up distributors to pay their bills. It wasn't my thing."

While the departure of one of its founders could have well been the death knell for another independent record label, Ahmet managed to replace Abramson with a man who would help make Atlantic even more successful than either of its original partners could ever have imagined. A year before Abramson was called up for duty, he and Ahmet had asked Jerry Wexler to join Atlantic as a promotion man who would also run their publishing company.

A former staff writer at *The Billboard*, Wexler had demonstrated an unerring knack for favorably reviewing records that then became hits. After going to work for a music publisher, Wexler had further proven his music business acumen by bringing "Cry," a huge hit for Johnnie Ray, and "Cold, Cold Heart," a Hank Williams song that became a million-seller for Tony Bennett, to his friend Mitch Miller, the head of A&R at Columbia Records.

By the time he sat down with Ahmet and Abramson at Atlantic in 1952, Wexler had already decided what he really wanted to do was make records. Wexler, who knew both partners well and "considered them among the most cultured cognoscenti in the city," told them he would not feel comfortable working for friends. When Ahmet asked what would make him comfortable, Wexler boldly replied, "Being your partner." Wexler would later write he was not at all surprised when Ahmet laughed and rejected his proposal.

With Abramson about to begin his military service, Ahmet went to Paul Ackerman, the well-respected editor who had been Wexler's "guru" at *Billboard*, for help in finding someone to join him at Atlantic. As Seymour Stein, the founder of Sire Records, who began working at *Billboard* when he was thirteen years old, later recalled, "Ackerman said, 'There are a number of people I could recommend but there's nobody better than Jerry Wexler.' "

A brilliant self-educated intellectual who never lost the guttural working-class accent of his youth, Gerald Wexler was born in New York City on January 10, 1917. After emigrating from Poland to America, his father, Harry, became a window washer who worked twelve hours a day at a job he hated for $4 a week. His mother, the former Elsa Spitz, was a formidable and eccentric figure who played piano, sang light opera, and wanted her son to write the Great American Novel.

Unlike his younger brother, Arthur, who joined the Communist Party and became "an ecstatic Marxist who followed Trotsky," Wexler was "always a flaming progressive, just short of the red carrying card, which my mother was. She was a Communist. And so was my brother. I grew up with very left-wing socialist leanings but I balked at the point where I think all smart people did at being directed how to think and what kind of movies to watch and what kind of books were okay to read. I didn't come close to toeing the party line. It was bullshit."

As a boy growing up in Washington Heights in northern Manhattan, Wexler had spent most of his free time hanging out with the tough guys who frequented Artie Goodman's pool hall on the corner of 181st Street and Bennett Avenue. Despite his mother's insistence that he excel at his studies, Wexler had little use for school, often skipped classes, and soon acquired a reputation in his neighborhood as someone who never walked away from a fight.

While attending George Washington High School, Wexler saw Fletcher Henderson, Bix Beiderbecke, Jimmie Lunceford, Roy Eldridge, and Red Allen perform at the Savoy Ballroom and the Apollo in Harlem. Like his future partner at Atlantic, he became a passionate collector of jazz records, most of which he bought in Salvation Army depots and junk shops.

A recurrent college dropout, Wexler left City College after two semesters and then spent most of his only term at New York University in the pool hall. After his mother learned the tuition for out-of-state students was just $100 a term, she took him to enroll in the Kansas State College of Agriculture and Applied Science (now Kansas State University) in Manhattan, Kansas.

Forsaking his studies, Wexler frequently made the hundred-mile journey to Kansas City to see Big Joe Turner, Bennie Moten, and Andy Kirk and His Clouds of Joy. As one of Wexler's professors wrote his mother, "Gerald is a young man of marked ability who is manifestly unable to integrate his own personality into the world. He is teacher's pet, yet teachers loathe him for his intolerable habit of trying—and too often succeeding—to steal their show."

After Wexler was asked to leave the school, his mother journeyed to Kansas to bring him home. On their way back to New York, she announced they would first be stopping off in Niagara Falls because,

"I've never had a honeymoon. This might be my only chance." Years later when someone asked her about the "oedipal implications" of her relationship with her son, she said, "Freud, shmeud. I loved Gerald, but I never wanted to fuck him."

Back in the city, Wexler joined his father in washing windows, a job he also thoroughly detested. He began hanging out at the Museum of Modern Art, where he watched foreign films and developed "an affinity for the Surrealists, particularly Magritte." During a Sunday afternoon jam session on 52nd Street, then the center of the jazz world, he got high for the first time by smoking a joint rolled by Mezz Mezzrow, who had regularly come to Sunday lunch with Ahmet and his brother at the Turkish embassy in Washington.

Drafted into the army after marrying Shirley Kampf in 1941, Wexler embraced the discipline and forced routine of military life and was assigned to the military police as a customs guard. Returning to Kansas after he was discharged, he completed his studies for a degree in journalism and then returned to New York City.

In 1949, he was hired as a $75 a week cub reporter for *Billboard* where, in his words, "I was the only guy who knew how to use a semicolon." When the magazine decided to change the name of its Race Records chart, Wexler threw out the term "rhythm and blues" and the name stuck. As he wrote later that year, "Rhythm and blues is a label more appropriate to more enlightened times."

A powerfully built man with dark hair and jug handle ears who had the rough-and-ready look of a dockworker, Wexler let his wife, Shirley, negotiate his deal at Atlantic with Ahmet and Herb and Miriam Abramson "because she had more confidence in me than I had in myself." In return for $2,063.25, Wexler received a 13 percent share in Atlantic Records and a weekly salary plus expenses that gave him a weekly draw of $300. Neatly defining what would become the nature of their relationship, Ahmet took the money Wexler had invested and used it as a down payment on a green Cadillac convertible. He then gave the only vehicle in which a real record man could be seen to Wexler to replace his aging Dodge.

On Wexler's first day on the job, Miriam Abramson dumped the mail on his desk and he "fell into the role I would play for the next fifteen years—I ran the candy store. I got there early and I left late.

I worried like crazy. I scrutinized bills, pored over details, supervised, and screamed when someone fucked up." Constitutionally unable to delegate authority to anyone, he "operated with a divine disbelief in the competence of the staff. Consequently my modus operandi drove my employees nuts . . . My goals were short-range and limited: tactics always, strategy never."

A human dynamo born with the kind of energy that sometimes verged on the manic, Wexler always felt he had something to prove to those who had preceded him at Atlantic. While he would later credit Jesse Stone for having taught him everything he knew "about our craft," Wexler was also keenly aware that Stone "always looked on me as an interloper with a slightly jaundiced eye. Because I came in to take Herb Abramson's place. I came in after him. He had already been part of the fabric of the company. I was a replacement."

Like Ahmet, Wexler was also a walking encyclopedia of jazz and blues. While the two men shared an overwhelming passion for all forms of black roots music, they could not have been more different in the way they conducted their business. "If I was a plodder," Wexler would later write, "Ahmet was an artist. He moved and managed by inspiration . . . He had phenomenal instincts, not simply as a talent scout but as a producer and songwriter as well . . . Fortunately, we complemented one another. Like a good rhythm section, we swung as a unit."

In every sense, their brand-new partnership was a marriage of opposites. While Ahmet was always cool, Wexler burned with a red hot flame. Born with a sense of entitlement second to none, Ahmet made it seem he had nothing to prove and wanted only to have a good time. A true child of the Depression, Wexler saw the rain cloud lurking behind every brilliant ray of sunshine. Because his father had fallen short of making his own mark in the world, Wexler was driven by "ravening fear." Ahmet was hip. Wexler was a hipster. And yet at Atlantic they soon became a perfectly matched pair, the record business equivalent of Mr. Inside and Mr. Outside.

In large part this was due to Ahmet's ability to harness Wexler's immense talent. Having grown up in thrall to his older brother, Ahmet had further refined his skill at playing the supporting role in the double act during his years with Herb Abramson. In Jerry Wexler, who was determined to make the best of his first real shot at success in the record business by outworking all his competitors even if this also meant working himself and others to distraction, Ahmet had found the perfect partner. With Jerry Wexler firmly ensconced in the chair where Herb Abramson had once sat, the label was ready to rock.

## 2

When they went out on the road together for the first time to push Atlantic's latest product by talking to disc jockeys, record retailers, and distributors in New Orleans and Chicago while looking for talent no one else had signed, Ahmet and Jerry Wexler discovered they had far more in common than their love for music and an overwhelming desire to make hits. As Wexler would later say, "We were very similar because we were both driven by a very heightened sense of irony. Irony prevailed. Discerning the ridiculous in the bourgeois around us and playing off that."

Seven years older than Ahmet and married, Herb Abramson had always been a steadying influence on his junior partner whenever they had set off on such trips together. Unlike Abramson, Jerry Wexler was up for everything and not about to judge the man for whom he was now working, thereby freeing Ahmet to indulge in outrageous behavior on the road.

With money in their pockets and an insatiable appetite for having as much fun as humanly possible, Ahmet and Wexler amused themselves by goofing on everyone they met. Feeding off one another like a pair of seasoned actors who had seen too many Bob Hope and Bing Crosby road movies, they regularly put on what Wexler called "little playlets" in which Ahmet assumed the role of the fast-talking sharpie while Wexler played along as the unwitting stooge who could never quite grasp that his partner was robbing him blind in every possible way.

In a pawnbroker's shop in New Orleans, a city where Wexler had never been before, Ahmet helped himself to a stack of twenty-dollar bills an inch at a time while generously telling his partner to do the same with a stack of singles, a routine inspired by a lengthy profile of the legendary playboy, gambler, and playwright Wilson Mizner in *The*

*New Yorker.* Knowing they were smarter than anyone with whom they came into contact, Ahmet and Wexler believed they could get away with just about anything on the road.

Wherever the two men went, Ahmet always knew everyone who mattered and where to go to hear great music while having more than one cocktail to make the night pass more quickly. Even then, Ahmet could drink most men under the table. Although no one could keep up with Ahmet, Wexler did his best to try.

During their first visit to New Orleans, Wexler got so drunk one night at the legendary Dew Drop Inn that he could not make it back to the hotel and instead spent the night there with "two 'Miss Fines' to keep me warm." When he stumbled downstairs in the morning, Wexler discovered Big Joe Turner eating breakfast in his undershirt with singers Smiley Lewis and Lloyd Price of "Stagger Lee" fame, who then went to the piano to accompany Turner as he sang. As Wexler would later say, "The road trips with Ahmet were like a total release. We were goofing on people and they had absolutely never seen white guys like us before. We used to have so much fun."

While on the road together, the two men also somehow managed to get their business done, recording Turner, Professor Longhair, Guitar Slim, and Champion Jack Dupree in New Orleans and then cutting a Joe Turner session with Elmore James on guitar at the Chess Records studio on the South Side of Chicago on October 7, 1953. When Leonard and Phil Chess showed up that night, four of the reigning kings of the independent record business sat down together to talk like friends.

The sons of an itinerant Jewish shoemaker, Leonard and Phil Chess had been born in a Polish shtetl. Eleven years old when his family emigrated to America, Leonard had come up from the street in the roughest way imaginable. After working with his father as a junk dealer, he began running the Macomba Lounge in the tough Cottage Grove section of Chicago. To ensure no one would even think of trying to rob him when he left the bar with cash, Leonard bought himself a chrome-plated pearl-handled .44 revolver, which he strapped to his waist so it would be clearly visible. As he told his son Marshall, a gun in the pocket would "do you no good."

Having been around black people his entire life, Leonard used the language of the street in a manner that caused some who had only ever spoken to him on the phone to assume he was black. Phil Chess, who was rounder and softer-looking than his older brother, was in many ways also easier to deal with than Leonard. "He was like Nesuhi," Marshall Chess would say of his uncle. "Ahmet could not have done it without Nesuhi just like my father could not have done it without Phil."

Although they were competitors, the Chess brothers and Ahmet and Wexler were also friends. Leonard regularly referred to them as "the New York Jews" and both men attended Marshall's bar mitzvah. While the Chess brothers would sometimes help the partners at Atlantic by pressing copies of a big hit at one of their plants, the way in which they did business at their respective companies was completely different.

Running their label like the company store many of their artists had frequented as children while growing up dirt poor in the rural South, the Chess brothers gave their performers money and cars when their records hit big on the charts. They bought them clothing, paid their rent and legal and medical bills, and then deducted what they had spent from the artists' royalties. Concerning the generous advances the brothers lavished on their most successful performers, Wexler would later say although he and Ahmet also "poured them out . . . we didn't make their car payments . . . we didn't pay their mortgages . . . we didn't dress them. We were not lords of the manor."

Wexler was also offended that the brothers sometimes referred to their artists as *"chaya,"* which in Yiddish means "animals." "The Chess brothers," Wexler said, "did have a plantation mentality. You better believe it. Phil Chess once asked me, 'Do you pay royalties on a continuous basis?' I said, 'Sure.' He said, 'We just cut them out after a while.'"

On the night they all sat down together in Chicago, Ahmet told Leonard Chess he had recently been listening to the radio as he drove through Atlanta but had not heard a single Chess record. Pulling over to the side of the road, Ahmet said he had called the deejay and said, " 'Listen, motherfucker, this is Chess Records. Have you got a wife and a family? You want 'em to live? Well you better start playin' our records.' That's what I call promoting records. Now, what are you doing for Atlantic in Chicago?" Not realizing Ahmet was putting him on,

Chess responded, "Come on, man, you didn't! Now I got trouble in Atlanta." As Wexler would later say, "Ahmet used to torture them with practical jokes."

Wexler, who had far more in common with the Chess brothers than Ahmet, told Leonard he was crazy to have gone into business with Benny Goodman's brothers Gene and Harry to set up Arc Music, thereby giving away half of his publishing company to them. Wexler offered to have Atlantic handle the Chess copyrights through Atlantic's Progressive Music for a 15 percent share of the profits only to have Leonard dismiss the idea by saying, "I can't bother with that."

Throughout the course of their conversation that night, Ahmet continued to play the joker. When Leonard said he had made an agreement with Muddy Waters, whom Marshall Chess would later remember as having always been treated like a member of his family, to come over to the Chess house to do the gardening once his records stopped selling, Ahmet said he had cut a different deal with Big Joe Turner. "If his records don't sell," Ahmet said, "I can be *his* chauffeur."

While varying stories about Muddy Waters doing manual labor for the Chess brothers have been disputed, Ahmet would later say that when he visited Chess Records, Leonard, who "was a good friend of mine, took me around. The office was a storefront and there was a receptionist when you walked into the office who had a phone and a typewriter. There was a fellow sweeping up. Leonard Chess introduced me to this guy. His name was Muddy Waters. He hired him part-time to do the cleaning in the office. He was also one of the artists. I said to Leonard Chess, 'Where is your accounting department?' He looked at me and said, 'Accounting department? Oh, our accountant is that girl at the entrance.' I said, 'She's the receptionist and she's also answering the phone and she's also typing your letters and she's also the accountant?' 'Yeah,' he said. When I asked him about royalties, he said, 'Royalties?' And he smiled and we didn't go further into that. We were not run that way. Other independent labels were selling records for cash and didn't even deny it. They were proud of it."

"I liked Leonard and I liked Phil," Wexler recalled. "Were we on a different level? We were college graduates. They came over and rode a junk wagon with their father collecting bottles and rags. That was how they started. More power to them. Anybody that had any knowledge of who we were would realize that we were cut from different cloth from Leonard Chess and Herman Lubinsky and the Mesner brothers at Aladdin Records. We were head and shoulders above that."

Unlike Ahmet and Wexler, Leonard and Phil Chess had gotten into the independent record business to make more money than they could have ever earned by running a bar. Although they had not grown up listening to black roots music, both men had a deep, instinctive feeling for the blues. The way in which they made their records was also entirely different from how the partners at Atlantic approached the process. As Wexler would later note, Leonard Chess would see Muddy Waters in a bar, take him into the studio, and tell him to play what he had played the night before.

In fact, Leonard Chess took a completely hands-on approach to making records. After Muddy Waters' drummer could not get the beat right on a track, Leonard told him, "Get the fuck out of the way, I'll do that," and then sat down behind the drum kit to provide "a steady, serviceable thud." Nor was he ever hesitant when it came to telling a performer how to sing. As Bo Diddley was about to cut his signature track, the eponymous "Bo Diddley," Leonard ordered, "Motherfucker, sing like a man. The beat has got to move at all times." Not surprisingly, Atlantic's records never had the raw, gutbucket power that defined the Chess catalogue.

Far more than the Chess brothers, Ahmet and Wexler already understood the power of the media. Over the years, both men would do countless interviews in which they made it plain how much of a contribution they had made to the growth of the independent record business in America while creating some of the greatest music of all time.

Shortly before his death at the age of ninety-one in 2008, Wexler said, "It's fashionable to present me as this street-wise kid stickball player from Washington Heights and Ahmet as the intellectual. That's the big mistake. Because he came from the gilded palace and he was the son of the ambassador and I came from the street. Bullshit! I was a thousand times the intellectual that Ahmet was. I read a thousand times more books than he did. But that is not the public picture, is it? I was the street-wise kid. The street-wise kid was going home at night and reading Sherwood Anderson and listening to broadcasts of Fletcher Henderson."

On the night these four men sat down together in Chicago to talk, Wexler was still completely in thrall to the man who was showing him the inside workings of the business in which they would both spend the rest of their lives. Insofar as the two new partners at Atlantic were concerned, everything was still, as Wexler himself might have said, completely copacetic.

## 3

To stay in business, Atlantic had to sell sixty thousand singles a month and so Ahmet and Wexler often found themselves in the studio four nights a week. A hit record on the label would usually sell between 200,000 and 300,000 copies, but there were always far more misses than hits, and so the pressure to continue generating commercially successful material on a regular basis was unrelenting. As Wexler would later write, "We weren't looking for canonization; we lusted for hits. Hits were the cash flow, the lifeblood, the heavenly ichor—the wherewithal of survival."

Within the short space of nine months in 1954, Ahmet and Jerry Wexler cut two songs that became big hits and also changed the face of popular music. On February 15 in the Atlantic office, the partners recorded their first smash with Big Joe Turner, "The Boss of the Blues."

Standing six foot two and weighing three hundred pounds, Joseph Vernon Turner Jr. was born on May 18, 1911, in Kansas City, Missouri. Leaving school at the age of fourteen, he began working as a cook and then a singing bartender in the clubs and bars on 12th Street in what was then a wide-open city run by "Boss" Tom Pendergast. In 1936, Turner performed in New York City for the first time on a bill with Benny Goodman and then appeared at the first of John Hammond's legendary "From Spirituals to Swing" concerts at Carnegie Hall in 1938.

After performing on the first show Nesuhi and Ahmet put on in Washington, in 1945, Turner signed with National Records, where he was produced by Herb Abramson. A huge physical presence with a wide, soft face, sleepy eyes, and a neatly trimmed mustache, Turner was a blues shouter who could perform in a variety of genres, jazz, big band, jump blues, rhythm and blues, and what was about to become known as rock 'n' roll.

Ahmet signed Big Joe Turner to the label in March 1951 after seeing him perform at the Apollo with the Count Basie band. Hurried in without a rehearsal as a last-minute replacement for the band's ailing regular singer, Jimmy Rushing, Turner's first performance turned out to be a disaster. As Ahmet later described the evening, "The Basie Band had intricate arrangements that were not exactly 12-bar blues. In between the blues, there would be maybe 18, 20, 24-bars. Joe couldn't read music . . . So he was singing with the band, but he would come back in in the wrong place; and the band would clash with what he was doing. Then the band finished and he was still singing!"

The audience at the Apollo was known even then for being "the toughest and very critical—so at the end of this tragic moment for Joe, they started hooting, howling, jeering, and laughed him off the stage." Rushing backstage to console Turner, Ahmet was told the singer had already left. Finding him in the bar of the Braddock Hotel next door, Ahmet told Turner he "shouldn't be a sideman with an orchestra anyway; you're a star in your own right—we want to make you a big star. Come and make records with us."

A seasoned veteran who knew how the record business worked, Turner replied, "Okay, if you pay me money." When Ahmet said he could come up with $500, Turner said, "Yeah, that's good." Quickly, Ahmet then added, "For four sides." Turner, who always called Ahmet "cuz," said, "All right, cuz. I'll go with you and see what happens." With Ahmet whispering the lyrics of a song he had written for him in his ear, Turner cut "Chains of Love" and then "Honey Hush" for Atlantic, both of which became R&B hits.

Jesse Stone would later say Herb Abramson had come to him before Turner's session at Atlantic on February 15, 1954, to say he wanted to find an up-tempo blues number for Turner to sing for a change. As Abramson was then in the army, it must have been Ahmet who made the request. In Stone's words, "I threw a bunch of phonetic phrases together—'shake, rattle, and roll,' 'flip, flop, and fly'—and I came up with thirty or forty verses. Then I picked over them."

Writing under the name Charles Calhoun, Stone came up with

five verses and a chorus for "Shake, Rattle and Roll." While the title describes someone about to roll a pair of dice from a cup, it was also widely understood to be a euphemism for sexual intercourse. The song itself became what writer Nick Tosches would later call "the perfect record" with lascivious lyrics that were not quite dirty enough to keep it from being played on the radio. Perfectly paced to the rocking beat, the chorus was so simple and infectious even a child could sing it.

With Stone on piano, Mickey "Guitar" Baker—later of Mickey and Sylvia fame—on guitar, Connie Kay on drums, Wilbur DeParis on trombone, and Sam "The Man" Taylor blowing a killer solo on tenor sax, "Shake, Rattle and Roll" was, as rock critic Greil Marcus would later write, "a story of domestic lust, lustful impatience, sexual wonder, and sex—grinding—that at once goes far beyond the salaciousness of the R&B hits of the time and is somehow as clean, healthy (and perhaps as dutiful) as hard work." As Marcus also noted, it was the chorus that sold the song. If in "Shake, Rattle and Roll," Big Joe Turner was "a great actor more than a great singer," then Stone, Ahmet, and Wexler, who were wearing white shirts and black ties and clapping their hands as they shouted "their heads off behind him" gave it "a flashy, white, drunken frat-boy edge."

Turner had cut twenty sides for Atlantic before making "Shake, Rattle and Roll," but nothing he had ever done for the label compared to this record. Going to number one on the R&B charts after it was released in April, "Shake, Rattle and Roll" stayed there for eleven weeks. The song was then covered with sanitized lyrics by Bill Haley and the Comets on Decca. Released in July 1954, that version became the first rock 'n' roll song to sell a million copies.

While the cover did not have the filthy groove and low-down funk of the original, it did open the ears of white teenagers across America to a sound they had never heard before. While the question of what was actually the first rock 'n' roll song remains a source of debate among music historians and critics, "Shake, Rattle and Roll" ranks high on any list. Using the original lyrics, Elvis Presley also cut his own version of the song as a demo for Sam Phillips at Sun Records in 1955 and the song then became a hit for him as well. In time, "Shake, Rattle and Roll" would help launch Atlantic's rise to the forefront of the independent record business. As Greil Marcus wrote, the record "still sounds like a door being flung open. But it doesn't quite sound as if people have made it to the other side."

Six months later under completely different circumstances, Ahmet and Wexler recorded another song that helped break down the barriers between black music and the white audience that was still learning to appreciate it. Before Ray Charles cut what would become his break-through hit on Atlantic, he had already recorded thirty-eight sides for the label without finding the distinctive sound on which he would base his career. As Paul Wexler, himself a record producer, would say of Ahmet and his father, "These guys were so attuned to black popular music at that point that they could hear the talent in its rawest form before even the talent knew what it wanted to do."

Ray Charles had written what would become his first great song while lying in the backseat of a car rolling through Tennessee, Kentucky, and Indiana as he was touring with his band. Smoking cigarettes and marijuana, Charles heard a gospel song entitled "Jesus Is All the World to Me" on the radio and began singing along to it with trumpet player Renald Richard, who then wrote down the lyrics and added a bridge from another song.

Calling Ahmet and Wexler in New York, Charles asked if they would come to Atlanta, where he would be performing at the Royal Peacock Club at 186 Auburn Avenue in the black section of the city. Flying to Atlanta, the partners took a cab to the "very inexpensive motel that went with the club." Saying, "I've got something you boys need to hear," Charles suddenly took off down the stairs. Because the singer had already plotted out his route to the club, the partners had to struggle to keep up with him.

In an empty club in the middle of the afternoon, Charles's seven-piece band was already onstage. As soon as Charles heard Ahmet and Wexler walk in behind him, he counted off "I Got a Woman" and the band tore into it. Ahmet and a "stunned" Wexler were deluged by what Wexler would call "an amazing succession of songs." Both partners knew they needed to find a studio to record the material they had just heard.

Through Xenas Sears, a local R&B disc jockey, the partners booked studio time on November 18, 1954, at WGST, the Georgia Tech University radio station. Throughout the session, they had to stop recording every hour on the hour so the staff announcer could read the news. Making the situation more difficult, the station's elderly engineer kept missing Ahmet's frantic cues to adjust the microphones for solos and ensemble passages.

When Charles had recorded "Mess Around" in New York City nine months earlier, Wexler, who was then still coming onboard at Atlantic, had listened quietly without offering any input. During this session, Wexler's "anxious stream of suggestions" irritated Charles. Despite the chaotic nature of the session, the partners cut four songs. While listening to playbacks of "I Got a Woman," both Ahmet and Wexler felt certain they "had found Ray's breakthrough smash at last."

Released in December 1954, the record became Ray Charles's first number one R&B hit. As Charles's biographer Michael Lydon wrote, "The record blended elements like a hybrid flower. It had a dancing beat like a jump blues, but it was based on gospel's 'rise to glory' chords, and the cheerful lyric, infectiously delivered by Ray, gave that mix a pop music gloss." Charles repeated the phrase "I got a woman, way over town" so often during the song that the partners hoped it would become "a sing-along line people would plug nickels into jukeboxes to hear over and over again."

For the first time in the history of popular music, an artist had blended the blues and gospel into a single song. By doing so, Ray Charles had taken a giant step in creating the new musical genre that would come to be known as "soul." Concerning their session in Atlanta, Ahmet would later say, "It was a real lesson for me to see an artist of his stature at work."

By now, Ahmet had formed a close personal relationship with Charles. A "quick mimic" who "played a mean game of checkers," Charles's incredible self-confidence allowed him to maneuver with consummate skill through a world he could not see. "Totally focused" on his own music, Charles always knew exactly what was going on around him and unlike many other musicians "followed the news on the radio and could talk about what was going on in the world." In a manner Ahmet could never have anticipated, Ray Charles would eventually teach him more about the record business than any other artist.

In the short space of six months, Atlantic had released two songs that would define the future of the record business in America. "Shake,

Rattle and Roll" helped begin rock 'n' roll. "I Got a Woman" established soul. What the two songs had in common were Ahmet and Wexler. While even they knew there was always an element of luck involved in everything they did, the partners at Atlantic were now well on their way to becoming the greatest team in the history of the record business.

business.

# SEVEN

## *Brothers in Arms*

*"Ahmet looked upon Herb Abramson as a brother and the deteriora-
tion of that relationship was painful for all of us."*

—Jerry Wexler

## 1

On April 25, 1955, *News from Atlantic*, the label's weekly press handout,
happily announced the long awaited return of the company's president and cofounder. Beneath a headline reading, "Herb's Back: Prexy
Herb Abramson Returns to Atlantic After GI Stint," the release noted
that after having spent two years overseas "as a dentist in the [sic] Air
Force," during which time he had attained the rank of captain, "Herb
Abramson . . . returns to active service in N.Y.C. this week" and "will
jump into the a.&r. picture immediately to speed execution of the
expansion and improvement plans long contemplated by the organization."

Since Abramson had left the label, the release noted that Jerry
Wexler had joined Atlantic as a vice president and "teamed with v.p.'s
Ertegun and Miriam Abramson to continue the company's success
along the original lines." Atlantic had actively gone into music publishing with Progressive Music, launched a new subsidiary label named
Cat, and had most recently added Nesuhi Ertegun to the company "as
a v.p. in charge of a new jazz and Album program."

As "Herb earned his reputation as an 'idea man,' " and Atlantic was
"no longer a specialty label" but was now approaching "major status in
the general record business . . . Herb's return signals the beginning of a

great new era of expansion with full executive force." Planning to "open new vistas for Atlantic along electronic lines," especially in the field of binaural (stereo) recording, Abramson would be devoting "much effort to hi-fi techniques, quality control and general product improvement, with an eye also to the developing tape market."

Noting Abramson had just been granted a patent "for his invention of the trick-track children's records, two of which Atlantic issued several years ago" that allowed a phonograph needle to randomly select various tracks so 256 different stories could be told on four 78 RPM sides, the handout concluded by stating, "You can expect plenty of surprises with this Abramson cat around!" In ways no press release could have ever adequately explained, no truer words had ever been written.

Herb Abramson was in fact returning to a company that bore little resemblance to the struggling independent label he had left two years earlier. While he had been gone, Big Joe Turner had hit it big with "Shake, Rattle and Roll." The Drifters had scored a number one R&B record with "Honey Love," a song written by Clyde McPhatter and Wexler. Ray Charles had gone to the top of the R&B chart with "I Got a Woman." The Clovers had cut four Top Ten R&B hits, among them "Lovey Dovey," which Ahmet had written.

In an essay in *Cashbox* magazine in 1954 credited to Ahmet and Wexler but most likely written by Wexler, the partners had explained how the blues would have to change to meet the tastes of the label's new target audience, "the bobby soxers," who in great numbers were now looking to find their own sound. Having coined the phrase "rhythm and blues," Wexler borrowed a term being used to describe music popular in the South and the Southwest and decided to call this new form "cat music." As he explained in the essay, cat music would be "Up-to-date blues with a beat, and infectious catch phrases, and danceable rhythms . . . It has to kick and it has to have a message for the sharp youngsters who dig it."

While the term never caught on, Wexler did establish a short-lived subsidiary label at Atlantic called Cat on which the Chords recorded "Sh-Boom." The song went to number two on the *Billboard* R&B chart and then became the first doo-wop record to enter the Top Ten on the pop chart, rising to number five. Covered by the Crew Cuts on Mercury for a white audience, the song was the number one record for nine weeks in August and September of 1954. In no small part, this was because Tom Dowd was then still regularly being hired by major labels to produce white cover versions of Atlantic's R&B hits that sounded as much like the original as possible.

Even after Herb Abramson rejoined Atlantic, Ahmet and Wexler continued going out on the road together. Journeying to Memphis to hang out with legendary disc jockey Dewey Phillips while he was on the air at WHBQ, they then accompanied him to the Variety Club, where Elvis Presley happened to be having a beer. The partners had already tried to buy Presley's contract from Sam Phillips at Sun Records for the astronomical sum of $30,000 only to have Phillips accept RCA's offer of $40,000 with a $5,000 bonus thrown in to sweeten the deal. If in fact Elvis had accepted their offer, the partners would have been hard pressed to come up with the money.

While Herb Abramson had in fact been very much like a brother to Ahmet before leaving Atlantic, Ahmet's brother was now at the label as well. Unable to bear the thought of Nesuhi going to work for Lew Chudd at Imperial Records in Los Angeles, Ahmet had told him, "You can't do that. We'll make you a partner in Atlantic." As Abramson would later say, "So, foolish me, I said to Ahmet, 'Give Nesuhi some of your stock, that doesn't cost me anything.' Then boom, what do I know, there is another hostile partner. Ahmet and Nesuhi used to talk in Turkish in my presence to say things I wasn't supposed to know." As Wexler would describe it, Ahmet and Nesuhi's relationship was based on "exasperation and exacerbation." There were times when he was closer to them than they were to each other "except when it came to the bone, the Turkish nitty-gritty."

Moving to New York, where he would soon marry for the second time, Nesuhi took over production of Atlantic's jazz records while also overseeing the label's entry into the burgeoning market for albums recorded in the long-playing 33⅓ format. With an eye for design and packaging second to none, Nesuhi personally approved all the artwork that appeared on the label's album covers while also signing and/or producing the Modern Jazz Quartet, John Coltrane, Ornette Coleman, Charles Mingus, Thelonious Monk, Rahsaan Roland Kirk, and Keith Jarrett.

As the noted jazz critic Nat Hentoff would later write, "Nesuhi was the most respected figure in jazz recording among musicians and, indeed, among his competitors. He had—to begin with—unerring taste. With that taste went standards. His love for the music prevented him from lowering his standards. And he had genuine respect for the musicians he signed for the label."

Unlike Ahmet, who often took control of a recording session in order to come up with a hit, Nesuhi was always a far more supportive presence in the studio. In the words of John Lewis of the Modern Jazz Quartet, Nesuhi "let us decide what we wanted to play." Both Mingus and Coltrane trusted him implicitly because "they knew Nesuhi knew how to listen." Hentoff added, "There was also his abiding curiosity. He was not afraid of being surprised, or even startled, by sounds he had never heard before . . . he became, in essence, one of the musicians. A description he would prize."

Although Atlantic's jazz records never sold nearly as much as the hits produced by Ahmet and Wexler, both men recognized the need to keep this form of music alive by giving Nesuhi free rein to sign artists he believed were doing significant work. By making it plain he did not share their feelings about this situation, Herb Abramson further complicated his already difficult reentry at the label. Until he joined Atlantic, Nesuhi had made only what Abramson called "moldy fig" records. "That was a very fine little hobby," Abramson would later say, "but he wasn't in the mainstream of the record business."

Now that both Nesuhi and Wexler were at Atlantic, Abramson no longer had the direct connection to Ahmet that had bound the two men together when they were struggling to get the company off the ground. Nor was Ahmet the same person he had been when Abramson had last worked with him on a daily basis. For the past two years, Ahmet had been in charge at Atlantic and was now far more assured and self-confident than he had been when the partners had worked side by side.

As Miriam Abramson would later say, "When Herb came back from the army in 1955, we were doing pretty well—everybody had cars . . . This whole shift in balance was something he couldn't adjust to. He couldn't come back as number one, and he certainly couldn't come back as number three. He had an ego, because he had started the company and he had experience. So it was rather an awkward situation. I think neither Jerry nor Ahmet felt comfortable working with him.

They'd had it with Herb from the minute he came back from Germany. He drove them crazy and he was driven mad by the fact that his place had been usurped."

In the record business, especially at a label like Atlantic that was now growing by leaps and bounds as the new white teenage market kept expanding, two years was an eternity. Despite all the changes that had occurred at the company while Abramson had been away, he could have still found a way to fit in if the same man who had gone off to serve his country had returned. But by all accounts, Herb Abramson in the spring of 1955 did not resemble the person he had once been. In Wexler's words, "Herb came back a little bit nutso." The songwriter Doc Pomus, who had worked with Abramson during Atlantic's first days at the Hotel Jefferson, called him "an absolutely professional flake" whose behavior grew more erratic by the day. "He fancied himself as a songwriter, and always called me up in the middle of the night to help him write a song. He grew weirder as time went on. Even so, he really was a lovely guy."

While it was obvious to those who knew Abramson that his personality had undergone a radical transformation during his time in Germany, they could only speculate as to the cause. As his wife Miriam, who had spent three months with her husband while he was stationed overseas and did not find him to be depressed, would later say, "Herb lost the impetus. He was gone and he lost it. His mind was altered. He did a lot of pot." In the words of Delia Gottlieb, who had first met Abramson more than a decade earlier in Washington, "I think Herb very definitely got into drugs in Germany and came back changed because he had been isolated from what he knew."

Although Abramson's third wife, Barbara, said she "never knew Herb to do cocaine," dentists did then have the legal right to possess and prescribe the substance as a topical anesthetic. "Herb was snorting cocaine," someone who knew Abramson well during this period would later confirm. "He was a dentist and would write his own prescriptions. He had a guy working for him who would run and get the drugs for him in the studio. It was all cocaine behavior. He must have gotten hooked in Germany."

Whether it was the loneliness and isolation Abramson felt while spending two years overseas as a military dentist when he really wanted to be making records that caused him to begin using the drug, no one can say for sure. Twenty years before cocaine would become the drug of choice for artists as well as many of the top-ranking executives in the record business, Herb Abramson had come back from Germany with a habit that would have made it difficult for anyone to work with him under any circumstances. Nor did he come home alone.

Herb Abramson brought with him from Germany a woman he wanted to marry. As Wexler would later say, "He came back with a Brunhilde!" Although Abramson had a two-year-old son he barely knew, he went with his German girlfriend to Reno to establish residency for a Nevada divorce, and it was there she became pregnant with his child. The two soon married but, in Miriam Abramson's words, "She was very unhappy in the United States. She hated it. And she went to group therapy and ran away with somebody else. From group therapy."

While her husband had been in the army, Miriam had continued to receive his full salary as the president of the label. Now that their marriage was over, new financial arrangements had to be made so they could both continue working at Atlantic. "To this point," she said, "I'd never had my own salary. I just had his. When we got the divorce, I got no alimony. Herb said if he gave me stock instead of alimony, I would say it was okay for Nesuhi to come in. So Nesuhi and I got stock at about the same time."

With his former wife running day-to-day operations at the label, and Ahmet, Wexler, and Nesuhi doing business together in one office, Abramson set up shop in another office with a conference room between them. What must have been a fairly intolerable situation for all concerned lasted a few tense months until Ahmet and Wexler decided Abramson should have his own subsidiary label at Atlantic, to be known as Atco (shorthand for the Atlantic Corporation), thereby giving him the chance, as Charlie Gillett would later write, "to prove that he had not lost his touch, that Ahmet was mistaken if he thought Jerry Wexler was any kind of substitute as a producer."

The partners also set up Atco because, as Wexler explained, "It behooved us to create another label, another logo, that could be handled by distributors other than the ones we had to give us more outlets for our product. It was a way to diversify." While Herb Abramson was now back at the label, the writing on the wall was plain for everyone to see. It was just a matter of time until he would be gone for good.

## 2

By 1957, a year in which the partners at Atlantic were forced to reduce their weekly salaries despite releasing hits by the Coasters, Chuck Willis, Clyde McPhatter, and the Bobbettes, Ahmet had shifted into full playboy mode and could be found out on the town night after night enjoying life to the fullest. Not yet the A-list celebrity he would eventually become, his divorce from Jan Holm was noted only in the somewhat lowly *New York Journal-American* by gossip columnist Louis Sobol, who on November 20, 1957, wrote, "The Ahmet Ertigons [*sic*] (he heads a record firm) have parted. His pop was once Turkish Ambassador to the US."

Still somewhat insecure about his own appearance, Ahmet had experienced a personal breakthrough in his dating life after being told that even the most beautiful models in New York were like teenage girls who liked to go out at night so they could be seen in the most fashionable places. Armed with this bit of invaluable information, he began keeping company with a succession of well-known models on a regular basis. The very sleek, racy-looking 1955 Aston Martin DB2/4 coupe Ahmet was now driving around Manhattan also did nothing to hurt his cause.

While Ahmet's former wife had been a model, she had never attained the lofty status of Pat Jones, who, in Miriam Abramson's words, was "the muse for James Galanos, the famous California designer. They used to have dancing in the Persian Room of the Plaza Hotel and when she and Ahmet would come in together, the band would play 'Have You Met Miss Jones?' " After Pat Jones introduced Ahmet to her friend Betsy Pickering, a former Sarah Lawrence student whom *Time* magazine described as one of "the cool all-American beauties . . . of the 50's," Ahmet began dating her as well.

A stunning dark-haired, dark-eyed beauty who looked somewhat like Audrey Hepburn and had already appeared on the cover of *Vogue*, Pickering sent Ahmet a postcard from Paris while waiting to be photographed in a Dior gown at the Château de Malmaison to say how hard she had been working and how much she missed him. Confessing she was not having much of a social life because she had been working so hard, Pickering ended her note by sending him her love.

As Ahmet would later describe this period, "The girls I was going out with included some sub-deb types or post-deb types who were very American, some bohemian girls who were Village intellectuals, and many girls like Pat Jones, who was the number one model in California in those days, and Betsy Pickering, who I was living with at that time. These girls were very fun, charming, and amusing people and in some cases very good-hearted and in some cases very bitchy."

Ahmet's boon companion during this period was Julio Mario Santo Domingo. Born into a very wealthy Colombian family, Santo Domingo had first met Ahmet in Washington while he was attending George-town and Ahmet was at St. John's. A good friend of future Nobel Prize–winning author Gabriel García Márquez, Santo Domingo would become the chairman of Avianca Airlines while amassing a personal fortune of $4 billion through his control of more than one hundred companies.

The two men shared an unrelenting love of the good times they always had when they were together, most often in New York. As Santo Domingo would later say, "Ahmet and I did not see each other in the daytime. Daytime was for sleeping. We used to go to El Morocco practically every night." Spectacularly politically incorrect long before the term was invented, Ahmet once went to greet his good friend at La Guardia Airport with a sign that read, "Welcome home, spic."

"In those days," Ahmet recalled, "when I don't think I had ten thousand dollars in the bank, the society columns used to refer to me as 'Ahmet Ertegun, the Turkish millionaire.'" One reason they did so was that after he had been given too many tickets, Ahmet decided he could no longer drive himself around Manhattan and so traded in his "Aston Martin for a used Rolls-Royce and I got this fellow—his name was Frank—who was an old Irish retired policeman. I think I was pay-ing him like 75 cents an hour. He was always very well dressed with a chauffeur's cap and had white hair and with a Rolls-Royce, he looked very, very stately. We'd be somewhere and we'd all get in the car and I'd say, 'Take us home, Frank.' Which meant El Morocco, which was at 54th Street between Third and Lexington, an elegant club."

Known to its habitués as "Elmer's," El Morocco was then the place to be seen in Manhattan. The first club to use a velvet rope to separate its customers from the hoi polloi, El Morocco was famous for its blue zebra-stripe banquettes, where club photographer Jerome Zerbe regularly snapped photographs of celebrities like Cary Grant and Marlene Dietrich consorting with the Vanderbilts, the Astors, and the well-known and much married Dominican playboy Porfirio Rubirosa that appeared in New York's society columns. Not surprisingly, Ahmet took to the place like a duck to water.

In Ahmet's words, "I made a deal with John Perona, who was the owner of El Morocco that I would always have a check for $12. If I came and had one drink or I had dinner for ten people, I had one check for $12. It was a very small amount because I came there at least three or four times a week and I always came with a good-looking girl and maybe two or three other couples and we knew everybody. It was part of a scene and that made the club."

To accommodate all the friends he liked having with him at night, Ahmet began renting a bus for $3 an hour that he outfitted with a bar and enough room for a three-piece band. Stocking the bar with champagne, he hired a bartender "and a band of out-of-work immigrant musicians, and rode around town livening up parties." While visiting Birdland one night, the basement jazz club on 52nd Street owned by Roulette Records founder Morris Levy, Ahmet kidnapped the entire Count Basie band and drove off with them on the bus. "Of course, they missed their next set. Those were very fun, marvelous days. I was a bachelor, loose on the town. I really started to go out with a lot of girls. I didn't have very much home life."

Although Ahmet and Herb Abramson no longer traveled in the same social circles, Abramson was also living well in the luxurious San Remo building on Central Park West between 74th and 75th Streets. After having gone to Mexico in February 1957 to finalize his divorce from the woman he had brought back with him from Germany, Abramson began keeping company with Barbara Heaton, a coat and suit model who was attending Hunter College at night. After the two were married at the end of the year, they moved into a duplex with five bathrooms in the equally elegant El Dorado on Central Park West between 90th and 91st Streets.

By 1957, as Abramson himself seems to have clearly understood, music in America had definitely changed. Although Atlantic was doing all it could to sell records to what was now primarily a white teenage market, Elvis Presley, Chuck Berry, Little Richard, Jerry Lee Lewis, Fats Domino, the Everly Brothers, and Buddy Holly were all recording for other labels. No longer at the cutting edge of the business, Atlantic found itself competing with labels whose records were more in tune with the musical tastes of these new consumers.

In a very thoughtful and well-considered essay entitled "Rock 'N' Roll—Seen in Perspective" in *Cash Box* magazine on July 28, 1956, Abramson had written, "No future history concerned with the life and times of the 20th Century can leave out Rock 'N' Roll. It's that important . . . it is the best dance music there is . . . Like the jazz and blues from which it is derived, good Rock 'N' Roll is always fresh in improvisation and always swinging with a beat."

Having accurately assessed this new musical form, Abramson began trying to find an artist who could make the kind of records he had described in his essay. After being told by his partners that he had to choose between a black male baritone singer and a young white kid who sounded black, Abramson decided that what he really needed was an artist who could do for his new label what Elvis Presley had done for RCA. Passing on Brook Benton in the hope he could pick him up later, Abramson signed Bobby Darin to a recording contract at Atco.

As a boy growing up in a working-class Italian American family in the Bronx, Bobby Darin—born Walden Robert Cassotto—had suffered from repeated bouts of rheumatic fever that left his heart so weakened that one doctor thought he would be lucky to live to be sixteen. After graduating from the Bronx High School of Science, Darin attended Hunter College on a scholarship but soon dropped out to pursue a career in music.

After working as a busboy in resort hotels in the Catskill mountains, where he performed as a comedy drummer and singer, Darin began writing songs with fellow Bronx High School of Science student Don Kirshner. In 1956, Darin signed with Decca Records and recorded his own version of "Rock Island Line." A Lead Belly song that had been a huge skiffle hit for Lonnie Donegan in England, the record went nowhere in America.

A driven and astonishingly talented performer with great personal charm who onstage projected his own version of Frank Sinatra's ineffable cool, Darin had not yet decided in which musical genre he wanted to make his career. In 1957, Herb Abramson released three singles by Darin on Atco, among them the 1931 standard "(I Found) A Million Dollar Baby." Spending what his partners at Atlantic considered to be an inordinate amount of money to promote these records, Abramson issued three more Darin sides during the following year. None of them made their way onto the charts.

In a business where the brutal monthly bottom line could be met only by churning out a steady stream of hits, Herb Abramson was now mired in an authentic dry spell. Had he been able to strike gold by coming up with at least one big record, Ahmet would have most certainly found a way to accommodate him at Atlantic. Unfortunately, this did not prove to be the case.

## 3

For Ahmet as well as every other record company executive trying to gain entry to the white teenage market, the most powerful sales medium was radio and the most powerful man in radio was Alan Freed. After bringing his "Moondog" show from Cleveland to WINS in New York in September 1954, Freed changed the name of his program to *The Rock 'n' Roll Party* and began popularizing the use of this term (which he also tried to copyright) to describe the music he played each night for his dedicated young followers.

Talking nonstop as he introduced records that often became hits simply because he was playing them, Freed would "shout incessantly into his open mike" as he kept time by ringing a cowbell or pounding his hand on a telephone directory. Backed by his business partner Morris Levy, Freed began hosting and promoting what soon became an immensely popular series of live rock 'n' roll cavalcade shows where the audience was equally divided between blacks and whites. Adding to his considerable income, Freed also managed groups who performed at his shows and whose records he plugged on the radio.

Although Herb Abramson was one of Freed's good friends, Jerry Wexler was the one who went to a cloakroom in the Brill Building at 1619 Broadway on the first Monday of every month to hand either

Freed or his representative a paper bag containing $600 in cash. "The baksheesh didn't guarantee play for any particular record; we were only buying access," Wexler would later write. "He viewed the Erteguns and me as marks, paying customers."

When times got hard for the partners at Atlantic, Wexler felt certain Freed would understand their situation and asked the disc jockey if he would agree to play their records for free for a few months. Freed's succinct reply, which Wexler would later say the deejay sent him in a letter from Cleveland, was, "I'd love to, Wex, but I can't do it. That's taking the bread out of my children's mouths." Freed then promptly stopped playing Atlantic's records.

The label had actually been paying Freed far more than $600 a month to play its records on the radio and book its artists on his live shows. To curry favor with him, Ahmet and Wexler had sent a bulldozer to dig the hole for a swimming pool they then paid for at Grey Cliffe, Freed's sixteen-room stucco mansion on Wallack's Point not far from where conservative pundit William F. Buckley Jr. lived in Stamford, Connecticut.

Although Freed would proudly point to the pool as the most expensive feature of his house, he did not respond to this generous gift by playing Atlantic's latest releases on his show. Interceding on behalf of his good friends at the label, Morris Levy went to the deejay and asked why he was doing this only to have Freed reply that just because Ahmet and Wexler had bought him a pool, they didn't own him. Telling Levy he would begin featuring Atlantic records on his show as soon as they released something "good enough" for him to play, Freed added that if the partners at Atlantic did not like what he was doing, they could come and fill in the pool.

Despite the friction between them, Ahmet and Wexler attended Freed's annual end-of-summer record business party at Grey Cliffe on August 26, 1957. Herb Abramson and his future wife, Barbara, were also there as were Morris Levy, Bob Rolontz of RCA, Bob Thiele of Coral, and Sam Clark of ABC-Paramount. As everyone stood around the pool, Abramson went into the house and found a pair of swim trunks. He and Thiele then began, in Barbara Abramson's words, "doing dives, enjoying themselves, and cooling down so that other people began wishing they had their bathing suits."

Wearing high heels, a tight red cotton Chinese dress, and "a beautiful $80 golden stole Herb had just bought me," she suddenly felt Ahmet grab her arm and pull her toward the pool. "No, don't do that," she told him. "Herb just bought me this stole and it will get ruined." Letting go of her arm, Ahmet said, "Oh, I didn't realize. Here, let me fold it for you." Taking the stole from her, "he folded it very, very nicely like a real gentleman and put it in the second row of chairs and I thought, 'This is a very nice person. He doesn't even want me to get splashed by people in the swimming pool.' "

Walking back to her "with this beguiling smile on his face, he grabbed my arm again and threw me in the goddamn pool without even asking me if I could swim." When Abramson dropped her off at her parents' apartment that night, she "was missing one shoe, all the curl was washed out of my hair, my makeup was washed off, and the dress was all wrinkled and that was when my father said to Herb at two A.M., 'What are your intentions regarding my daughter?' " A week later, Abramson presented her with an engagement ring.

While the sight of Herb Abramson's good-looking new girlfriend standing beside a pool for which Atlantic had paid may have just seemed like too good an opportunity for an inveterate practical joker like Ahmet to ignore, he would never have contemplated pulling such a stunt with Herb's former wife Miriam. By acting like what Barbara Abramson would later call one of "the boys down at the public swimming pool at 59th Street tossing the girls in to get wet as part of rough horseplay," Ahmet had clearly demonstrated how he now felt about his longtime partner. As he would soon prove, Ahmet's patience with Herb Abramson's role as the president of a label he was no longer actually running was nearing an end.

On February 11, 1958, Paul G. Marshall of the law firm Marshall & Ziffer sent the "Principals of Atlantic Recording Co." a memo in which he discussed overtures made by Max Youngstein of United Artists to purchase Atlantic Records with negotiations to "take place around a central figure of two million, five hundred thousand dollars but actually would be based on a formula of five times net before taxes or four times net before taxes, officers' salaries." As Marshall also noted, "Mr. Youngstein asked which of the personnel would come along in the deal. I refrained from comment and he ventured the opinion based on what he had been told, a minimum of three principals must come with the deal. Namely, Ahmet, Jerry, and Nesuhi."

Then just twenty-five years old, Paul Marshall would over the course of his long legal career sell the music and movie rights to the Woodstock Festival while also representing a list of clients that included the Beatles, Akira Kurosawa, David Frost, Jacques Brel, Isaac Bashevis Singer, and Suge Knight. As he would later say, "I am the ancient history of the music business. Someone once asked me who was my first client. And I said, 'Mozart.' "

In Marshall's words, "Max Youngstein came to me. United Artists was then just a film company that was going into the record business and they had two choices. They could either start up or buy. The reason Herb was not mentioned in the memo was very simple. Herb was in trouble in the industry and people knew it. In my first meeting with Jerry Wexler, he mentioned that Herb was not coming along if the company was sold."

Beginning a pattern that would continue throughout his years at Atlantic, Wexler was eager to make the deal. "Herb always told me," Barbara Abramson would later say, "that Jerry used the oft-quoted phrase, 'This is just a horse race. It can stop anyday now.' So Jerry felt, 'Cash in while it's good. And get the money.' " In Marshall's words, "Jerry was a very sound man who I really loved but he was always interested in selling. Always, always. He wanted to put money away. He hadn't come from wealth and he was not financially secure and he had a wife and kid and the record business then was a fly-by-night business."

Although "the United Artists offer didn't proceed much further," Ahmet and Wexler used it as the impetus to change the long-standing corporate structure at Atlantic. "Herb didn't particularly want to sell," Barbara Abramson would later recall, "and Ahmet came to him and said, 'We want to have another election because it won't look good for a sale if in all these years, we've never had an election of a different set of officers.' I said to Herb, 'How do you feel about that?' And he said, 'I don't like it at all. It's like a gang-up.' "

Having already given his former wife Miriam more than half of his original 30 percent share of Atlantic, Abramson knew the vote would go against him. "It was a cabal because they were also trying to freeze Miriam out," Barbara Abramson recalled. "Herb spoke to me about it a number of times and said, 'I should have told them, "Okay, you want to be president? I'll be chairman of the board." ' But obviously they wouldn't have liked that either."

"Let me tell you the key to everything," Wexler later said. "While Herb was gone, he got everything we got. Salary, cash, whatever it was, he got. When he came back, we gave him Atco to run but he started to act kind of eccentric and crazy. So Ahmet and I got together and said, 'We're going to have to do something about this.' We decided to make Ahmet president and reduce Herb to executive vice president. When we called Herb in and told him that, he walked out and said, 'See my lawyers.' He could have stayed forever. We were not the kind of people that would get rid of breathing bodies, warm human beings." In Ahmet's words, "Herb insisted on being bought out. He didn't have to go."

More than thirty years later, Abramson would admit, "I had a big ego and after a while I couldn't take it, so I said, 'Buy me out.' It was the stupidest thing I ever said, but that was it. In entertainment entities there is cutthroat politics, but it is the way of the world." After Abramson stalked out of the meeting at Atlantic, the partners began protracted deliberations with him during which, as Ahmet later said, "Herb tried to blackmail us to get the price up. He threatened us. So anyway, we paid him off and got him out. And I said, 'Well, good riddance.' We didn't part as friends."

Although Wexler would later write that like all independent record labels, Atlantic was then cash poor, the partners managed to raise $300,000 to buy out Abramson. Using what would be today's equivalent of about $2.4 million, Herb Abramson then founded the Triumph, Blaze, and Festival record labels, none of which was particularly successful. He produced "High Heel Sneakers," a hit for Tommy Tucker on Chess Records, and cowrote "Long Tall Shorty" with Don Covay.

Moving with his wife and young daughter to the fashionable Belnord apartment building at 225 West 86th Street, Abramson built and ran the A-1 recording studio, which was originally located in Atlantic's former offices at 234 West 56th Street before moving to the ground floor of a hotel at Broadway and 72nd Street. Shortly after leaving Atlantic, Abramson also sold his "trick-track record" patent to the Mattel Corporation for use in its very popular "Chatty Cathy" doll, which uttered a variety of recorded phrases through the use of a pull string.

As Herb Abramson got older, his kidneys began to fail. Insisting this "was not for publication," Ahmet would tell an interviewer that after Abramson had "lost all his money, I put him on a salary that nobody knew about. I guess I had him for the last twenty years of his life." One week before his eighty-third birthday on November 9, 1999, Herb Abramson died of kidney failure. Through Atlantic Records, Ahmet paid for his cremation.

In time, Abramson's decision to sell his interest in Atlantic before the company began generating huge profits came to be viewed in the record business as a mistake of historic proportions. Abramson himself seems to have dealt with it with a kind of equanimity shared by few others in an industry he had helped create. As he would later say, "I sometimes look at it like a poker game, in that originally there are quite a few participants, but some of them are dealt out, and some of them end up with all the chips. That is the way the cookie crumbles."

In a letter of condolence he sent to Barbara Abramson shortly after her husband's death, Jerry Wexler wrote, "Herb was a wonderful man. Not only for his talent and role as a pioneer in recorded music but for the fine character and inherent decency that was so basic to his nature. Life had not always been kind to him and although we rarely communicated through the years, I sensed that he never let misfortune embitter him or turn him against others."

Wexler concluded his letter by writing, "He welcomed me into the firm and as he said goodbye to us for his tour of Army duty, he left me with this counsel. 'No matter what, don't ever stop making records.' Simplistic on the face of it but it turned out to be the most important single rule to go by through all the vicissitudes of a very tough occupation."

At Atlantic Records, Ahmet, Wexler, and Nesuhi were now in control. Within a matter of weeks after Herb Abramson had walked out of their offices for the final time, Ahmet came up with the huge hit that finally crossed the label over into the white teenage market it had been pursuing for so long.

# EIGHT

# Splish Splash

*"Splish splash/I was takin' a bath/Long about a Saturday night."*
—Bobby Darin, Murray Kaufman, and Jean Murray

1

As he sat in the bleachers surrounded by teenagers in a television studio at WFIL in Philadelphia with a microphone in his hand, a very youthful-looking and impossibly handsome Dick Clark leaned into the camera to introduce an artist he was proud to say was also a personal friend. After telling Clark he had no idea what was happening across the country because everywhere he went throughout the land, people were saying the best show on television was Dick Clark's *American Bandstand*, Bobby Darin said he was about to introduce a new song he thought could be pretty big.

Moving off to where performers like Frankie Avalon, Connie Francis, and Dion and the Belmonts lip-synched their latest releases on the show teenagers all over America rushed home from school each day to watch, Darin began snapping his fingers and rolling his shoulders to the infectious beat of "Splish Splash." Due in no small part to the exposure Dick Clark gave the song on *Bandstand* as well as his wildly popular Saturday night show on ABC, the record became a million-seller and rose to the top of the R&B charts.

With the possible exception of Jerry Blavat, who in time would become a fast-talking radio disc jockey known as "The Geater with the Heater" and "The Big Boss with the Hot Sauce," none of the teenagers who danced regularly on *Bandstand* and so had themselves become pop stars, had ever heard of Ahmet Ertegun. Nor would they have understood how a man twice their age could have known that a song with nursery rhyme lyrics and a rocking beat would allow Atlantic Records to finally tap into the brand-new market *American Bandstand* as well as a slew of locally televised teenage dance shows had created.

With Alan Freed's own nationally televised *Big Beat* show having been canceled when ABC affiliates in the South became outraged by the sight of singer Frankie Lymon dancing with a white girl as the show's closing credits rolled, Dick Clark had become the man who could make or break a record in America. In small towns all over the country, teenagers would vanish from the streets as soon as *American Bandstand* came on at three, not to be seen again until the program ended at four-thirty.

While AM radio remained the mainstay for teenagers who listened to rock 'n' roll, they could now for the first time sit in their parents' living rooms and actually watch performers whom they had only ever heard before. The new medium was ideally suited for an artist like Bobby Darin, who with his good looks and brash, self-assured stage presence could sell a song like no one but Elvis.

Although Herb Abramson had recognized Darin's talent by signing him to Atco, he had never known what to do with him in the studio and actually delayed a session at which Darin wanted to record "Splish Splash" until the artist came up with "better material." Darin had written the song in disc jockey Murray "The K" Kaufman's New York apartment while they were "shooting the shit one night" and "talking about writing songs." Opening his "big mouth," Darin boasted he could write a song "off any idea: give me an idea and you got a song. So Murray says, 'Okay, wise guy. Write me a song that has "splish splash I was takin' a bath" as one of the lines.' I went right to his piano and did it." In truth, Kaufman's mother, Jean Murray, had suggested the line to him over the phone and she then collaborated with Darin and Kaufman on the music.

Had it not been for the ongoing tension between the partners at Atlantic, Darin might never have recorded what became his breakthrough hit. In Ahmet's words, "Bobby Darin used to come see Herb, and Herb would keep him waiting, sometimes an hour before he could see him. He didn't care. The records weren't selling . . . Herb was keeping him waiting and he would be in the waiting room next to my office where there was a piano and he would sit and play . . . I thought, 'My God, this kid is terrific.' "

When Ahmet learned Darin's one-year contract with Atco was about to expire and Abramson intended to release him, he decided to produce the artist on his own. Although by now Ahmet was no longer doing much actual recording, he took Darin into the Atlantic office at 234 West 56th on April 10, 1958, for a split session with jazz singer Morgana King, whom he had just signed to Atlantic. "Can you imagine?" Jerry Wexler recalled, "the disparity between a Morgana King and a Bobby Darin? In a single session?"

Realizing Darin had been "creating a completely different kind of music," Ahmet decided "he needed a much funkier backing than he had been getting" and put together "a little rhythm section" of good R&B players Darin knew and liked. Together, they selected the sides Darin would cut in his hour and a half of studio time. Ahmet also insisted Darin play piano on the session "because that was one of the things that got me about him—the basic rhythm that he put into his songs."

With Tom Dowd at the board of the brand-new eight-track Ampex 300 recording console he had persuaded the partners at Atlantic to let him buy for $11,000 and Ahmet instructing drummer Panama Francis to lay back on the "eights" he was playing on his cymbals, Darin did seven takes of the song before they had it down. "When I cut the record," Ahmet would later say, "I thought it was going to the top. It was a cute novelty lyric, and everybody dug it. Without the lyric, it would have been a hit because of the music and the track. It was just there."

Confirming that Ahmet was already light-years ahead of his partners when it came to understanding the kind of records kids who watched *American Bandstand* would buy, Wexler said, "I thought 'Splish Splash' was an abominable piece of shit, but Ahmet saw it and that was why he did it and that was the beginning of Bobby Darin."

During the same session, Darin cut "Queen of the Hop," which also became a Top Ten hit. Earlier in the day, Ahmet had learned that Chuck Willis, who in 1957 had cut "C.C. Rider" for Atlantic, thereby inspiring the Stroll dance craze, had died on an operating table in Atlanta, Georgia, at the age of thirty. "It was our first experience of a great artist being taken away from us, suddenly out of the blue," Ahmet would later say. "It was a terrible tragedy and a devastating shock to all of us." Despite the bad news, Ahmet managed to produce two hits for Darin in that day.

In the mistaken belief he was still going to be cut loose from his Atco contract, Darin went into Decca's New York studio two weeks later and cut "Early in the Morning," a song that bore a great resemblance to Ray Charles's "I Got a Woman." When Decca learned Darin had re-signed with Atco, the company credited the song to "The Ding Dongs" and released it on its Brunswick label eight days after "Splish Splash" hit the stores.

"Bobby Darin snuck off with Murray the K and they went out and cut a record and then gave it to Decca under another name," Paul Marshall, who was then handling Atlantic's legal affairs, recalled. "Darin was called in with his lawyer and his manager and we had this meeting with Ahmet and Jerry. I pointed out he was a young man with a great start to a career and the last thing he needed was people like me on his case to stop this record and what would he get from it? Murray the K would have made some money but not him. I said, 'You just made a terrible mistake. Because I'm going to beat you.' "

After Darin had signed a statement retracting Decca's right to release the record, Marshall called Murray the K, who "took a very harsh line and had a chip on his shoulder." Walking over to the phone on Ahmet's desk, Marshall picked it up and said, "Get me the manager for WINS." Suddenly nervous, Murray the K demanded to know why Marshall was calling his radio station. "Murray," Marshall told him, "if we're going to sue somebody who plays our records, it's wise for us to warn them that we're going to do it."

Faced with a lawsuit Decca knew it could not win, the label surrendered the masters to Atco but then rushed Buddy Holly into the studio to record his own version of the song, which they then released before Atco could issue the original verson credited to Bobby Darin and the Rinky Dinks. Both versions became minor hits, with the original rising slightly higher on the charts than the cover. "I wish somebody could catch the glamour and glory of the fifties," Marshall would later say. "Those days were so much fun. The majors lost control. Rock 'n' roll came and they didn't believe in it and all these guys came out of the woods and a lot of them were characters. There were no MBAs. Just people who loved records."

Six months after "Splish Splash" had made Bobby Darin a star, Ahmet was having lunch with his friend the well-known Austrian singer and actress Lotte Lenya who as Jenny Diver in the 1928 stage version of her husband, Kurt Weill's, *The Threepenny Opera* had introduced the song "Mack the Knife," with lyrics written by Bertolt Brecht. At some point, she asked Ahmet why he had never made a recording of any of her husband's songs. Ahmet told her he didn't make that kind of record at his company but when she asked him to promise he would try, Ahmet said, "Well, maybe we will."

A few days later, Darin came to see Ahmet with the version of "Mack the Knife" Louis Armstrong had cut in 1956. "I know this sounds pretty weird," Darin said, "but I think I could make a great version of this—I should do it." Then twenty-three years old, Darin loved big band arrangements and songs that were standards. After seeing *The Threepenny Opera* in Greenwich Village, Darin had begun performing "Mack the Knife" on tour.

When Darin told Ahmet he wanted to cut the song so he could be more than "a teen idol," Ahmet's initial response was, "What are you talking about? You'll ruin your career." Nor was he alone in this opinion. Dick Clark told Darin he was crazy to want to record "Mack the Knife" and "he was going to die with the song." Still owed royalties for "Splish Splash," Darin told Ahmet he was willing to roll the money over and pay for the session at his own expense. Backed by a full orchestra conducted by Richard Weiss and with Ahmet, Nesuhi, and Wexler producing, Darin cut the song in December 1958.

"As we were cutting 'Mack the Knife,'" Ahmet recalled, "everybody knew that this was going to be a number one record. Then I realized that having done the rock thing, Bobby was now going to have a big pop hit. He was going to be a major, major star . . . But we knew as we were cutting it. We were jumping up and down. After the first take, I said, 'You've got it. That's it.'"

Despite Ahmet's enthusiastic reaction during the session, it was not until "Dream Lover," a record Ahmet and Wexler also produced, had gone to number two in the pop charts and Darin's manager had urged Ahmet to put out "Mack the Knife" as a single that the song was finally released in August 1959. Darin's jumping, swinging version of the song, in which he improvised Lotte Lenya's name into two different verses, went to number one three months later and stayed there for nine weeks. The only number one hit Darin would have in his career, the record remained in the Top Ten for a year and sold two million copies. "Mack the Knife" won the 1959 Grammy Award for Best Record of the Year and Darin was named Best New Artist.

When "Beyond the Sea," Darin's version of Charles Trenet's "La Mer," became a hit as well, the singer could do no wrong and began appearing at the Copacabana nightclub in New York, where he set the all-time attendance record. In time, Darin would record twenty hits for Atco, the label from which he had nearly been released by Herb Abramson.

For the partners at Atlantic, the good news was that the dry spell in which they had been mired throughout 1957 was over. "Two records got us back in the game," Wexler would later write. "These tunes were so winning, so widely popular, so immediately irresistible, no one could keep them off the air." One of those songs was "Yakety Yak" by the Coasters. The other was "Splish Splash." "Each sold well over a million. At wholesale, that meant $400,000 or $500,000 in revenue."

Despite a decade of success at Atlantic, two records with a combined running time of about four minutes had made it possible for the partners to cover their operating costs while also providing them with their yearly income. In an era when the independent record business was still a crap shoot of major proportions and the pressure to come up with hits was unrelenting, Ahmet had proven yet again he had a set of magic ears.

## 2

Atlantic chose to celebrate its tenth year in the record business by filling the January 13, 1958, edition of *Billboard* with nineteen pages of articles and congratulatory ads that purported to tell the real story of how the company had grown "during one of the industry's liveliest ten year periods" and so was now poised to become a major label. Both Ahmet and Nesuhi contributed signed pieces in which they discussed Atlantic's humble beginnings as well as its very bright future in the jazz LP field.

In alphabetical order beneath their photographs, Atlantic's brightest stars were profiled while being featured in quarter-page ads bearing their likeness, for which they had most likely paid. Now married to Freddy Bienstock, an Austrian-born executive at Hill & Range, the music publishing company whose number one client was Elvis Presley, the former Miriam Abramson was lauded for her vital role in having kept the label afloat in an article entitled "Atlantic's 'Money Man' Is a Woman."

While Jerry Wexler received scant notice in the extensive outlay, he did sign (as Gerald Wexler) an introductory statement in which the partners (including Herb Abramson) proudly noted that during the past decade Atlantic had issued 425 singles, 100 LPs, and 109 extended play records. "We started as young collectors and jazz enthusiasts," the statement read, "and thought (naively, perhaps) that it would be a 'ball' to combine business with our main source of pleasure in life. If the truth be told, we are still fans and amateurs—and hope that we'll never get so old that we'll change in this respect."

After thanking all the distributors, disc jockeys, retailers, and jukebox operators who had kept Atlantic "alive and healthy for a decade," the partners concluded by writing, "Our pleasant association with them makes us look forward with keen anticipation to another decade of progress." A photograph of ten birthday candles blazing away on a turntable strewn with ribbons filled the rest of the page.

On every level, "The Atlantic Records Story, 1948–1958" was an impeccable piece of record business publicity. What seems most remarkable about it now is the incredible litany of companies that felt compelled to take out ads to congratulate the label on its success. In what was then still very much a business of personal relationships where everyone had to stay on the good side of those who paid their bills on time, companies indebted to Atlantic for their continued survival were only too happy to publicly proclaim their loyalty. Nowhere in this extended promotional package could the names of any disc jockeys or the radio stations for whom they worked be found. Insofar as they were concerned, Atlantic was but one of the many suitors vying for attention on their weekly play lists.

To court their favor, Atlantic played a prominent role in the legendary second annual disc jockey convention sponsored by Todd Storz, the creator of the Top 40 radio format, at the Americana Hotel in Bal Harbour, Florida, during the 1959 Memorial Day weekend. At an event that would spawn a thousand stories and be immortalized in a *Miami News* headline reading, "FOR DEEJAYS: BABES, BOOZE, AND BRIBES," Ahmet chose to promote his label in his own unique manner.

Sponsored by nearly fifty record companies including all of the major labels, the convention was "a lavish and lascivious four-day bacchanal" at which 2,500 disc jockeys from all over the country were treated free of charge to "around-the-clock receptions, parties, concerts, and gambling junkets to Havana." When they arrived at the convention, the deejays were each handed a million dollars in "play money" by RCA so they could begin gambling with it. For every visit they paid to the company's hospitality suite where "liquid refreshments" were available for free, they received another $5,000 in scrip. On Memorial Day in exchange for the play money, RCA auctioned off a stereo set, a color TV, $500 worth of clothing, a trip for two to Europe, and a Studebaker Lark.

As Joe Smith, a Yale graduate who would become the president of Warner Bros. Records but was then a very popular AM disc jockey in Boston, would later say, "I was one of the board members of that convention in Miami Beach. I had just been married so I took my wife there. I was playing blackjack and I went bust and the guy gave me more chips. She said, 'Aren't you supposed to lose?' I said, 'Shhh. I can never lose. So long as my ratings are up there.'"

Nonstop gambling was not the only divertissement offered to the disc jockeys over the course of the holiday weekend. Then seventeen years old, Marshall Chess would remember smoking pot for the first time at the convention. Long before it became a staple of the hippie culture during the 1960s, marijuana was widely available in the music business and, as he recalled, "They were bringing pot into the Brill Building in New York in these big garbage bags and selling it for twenty dollars an ounce. They called it 'mezz.'"

The convention also featured what writer William Barlow called "one of the largest contingents of hookers ever assembled at a hotel in Miami Beach" with some prostitutes having been "recruited from as far away as New York City." In Marshall Chess's words, "I remember Ahmet and all these other guys at the convention standing in a circle and there was a guy in the middle fucking a whore and everyone was throwing hundred-dollar bills betting on how long he could fuck her."

In the words of Paul Marshall, who attended the event, "Ahmet hired a certain number of hookers. However, he got them gowns and introduced them as the cream of Miami debutante society. And he told them he would double their fee if they did not have sex with the guests. After Jerry Blaine had danced with them all, he made a pass at one and she slapped him across the face. We were all beside ourselves because all the Atlantic people knew they were hookers."

Morris Levy of Roulette Records, who in Paul Marshall's words was "in the mob" and "ran about eighty or ninety hat check concessions in nightclubs" in New York City, spent $15,000 for an all-night barbecue that featured the Count Basie band. Half the money went to pay for two thousand bottles of bourbon. All told, the estimated cost of the weekend for the record companies was $250,000.

At "a great breakfast Atlantic gave at that convention," the featured speaker was the comedian Professor Irwin Corey. Decked out in seedy formal attire and sneakers, Corey, who billed himself as "The World's Foremost Authority," would deliver long, rambling monologues filled with double talk that would suddenly make eminent sense while also being incredibly funny. "Remember," Marshall would later say, "these were disc jockeys from Keokuk, Iowa. They introduced him as 'Professor Irwin Corey from Harvard University, an expert in the field,' and he said, 'And, as one of the great leaders of the phonographic industry, Mr. Morris Levy, has said, "A man can get further in the music industry with a kind word and a gun than with a kind word alone." ' And nobody laughed. But at the dais, we all fell over."

The event was such an ostentatious public demonstration of the overwhelming power wielded by the nation's disc jockeys as well as the outrageous lengths to which record companies would go to service their every need that the ensuing "media frenzy" over what was characterized as a full-fledged orgy caught the attention of the Legislative Oversight Subcommittee of the United States House Interstate Commerce Committee. In February 1960, fresh from its news-making exposé of the networks' rigged quiz shows, the subcommittee began public hearings into payola, the form of commercial bribery that had for years been standard practice in the music industry.

"When I first started working for King Records in 1958," Bob Krasnow, the founder of Blue Thumb Records, remembered, "I paid off everybody. It was just the thing to do. If you didn't pay to play, you didn't get played. One of my jobs was to call on Dick Clark. I couldn't pay off Dick so I figured out if I could get my records on WIBG radio in Philadelphia, Dick would hear them and that would grease the way."

The top jock at WIBG was Tom "Big Daddy" Donahue, who after the payola scandal broke moved to San Francisco, where in 1967 he transformed KMPX into the first alternative free-form FM rock radio station in America. "Tom Donahue was one of my great mentors," Krasnow recalled, "and I was awed by him. I brought him a record one day and I had money on me to take care of him and he listened to the record and he said, 'Wow, that's a grand record, man.' Then he looked me straight in the face and said, 'No, Bob, that's a *two* grand record.' I realized what mercenaries they were. I thought the guy liked me."

On May 19, 1960, along with the program director at WINS and five other deejays, among them Hal Jackson, for whom Ahmet had written "The House That Jack Built," which became Jackson's radio show theme song in Washington, Alan Freed was arrested for taking payola. In a continuing drama reminiscent of the recent quiz show hearings that received front-page newspaper coverage all over the country, one well-known disc jockey after another appeared before the committee to admit their complicity in a practice that had been an industry standard for decades.

The hearings effectively destroyed Alan Freed's career, and he died a broken man five years later at the age of forty-four. Dick Clark, who was also called to testify before the subcommittee and steadfastly denied ever taking payola, survived as the host of *American Bandstand* after being forced by ABC television to divest himself of his own extensive record business interests.

The only two labels who never signed the Federal Trade Commission consent decree stipulating that record companies would no longer engage in payola were Chess and Atlantic, both of whom were represented by Paul Marshall. As he would later say, "When I read the decree, I noticed the big companies like RCA and CBS had signed it but that my clients were being asked to sign it as corporations and as individuals. So I looked up the law and I determined there was no crime. There was no statute which made payola illegal."

The theory behind the commercial bribery statute under which Alan Freed had been prosecuted for taking payola was that money paid to the deejays should have been paid to their employers. However, existing Federal Communications Commission rules prohibited radio station owners from receiving such payments. "Therefore the money wasn't being diverted," Marshall contended. "They weren't paying the owner and they couldn't pay the owner. They paid the disc jockey. And I likened it to a tip. If any establishment says you can give our employees special favors or benefits, then it didn't lose anything. Ergo, there was no money stolen."

Marshall also argued that the only deejays paid to play music on the air were those who already had "a very substantial audience." Since "the crime consisted of changing and affecting public taste," the fact that "people had already accepted these guys before they ever got paid" made this charge also impossible to prove. In Marshall's words, "There used to be songs called 'turntable hits' which got a lot of play but never sold a record."

In the end, the 1960 payola scandal affected only the major labels, which then began hiring third-party promotion men who would sign contracts acknowledging they could, in Marshall's words, "never talk to a disc jockey even if he was his brother. By signing it, they made the government happy and they could say, 'Look, they're doing what they can do.' It was all bullshit."

"In the very beginning," Ahmet admitted, "I made a lot of friends among disc jockeys and they played my records. A few would look for favors of one kind or another. And we were in a position where we really had to deliver some favors to get our records played. When there were very important stations that were playing our competition much more than us, we would go see what we could do to befriend those people. And sometimes they would ask for some remuneration which we very often came through with. After the first payola investigations, we hired other people to look after that and I think that was the position most record companies were in all over the world."

At both the convention in Miami Beach and then during the public hearings that ruined the lives and careers of disc jockeys throughout America, Ahmet and his label somehow managed yet again to emerge unscathed. The partners at Atlantic went right on doing business as usual by putting money into the hands of those who could make or break their latest releases by playing them on the air.

## 3

Far more than the death of his father or the failure of his marriage, the overwhelming sense of personal loss Ahmet experienced when the artist he loved and respected above all others left Atlantic shook him to the very core of his being. After a decade in the business, Ahmet learned for the first time that his relationship with those who recorded for him was based on mutual need and so would always end in time. Despite how close he would become to many of his artists over the next five decades, Ahmet never made the same mistake again.

Along with Jerry Wexler, Ahmet was in the Atlantic office on the night of February 18, 1959, when his great favorite Ray Charles cut a song he had regularly been performing with his band. Running more than seven and a half minutes, "What'd I Say" began with Charles playing a very rapid, raunchy, and completely irresistible riff on electric piano for a minute and a half before finally singing a series of lines including the one about the girl with the diamond ring who really knew how to shake that thing from "Mess Around."

More than four minutes into the track, Charles suddenly stopped singing and playing. As his biographer Michael Lydon wrote, "Immediately a gaggle of men and women's voices rise in protest. They want the music to keep going, and though pretending he doesn't understand, Ray starts again" by exchanging a series of guttural sexual moans and grunts with his female backup singers, "the grunts each time becoming more edged with sexual pleasure until Ray is screaming, the ladies moaning, and the band rocking. Out of the ecstatic tumult come exhortations to 'Shake that thing,' and the general agreement, 'Don't it make you feel all right!'"

Combining elements of jazz, gospel, and the call-and-response of Mississippi Delta field blues into a mind-blowing synthesis of filthy funk and nonstop driving rhythm, the track was unlike anything anyone had ever heard before, much less recorded. Understandably, neither Ahmet nor Wexler knew what to do with a cut they thought had "dance-craze possibilities" until Tom Dowd edited out "unwanted choruses and telescoped the track to two three-minute sides of a 45 entitled "What'd I Say Parts I & II."

Realizing "they had a record too hot for spring release," the partners decided to hold it back until June so it could become "the dance hit of the summer." Ray Charles's first Top Ten hit, "What'd I Say" spent fifteen weeks on the pop charts and became the number one R&B single. The song sold a million copies, making it the artist's first gold record.

A landmark track that broke down the barriers of what was then considered suitable for radio play, "What'd I Say" became, as Lydon wrote, "the life of a million parties, the spark of as many romances, a song to date the summer by." When a seventeen-year-old bass player named Paul McCartney first heard the song in Liverpool, chills went up and down his spine and he suddenly knew what he wanted to do with his musical career.

A bigger hit by far than "I Got a Woman" had been four years earlier, "What'd I Say" brought Ray Charles the largest royalties of his career. It also raised his price on the road and made "a fortune" for Atlantic by contributing to "the label's first-ever million-dollar month in gross sales." For Ahmet and Wexler, the only bad news was that since Ray Charles's contract with the label was about to expire in the fall, they would now have to come up with a much better offer to re-sign him.

Aside from how much both partners valued Ray Charles as an artist, their need to keep him on Atlantic was compounded by the fact that when Clyde McPhatter's contract with Atlantic had ended in March, he had signed with MGM Records for a guaranteed income of $50,000 a year. United Artists and Warner Bros. Records had also bid for his services, thereby making it plain that major labels were now eager to acquire black artists.

A performer whom Ahmet called "a singer from heaven with the most lyrical voice," McPhatter had put together the Drifters after being fired from Billy Ward and the Dominoes. At his first session for Atlantic, Wexler cut "Money Honey" with him and the cut went to number one on the R&B charts. Ahmet then wrote what Wexler considered his greatest song for McPhatter, a direct forerunner of "The Twist" entitled "Whatcha Gonna Do," but the record went nowhere. McPhatter had another hit with "Honey Love," which Wexler cowrote. Then McPhatter was drafted. When he returned from the army, Herb Abramson produced a hit entitled "Seven Days" and then had him cut "Treasure of Love," a number one R&B hit in 1956.

After finally breaking through to the white market with "A Lover's Question" in 1958, McPhatter jumped ship at Atlantic and took the big money offered by MGM. Despite what McPhatter had done, Ahmet and Wexler still felt that they could re-sign Ray Charles.

What neither man knew was that Larry Myers, a young agent in the Billy Shaw agency, had already decided the best thing he could do for Ray Charles was get him off Atlantic. By continuing to record for what Myers viewed as a black label, Charles, who was then earning a thousand dollars a night on the road, would remain "stuck in a black world" and would never be able to make the kind of money paid only to musicians who entertained white audiences in America.

When Myers presented his case to Milt Shaw, who after the death of his brother Billy had begun managing Charles, Shaw told him Atlantic had been doing a great job with the singer and he was not eager to encourage him to leave the label. Myers eventually persuaded Shaw to tell Charles he should wait to re-sign with Atlantic in the hope a major label might offer him a better deal. What in time would become a classic music business ploy achieved one immediate result.

Suddenly worried that Charles might actually be thinking about leaving Atlantic, Ahmet and Wexler began doing all they could to re-sign him. Ahmet flew to the Midwest twice with a contract for Charles to sign only to realize the artist was avoiding him. To no avail, Ahmet offered one of Charles's close associates a payment of $5,000 or $10,000 if he could persuade the singer to stay at Atlantic.

Working behind the scenes, Myers went to ABC-Paramount Records, a major label that had been founded four years earlier by Sam Clark, a record distributor from Boston who had been given half a million dollars by Leonard Goldenson to bring ABC into the record business. A most unlikely bidder for Charles's services, the label had released thoroughly white-bread hits like "A Rose and a Baby Ruth" by George Hamilton IV and Paul Anka's "Diana" while also distributing teenage smashes on the Chancellor label by *American Bandstand* pop idols Frankie Avalon and Fabian. Lloyd Price, their first black artist, had scored a hit with "Personality" but the song had little in common with the kind of gutbucket soul that had become Ray Charles's stock in trade.

As Myers soon learned, ABC-Paramount was not only eager to sign Ray Charles but were also willing to offer him the kind of deal no artist in the record business had ever been given before. After Milt Shaw told Charles to meet with ABC-Paramount in October 1959, Sam Clark offered to let Charles produce his own records, which the label would then distribute for a fee. Clark told Charles he would sell far more records on a major label, thereby enabling him to attract white audiences to his shows. Once his records had earned back their advance, Charles would earn 75 cents on the dollar for each copy sold. The singer would also be guaranteed an annual income of $50,000 on a three-year contract.

After telling Clark to write up a formal proposal so he could show it to the partners at Atlantic and give them a chance to match the offer, Charles said he also wanted to own his masters. By doing so, he would control all the rights to recordings he would make for ABC-Paramount, thereby cutting the label out of all future profits after his contract with them was over.

As no record company had ever before entered into such an agreement, Clark told him this would not be possible. Charles, who was bluffing and was already willing to accept the offer, insisted that without this provision there would be no deal. After thinking about it, Clark offered to let Charles have his masters back after five years. As Charles's lawyer told him, not even Frank Sinatra had ever gotten this kind of deal.

Taking the ABC-Paramount offer to Ahmet and Wexler, Charles said if they matched it, he would stay at Atlantic. Telling the artist they loved him, the partners said they could not possibly agree to such a deal but left the meeting thinking negotiations had only just begun and they would have the opportunity to talk with him again. Ahmet in particular was confident the deal would eventually be done because he was not only the first to have recognized Ray Charles's talent but had also allowed him to do as he liked in the studio, thereby enabling Charles to transform himself into the great artist he had become.

While Charles had rewarded Ahmet's faith by making great records, both partners had also done all they could to push his releases because of their unwavering faith in him. Both Ahmet and Wexler felt certain Charles would stay on the label that had for so long been his home rather than sign with a "soulless corporation" where no one would ever love or understand his music as well as they did.

At what was then the most expensive session in the history of Atlantic, Nesuhi had brought in the entire Count Basie band and half of the Duke Ellington orchestra to join Ray Charles's own band in the studio. With more than forty musicians behind him, the singer cut twelve standards (six of which were produced by Wexler), thereby demonstrating he could do far more than sing his own brand of gospel-charged rhythm and blues.

When Atlantic released *The Genius of Ray Charles* album in November, it sent more than three thousand promotional EPs to disc jockeys and took out the first full-page ad for Ray Charles in *Billboard*. When the month ended without either Ahmet or Wexler having heard from Charles or his manager, someone called Atlantic to say the word on the street was that Charles had already signed with ABC-Paramount and the contract was on file with the musicians' union.

On December 7, 1959, *Billboard* announced the deal. A week later, the trade paper provided details of the "exceptional" 75–25 split Charles had been given at ABC-Paramount. Ahmet would later say that for him the news was "emotionally, a great blow." Having always considered Ray Charles his friend, Ahmet could not understand why the artist had never given Atlantic a chance to come back with a second offer.

Even though he had been considerably less personally involved with the artist than Ahmet, Jerry Wexler now had a real reason to worry and lay awake one night until dawn wondering what would become of Atlantic. Now that Ray Charles had left the label, Wexler feared they might also lose performers like Bobby Darin and perhaps even cease to exist. Expressing what everyone at Atlantic was then feeling, Herb Abramson's former wife Miriam Bienstock would say, "We felt betrayed, it was a terrible thing."

No one at the label was more upset by what Charles had done than Ahmet. Unable to accept that Charles himself had actually done this to him, Ahmet would say he believed Charles's personal valet, "the guy who was doing everything for him, including buying dope and getting girls" had been taken care of by ABC-Paramount and then persuaded Charles to agree to the deal because, "in those days with Ray Charles, his signature was an 'X' so someone had to bring him in to put the cross in and I don't know to what extent Ray knew about it."

Larry Myers would later say, "I would be glad to convince Ahmet and Jerry that Ray knew all about it. Nobody put anything over on Ray." Explaining his decision in his own words, Charles said, "Seventy-five cents out of a dollar and owning my own masters, that's why I left Atlantic." In Ahmet's words, "Afterwards when there were explanations of how it happened, even though I knew it wasn't so, I never said anything 'cause it didn't matter, the fact is that we lost him."

"I worked with Chris Blackwell at Island Records after Bob Marley died," Paul Wexler recalled, "and I saw that some of the joy of being a record man had gone out of Chris when his genius went away. Who was Ahmet's genius? Ray Charles. Ray went away. And Ahmet never fell in love with another artist like that again. And to a great extent, he was also out of the studio after that point."

For Ahmet, the first cut was the deepest and he never did get over losing Ray Charles. Seven years after the artist had walked out on him, Ahmet was still carrying the torch. As a woman he was then seeing in Los Angeles recalled, "He was brokenhearted over Ray Charles leaving him."

By then, the real power in the record business was being wielded by the artists. Unlike Wexler, who refused to accommodate himself to the impossible demands of rock stars accustomed to having their every whim catered to like divine right kings, Ahmet always found a way to deal with them. In the most painful way imaginable, he had already been through it all with Ray Charles.

# NINE

# Love and Marriage

*"I fell in love with Mica. I really wanted to marry her and I had to talk her into it. She had a greater elegance and aristocracy than any of the girls I knew. She was much more of a lady and it showed through and I think the most important choice I ever made in my life was to marry her."*

—Ahmet Ertegun

1

In the spring of 1960, Phil Spector blew into Ahmet's life like a wild storm from the West Coast. Born on December 26, 1939, into a lower-middle-class Jewish family in the Bronx, Spector was nine years old when his father committed suicide. Four years later, he moved with his mother and older sister to Los Angeles, where he attended Fairfax High.

After forming the Teddy Bears in 1958, Spector changed the inscription from his father's gravestone in the Beth David cemetery in Elmont, Long Island, into the present tense and used it as the title for "To Know Him Is to Love Him." A mellow doo-wop ballad that became a slow dance staple at teenage makeout parties all over America, the record sold a million copies and went to number one on the *Billboard* pop chart but offered no indication of the work Spector would do as a producer once he loosed his trademark "Wall of Sound" upon the world.

A year later, Spector began working for Lester Sill, who had discovered Jerry Leiber and Mike Stoller. The songwriting duo had then written, arranged, and produced one big hit after another for Atlantic with the Coasters and the Drifters. At Sill's urging in the spring of 1960, Leiber paid for Spector's airplane ticket to New York. The songwriters signed Spector to an exclusive publishing contract, gave him a monthly advance, and made him their fifth guitar player on sessions. With a kind of self-confidence that verged on the monomaniacal, Spector regularly told everyone he met that he was a genius.

Blessed with what his biographer called the ability to "find his way around almost any instrument" as well as "a natural gift for sight-reading and improvisation," Spector wrote the haunting melody for Leiber's lyrics on "Spanish Harlem." Ben E. King, the former lead singer of the Drifters, then beginning his solo career, recorded the song on October 27, 1960, and it went to number fifteen on the R&B charts.

Having lost his father under the most tragic circumstances, Spector also had, according to Leiber, a "terrific fear of abandonment" and "was frightened to death of being left alone." His psychological profile made him the first in a long line of eager young record business men who adopted Ahmet as both mentor and surrogate father. "I'd never seen anybody like Phil before," Ahmet would later say, "and I'm sure I'll never see anybody like him again . . . He was really crazy, but charming, super-intelligent, and really talented."

Jiving with one another in their own version of Mezz Mezzrow's brand of hipster slang, the two very unlikely companions began going out on the town together night after night. Despite the disparity in their backgrounds and the sixteen-year difference in their ages, they soon became inseparable. Ahmet then offered Spector a job as his personal assistant and as a staff producer at Atlantic. For a twenty-one-year-old kid on the make, it was the opportunity of a lifetime.

The fact that he had already signed a contract with Leiber and Stoller did not trouble Spector in the least and the contract itself soon somehow disappeared from their files. Adding insult to injury, Spector also signed a contract with the Hill & Range music publishing company, thereby making him "one hundred percent exclusive" with all three entities at once. Spector then began sleeping at night in the Atlantic office, while persuading the switchboard operator to let him call home long-distance as often as he liked at the company's expense.

In vain, Wexler kept waiting for the pint-sized producer with the gargantuan ego to deliver the big hits he claimed he had come from

California to make. In the studio, the two men clashed constantly. Working together in the worst possible way with a group called the Top Notes, they managed to screw up "Twist and Shout," a Bert Berns composition Wexler would later call "a natural hit."

Miriam Bienstock also soon came to dislike Spector because he would book studio rehearsal time at Atlantic and then turn up late or not show up at all, thereby forcing artists who had waited for him to return the next day. Despite his undeniable talent, the kindest thing many of those who met Spector during this period had to say about him was that he was an asshole. Others thought he was insane.

Overlooking flaws in Spector's outsized personality that would have caused anyone else to fire him, Ahmet felt certain that in time the hits were "going to come. In the meantime, he and I were going out to clubs . . . and having a terrific time." As Paul Marshall would later say, "I don't know why Ahmet liked hanging out with Phil because I couldn't stand him. He was not a lovable guy. He was egoistic and always rude to musicians and assistant engineers."

Marshall was in the studio one night while Spector was recording when Spector received a telegram informing him he had been drafted and was being ordered to report for duty at Vance Air Force Base in Enid, Oklahoma. The telegram was signed by General Curtis LeMay, the United States Air Force chief of staff. "Phil went crazy," Marshall would later say. "Absolutely crazy. 'They're out to kill me! They're out to destroy my career!' I knew Ahmet had sent it so I called him and said, 'This is great!' " After Marshall told Ahmet how badly Spector was melting down in the studio, "We got another telegram, 'Orders canceled!' "

Whenever they found themselves together in Los Angeles, Ahmet loved roaring around the city in a souped-up Ford Thunderbird Spector had equipped with a 45 RPM record player under the dashboard. Whenever a music publisher wanted them to listen to new material, they would insist he get into the backseat and then take off at ninety miles an hour on Sunset Boulevard as the publisher screamed, "Let me out of here—I don't care if you ever record one of my songs—just let me out of the car!"

In Los Angeles, Ahmet also took Spector to see Bobby Darin, who by then had married sixteen-year-old Sandra Dee, the beautiful blond actress who had played the title role in *Gidget*. After a couple of drinks as they sat around his pool, Darin picked up his guitar and began playing a new song he had written that did not impress Ahmet in the least. "That's terrific," Ahmet told him. Darin then played five more songs, each no better than the first. All the while, Ahmet kept telling him they were "fabulous."

Unable to take it anymore, Spector finally exploded. "Are you fucking crazy, or am I? He can't record these songs. These songs are pure shit!" Demanding to know who the hell Spector was, an incensed Darin screamed, "Get him the fuck out of here!" In need of a hit some months later, Darin told Ahmet it might be wise if they found "some new blood" to produce his next record. "There's this kid, Phil Spector," Darin said, "do you think you could get him to work with us?" Ahmet replied, "That's the guy you threw out of your house!" In the end, Darin never worked with Spector.

After making a series of very conventional big band records for Atlantic that went nowhere, Darin eventually "succumbed to Hollywood pressure" from his managers and agents to begin recording for a major label. When his contract with Atlantic expired in the fall of 1962, Darin signed with Capitol. Ahmet accepted the loss of Atlantic's first white star with an equanimity he had not had when Ray Charles left him.

By the spring of 1961, Ahmet's social relationship with Spector had also ended. Having met the woman he was about to marry, Ahmet no longer needed someone to go out with every night. Spector formally left Atlantic on April 6, 1961, Ahmet's wedding day.

Constitutionally unable ever to work for anyone else, Spector founded Philles Records with his mentor Lester Sill, whom he then forced out of the company. Producing one huge hit after another for the Ronettes, the Crystals, and the Righteous Brothers, Spector earned $2 million by the time he was twenty-six and became the subject of a memorable profile by Tom Wolfe entitled "The First Tycoon of Teen."

In a scene that would not have been out of place in a 1930s Hollywood movie, Spector was recording in Los Angeles when he crossed paths with a twenty-year-old starstruck kid from Brooklyn who in time would also come to regard Ahmet as his mentor. Going out of his way to humiliate David Geffen, Spector made him sit with his chauffeur at another table when everyone went out to eat after a night in the studio.

In 1966, Spector recorded what would come to be regarded as his masterpiece, "River Deep—Mountain High" by Ike and Tina Turner. He then went on to produce *Let It Be* by the Beatles as well as George Harrison's multi-platinum album *All Things Must Pass.* His relationship with John Lennon ended in 1973 when Spector reportedly brandished a gun in the studio and then disappeared with the master tapes of the album the two were recording.

While Ahmet and Phil Spector never worked together again after he left Atlantic, they did remain good friends throughout their lives. As Jann Wenner, the founder of *Rolling Stone* magazine, would recall, "Ahmet loved Phil Spector for all kinds of reasons but one of them was that Phil was just incredibly witty and dark in that Lenny Bruce kind of way. Ahmet recognized Phil's genius and thought he was this wonderful character because Ahmet always loved crazy, larger-than-life people."

In Los Angeles during the mid-1960s, Ahmet and his former protégé shared many wild nights. By then, Spector had already begun exhibiting the kind of behavior that would doom him. "Even in those days," Ahmet would later say, "Phil hated for anybody to leave and was known to sort of lock up people in his house and not let them go. He was always flashing his gun around but I never thought he would shoot it."

On February 3, 2003, Phil Spector shot and killed Lana Clarkson, a forty-year-old former B-movie actress he had picked up in the House of Blues on the Sunset Strip, where she was working as a hostess in the VIP room. Found guilty of murder in the second degree in April 2009, he was sentenced at the age of sixty-nine to nineteen years to life in the California state prison system.

"Ahmet brought Phil in," Keith Richards of the Rolling Stones said. "But nobody could control Phil." Although even Ahmet soon learned this was true, he had still been perfectly willing to delegate responsibility in the studio to Spector in the hope he would come up with a series of monster hits for Atlantic. While the first boy wonder in whom he had invested his time and energy failed to fulfill his expectations, Ahmet never stopped looking for the next young genius who might help keep his label at the top of the charts.

## 2

On the night Ahmet met his future wife through mutual friends in the Bon Soir, a small, crowded, and famously dark cabaret on Eighth Street in Greenwich Village, marriage was the last thing on his mind. Still operating in full bachelor mode, he was seeing three different well-known models on both coasts while also escorting a variety of other girls on his nightly outings to Birdland, El Morocco, and the city's newest hot spot, the Peppermint Lounge.

The only woman at the table that night whom Ahmet did not know spoke with a continental accent that immediately defined her upbringing. Svelte with long black hair and the regal bearing of what he would later call "a natural aristocrat," she had come to New York hoping to find someone who could help get her cancer-ridden father out of Romania, which was then still under communist control. Because she seemed "so sad," the wife of the Turkish ambassador to the United Nations, with whom she was staying, arranged for her to join the dinner party.

"At the end of the evening," Ahmet would recall, "instead of her going home with the person who brought her, I took her home and we became friends." The next day, he called and they went out to dinner. After she returned to her home on a farm in Canada a few days later, Ahmet began calling her regularly. As he would soon learn, she was also a child of history whose background was in many ways as complex as his own. For the first time in his life, Ahmet was involved in a relationship that was a meeting of equals.

Born into a wealthy landowning family in Bucharest on October 21, 1926, Ioana Maria Banu was the only child of Natalia Gologan and Dr. Georghe Banu, a well-known physician who served as secretary of health in the right-wing government that ruled the country under King Carol II. As a young girl, she acquired the name by which she would be known. Because her German nurse kept hearing her father call her "the little one" in Romanian, "she thought that was my name. In Romanian, 'mic,' which is pronounced 'meek,' means 'small.' She kept saying, 'Mica is here. Mica is there.' And it stuck."

After her parents' short-lived marriage ended in divorce when she was eight years old, Mica was raised by her mother and grandmother. Although her father was "very caring" and she sometimes preferred him to her mother, he was also "very busy. He wrote a lot of books and helped pass a law that everybody in Romania had to be tested for syphilis before they got married."

In 1939, Dr. Georghe Banu published a book about eugenics, in which he advocated a set of scientific beliefs very much in accord with the views of the Nazi government in Germany. Banu argued for the use of preventive sterilization of "pathological individuals" including "imbeciles, idiots, epileptics, criminals, and those affected by diverse psychoses" as well as those suffering from syphilis, tuberculosis, and leprosy. He wrote that sterilization was "a necessary formula for the conservation and improvement of the race."

Too young to understand the full import of her father's work, Mica was fourteen years old when half a million Nazi troops occupied Romania, then still a neutral country. On November 23, 1940, Romania joined the Axis and began supplying Germany with oil, grain, and industrial products. On August 1, 1943, the Romanian oil fields were bombed by the Allies.

"Of course, I saw the bombardments," she recalled. "I was going to school and the car was supposed to come pick me up because the planes took off from a place in Italy called Foggia and so you knew from the radio exactly when they had taken off and when they were coming." Driven from Bucharest to her family's country house in Baragan, where she "was shoved every holiday," she would then return to the city once the raids were over.

Raised "to be a nothing," as she put it, Mica was sixteen when she met Stephen Grecianu, whom she then married against her father's wishes in 1942. Fifteen years older than Mica, Grecianu was the son of a wealthy landowner and had grown up in and around the royal court in Bucharest. Educated in Paris, he was serving as a pilot in the Romanian air force flying German Messerschmitt fighter planes into aerial battles against the Allies.

On January 10, 1948, a week after King Michael, who had succeeded Carol II, had left the country after being deposed at gunpoint, Mica and her husband, whose mother had served as lady in waiting to Queen Marie, left Romania on the same train as the king's aunts,

Princess Elisabeth, the former Queen of Greece, and Princess Ileana, the wife of Austrian Archduke Anton. Traveling on Nansen passports issued to stateless people by the League of Nations, the couple ended up in "the Dolder Grand, the most luxurious hotel in Zurich, but we didn't have a dime because after everybody put all their jewelry with the Queen, they confiscated everything the night before we left."

Mica and her husband stayed in Switzerland for a year. Along with many of the other high-born members of the Romanian court who were then living in exile at the hotel, they were about to emigrate as a group to Paraguay, where the authorities had said "we wouldn't pay taxes for twenty years and they would help everybody to start industries," until they were shown a movie about the country. "When they showed us the movie, it was such a catastrophe that nobody wanted to go. It was horrible. Absolutely horrendous. So then we each went our different ways."

The couple moved to Paris, where Stephen Grecianu "tried to find a job which was very difficult although he spoke the language." While staying at the Dolder Grand Hotel, Mica had met the man who ran Bruyère, a couture fashion house on the Place Vendôme. "I put some clothes on and walked on the runway as a model but that only lasted for three or four months." Some "very rich Canadians" whom the couple had also met in Switzerland then helped them go to Canada and lent them "some money to buy a farm."

In 1951, the couple emigrated and purchased a dairy farm on Lake Ontario. Her husband then converted the property into a chicken farm. "We had five thousand chickens and I would get up at five in the morning. The funny thing is you have to clean the eggs. You gather them three times a day and then you have to clean them and put them in cardboard and ship them. That's why I really can't look at a chicken anymore. But when you are young, everything is great. We were happy to be free. We were happy not to be persecuted."

The couple became Canadian citizens and although "it was pretty grim in the winter," they stayed on the farm until the fall of 1960, when Mica came to New York to see if the Turkish ambassador to the United Nations, who had met her father while serving in Romania, could help her get him out of the country. "I was married and I was quite happy and I didn't come with any idea of finding a man. I really didn't but then it just happened. It just clicked. Ahmet didn't have much money then but he had marvelous cars and chauffeurs and he went out every night. El Morocco was his stomping ground, and Birdland. He was always living well and going to expensive restaurants and running to Fire Island every weekend. He fascinated me."

After Mica returned to Canada, Ahmet called her constantly on the farm, where she talked to him on a hand-cranked phone. A month later, Mica told her husband she had to return to New York to visit a friend and it was then that she and Ahmet began their affair. As he would later say, "If you see pictures of Mica in those days, she really was a beautiful young girl . . . Even though I think she was virtually penniless, she had an air about her."

During his whirlwind courtship of Mica, Ahmet ended his relationship with Betsy Pickering. At one point, however, he and Mica "nearly split" and she returned to Canada only to have Ahmet come with his sister and nephews to visit her at the farm. As she recalled, "Ahmet adored my husband. The two of them got along very well." In an incredibly stylish gesture right out of one of the Fred Astaire and Ginger Rogers movies Ahmet had loved as a boy, he arranged for a band to emerge from the closet of her suite at the Ritz-Carlton in Montreal to play "Puttin' on the Ritz."

After spending six difficult weeks together in New York, Mica left for Europe without Ahmet and went to stay with a friend who "was against me getting married. Everybody said I would regret it and it would be a disaster and last two months." From Baden-Baden in Germany, Mica sent Ahmet a letter in which she wrote, "I do not know if I am capable of fulfilling all your desires . . . in my own way I am very simple and I like to have a closeness and an understanding that is above all the problems life is presenting . . . I will always love you but I do not want to make you unhappy—I would have loved to be with you and close to you. I hold you in my heart."

On her way back to Canada after a Black Sea cruise that included a visit to Ahmet's mother and sister in Turkey, Mica was changing planes in upstate New York when she heard herself being paged. Over the phone, Ahmet proposed to her. On Thursday, April 6, 1961, the two were married by a judge in an apartment in Manhattan with thirty people present, among them Nesuhi, Julio Mario Santo Domingo, Miriam Bienstock, and Jerry Wexler.

As Ahmet would later say, "Mica is a very, very steadfast person.

Where before I was kind of wandering around aimlessly, she suddenly gave me an anchor. We began having dinner parties with nicer and more interesting people and less bimbos. It was a delight to be married to someone who was so intelligent and had so much common sense and she lifted my spirits every day and really inspired me to work harder. But part of my life was going out to clubs and that I didn't stop."

Ahmet also did not stop seeing other women. Even while he had been pursuing Mica, she knew "he was coming back to New York and going out with other people." As Jean Pigozzi, the art collector and photographer who became one of Ahmet's closest friends, said, "I really don't think Ahmet ever got emotional about any of those girls. Zero." By marrying Mica, Ahmet made it plain she was the one with whom he wanted to spend his life.

## 3

Always at the forefront of what was happening at night in the city, Ahmet was one of the first to make the scene at the Peppermint Lounge, a mob joint on 45th Street where formerly only hookers, dancers, and musicians from nearby clubs could be found. The shift in action from the elegant El Morocco to a seedy hole-in-the-wall near Times Square where Joey Dee & the Starliters performed "The Peppermint Twist" each night as frenzied socialites threw themselves about on "a dance floor the size of somebody's kitchen" marked the end of the 1950s in New York as well as the start of a musically charged social and cultural revolution that would churn through America for the next half-century.

Unlike most of those who lined up in the street each night to get inside the Peppermint Lounge while "laying fives, tens, and twenty dollar bills on cops, doormen, and a couple sets of maître d's to get within sight of the bandstand," Ahmet knew "The Twist" had originally been recorded by Hank Ballard and the Midnighters on King Records two years before Chubby Checker cut his version and popularized the dance on *American Bandstand*.

In October 1961, as Tom Wolfe wrote, "a few socialites, riding hard under the crop of a couple of New York columnists, discovered the

Peppermint Lounge." Greta Garbo, Elsa Maxwell, Countess Berna-
dotte, Noël Coward, Tennessee Williams, Judy Garland, Jayne Mans-
field, Perle Mesta, Jackie Kennedy, and the Duke of Bedford were soon
among those doing the Twist alongside "sailors, leather-jacketed drifters, and girls in toreador pants." A month later, Joey Dee, then twenty-
two years old, was performing at a gala "fund-raising champagne
dinner" at the Four Seasons restaurant as well as "a hundred dollar a
plate Party of the Year at the Metropolitan Museum of Art."

With Mica by his side, Ahmet was at the Peppermint Lounge
every night. The sheer incongruity of well-to-do socialites who knew
nothing about this kind of music trying to dance to it like hormon-
ally crazed teenagers made the scene irresistible. While living on their
chicken farm in Canada, Mica and her husband had brought some girls
in from the local village to help them package eggs "and I remember
there was an Elvis Presley song playing on the radio and the girls were
gyrating while they were cleaning those eggs and I was looking at them
and I said, 'They must be totally degenerated. What the hell are they
doing?' Little did I know."

As Arthur Gelb noted in the still very staid *New York Times*, "Café
society has not gone slumming with such energy since its forays into
Harlem in the Twenties." Much like the Charleston and the Shimmy,
two dances adored by bathtub-gin-swilling flappers during that era, the
Twist was not only fun but also an authentic form of physical libera-
tion, allowing people to dance alone with one another. The first teenage
dance craze to be seized upon by adults, the Twist launched America's
newfound fixation with youth culture as well as a form of music that
had previously been considered the exclusive province of juveniles se-
duced by what some in the South still called "jungle rhythms."

Even as Ahmet was twisting the night away at the Peppermint
Lounge, he was trying to sign Joey Dee & the Starliters. After learning
through the mob guys who ran the place that Morris Levy of Roulette
had gotten to the band first, Ahmet began repackaging cuts he had
already released into albums entitled *Do the Twist with Ray Charles* and
*Twist with Bobby Darin*. These albums then became popular with "a
dance crowd" who "had never heard these records before."

Able as a couple to fit into virtually any kind of social milieu,
Ahmet and Mica quickly slipped in and then out of the scene at the

Peppermint Lounge. Although neither of them realized it at the time, the new life they were now sharing helped create what would become an ever widening rupture between Ahmet and the man who looked up to him as not just a business partner but also a mentor and friend.

While Mica had been living on the farm in Canada, in Ahmet's words, "She did the beds, she did the cooking, and she did the farming with the tractor. She worked eighteen hours a day. When we could afford it, the first thing she wanted was neither a Cadillac nor a Rolls-Royce nor a diamond. She wanted to spend money on our style of life, which meant that we would have service. She wanted someone who would iron her dress or bring her breakfast in the morning. And she wanted me to have what I'd had as a child. As soon as I married Mica, I was back living the way I used to live when I was a kid which was wonderful because I also understood the value of that."

After Ahmet purchased a five-story brownstone on East 81st Street for $100,000 that Mica then began renovating and redecorating, Jerry Wexler dropped by one day and Ahmet invited him to stay for lunch. "When Jerry saw there was a cook and a butler to serve the lunch," Ahmet recalled, "he turned to me and said, 'Do you always live like this?' As if to say, 'This is not right.' Living like that would never have occurred to him but I was very happy to get back to what I considered normal."

Wexler would later write that he and Ahmet had "begun moving in different directions back in the late fifties, early sixties . . . Gone were the days when Ahmet and I went off together to explore the back alleys of New Orleans." In part, this was because "the business had gotten too big. Domains were separating, demands diverging."

When Atlantic moved its offices from 234 West 56th Street to 157 West 57th Street, directly across from Carnegie Hall and the partners' favored spot for lunch, the Russian Tea Room, the two men still shared an office in which they faced one another, but with a sliding door between them that was often shut. When Atlantic moved again, to 1841 Broadway, between 60th and 61st Streets, the two men were separated by a long hallway.

Despite Wexler's great sophistication, his inability to realize that Ahmet's marriage would also cause their relationship to change seems difficult to understand. The way in which Wexler chose to discuss this issue in his autobiography speaks to the incredible depth of feeling he always had for the man who had given him his start in the record business as well as how painful it was for him no longer to be the number one person in Ahmet's life. Nor was it only Mica's influence that caused them to grow apart. As always where these two men were concerned, the primary issue was music. While Ahmet was perfectly willing to accommodate himself to white rock 'n' roll, Wexler preferred to continue producing the kind of black roots music he had always loved.

The other issue was social class. While Wexler lived very well with his wife and three children in a house in Great Neck, Long Island, where he regularly hosted disc jockeys and promotion men at backyard barbecues, he was always too busy working and worrying about the future of the company to waste his nights in the Peppermint Lounge. Nor was it surprising he would view those who prepared and served Ahmet and Mica lunch in their East Side brownstone with the attitude of a kid from Washington Heights who had gotten his real primary education in a pool hall.

Despite the growing tension between the two men, they continued to work well together at Atlantic. And then as just about every kid in America sat with his parents in front of the television set on the first Sunday night in February 1964, the impossibly cute and cuddly Beatles began shaking their moptops on Ed Sullivan's very popular CBS television show. Suddenly, the bottom dropped out of the white teenage market for black music that had been keeping Atlantic in business.

Once the British Invasion began in earnest, Ahmet and Wexler were no longer able to make the kind of music other labels could only envy. Instead, they had to start scrambling just to keep their company alive.

Ahmet, eight years old, on the beach in Deauville, France, in 1931 with his brother, Nesuhi, standing behind him.

Ahmet being read to by his father, Mehmet Munir, in the embassy in London.

3

Ahmet with his sister, Selma, at the piano and his brother, Nesuhi, in the Turkish embassy in Washington, D.C.

4

Top row, left to right: Sadi Koylan, Nesuhi, Selma, Dr. Vahdi Sabit, a family friend, and Ahmet. Ahmet's father and his mother, Hayrunnisa, sit beside one another in the center of the first row.

Ahmet with drink in hand, Duke Ellington, Bill Gottlieb, unidentified woman, Dave Stewart, and Nesuhi in Gottlieb's home, 1941.

Jerry Wexler, Ahmet, and Miriam Abramson with the Cash Box Award at Atlantic Records, 1954.

Jerry Wexler and Ahmet presenting Ruth Brown with a gold record on-stage at the Apollo Theater in Harlem, 1956.

The great Ray Charles at the piano.

9

Jerry Wexler, Alan Freed, and Ahmet (front row) onstage with Big Joe Turner at Freed's *Rock 'n' Roll Party* at the St. Nicholas Arena, January 14, 1955. Ahmet's wife, Jan Holm, stands behind him.

10

Herb Abramson, Jerry Wexler, Ahmet, and Clyde McPhatter, February 25, 1958.

Jerry Wexler and Ahmet with Jesse Stone behind them in the recording booth, February 27, 1958.

11

Beaming in sharp suits, Jerry Wexler, Nesuhi, Bobby Darin, and Ahmet.

12

Sonny and Cher at Atlantic with their gold record for "I Got You Babe," August 15, 1965.

13

The Buffalo Springfield fooling around under the pier in Malibu, 1967. From left to right, Richie Furay, Stephen Stills, Dewey Martin, Bruce Palmer, and Neil Young.

Graham Nash, Neil Young, Stephen Stills, and David Crosby rehearsing at Neil Young's ranch, 1974.

Ahmet and Mick Jagger.

Clockwise from left: John Bonham, Jimmy Page, Robert Plant, and John Paul Jones of Led Zeppelin.

18

Ahmet in excelsis, celebrating the Cosmos' championship victory with coach Eddie Firmani, August 14, 1977.

19

Mica and Ahmet.

Steve Ross and Ahmet partying together, September 1989.

Henry Kissinger and Ahmet.

Ahmet and Phil Spector, 1990.

Ahmet, Seymour Stein, and Jann Wenner, 1991.

24

Mica and Ahmet playing backgammon in the study of their town house.

Kid Rock on tour, 2010.

25

# TEN

# The Oak Room

*"If you didn't have the Beatles in 1964, you didn't have anything."*
—Jerry Wexler

## 1

Shortly after the Beatles changed the nature of the record business in January 1964 by selling more than a million copies of their debut album in America on both Vee-Jay and Capitol, Ahmet informed attorney Paul Marshall that his services would no longer be needed at Atlantic. While Ahmet did not explain the reason for his decision, Marshall knew exactly why he was being let go. As he would later say, "Ahmet and I were friendly and he thought I had screwed him and been disloyal by not bringing the Beatles to Atlantic. I should have raised the issue of why he was letting me go but I didn't. I had too much false pride. I wasn't going to say a thing."

For Ahmet, who always prized loyalty above all other virtues in those who worked for him, Marshall's decision to place the group with another independent label (who then lost their rights to Capitol when they failed to pay royalties) became a crime of major proportions as the Beatles put an unprecedented twelve songs on the *Billboard* Hot 100 during the first week in April 1964. Before the year was out, the group would release nine singles and six LPs that sold 25 million copies in America, thereby comprising an astonishing 60 percent of all the records sold on all labels in the United States.

At the beginning of what everyone soon realized was an authentic worldwide revolution in popular music, Atlantic suddenly found itself watching from the sidelines as the money Ahmet believed should have been his poured instead into other companies. While Ahmet continued doing business with Paul Marshall over the years, his personal relationship with the attorney ended on the day he let him go.

While on holiday with his family in Turkey many years later, Marshall paid a social visit to Ahmet and Mica at their summer home in Bodrum. As they all sat down to lunch, Ahmet, in Marshall's words, "began laughing and said, 'You're the guy who took the Beatles from me.' And I said, 'It's not true. That's not true.' " What Ahmet had never known until that day was that, as Marshall would recall, "The first person I had offered the Beatles to was Jerry Wexler, who was my primary contact at Atlantic. I was EMI's general counsel and I had gotten this call from them, 'Please can you do something to help because Capitol has turned the Beatles down.' So I went to my friends at Atlantic and sent the record to Noreen Woods, who was Ahmet and Jerry's secretary."

Marshall did not consider himself a musical expert and so "if someone asked me to listen to a record, I would double my fee." Without ever having heard the music on the album that would be entitled *Introducing . . . The Beatles*, Marshall offered Atlantic the first shot at an LP that included smash single hits like "Please Please Me," "Love Me Do," "Do You Want to Know a Secret," as well as the Beatles' killer cover version of Bert Berns's "Twist and Shout," a song first recorded by Jerry Wexler and Phil Spector on Atlantic.

"A couple of days later," Marshall would later say, "Noreen Woods came back to me and said, 'Jerry said they're derivative.' And that was it. It happened and I never discussed it with anyone and then after I had offered them to Atlantic, I placed the Beatles on Vee-Jay."

With good reason, Jerry Wexler himself chose to never mention this story in any of the countless interviews he did during his lifetime. Nor did he write about it in his autobiography. However, as he would say, "I was not anti–rock 'n' roll. But if it didn't have the blues in it, I couldn't give it house room. That was why I didn't care about the Beatles and I did like the Rolling Stones. The Beatles were totally devoid of a blues element but the Rolling Stones, that was in their DNA."

While no one could have known the Beatles would become the most significant group in the history of popular music and eventually sell more than a billion units worldwide, Wexler's decision to pass on them must rank as one of the most grievous errors in the history of the record business. Over the years, every great record man, Ahmet among them, made mistakes that in hindsight seem impossible to understand only to then bury them by going on to make hits with artists no one else might have signed.

That Ahmet never knew what Wexler had done speaks to the increasingly separate lives the two men had begun to lead. It also reflects the degree to which Ahmet had delegated his day-to-day responsibilities at the label to his partner. As songwriter Mike Stoller recalled, "In the late Fifties, Ahmet used to come into the Atlantic office at four in the afternoon—and leave at six." Although once the Beatles hit it big in America, EMI would have done everything in its power to move them to Capitol, Atlantic would never have been so foolish or disorganized as to risk doing anything to lose them.

The constant anxiety that had kept Wexler working long hours for more than a decade at Atlantic had now been compounded by a secret he could not share with anyone, his good friend and partner most of all. At a time when a host of other independent labels were experiencing hard times and being sold by their founders to bigger companies or cutting back on their releases, Atlantic in 1964 failed for the first time to increase its profits from the previous year. To survive, Ahmet and Wexler were forced to cut their own pay and then sold the Progressive Music publishing catalogue to Hill & Range, thereby giving up all future rights to songs like "Shake, Rattle and Roll," "Money Honey," and "Since I Met You Baby."

Desperate to latch on to the British Invasion in any way possible, Atlantic did release an album entitled *Ain't She Sweet* in October 1964. The LP included four tracks recorded in 1961 by English rocker Tony Sheridan with the Beatles in Hamburg, Germany, as well as eight cover versions of Beatles songs by a group called the Swallows. Not surprisingly, the album did not sell.

With all this as backdrop and subtext, the stage had now been set for a melodramatic lunch in the Oak Room of the Plaza Hotel that would set Ahmet at odds with his partner for years while leaving Jerry Wexler wondering exactly what he had done to cause his friend to think he had betrayed him.

## 2

Arguably the greatest songwriting duo in the history of rock 'n' roll, Jerry Leiber and Mike Stoller first met Ahmet and Jerry Wexler in the Russian Tea Room on the night of July 26, 1956, a date Stoller would never forget for more than one reason. Earlier in the day, he and his wife had arrived safely in New York after having been rescued at sea following the collision in heavy fog of the *Andrea Doria,* the Italian ocean liner on which they had been traveling, with the *Stockholm* of the Swedish American Line.

Having survived an authentic maritime disaster in which forty-six of their fellow passengers on the *Andrea Doria* as well as five crew members on the *Stockholm* had been killed, Stoller and his wife were greeted on the dock by Jerry Leiber, who had flown in from Los Angeles to meet them with some incredibly good news. Elvis Presley had just covered "Hound Dog," a song the duo had written for Big Mama Thornton that had gone to number one on the R&B charts. Backed with "Don't Be Cruel," Presley's version became a smash hit that sold four million copies.

Then just twenty-three years old, Leiber and Stoller had already established a track record as songwriters that was second to none. As teenagers in Los Angeles, they had written hits like "Riot in Cell Block #9" and "Kansas City." Going into business with Lester Sill, who had discovered Leiber while he was working in a record store on Fairfax Avenue, they founded Spark Records and released "Smokey Joe's Cafe" by a five-man vocal group known as the Robins. Impressed by their talent, Nesuhi sent the record to Ahmet in New York.

When Spark folded, Ahmet and Wexler picked up the record and put it out on Atco, where it sold a quarter of a million copies. Leiber and Stoller then began writing and producing songs by the Coasters, a group formed from the remnants of the Robins, with Carl Gardner singing lead, that were released on Atco. The two sets of partners did not meet until they all found themselves in New York. The four men hit it off immediately and began a fantastic run of success for all concerned.

A musical genius who had begun taking piano lessons when he

was five years old, Mike Stoller had studied with James P. Johnson, whom Ahmet had met during his wild night out in New York City at the age of thirteen. Born into a Yiddish-speaking household in a tough working-class neighborhood in Baltimore, Maryland, the brilliant lyricist Jerry Leiber was by far the more boisterous and aggressive of the partners. Much like Jerry Wexler, Leiber had also never walked away from a fight while growing up.

In 1957, Leiber and Stoller, who by then had signed a distribution deal with Atlantic, moved to New York to set up shop. A year later, their incredibly infectious "Yakety Yak" by the Coasters helped Atlantic cross over into the white teenage market. As both Ahmet and Wexler would soon learn, they had finally met a pair of partners who were as difficult to control as they.

After cutting "There Goes My Baby" with the Drifters in March 1959, Leiber and Stoller brought the tape to Wexler, who was so offended by it that he "automatically started yelling while eating a tuna fish sandwich—bits of which consequently ended up all over the wall as he kept shouting, 'Goddamn awful trash! How can you play a tape like that for me? That tune is being played in three different keys, it sounds like three stations playing at the same time coming through on one very bad car radio!' "

Stoller would later remember Ahmet trying to be diplomatic by explaining that although the duo made great records, no one could "hit a home run every time." Depending on which version of the story Leiber chose to tell, Ahmet said the song was interesting, thereby causing Wexler to stalk out of the room, or, even as Leiber was apologizing for the track, Ahmet said, "Smash! You've got a hit record and you don't even know it." When Leiber replied, "This is a full-of-shit record," Ahmet said, "Boy, that's the kind of shit I need." After Leiber and Tom Dowd remixed the song, it went to number one on both the R&B and pop charts.

That four men with such powerful personalities could agree on anything was a minor miracle. In 1961, after Phil Spector had established himself as the first superstar producer, Leiber and Stoller asked that their names also be included as producers on their records. Outraged by what then became standard practice in the industry, Wexler was eventually forced to concede to their demand.

As always in the record business, the real issue was money. In addition to being given credit for their work in the studio, Leiber and Stoller also wanted to be paid a producer's royalty on each record sold. "At that time," Miriam Bienstock would later say, "there weren't many producers—especially ones getting royalties. As a principal in the company, I just didn't want to pay it."

Knowing they could not afford to offend the hit makers who were helping keep Atlantic in business, Ahmet and Wexler gave in on this point as well. Because the agreement was informal, Leiber and Stoller's attorney then asked to audit Atlantic's books. The request mightily offended Wexler, who began referring to the pair as "Mr. Lust and Mr. Greed." In his autobiography, Wexler would also call Leiber, with whom he had much in common, "Mr. Disorderly Conduct."

When the audit revealed that during their six years at Atlantic the duo had been underpaid by $18,000, Leiber was willing to drop the issue and just go on doing business as they had before. Stoller however wanted the full amount to be paid. At what began as a "relaxed and friendly" meeting, the pair presented their case to Ahmet and Wexler. "Fine," Ahmet said. "I'll pay the eighteen thousand, but I don't ever want to do business with you guys again." Taking the same position, Wexler said the pair could have their money but forget about ever working again with the Drifters, the Coasters, or Ben E. King.

Leiber and Stoller dropped their demand but when Ahmet and Wexler assigned Spector to work with the Drifters in the studio on a record the duo thought they would be producing, they left Atlantic and went to work for United Artists. While, in Leiber's words, "the big falling out was really with Jerry," the more lasting rift was with Ahmet, who "took offense at a situation in which *we* were wronged. He has always been like that. I think he was offended because *he* was in the wrong, and I think he was embarrassed. I don't think he has ever gotten over it."

After forming two unsuccessful labels, Leiber and Stoller reached out to a fabled record business character named George Goldner with an offer he was in no financial position to refuse. If Goldner could successfully promote the first release on the songwriters' new label, Red Bird Records, they would give him a stake in the company. After "Chapel of Love" by the Dixie Cups became the first in a long string of hits

by the Shangri-Las, the Jellybeans, and the Ad-Libs, Goldner joined
the label as a partner.

A man who dressed like Jay Gatsby but lived like Meyer Wolfsheim,
George Goldner had by the time he went into business with Leiber and
Stoller already founded Tico, Gee, Rama, Gone, End, and Roulette
Records only to be forced to sell them all to Morris Levy to cover his
gambling debts. Known as "The Mambo King" for his lifelong love
of Latin music, Goldner had also discovered and produced Frankie
Lymon & the Teenagers, Little Anthony & the Imperials, the Flamin-
gos, the Cleftones, and the Chantels.

In the words of Sire Records founder Seymour Stein, who worked
as Goldner's assistant at Red Bird, "George was a reckless gambler who
had amazing ears. He was very good-looking, vain, well dressed, and
immaculate and he bought all his clothes at Cy Martin, a famous store
on Broadway. George not only gambled at the racetrack, he would
gamble looking at a girl in the street wondering which way she would
cross it."

At Red Bird, Leiber and Stoller soon discovered Goldner was making money by pressing and shipping thousands of copies of every hit
on the label to California, where they were then sold for the benefit of
George Goldner Enterprises. Deciding they could neither afford to lose
Goldner nor continue supporting "his destructive addiction to the racetrack," the songwriters began looking for a way to control him. It was
then, as Leiber recalled, that Jerry Wexler called the duo from "out of
the blue" to propose a merger between Red Bird and Atlantic.

At a time when "Red Bird was red hot and Atlantic was ice cold,"
the merger seemed like a marriage made in heaven. Leiber and Stoller
had the creativity and Atlantic had a first-rate sales and distribution
setup. Accepting Wexler's invitation to get together and talk, Leiber
said he would bring Stoller and Goldner to a meeting over lunch at the
Oak Room at the Plaza Hotel along with their attorney, Lee Eastman,
whose daughter Linda would later marry Paul McCartney. Born Leo-
pold Epstein, Eastman had already incurred the wrath of the partners
at Atlantic when he insisted his clients audit the label's books.

While the songwriters would later say the merger would have profited all concerned while also putting Goldner under the watchful eye
of Jerry Wexler, "who would catch him if he were stealing," an entirely
different plan may have also been in place. Seymour Stein would later

recall Goldner telling him before the meeting, "Can you believe it? We may be buying Atlantic Records."

Sitting down under the high-vaulted ceiling of the Oak Room, the six men set about discussing their business. Setting the tone for what was to come by putting away two martinis before the salads had been served, Goldner was working on a third when he looked across the table at Ahmet and said, "Who needs a label that's going down the toilet?" When Ahmet replied, "We're hardly going down the toilet," Goldner retorted, "With the shit you're putting out, it won't be long."

Apologizing for their partner's behavior, Leiber and Stoller cancelled Goldner's order for a fourth martini. As the conversation turned to the subject at hand, Eastman kept up the assault by pointing out "it was absolutely unreasonable to see how this merger could benefit anyone but Atlantic." When Wexler protested that no one had yet even heard the terms, Eastman said the terms were beside the point—Atlantic had little to offer and Red Bird had everything. Having not yet fully grasped what was going on, Ahmet said, "I didn't know we were prepared to make a formal offer."

Heaping more fuel on the roaring fire he had helped start, Goldner said, "Him and Wexler are supposed to be running Atlantic, but the right hand doesn't know what the left hand is doing. Looks to me like they're just jerking each other off. Aside from a free lunch, this is a waste of time." When Eastman agreed, Leiber and Stoller looked at one another in confusion but by then Ahmet and Wexler had already left the table. "Can you imagine?" Leiber would later say. "George is like a beggar that came out of the gutter and all of a sudden he put on king's clothing, and was sitting at a table with Ahmet, who was the duke of Windsor—all of a sudden this panhandler was making demands of the duke of Windsor."

Both songwriters would later insist Goldner had done all he could to sabotage the deal so he could keep his profitable backdoor operation going by not having to report to the partners at Atlantic. They also maintained that Lee Eastman, who was receiving 5 percent of the duo's writing and producing income while also being paid to represent Red Bird, did not want the merger to go through because Leiber and Stoller would then be using Atlantic's lawyers rather than him.

But it was not Lee Eastman or George Goldner who upset Ahmet at the Oak Room that day. At some point during the conversation, Leiber said that he and Stoller, Goldner, and Wexler had been talking about buying out Ahmet. According to Ahmet, Leiber also said if Ahmet refused the offer, Wexler had told them he would do the deal without him. In Ahmet's words, "There was only one problem—it was my company." And there it was. The bone of contention that would stick in Ahmet's throat for the rest of his life.

What Ahmet believed Paul Marshall had done to him with the Beatles was nothing compared to this. Without his knowledge, Jerry Wexler had gone behind his back to talk to others about buying Atlantic. For Ahmet, there could be no greater sin. When he went home that day, Ahmet was, in Mica's words, "truly upset and said Jerry had tried to take the company from him." As Ahmet would later say, "That was the beginning of a break of faith between myself and Jerry."

Admitting the merger was "mishandled" and "There are some things in life that you wish you could go back and do differently," Wexler would always insist that taking Atlantic away from Ahmet was never what he had intended. In a chapter in his autobiography aptly entitled "Rashomon at the Oak Room," Wexler would go to great lengths to flatly deny the charge.

Not that the partners ever discussed the matter. To have even brought it up would have been for Ahmet an admission of weakness as well as an acknowledgment of how badly the partners still needed one another to keep the label going. And so Ahmet let the wound fester. This too was entirely in keeping with his character. Years later, Ahmet said, "It is a testament to my relationship with Jerry Wexler that we could continue to be on friendly terms." The sad fact of the matter was that after that fateful lunch at the Oak Room, nothing between two of the greatest record men in history was ever the same again.

## 3

Because records were sold for cash, it was always a business that interested the mob. On any given evening in New York City, wiseguys in expensive suits could be found in many of the clubs Ahmet frequented and it always pleased them to be seated at the best table in the house and then be able to impress their wives, mistresses, or girlfriends by having the featured performer show respect by stopping by for a drink and some pleasant conversation.

Since none of the mobsters knew the first thing about how records were actually made, it was virtually impossible for them to control the product on which the industry was based. Instead, they lurked in the shadows, looking to pick up loose change whenever and wherever they could. As Wexler described the mob's involvement, "The Mafia would like to control the record industry, but they have never managed to. They're just on the fringes: selling cut-out records, pressing, independent promotion."

The most notable exception was Morris Levy, who was connected and so was able to run Roulette Records with impunity. While "Moish," as he was known to his many friends in the industry, has become the whipping boy for organized crime in the record business, those who did not have to do business with him had nothing but good things to say about the man. In Paul Marshall's words, "Morris looked like an animal and talked like he was out of the movies and his house in New Jersey was really a funny place to be. I remember sitting by his pool one day having a discussion about philosophy and he said, 'Well, Koik-a-gahd said . . . You know, Koik-a-gahd.' He was talking about Kierkegaard and I was sitting there trying to keep a straight face."

After Mica met Levy for the first time at the Peppermint Lounge, she told Ahmet, "He invited us to go to his house in New Jersey. How exciting. And Ahmet said, 'You'll never go there. I want to be on good terms with him but never get too close.' " Despite how charming Levy could be, Ahmet was always careful to maintain his distance from him as well as all those in the business whom he knew had mob connections.

It was a lesson Blue Thumb Records founder Bob Krasnow learned one day when he walked into the Roulette Records office to collect some money Levy owed him. "I brought this guy with me who was like six-five and could barely speak, not even Italian," Krasnow recalled. "I said, 'I don't need to see Mr. Levy. Just give me my money.' And they said, 'What money?' I never got the money and they told me to leave the country. That was when in the record business, there was an adventure every five minutes."

When Jerry Wexler was interviewed by Dorothy Wade and Justine Picardie in 1989 for their book, *Music Man,* he offered up a veritable primer on Mafia involvement in the record business. Wexler told the English journalists the easiest way for the mob to gain control of a record label was when some highly placed executive came to them for money he could find nowhere else and then made the wiseguys "silent partners" in the enterprise. After Leiber and Stoller realized this was precisely what George Goldner had done at Red Bird Records, they sold the label to him for a dollar. A few months later, Goldner sold off all the Red Bird masters to raise yet more cash.

According to Wexler, a label could also find itself in business with the mob if it asked for "a favor" for which the company would then be expected to do something in return. In Wexler's words, "We were very, very careful not to do any of those things." Despite his staunch disclaimer, Wexler's expertise on the subject came from firsthand experience. In 1965, the partners at Atlantic went into business with Bert Berns, a brilliant songwriter and producer who belongs in the Rock and Roll Hall of Fame. Using the first letter of each of the partners' names (Bert, Ahmet, Nesuhi, and Gerald), they formed an offshoot of Atlantic entitled Bang Records whose label bore the unfortunate but very telling image of a gun.

Over the course of his brilliant career, Bert Berns wrote and produced hits like "A Little Bit of Soap" by the Jarmels, "Twist and Shout" by the Isley Brothers, "Cry to Me" and "Everybody Needs Somebody to Love" by Solomon Burke (which then became a hit for Wilson Pickett), "Tell Him" by the Exciters, "Cry Baby" by Garnet Mimms and the Enchanters, "Baby I'm Yours" by Barbara Lewis, "Here Comes the Night" by Them, with Van Morrison, "I Want Candy" by the Strangeloves, "Hang on Sloopy" by the McCoys, "Are You Lonely for Me, Baby" by Freddie Scott, and "Piece of My Heart," a song originally recorded by Erma Franklin that then became a breakthrough smash for Big Brother and the Holding Company with Janis Joplin singing lead.

In the words of Paul Marshall, who represented Berns, "Bert knew people in the mob and he liked to hang out with them and he carried a gun which I thought was very Freudian because he doubted his own masculinity. He had this whole thing about being tough and he wasn't at all. It was a pose. He was a great songwriter, a remarkable talent, and a sensitive man. Had he lived, he would have been a great star. I liked him but I knew he was absolutely nuts."

One day, Berns asked if he could introduce Marshall to some friends who were seeking legal representation. The friends turned out to be Tommy Lucchese, aka "Three Finger Brown," the cofounder of the Lucchese crime family in New York, and Pat Pagano, a capo in the Genovese family. The two mobsters needed legal advice because they had just acquired a recording studio on 42nd Street where some "amateur" had been duplicating pirated masters and, in Marshall's words, "they had taken the opportunity to have a discussion that helped him walk away from it."

After he expressed his "enormous respect for them," Marshall explained he could not act as their lawyer and advised them to seek representation elsewhere. Lucchese then hired another attorney, who came to Marshall for advice, which was not "of any criminal consequence." When Marshall went to his summer house in the country, he found a thank-you gift from the mobsters—a purple Cadillac convertible. Marshall kept the car for the summer but then returned it. "I didn't hand it back immediately because that would have been rude. It takes tact."

Over lunch in Florida many years later, Wexler would tell a friend that during this period he and Ahmet discovered someone had "set up a pressing plant in the forests of New Jersey" where they were making and selling fake Atlantic 45s. Bert Berns seems to have offered to solve this problem by having "some mobsters go in with a baseball bat and destroy the record press and maybe whoever was running it as well." According to Wexler, Ahmet not only knew about the plan but also "orchestrated or authorized" it.

That might have well been the end of it if not for what Wexler would later call Bert Berns's "obsession with power." When Berns demanded full control of the publishing company Atlantic had also established with him, Ahmet and Wexler refused to give it to him, and Berns then filed suit against them for breach of contract.

"The breach of contract suit was not particularly bitter or angry," Paul Marshall recalled. "They were yelling at each other but it was just the usual lather, you don't pay me my royalties correctly and that kind of thing." Understandably, no one at Atlantic would have wanted to lose a skilled hit maker like Bert Berns. But as Wexler would later say,

"When the Bang fallout began, the mob said, 'You're fucked. We did this for you. We own you. But we'll just take Bang Records and call it a day.'"

In actual fact, it took more than just a threatening conversation to persuade Wexler to let Bert Berns leave Atlantic with artists like Neil Diamond, Van Morrison, and the McCoys in tow. Wexler's daughter Anita was then fourteen years old. As her boyfriend at the time recalled, "I know there was one time that somebody had apparently threatened to break her legs. I think they threatened Jerry by using her. Apparently, Jerry had a very bitter breakup with Bert Berns and Morris Levy's name was in the mix at some point too." After the mob threatened Jerry's daughter, the partners at Atlantic had no choice but to let Berns leave the label. According to Mica, "I think the mob threat came from Bert Berns but Ahmet told me not to talk about it."

In a cash business where distributors had to make their own deals with local trucking companies and shippers, no independent record company could ever say it was completely free of mob influence. So they could shut down an illegal record pressing operation that was taking money out of their pockets on a regular basis, the partners at Atlantic made a decision that cost them more than they had been losing at the time. Having suffered from rheumatic fever as a child, Bert Berns died of heart failure at the age of thirty-eight. In his autobiography, Jerry Wexler made a point of noting that he did not attend the funeral.

## ELEVEN

# I Got You Babe

*"After Sonny and Cher had become huge stars, we gave a press party for them in L.A. and invited all the Hollywood press and we had a receiving line that included Sonny and Cher and myself and some people from the company. One lady stopped and said, 'Are you Mr. Mica Ertegun?' I said, 'What publication are you from?' She said, 'I'm from* Vogue *magazine.' So I said, 'Oh yes, I am Mr. Mica Ertegun.' She said, 'Who did you think I was?' I said, 'I thought maybe you were* Women's Wear Daily.' "

—Ahmet Ertegun

## 1

Forty-two years old, Ahmet now bore little physical resemblance to the gawky teenager in an oversized zoot suit he had once been. Sporting a full black goatee streaked with gray on either side and sharp black glasses through which his large dark eyes could be clearly seen, he projected an air of magnetic self-assurance that defined him as a serious player in the record business as well as a member in good standing of the rarefied social circle through which he and Mica now moved.

Blessed with a sense of personal style that transcended fashion, Ahmet and Mica had themselves become fashionable and were spending their evenings on the town with hip New York movers and shakers like Bill and Chessy Rayner; Baby Jane Holzer, whom Tom Wolfe had immortalized in 1964 as "The Girl of the Year"; her good friend Nicky Haslam, the British art director of *Show* magazine; Andy Warhol; and Diana Vreeland, the legendary editor of *Vogue*.

Along with his great fashion idol Fred Astaire, Dean Acheson, Bill Blass, Miles Davis, Douglas Fairbanks Jr., Clark Gable, Cary Grant, and Diana Vreeland's husband, banker Thomas Reed Vreeland, Ahmet had been named as one of the best-dressed men in the world in a piece entitled "The Art of Wearing Clothes" by his good friend George Frazier in the September 1960 issue of *Esquire* magazine. "Dedicated to chic living," Ahmet, in Frazier's words, "buys ready-made suits at J. Press (around $100 each and has them recut for around $50)" by "the legendary valet of the Algonquin Hotel in New York."

Frazier also noted that when Ahmet "somehow came into possession of a suit" made by the famed tailor E. Tautz of Savile Row in London in 1923, the year of his birth, "he promptly put it into a protective cellophane covering and hung it in a closet. It has remained there ever since, emerging only when he wears it on some opulent occasion or when he permits clothes-conscious male visitors the privilege of admiring its splendid cut, caressing its incomparable stitching." As Miriam Bienstock would later say, "Ahmet and George Frazier used to talk to each other about clothes like two girls shopping."

In what even then seemed like the most unlikely manner imaginable, Ahmet put an end to the long dry spell at Atlantic by signing a husband-and-wife duo whose onstage garb became as vital to their success as their music. At a time when the hippie revolution was just getting underway in California, no one on the East Coast had ever seen anyone who looked or dressed like Sonny and Cher. And while the pair did not sound like anyone who had ever recorded for his label, Ahmet still somehow managed to hear money in their music.

The son of Italian immigrant parents from Detroit, Salvatore Philip "Sonny" Bono dropped out of high school in Los Angeles and went to work as a box boy and a meat truck driver before he started writing songs for Art Rupe at Speciality Records. After replacing the legendary Bumps Blackwell as a staff producer there, Bono left the label and began working for Phil Spector at Gold Star Studios in Hollywood.

With songwriter and arranger Jack Nitzsche, whom Keith Richards would later call "the man who actually made Phil Spector by putting the sounds together," Sonny wrote "Needles and Pins," a hit for Jackie DeShannon and later for the Searchers. A music business veteran who had not yet really made a name for himself, he was twenty-eight years old when he met his future wife and singing partner in Aldo's Coffee Shop, a celebrity hangout in L.A.

Then sixteen years old, Cherilyn Sarkisian had been born in El Centro, a small city fourteen miles north of the Mexican border in Imperial County, a largely agricultural area. Her father, an Armenian truck driver, and her mother, Georgia Holt, born Jackie Jean Crouch in Arkansas, divorced when she was a child. Severely dyslexic, Cher dropped out of high school and moved to Los Angeles, where her mother was then pursuing a career in acting and modeling.

After Sonny brought Cher to Gold Star, she sang backup vocals on legendary Phil Spector productions like "Be My Baby" by the Ronettes and "You've Lost That Loving Feeling" by the Righteous Brothers. Jack Nitzsche hired Sonny and Cher as backup singers for a recording session attended by most of Phil Spector's regular studio musicians, Brian Jones of the Rolling Stones, Jackie DeShannon, and Brian Wilson of the Beach Boys that Charlie Greene and Brian Stone were producing.

"There were thirty people singing background," Stone recalled, "but Cher had this killer voice. We had her standing like fifty feet from the mike all the way in the back of the studio but all you could hear was her. After the session that night, we took them back to our office and signed them to manage them." Greene and Stone also signed Sonny and Cher to recording and publishing contracts, thereby enabling them to control their future in the business.

As an agent would later describe the pair of legendary hustlers who would soon dominate the music management scene on the Sunset Strip, "Greene and Stone wore dollar signs on gold chains around their necks. That's how obvious they were. And they signed up everything that moved and wound up owning huge publishing rights on a lot of acts." In the words of bass player Bruce Palmer of Buffalo Springfield, whom the two men also managed, "Greene and Stone were the sleaziest, most underhanded, backstabbing motherfuckers in the business. They were the best."

Born Charles Greenberg on Long Island, New York, Greene had "ferried performers" like Bobby Darin, Sammy Davis, and Louis Prima and Keely Smith "around Manhattan nightclubs in his job as low-level press agent for Rogers & Cowan." Stone would later describe his boyhood friend and partner as "short and kind of stocky. He looked like John Belushi and he walked around with a phone attached to his head and he was a schmoozer. I had been an accountant and studied law and I was quiet and he was much more outgoing. That was why we were such a great team."

After working briefly as publicists for Lionel Hampton, the pair hitchhiked to Los Angeles, where they set up shop in an unlocked dressing room at Revue Studios and began soliciting work as press agents from actors. When the head of the studio learned what they were doing, he had them thrown off the lot.

By the time the pair signed Sonny and Cher to a management contract in return for 25 percent of their earnings, Greene and Stone were "living with two hookers in the Hollywood Hills. Sonny and Cher were broke so they came to live with us. Cher was a clueless kid with pimples all over her face. She had a big nose and would never wear a dress, always pants. She was like this crazy pachuco kid who was very quiet. Cher's mother was around but she didn't like Sonny and did not want them to be together."

While living with Greene and Stone, Sonny went to the piano one night and "wrote this song, 'Baby Don't Go.' He wrote the lyrics on a shirt cardboard and woke us up in the middle of the night and said, 'I want to play this for you,' and we said, 'We love it. It's a great song. We gotta go record this.' He said, 'You think so?' We had no money so we hocked this old dictating equipment from our office for five hundred bucks to a friend and went into the studio the next day."

Greene and Stone then called the A&R man at Warner-Reprise Records with whom Sonny and Cher had already made a verbal agreement to release their remake of Mickey & Sylvia's "Love Is Strange" under the name Caesar and Cleo. Because the managers "just wanted our five hundred bucks back," they persuaded Mo Ostin to come to their office at 7715 Sunset Strip to listen to their new demo. Born Morris Meyer Ostrovsky in New York City, Ostin had worked as Frank Sinatra's accountant before being hired by the singer to head his label, Reprise Records, which was subsequently bought by Warner Brothers.

In Stone's words, "We play him 'Baby Don't Go.' He says, 'I love this record.' We say, 'You're going to be a little stunned by this. But this is Caesar and Cleo. Kill the other record and put this one out.' 'I can't,' he says. 'It's scheduled to come out in a week.' Charlie and I went crazy.

We said, 'Mo, put this out too. Under another name. Whichever one hits, you'll have it.' He says, 'What do I call them?' We say, 'Why don't you call them Sonny and Cher?' "

When Ostin asked the managers what they wanted from the deal, they told him Caesar and Cleo "were five percent artists. 'Make it eight and a half percent and we'll take a little piece of the override and give us back our $500. Send us the agreement and it's yours.' What we didn't realize was that he was steaming about it. We expected them to sign Sonny to a long-term contract but they were so pissed off that they made it a one-record deal for 'Baby Don't Go' for eight and a half percent and a thousand bucks and we signed it and said, 'Sonny, you're free. We can now sign you and Cher as a separate act to another label.' "

Although "Love Is Strange" by Caesar and Cleo went nowhere, "Baby Don't Go" became a hit in Los Angeles and Dallas. After doing a session in L.A. with Nino Tempo and April Stevens, a brother-and-sister act for whom he had produced an unlikely B-side hit entitled "Deep Purple" on Atco in 1964, Ahmet and Nino Tempo were driving down Sunset Boulevard "with the radio on in the car" when Tempo said, "How can I get a sound like the drummer on this record?" Ahmet asked him who they were, "and he told me Sonny and Cher. I said, 'Wait a minute. Sonny and Cher? That's Caesar and Cleo.' "

Ahmet already knew Sonny as the "young man" who "played the tambourine and helped me get musicians when we had sessions in California. I put him in the band with the tambourine so he could get scale and make some extra money and he was very nice. He was a friend of Phil Spector's and he had a girlfriend and he wanted to make records and they called themselves Caesar and Cleo."

After contacting Greene and Stone, Ahmet, in Stone's words, "came up to our office. I had never met him before but I knew who Atlantic was and I idolized the label. Sonny loved Ahmet and we adored him and he said, 'I wanna sign this act.' " Even though love was flowing like water in Greene and Stone's office on the Sunset Strip that day, the managers were not about to put Sonny and Cher on Atlantic without first determining how much Ahmet really loved them.

"We said, 'Ahmet, we love you and Sonny loves you and we think you're the greatest and we idolize you and Atlantic is the greatest. But you're a black label. How are you going to break a white pop act?' And he said, 'Man, listen, no problem. Just in case you forgot, we had Bobby Darin.' By then, Bobby was already long gone from Atlantic. 'Ahmet, will you be able to break a pop act?' And he said, 'Man, I'm gonna tell you something. I'm going to make this label a pop label.' We said, 'Ahmet, come on, man.' And he said, 'I'm gonna bust my ass to break this act. They're great.' "

When Greene and Stone asked for an 8½ percent deal for Sonny and Cher, Ahmet said, "No problem, man." After the managers informed Ahmet they had also signed Cher as a solo act on Imperial Records, Ahmet replied, "Doesn't bother me, man. I want the act. I want Sonny and Cher." In Stone's words, "So we ended up with three separate agreements. Each label allowed they knew of the other and everything was fine."

What possessed Ahmet to give Greene and Stone everything they wanted in return for Sonny and Cher, whose music was as far from his own taste as possible, no one can ever say for sure. Tuned into a frequency only he could hear, Ahmet had recognized something in "Baby Don't Go" that led him to believe Atlantic could achieve commercial success with a sound that can most charitably be described as pop masquerading as fake folk rock.

Although Stone would later say that "Ahmet had no clue as to what was then happening on the Sunset Strip," he did understand that songs about youthful rebellion and teenage angst had always sold well. And while Sonny and Cher had already packaged themselves as a pair of shaggy-haired, vaguely psychedelic social outcasts, their onstage demeanor echoed that of a duo whose music Ahmet knew very well indeed.

As Brian Stone recalled, "Charlie and I had come out of New York where two of our best friends had been Keely Smith and Louie Prima. We used to handle them and they were our heroes and that was who we wanted Sonny and Cher to become. When they did their show onstage, they would be like loxes. Sonny would be a little more animated than Cher but kids really responded to them and loved this little love thing they had. They were like teenaged lovers. Although we never formulated it that way, Sonny and Cher were like a teenaged Keely Smith and Louie Prima. Years later, Keely ran into Cher at a party and she ignored her and Keely said, 'She's me. Doesn't she know that?' "

A year after "Baby Don't Go" became a hit, Sonny came up with "I Got You Babe." Greene and Stone loved the song and when Bob Skaff at Imperial Records, who "had great ears" heard it, "He said, 'That's my record. I want that record. That's the greatest song I ever heard. It's a number one song.' Ahmet heard the song but he didn't get it. The other side of 'I Got You Babe' was 'It's Gonna Rain Outside.' Nesuhi heard that first and said it was the hit. Ahmet wasn't blown away by 'I Got You Babe' but we knew it was a big record, a smash, so we put it out."

Promoting the duo as "the greatest act you've ever seen," Greene and Stone decided to break Sonny and Cher internationally. "Only two or three companies had international distribution so we had to release it country by country on the different labels Atlantic had deals with in each country." Once the record began climbing up the charts, the managers asked Ahmet to put up the money so Sonny and Cher could tour overseas.

"We told Ahmet we wanted to take them to Europe to tour so we could break them across the world. We said, 'Ahmet, we're going to bring a film crew and make a film called *Sonny and Cher in London.* He said, 'You guys are crazy. How much is it going to cost?' He never wanted to part with any money but we finally got him to agree to do it."

On their first day in London as Greene and Stone were checking into the Hilton with Sonny and Cher, "They saw what we looked like and would not let us in. Charlie was a hothead and he leaped across the desk and punched the guy. They said, 'Get out of here,' and we called a press conference outside the hotel. No one knew who Sonny and Cher were but we were on the front pages of all the newspapers for being kicked out of the hotel."

Years later, Greene and Stone would learn that "Ahmet, Jerry, and Nesuhi were trying to sell Atlantic at this point to ABC-Paramount. They were in terrible, terrible condition and they had a deal pending for somewhere between three and seven million bucks for Atlantic. After 'I Got You Babe' became a monster smash, they killed the sale to ABC-Paramount and Ahmet told me this was the biggest record he'd ever had in his life. It was his first million-seller worldwide and crossed Atlantic over into new markets."

Released in July 1965, "I Got You Babe" went to number one on the American pop charts and stayed there for three weeks. Delighted by their success, Ahmet threw "a giant party" for Sonny and Cher when they returned to New York after their European tour at which they met Baby Jane Holzer and Andy Warhol, whose art would reflect the outsized, cartoonlike image of pop stardom the duo were already projecting.

Ahmet then called Greene and Stone in California to ask if Sonny and Cher could "play at this dinner party. It was the first time Jacqueline Kennedy was going out since Jack Kennedy had died and they asked her who she wanted to play and she asked for Sonny and Cher and we said yes, absolutely."

In less than two years, Sonny and Cher had gone from living with Charlie Greene and Brian Stone and two hookers in a house in the Hollywood Hills to mixing with the crème de la crème of café society in New York City. Their improbable rise from the street to a penthouse at the Waldorf Towers to perform for the former first lady was the stuff of dreams. It would soon become the paradigm for success in a business that Ahmet and Mica had somehow made socially acceptable.

## 2

Although Ahmet did not attend the dinner party for Jacqueline Kennedy, he did go to great expense to fly Sonny and Cher, their managers, and a five-piece band that included Mac Rebennack, soon to be known as Dr. John, first-class from Los Angeles to New York, where he put them all up in style at the Hampshire House on Central Park South. On the afternoon of the party, Greene and Stone went to the penthouse of the Waldorf-Astoria to check out the apartment owned by Charles Engelhard Jr. and his wife, Jane, a fabulously wealthy couple who were good friends of Ahmet and Mica. Known for his extensive mining interests in South Africa, Engelhard was the real-life inspiration for Ian Fleming's fictional character Auric Goldfinger.

"It was a regular living room," Stone would later say, "about fifteen-by-twenty and we set up a five-piece band. We didn't know where the hell we were and we were walking around this monstrous, unbelievable apartment with thousands of platinum plates on the wall and this daffy lady who turned out to be Mrs. Engelhard gave us a tip, a hundred-dollar bill, because she thought we were members of the band."

The guest list for the party was small, just thirteen people having been invited for dinner, Nesuhi and Diana Vreeland among them. Jackie Kennedy was so pleased by Sonny and Cher's performance that she asked them to repeat it. After they had done so, the former first lady complimented Sonny by telling him he looked "rather Shakespearean" and then made pleasant conversation with the band.

Decked out in a pair of tight hip-high green suede pants and a short military jacket with a double row of buttons she had bought that day at Bendel's, Cher caught the eye of Diana Vreeland. "My dear," the esteemed editor of *Vogue* told her, "you have a pointed head! You're absolutely beautiful." As Cher recalled, "And the next thing I knew, Richard Avedon was coming out to take my picture." At some point during Cher's visit to New York, the usually taciturn singer also supplied Ahmet with the punch line for a story he never tired of telling.

At a dinner party in Los Angeles some years before, Ahmet had met this "very tall, statuesque lady" who "looked as though she could have been a showgirl in Las Vegas." When Ahmet asked her what she did, she told him she was interested in metaphysics. "Oh," Ahmet said. "You mean Plato, Aristotle, that sort of thing. She said, 'Oh, no, Dr. Wilson who has the Church of Metaphysical Science.' "

Ahmet then said something that made everyone laugh "but she started to cry and said I was insulting her religion." After Ahmet apologized for his remark, she told him, "I'll only forgive you if you promise to go to the church with me tomorrow." The next morning, Ahmet escorted her to Grauman's Chinese Theatre on Hollywood Boulevard. After being ushered into a private box where "the only other occupant was the actor and fellow church member Mickey Rooney," Ahmet dutifully listened to "a good sermon" that was "a cross between the usual kind of born-again Christian doctrine and Dale Carnegie advice on how to be successful in life."

After he had seen the woman a few more times, she said, "You know, I have a daughter who is a great singer." Ahmet replied, "Listen, if we're going to be friends, let's not talk about daughters who are going to be singers, uncles who write songs, and so forth. It never seems to work." She agreed and the two eventually ended their relationship.

During Cher's visit to New York to perform for Jackie Kennedy, the singer told Ahmet, "I was very surprised to find out that you were friends with my mother." Perplexed, he replied, "What are you talking about? I don't know your mother." Cher said, "Yes, you do." At which point her mother, Georgia Holt, walked into the room. As Ahmet would later say, "Who is it, except this woman who was interested in metaphysical science. She said, 'I told you I had a daughter who sings.' I said, 'Oh, good Lord!' "

### 3

Emboldened by their success, Charlie Greene and Brian Stone continued doing all they could to promote Sonny and Cher in Los Angeles. Greene, who invented the term "heavy" to describe a song and then persuaded deejay The Real Don Steele to use the phrase as often as possible on his popular KHJ radio show, began offering the station the right to air exclusive advance copies of English hits for a week. "And in return," Stone would later say, "they had to play us so many times and Ahmet would go crazy because we would put the record on the radio before there were even records pressed. We were acting like promotion guys."

Because a record could not be played on KHJ "unless it was in the charts," Greene and Stone "had people who worked for us call stores and make orders and we sent people in to buy the record. KFWB and KRLA were in the same market and they would call Ahmet and scream at him and Ahmet would blow his top and call me and say, 'You're killing me with the radio stations!' They would tell him they weren't going to play any Atlantic records. He would say, 'How did that record get on the radio?' And we would say, 'Ahmet, we don't know. We're not sure.' He knew we were full of shit. But he forgave it all because we were making him money."

After the managers had set up a film deal for Sonny and Cher with William Friedkin slated to direct his first full-length movie, "Sonny became a real power freak and began going to all the writers' meetings and telling everybody what to do and everybody was freaking out. His agents were with him all the time and they were saying how much do your managers get and he would say 25 percent and they would say, 'What? Are you out of your mind? I'll do that for less.'"

The rapidly deteriorating relationship between Sonny and his managers came to an end when a story about Sonny and Cher entitled "The Children of Bob Dylan" appeared in *Life* magazine. "There was a big giant picture of them and on the fifth page, there was a half-page photo of Charlie and me sitting in our limousine. We bought it because Ahmet had a limousine. 'Oh, he has a limousine? We have to get a limousine.'" As Jimmy McDonough would later write, Greene and Stone bought "an $18,500 Lincoln limousine with a Blackgama mink interior, a bar with full sterling service, and an eight track player, with an elegant white-gloved black chauffeur with a sideline in all sorts of contraband."

When the *Life* magazine article appeared, "Sonny was really infuriated. He said, 'That should have been a page on me. How did that happen?' He was really pissed at us. Shortly after that, we got a letter from an attorney Sonny had hired who said our agreements with Sonny and Cher were terminated. Sonny never even called us. We never talked to them again. It wasn't that our careers were dead. These were like our best friends who had left us without saying a word and wouldn't talk to us anymore. We were broken."

Greene and Stone however did have Sonny and Cher "locked up in ironclad contracts." When Ahmet began demanding that the duo get back into the studio, the managers told him Sonny and Cher had signed with them as recording artists and so he could not put out anything by them until the conflict had been resolved. "Ahmet was freaking out of his mind. He had this giant act and we had said no. And he said, 'They don't want anything to do with you anymore.' We said, 'Ahmet, we don't care what they want. If they want out, they have to buy us out.' Sonny hated us but he had no real money. We were in a deadlock that went for weeks."

In need of new product to feed the market Sonny and Cher had created for their music, Ahmet found himself in the middle of a dispute that was hurting not only his label but also all concerned. Stone then called Ahmet in the middle of the night and said, "Ahmet, I've got the solution for this. 'What are you talking about, man?' 'I know how to solve this. Sonny buys us out because you put up the money and when he does, we give up all our percentages and you recoup the money. It's airtight. You give us the cash and loan it to Sonny and you get your money back in front.' And Ahmet said, 'That's great, man. We can do that.'"

After a good deal of negotiating, the managers agreed to accept a buyout of $350,000. Greene and Stone also specified that the sum—today about $2.3 million—be paid to them in cash. The pair then flew to New York, where an Atlantic representative escorted them to the bank to withdraw the money. "We went in there with an attaché case and they had guards and we were in a private room counting it out. We had never seen that much money in our lives and then Charlie and I suddenly realized, 'Holy shit, we have to walk through the street with this.' So we hired an armed guard to protect us while we walked back to the Plaza Hotel. Charlie said, 'What if this guard hits us over the head while we're walking in the street?' We were so paranoid. We got back to the hotel and we were hysterical, playing cards with big bundles of cash and throwing it on the beds. If it would have gone into our account, we would never have seen it. We wanted to see it."

While Sonny and Cher did not go on "to make that much money for Atlantic" and left the label in 1971 after a period of declining popularity, the deal proved to be extremely profitable for Atlantic in the long run. In 2009, the gross earnings from Sonny Bono's songwriting copyrights were still "something like eight hundred thousand dollars, and that was for a quarter."

After their recording career ended, Sonny and Cher hosted a wildly popular variety show that ran on CBS until the couple divorced in 1974. A conservative Republican who served as the mayor of Palm Springs, California, for four years, Sonny was elected to the United States House of Representatives in 1994. While serving his second term as a congressman, he died in 1998 at the age of sixty-two as the result of injuries suffered in a skiing accident. Having won the Academy Award as Best Actress for her role in *Moonstruck* in 1988, Cher continues appearing in films and still performs on a regular basis in Las Vegas.

In retrospect, the most astonishing aspect of Ahmet's dealings with their managers was that he could come up with the money to pay off

Greene and Stone without having to ask for a loan or a line of credit. A payment that might have sunk a smaller independent label in 1966 did not even make a serious dent in the vast amount of cash the partners at Atlantic had by then salted away "in various and sundry places" to serve as the label's operating capital.

As well as anyone, Ahmet understood that the record industry was a business of personal relationships founded on money. On the night he had thrown his huge party in New York to celebrate Sonny and Cher's triumphant return from Europe, Ahmet had summoned Greene and Stone to a late night meeting with him, Nesuhi, and Jerry Wexler. After telling the managers how happy Atlantic was with what they had done and how proud of them they were, Ahmet said, " 'I'm raising your percentage from eight and a half to ten percent. And by the way, here.' And they gave us a hundred grand as a bonus. In cash. Not recoupable. We split it fifty-fifty with Sonny. He had never seen money like that and he was blown out by what Ahmet had done and so were we. You talk about locking in a client, man. That guy. What a mensch, man."

In a business where it was understood that for every favor done, another favor was expected in return, Charlie Greene and Brian Stone now owed Ahmet. And so when the pair found themselves managing one of the greatest American rock bands of all time, they brought them to Atlantic.

# TWELVE

# Hey, What's That Sound

*"When Ahmet walked into the room, you got good."*

—Neil Young

## 1

A lifelong devotee of the sport, Ahmet was in Mexico City on June 12, 1966, watching the Tottenham Hotspur football club defeat the Mexico World Cup soccer team 1–0 when Jerry Wexler called from New York to say that Charlie Greene and Brian Stone were trying to reach him about a very talented new group they were managing who had already built up quite a following. When Wexler told him there was a lot of interest from other companies, Ahmet decided that instead of going back to New York, he would fly from Mexico City to Los Angeles to see them. As Stone would later say, "We talked to Jerry first but Jerry hated pop acts. He didn't want to hear about it and hated all these scumbags. Only Ahmet would talk pop acts. So Ahmet came out and we all got together in my office."

The band Ahmet had flown to Los Angeles to meet was Buffalo Springfield. In his words, they were "very special in so many ways. First of all, the songs they wrote didn't resemble anything that anybody else was doing. They also had three outstanding lead singers who were also great guitar players—Neil Young, Stephen Stills, and Richie Furay. I mean, a rock 'n' roll band is lucky if it has one good singer and one guitar player who can really play—that alone can make them a great band. The power in Buffalo Springfield was too incredible. They were one of the greatest rock 'n' roll bands I've ever heard in my life."

Richie Furay first met Stephen Stills in Greenwich Village when they worked together in the Au Go Go Singers, the house band at the Cafe Au Go Go that Furay had formed in 1964. Born in Dallas, Texas, Stills had been raised in a military family that moved constantly. After graduating from high school in the Panama Canal Zone, he dropped out of the University of Florida to pursue a career in music.

While touring Canada as a member of a folk rock group called the Company, Stills met Neil Young, son of the noted Canadian sportswriter, newspaper columnist, and author Scott Young, who was then performing with a group called the Squires. Musically, Stills and Young hit it off immediately and Stills told Young if he ever went to New York, he should look up Richie Furay. "A nice, uncomplicated guy" who "could sing like a bird," Furay was so impressed by Young's songwriting talents after the two met that he began performing Young's "Nowadays Clancy Can't Even Sing" as part of his solo act.

Young and his friend bass player Bruce Palmer then drove Young's 1953 Pontiac hearse to Los Angeles to find Stills. After searching for him for days, they were about to leave the city when they ran into Stills and Furay stuck in traffic on Sunset Boulevard with "music business eccentric" Barry Friedman, in whose house both musicians were then living.

Smoking joints together, Stills, who along with Furay had already signed a personal management contract with Friedman, told Young he was going to start the "best band in Los Angeles" and invited him and Palmer to become part of it. After the four musicians added Canadian drummer Dewey Martin, who had played with Carl Perkins, the Everly Brothers, Patsy Cline, Roy Orbison, the Standells, and the Dillards, they decided to name themselves after a steamroller made by the Buffalo-Springfield Roller Company that happened to be parked on the street outside Friedman's house.

Buffalo Springfield played their first gig at the Troubadour Folk Den on the Sunset Strip on April 11, 1966. After seeing the show, Chris Hillman, the bass player for the Byrds, booked the band to open for his group four days later in San Bernardino. That gig led to a six-week engagement at the Whisky A Go Go, where the Springfield soon became the hottest band in L.A. By their fourth or fifth concert, as Stills would later say, "We were so good it was absolutely astounding, and the first week at the Whisky A Go Go was absolutely incredible. We were just incredible, man, that's when we peaked. After that, it was downhill."

By far the most ambitious member of the band, Stills had already asked Friedman's neighbor, Dickie Davis, who ran the lights at the Whisky and The Trip, to look at a music publishing contract the band had been offered. When Davis advised Stills not to sign it, he took over from Friedman as the Springfield's representative and began talking to A&R man Lenny Waronker at Warner Bros. Records. "Overwhelmed by the machinations of the deal," Davis went to Greene and Stone for advice and "they quickly took over."

Their first order of business was to free Stills and Furay from the personal management contracts they had signed with Friedman. According to one account, Greene took Friedman to New York, got him "outrageously stoned," and then drove him around in a limo without letting him eat until he finally signed a release letting them go. "They said we pulled a gun on Friedman to get the Springfield and that's not true," Brian Stone would later say. "The truth is Stephen said, 'You have to buy this guy out. Get the hippie out of this thing.' Charlie was going to meet with Friedman and he said, 'Give me a check for five thousand dollars.' I said, 'Charlie, not a check. Take cash.' Charlie showed him the money in the car. It was hard to turn down and he signed off on them."

On June 8, 1966, in return for a $5,000 advance and a 15 percent management fee, Greene and Stone signed Buffalo Springfield to a record deal on their own label, York/Pala Records. They also acquired a 75 percent share of the band's music publishing for their company, Ten-East Music. Four days later, Wexler called Ahmet in Mexico City with the news that Greene and Stone had an act they wanted him to sign. By then, the managers had already begun buying the band new instruments and renting them cars, for which the musicians would later be billed.

Despite the $100,000 handshake Ahmet had given Greene and Stone for having brought him Sonny and Cher, Ahmet realized that because other record companies were interested in the group, he would have to sell himself to them to close the deal. While there was no one in the business better suited to the task, he was now faced with the daunting prospect of having to schmooze five fairly stoned young musicians who already knew how good they were after having blown away audiences night after night on the Sunset Strip.

In a business where all credentials were personal and a big-money deal could hinge on how good a record executive was in the room, Ahmet immediately established his credentials by sitting down with the band on the floor of Greene and Stone's office so he could tell them why they should sign with Atlantic. As he recalled, "I'll never forget sitting on the floor in that office doing my best to convince them I was really into their music and they should go with me because of all I could do for their career. Neil looked up at me and asked if I could get him a membership in an L.A. golf club. I was thrown by that one but when I saw he was serious, I said I'd do my best."

While Brian Stone doubts "Neil Young ever said that, or if he did, he was joking, because they were kids," the fact that an elegantly dressed record business legend like Ahmet was perfectly willing to communicate with musicians half his age on their level convinced the band to give Greene and Stone the green light to sign them to Atco. In return for a $12,000 advance, Atlantic took half of the managers' 75 percent share of the Springfield's publishing, thereby leaving the five band members and Dickie Davis to split the remaining 25 percent six ways.

In practical terms, this meant that while Stills, Young, and Furay would receive full songwriting royalties for their work with Buffalo Springfield, each would be paid less than 4.2 percent of the publishing money. On March 15, 1967, Young received a royalty statement from Ten-East Music. The total he had earned amounted to $292.78. Less advances of $131.46 from November 1966 as well as $161.32 that had been applied against loans and advances, he was paid nothing at all.

While the publishing deal would later cause great acrimony between the band and its managers, a far more immediate set of problems began as soon as Greene and Stone took Buffalo Springfield into the studio in July to begin recording the series of singles that became its first album. As Ahmet would later say, "At one of our first sessions at the old Gold Star studio in Hollywood, the group was tuning up. They tuned up to one another. Then someone hit a note on the piano and they realized they were all out of tune. Then they broke up in hysterical laughter. They kept trying to tune up and kept laughing and this lasted approximately three hours. I finally went to a Spanish guitar maker who had a shop up the street to help them get it together. What they did when they played live never came off on their records because they became much more cerebral when they went into the studio."

Right from the start, there was also the inevitable clash of personalities between Stills and Young. "When the group started," Stone recalled, "they said to us that Richie Furay was the lead singer. Stephen was supposed to be the leader of the group and Neil and Stephen were the lead guitarists but they were always fighting over that. They were at each other's throats all the time and used to fight about this stuff and Neil eventually wanted to sing his own songs."

Even then Young was the loner in the group. His songs were so idiosyncratic and intensely personal that they bore little resemblance to the far more commercial material Stills seemed effortlessly able to generate. In Ahmet's words, "Stephen's poetry was earthy, based more on the blues, with a penchant towards Latin grooves. Neil's music was more abstract. He had a lot of musical thoughts which didn't make sense to me right away. His voice was odd, shaky. It's like looking at a Cubist painting in 1920——if you look at one Picasso, you would say, 'I don't know what this is.' But when you see the whole body of work, it's a great thing."

Except when they were driving one another to new heights while trading guitar leads on stage, Stills and Young had virtually nothing in common. Marching to the beat of a drummer only he could hear, Young would throughout his long career constantly reinvent himself as an artist by recording songs no one else could have written in a variety of musical genres. Far more ambitious and driven than Young, Stills, who in Young's words was "a great musician," desperately craved bigtime success and "wanted to hang out in London with the Beatles as soon as possible."

One day when Young failed to show up for a session or a rehearsal, the always combustible Stills burst into the bungalow where Young was living with his girlfriend in Laurel Canyon, picked up her guitar, and threatened to smash it over Young's head while screaming, "You're ruining my career! You're ruining my career!" When Young began suffering epileptic fits onstage, Stills thought, in Stone's words, that Young was "full of shit, having one of his phony spells. It was like, 'He doesn't want to play the date and now he's fainting.' "

Neither Stills nor Young liked what they would later say Greene and Stone did to their music in the studio. In Stone's words, "They were a bunch of kids who had never been in a studio in their lives and knew nothing about recording. They would sit on the floor and not know what they were doing. They would change the levels of their instruments during sessions. They were in the booth with us every minute of every day of everything we ever did. It wasn't like we took the record away from them. For years, Neil has contended that the record sucks. He and Stephen never stop saying this."

The day after the band finished recording the final track of their debut album, *Buffalo Springfield*, they phoned Greene and Stone and begged them to scrap everything and let them start all over again from scratch. Stone refused to do this and Ahmet, who was eager for product so he could break the Springfield nationwide, backed him up.

Calling Ahmet "a musician's businessman" who "knows music," Young would later say, "Ahmet always said, 'This record's not as good as the fuckin' demos, man.' . . . Ahmet heard those demos and, based on hearing those demos, signed us to Atlantic. And then Charlie and Brian made a record that was nowhere near as good as those fucking demos." In fact, Ahmet had already signed the band when they went into the studio to record the demos.

When the album was released in December 1966, it went nowhere and the group blamed Greene and Stone. Without a hit, the managers did not know how to promote the band. Unwilling to put the Springfield out on the road as an opening act or relegate them to the club circuit, Greene and Stone allowed the group to languish in L.A.

Fortunately for all concerned, as Stills drove down from Laurel Canyon on the night of November 13, 1966, he was confronted by a phalanx of helmeted LAPD troopers in full battle gear wielding billy clubs as they cleared thousands of protesters, Sonny and Cher among them, from in front of a club called Pandora's Box. Responding to demands from the owners of restaurants and nightclubs on Sunset Boulevard to enforce the ten P.M. curfew on the hordes of teenagers who had scared away their far more well-heeled patrons, the LAPD had shown up in force. As Stills would later say, "The Sunset Strip riot [was] just a funeral for a bar. But then you had the immortal genius of the idiots who ran the LAPD, who put all of those troopers in full battle array, looking like the Macedonian army, up against a bunch of kids."

After "ingesting hallucinogens," Stills wrote a song in fifteen minutes about what he had seen. Buffalo Springfield's only Top Ten hit, it became the first great anthem for the youth rebellion that changed the face of American culture—and helped Ahmet sell tons of records.

## 2

Walking into Brian Stone's office with his guitar in hand, Stephen Stills said, "Hey, I just wrote a song." In Stone's words, "So we walked into Charlie's office and we said, 'Let's hear it.' Stephen sits down on a chair and says, 'I'll play it, for what it's worth.' After he finished, we said, 'That's fantastic. We have to go right into the studio.' 'You like it?' 'Stephen, we love it. It's a great, great song.' 'Are you sure?' 'Absolutely. It's sensational.' "

The managers immediately booked studio time at Columbia and on December 5, 1966, Buffalo Springfield quickly cut a song Stills had loosely based on "Murder in My Heart for the Judge" and "The Other Side" by Moby Grape, one of San Francisco's great psychedelic bands. When Stills complained at the end of the session that he did not have a title for the song, Greene, in his words, said, "Yes, you do. You told me, 'Let me play this song for you, *for what it's worth*.' For once Stephen agreed with me."

With Stills sitting in their office a day later, Greene and Stone played a dub of the song over the phone for Ahmet in New York. "The guys in the band were all kind of neutral about it," Stone would later say, "and we didn't tell Ahmet who it was and he said, 'It's sensational, man. It's sensational. Who is it?' 'Ahmet, good news. It's Buffalo Springfield.' And he went crazy. He was just delirious. 'I love it, man. We gotta put that out right away. But I got a couple of comments. What's the name of it?' "

When the managers told him Stills called it "For What It's Worth," Ahmet said, "No, man. That's no good. You can't call it that. You can say it in the song. You should call it, 'Hey, What's That Sound?' " Stills, who was listening to every word, said he was not about to call it that and "was really pissed." Ahmet then said, "The line, 'There's a man with a gun over there,' that's bad. You gotta change that." In Stone's words, "He thought it was too explicit and he was right. We said, 'Stephen, Ahmet doesn't like that line. Is there anything you can do with that?' Stephen looked up and said, 'No, man. That's the song. I'm not changing it.' Ahmet said, 'Well, all right, man.' "

The first direct confrontation between the head of the label and his ambitious young artist ended in a grammatical draw. Stills got to keep the line about the man with a gun but Greene and Stone appeased Ahmet by enclosing the title he had suggested within a set of parentheses before the one Stills preferred.

Three days later, an acetate of "(Stop, Hey What's That Sound) For What It's Worth" was being played repeatedly in L.A. by Greene and Stone's favorite radio station, KHJ. Because Stills had so accurately "captured the paranoia in the air, circa early 1967," the song became a Top Ten hit. Doing all he could to break the band, Ahmet replaced "Don't Scold Me" with "For What It's Worth" on the Springfield's debut album and then rereleased it.

He also advanced Greene and Stone the money to bring the band to New York to play at Ondine's, a hip discotheque at 308 East 59th Street between First and Second Avenues where Jimi Hendrix had performed with Curtis Knight and the Squires in 1965 and where the Doors had made their New York debut a year later. On any given night, girls in miniskirts could be found dancing at Ondine's until three in the morning as Jackie Kennedy, Faye Dunaway, Sonny and Cher, celebrity hair dresser Monte Rock III, and Eric Burdon of the Animals mingled with bikers who had parked their motorcycles alongside the limousines outside the front door.

Most definitely Ahmet's kind of place, there could not have been a more unlikely venue for a band like Buffalo Springfield to make its East Coast debut. And yet, as he would later say, "When they performed there, man, there was no band I ever heard that had the electricity of that group. That was the most exciting group I've ever seen, bar none. It was just mind-boggling."

In New York, things went no better for the Springfield than they had in Los Angeles. Onstage one night in Ondine's, Stills slapped Bruce Palmer across the face because his bass was too loud. Palmer responded by knocking Stills through the drum set. After suffering a seizure onstage, Young staggered into a hallway at the disco, where a woman had to insert a pencil into his mouth to keep him from swallowing his tongue. After Palmer was busted for pot at the two-room suite at the Wellington Hotel, where all five musicians were staying while Greene and Stone resided in luxury at the Plaza, the bass player was sent back to Canada.

One night at Ondine's, the band did get to perform with one of the greatest soul singers who ever lived. "Dewey Martin knew Otis Redding," Stone recalled, "and he said, 'I called Otis and he's coming to see us tonight.' Everybody thought Dewey was full of shit." After Redding walked into the club, the band brought him up to the stage to join them but, as Atlantic's fast-talking FM promotion man Mario Medious recalled, "Otis was so drunk that when he took a bow, he fell over. But then he sang with them and he was fantastic."

Ahmet, who was also at the club that night, was delighted. By then, Wexler had already signed a lucrative distribution deal with Stax, the Memphis label for whom Redding recorded. The singer was doing so well for Atlantic that Ahmet never bothered to tell him his older brother's name was not "Nescafe." Nor did Ahmet correct Redding when he called him "Omelet" in the mistaken belief "that he liked omelets and that was why they called him that, like a guy who liked hamhocks would be called Hamhock."

On January 9, 1967, Buffalo Springfield cut Neil Young's "Mr. Soul" at the Atlantic studio at 1841 Broadway. Brian Stone would later confirm that Charlie Greene hit Stephen Stills in the mouth during this session. Whether or not this actually happened, it was the last time Greene, whom his partner would later describe as "kinda like the manager's equivalent to Stephen Stills," ever spoke to the musician. As Stone would also say, "Otis Redding was at that session. He said, 'Holy shit, I love that song, man. I want to record it. I'm gonna cut that song, man.' "

Without ever having done so, Redding died eleven months later at the age of twenty-six when the plane on which he was traveling with four members of his band crashed into a lake in Wisconsin. Wexler first heard the news at the airport just after he had picked up the master tapes of "Dock of the Bay," a song that then became a huge posthumous hit for Redding. When Ahmet came home to Mica that night, he sat down on the sofa and cried.

Although Charlie Greene and Brian Stone were credited as having produced "Mr. Soul," they never recorded the band again. "I never really thought of them as producers," Ahmet said. "Look, don't get me wrong—I like Greene and Stone. They were funny. They were also hustlers. And you know—you don't want to have a hustler hustle you." In Stone's words, "Ahmet used to say to us, 'Stop being producers. You're just managers. Why do you keep trying to make records? It causes such aggravation. Stop producing. Just manage.' " After Buffalo Springfield hired the same attorney Sonny and Cher had employed to free themselves from Greene and Stone, the band ended its relationship with its managers.

At some point during this period, Charlie Greene got married at the Plaza Hotel. Ahmet and Wexler attended the festivities. After the event, Greene asked Wexler for a $78,000 dollar loan. "They were repossessing our cars," Stone recalled. "We needed the loan because they were locking us out of our offices. Buffalo Springfield was not a giant act and on top of that, they were crazy and hating each other and wanted to split up."

In Jerry Wexler's words, "Greene and Stone were constantly hitting on us, and we were constantly bailing them out. They came to the well again and again until the pitcher broke. Listen, we were completely aware of their hype—it was a deal where they knew that we knew that they knew that we knew. But the bottom line was, it was a very productive relationship. Also—we enjoyed them. We enjoyed the scoundrel, scamp aspect of them." After Wexler had agreed to the advance, Ahmet, in Stone's words, "called Wexler from L.A. where he had been talking to the Springfield and said to Jerry, 'I'm flying back tonight. Don't give them any money till I get back. Not until I talk to them.' We were freaked out."

When the managers met with Ahmet the next day, he told them, as Stone said, " 'Listen, I'll loan you the money only on the condition you guys release the Buffalo Springfield.' He kept saying, 'I'm telling you, there's no more group. The guys are all splitting up. Neil is going off by himself. Stephen doesn't want anything to do with anybody. Richie is going to start another group.' I said to Ahmet, 'I will let these guys out on the condition that if they ever reassemble or you are in some way involved in their records, I get a piece.' And he said, 'Fine.' He never signed the agreement and we got nothing for Crosby, Stills,

Nash. Nothing. I did it because Ahmet said they were splitting up and because he was making us this loan but Ahmet kind of conned us into that. He really did."

Before their association with Atlantic ended, Greene and Stone also persuaded Ahmet to sign a band Neil Young had told them about. "Charlie and I went to see them and I thought they were shit, actually," Stone would later say. "Cacophonous. Out of tune. Awful. I called Ahmet and I said we had a new band and he saw them at the Purple Onion or some crazy place on the Sunset Strip and signed them. Iron Butterfly became such a giant act that it made Jerry Wexler go out and sign Led Zeppelin."

While Ahmet "didn't want to put out the Iron Butterfly album because all the singles were shit," college FM radio stations began playing the nearly eighteen-minute version of "In-A-Gadda-Da-Vida," a drunken misspelling of "In the Garden of Eden." As Jason Flom, who became cochairman of Atlantic Records, would later say, "It was so bad you could actually hear the drummer drop his stick during the song and they didn't want to spend the money to do another take. Just a disaster." When orders for the record began multiplying at an amazing rate, Ahmet called Greene in Los Angeles and said, in Flom's words, " 'This record is going crazy. You have to put this band on the road.' Charlie says, 'What band? There is no band.' Ahmet says, 'Go out and find the worst drummer in America because no one else is going to be able to duplicate it.' " While, in Stone's words, "Ahmet had no idea what the title meant, that record was number two for two years. Because of the FM stations."

In April 1967, Greene and Stone were no longer involved with Buffalo Springfield and Stills asked Jack Nitzsche to produce "Bluebird," the song he envisioned as the band's next single. Because Nitzsche was too busy working with Young, Stills inveigled Ahmet to do the job. In the studio, Stills and Young argued so contentiously about who would play the lead guitar solo that Young suffered a seizure in the control booth before finally acceding to Stills' demand.

Nitzsche, who was at the session, would later remember Ahmet trying to calm both musicians down by telling them, "You will have to stop this. This is ridiculous. You see, this is Jack Nitzsche over here, and if he picks up that guitar over there, and hits me in the head with it, that goes in *Cashbox* magazine—front page. If you two guys beat each other bloody, no one cares. No *Cashbox* magazine. Understand?" Ahmet's words fell on deaf ears but the song did appear on the band's second album, *Buffalo Springfield Again,* released on Atco in November 1967.

Five days after Buffalo Springfield appeared at the Long Beach Arena on May 5, 1968, the group called a meeting to announce they had officially broken up. In Ahmet's words, "They had a meeting in Hollywood with the lawyers in 1968 and the band told me they were going to break up. They wanted their release from Atlantic Records. And I tell you something, I begged them not to break up. I actually cried. Eventually I said okay . . . they could leave the label if they wanted." Two months later, Atco released a collection of tracks the band had already recorded as *Last Time Around.*

By then, Ahmet had already decided that Stills, with whom he had forged a close personal relationship, was the great commercial talent in the band. As Stills's future band mate Graham Nash would later say, "Stephen and Ahmet were tight, and in more ways than just music. Ahmet was a father figure to Stephen, no question. As he got older, Stephen began to turn into Ahmet. He started to dress like Ahmet and had this goatee like Ahmet and began wearing shoes that cost five thousand dollars."

After the members of Buffalo Springfield went their separate ways, Ahmet had to decide which of its musicians to keep on the label. "I had to make a choice. I don't think Neil and Stephen wanted to be on the same label, and it was a tough decision, but the decision was made for me by Neil, who said he wanted to go on Warner's with Jack Nitzsche and make some records that I thought could be financially disastrous— uncommercial and expensive. I figured he and Neil would go off on a wild tangent, so it seemed to me I had a very good shot with Steve."

Ahmet handled the situation so adroitly that Young would always revere him for having helped the Springfield rid themselves of Greene and Stone and for then allowing him to record for Mo Ostin at Warner- Reprise. When the first great rock supergroup emerged from the re- mains of Buffalo Springfield, Ahmet signed them to Atlantic.

# THIRTEEN

# *Selling Out*

*"We were all getting along, but it wasn't the happiest of moments for anybody. Jerry felt a need to consolidate what he was doing; he was concerned about the future and about getting enough money so that he didn't have to worry. Nesuhi, I think, just wanted to get out and do something else. I didn't want to sell the company—the company was my idea, it was my brainchild, and we were doing well. I saw no reason to think that disaster was imminent. However, they were so insistent on selling. I really didn't have an option."*

—Ahmet Ertegun

## 1

The overwhelming sense of regret Ahmet had experienced after losing Ray Charles paled in comparison to how he felt about letting his older brother and Jerry Wexler persuade him to sell Atlantic Records in October 1967 for a sum Wexler would later accurately describe as "something of a joke." In truth, Ahmet never really opposed the deal, a position that then made eminent sense.

Although Atlantic placed an unheard-of eighteen records in the Billboard Hot 100 in June 1967, with Jerry Wexler's landmark production of Aretha Franklin's "Respect" at number one and "Groovin' " by the Young Rascals in the second slot, the writing was clearly on the wall for independent record labels. In Chicago, Vee-Jay had gone bankrupt and would soon be forced to auction off five thousand priceless masters. In a steep decline as the market for the blues disappeared, Chess Records would in a year's time be sold for roughly a third of

Atlantic's purchase price to a California conglomerate that eventually destroyed the label.

Throughout the record business, there was also a good deal of fear that the FCC intended to reopen the secret payola hearings it had held in Los Angeles in June 1966. Despite the great run of success Atlantic had enjoyed by distributing hits by Stax-Volt artists like Otis Redding, Sam and Dave, Rufus and Carla Thomas, and Booker T. and the MG's, a new label had begun giving Ahmet fits in the market that his company had dominated for the past two decades.

As Ahmet would later say, "What the industry generally called 'The Atlantic Sound' was eventually superseded by the Motown Sound, which was fabulous. It got me right away and I didn't know how to reproduce it and it scared the shit out of me. We didn't understand how to write it, we didn't understand how to play it, we didn't understand how to sing it. It was newer and hipper than what we were doing and it got to the public in a very heavy way and became pop music."

Atlantic's predicament was further complicated by the fact that most of the black artists who were selling big on the label had been signed by Stax-Volt. Originally formed as Satellite Records by Jim Stewart, who was then joined by his sister Estelle Axton, the label had made a distribution deal with Atlantic in 1965. After Ahmet and Wexler signed Sam and Dave, they put them on Stax and allowed Stewart to record them in Memphis. Wexler and Stewart soon became so close that whenever Stewart came to New York, he would stay in Wexler's house on Long Island.

Having never read the contract they had both signed, what neither man knew was that attorney Paul Marshall had specified that Atlantic would own all of the Stax masters. As guitarist Steve Cropper would later say, "It was a terrible deal—Atlantic really used us. But we needed them badly, so we used them as well. We needed them because it's very hard for an independent to be heard anywhere outside of its own territory." While the deal proved incredibly favorable for Atlantic, yet another clause in the contract allowed Stax to end the agreement if Atlantic was ever sold, thereby diminishing Atlantic's potential value if it ever changed hands.

Along with Wexler and Nesuhi, Ahmet had already cleared the decks for a possible sale by buying out the company's other two stockholders. At Wexler's urging, Miriam Bienstock had been paid $600,000 for her 13 percent share of the label. As she would later say, "I didn't want them to sell the company but that was why I had to go. There was no great regret on my part when I left and I think Jerry was happy because now there was no obstacle in his path."

Between what he had been paid over the past twenty years and the buyout for his 50 percent share of the label, Dr. Vahdi Sabit received "between two or three million dollars from the company" for his initial $10,000 investment. Giving up his dentistry practice, Sabit, in Ahmet's words, "then moved to the south of France and gambled. He went to the casino every night and after about fifteen years, he lost it all and went back to Turkey. I didn't want Atlantic partners who were destitute so I put him and his wife on salary and for the rest of their lives they got $24,000 a year."

Now the majority partner at Atlantic, Ahmet had blocked the sale of the label to ABC Records for $4 million because of the company's demand that the partners indemnify it against potential lawsuits. In Paul Marshall's words, "I represented Atlantic when ABC was trying to buy them and Jerry was very upset with me because after having negotiated for three months and finding out that ABC was asking for things I would never advise my client to do, I really fought it. Jerry was furious with me because he really wanted that. He wanted the security."

In Wexler's words, "I had this feeling that a puff of wind could come along and blow us all away, instantly. All you had to do was make a succession of flop records, and you get blown away. The rewards were enormous—but so were the risks. [Atlantic was] like a little family corner store that used to be just plugging along with everybody very happy—it couldn't stay that way. It was either grow or disappear. And who's to predict? Everybody else disappeared."

Hitting his full stride as a producer, Wexler had decamped to Memphis and then Muscle Shoals, Alabama, where he began generating big hits with Wilson Pickett and Aretha Franklin that earned him the Record Executive of the Year award in 1968. Doing the brunt of the in-house studio work at Atlantic as Ahmet spent more time in Los Angeles pursuing white acts like Buffalo Springfield, Wexler had become so vital to the label's success that Ahmet could no longer withstand his partner's desire to cash out by selling the company to the highest bidder.

In Ahmet's words, "Wexler was sure that eventually our luck would run out. As he put it, if our luck ran out, we'd be back in the tenements somewhere so he figured, 'Let's get something so we know we're safe for the rest of our lives, right? Who cares, right? We had a good time. Made some terrific records, right? This company wants to buy it? That's it.' "

For far more personal reasons, Nesuhi was also willing to go along with the plan. As Mica would later say, "In the Eastern hierarchy, the elder son is the leader. For Nesuhi, it was very hard to accept that Ahmet was that person at Atlantic. He always tried to be on an equal basis with him but it didn't work. I think partly because of the complex of being with Ahmet, Nesuhi wanted to sell."

Although Ahmet, in his words, "could have put up the money to buy them out and I thought about that, I would then have had to run the company by myself and I wasn't ready to do all the work they were doing. It was like buying out the people who were responsible for a lot of the good things that were happening. If I had bought them out, then I would have had to say, 'Okay, you have to work for me for another two years.' They would show up and not do anything. So that was why I agreed to sell. I wanted to stay with them and for them to stay with me. They were so insistent that I gave in."

At Atlantic, the groundwork was now in place for a deal that would come to be regarded as one of the worst financial decisions in the history of the record business. A company that would eventually be valued at between $2 to $4 billion was about to be purchased for about as much money as it had in the bank.

## 2

About six months after Alan J. Hirschfield had left his position as an investment banker at Allen & Company to put together the acquisition of Warner Brothers by Seven Arts Productions for $32 million, he was contacted by his friend Tommy Kempner, a partner at Loeb, Rhoades "whose wife was Nan Kempner, a very prominent socialite, who was a good friend of Mica Ertegun." Having become the chief financial officer of the newly merged company, Hirschfield was also overseeing music operations at Warner Bros. and Reprise Records on the corporate level and so Kempner arranged for him "to meet Ahmet Ertegun and Jerry Wexler and that was how it all started."

Right from the start, the partners at Atlantic made it plain to Hirschfield they were "very anxious to sell" the label for a variety of reasons that included the looming payola scandal "mainly regarding the black acts," the future profitability of performers like Aretha Franklin, Otis Redding, Wilson Pickett, Sam and Dave, and Booker T. and the MG's, and their concern "the white acts they had that were then bubbling under would never replace those revenues."

Unlike Ahmet, Clive Davis, the president of Columbia Records, had attended the Monterey Pop Festival in May 1967. Having already outbid Ahmet for the seminal San Francisco band Moby Grape, who never hit it big, Davis had also signed Blood, Sweat & Tears, the Electric Flag, and Big Brother and the Holding Company, featuring Janis Joplin, to his label. For its share of the burgeoning white psychedelic rock market, Atlantic had to rely on Buffalo Springfield, Iron Butterfly, the Vanilla Fudge, and an English blues trio called Cream, who had yet to make it in America.

Because Ahmet and Wexler seemed eager to do a deal, in Hirschfield's words, "It was not a long negotiation. One of their problems was that they had about $6 million in cash in a lot of places that was company money. Some of it was in banks. Some of it was in cash in various and sundry places. It was all on the books but the problem was justifying where it had come from as well as how they were using it which would have been even more difficult because of what was in their files." The Atlantic files, which Hirschfield saw, "had every disc jockey in the United States' shoe size, hat size, preference in women, and drugs of choice. It was a very dirty business and the black side was particularly dirty and I think it is accurate to say that a lot of the cash was being used to pay disc jockeys."

Precisely where all the money had come from was another matter. As Hirschfield would later say, "Some of it could have come from cutouts [records sold at discount], or returns. Some could have come from record stores in direct payments that they turned to cash and didn't report to the artists or the government. Those would have been the most likely sources."

Because Atlantic was a private company, the partners had for years also "been paying themselves big salaries and charging everything they could to the business. Ahmet always lived off the business. So what happened was, we gave them twelve million up front, six of which was their own cash. We kind of laundered the money for them, which was a big inducement because now it was clean. So if they hadn't accounted for it to the IRS or the artists, it now got paid to them as a capital gain on which the tax rate was then around 25 percent rather than 60 percent on personal income. Which was perfectly legitimate but a great way to wash it." Hirschfield also offered the partners 66,000 shares of Warner-Seven Arts stock worth $3.5 million, a $2.5 million note, and a share of the profits in the merged venture that could amount to as much as another $4 million over the next three years.

To bring about the merger between Seven Arts and Warner Bros., Hirschfield had made a deal with Frank Sinatra, who owned one third of Reprise Records, and his lawyer Mickey Rudin. Sinatra had reduced his interest to 20 percent of the label in return for $3.2 million in cash and the guarantee that if Hirschfield acquired other music companies, the singer would receive one fifth of the purchase price as well. While Hirschfield kept his associates at Warner-Seven Arts apprised of his negotiations with the partners at Atlantic, Sinatra's lawyer Mickey Rudin was the one "who loved the deal. Frank didn't particularly understand it because he hadn't heard of anybody on the label. His world was Dean Martin and Sammy Davis and Petula Clark and Trini Lopez."

When Hirschfield finally reached "the point of deal or no deal, when even Jerry was nervous," he reached out to Sinatra for help. "I said, 'Francis, listen, we're on the verge of closing this deal but I've got some nervous sellers. One of them, Ahmet, is skeptical.' Ahmet could have cared less who Frank was. But Wexler would get tears in his eyes when he talked about Frank. He was his idol."

Hirschfield then asked Sinatra if he would host a cocktail party for the principals as well as their attorneys and accountants at the singer's apartment. "I explained to him who their acts were and who Aretha was and I said, 'There's this guy, Jerry Wexler,' who Frank had heard of as a great producer. I said, 'He's going to pee in his pants if you just give him a hug. Trust me. This is going to make you very rich.'"

After everyone had assembled in Sinatra's apartment, where "there was a great spread and Frank couldn't have been more gracious and welcoming," Sinatra went over to Wexler "and literally put his arm around him and said, 'Jerry, I hear you got this great kid, Aretha Franklin. I think she's great. Can I ask you a question?' Jerry could barely talk by that point. 'Anything, Frank. Anything.' He said, 'Do you think she'd do a duet with me?' At that point, I thought we were going to have to change Jerry's underwear. I looked at Frank and I couldn't believe what was coming out of his mouth and at that point I knew we were going to sign a deal within days."

Sinatra also charmed Ahmet and Nesuhi, with whom he talked about jazz and, as Hirschfield recalled, "That was how it happened. I remember it like yesterday. I got a hold of Frank and said, 'I knew you were good but I didn't know you were that good.' I gave him a big hug and the rest was history." Less than two years later when Warner-Seven Arts was acquired by Steve Ross and Kinney National, Sinatra was paid $25 million for his 20 percent share of the company.

The year after Warner-Seven Arts acquired Atlantic Records for about $17.5 million (the modern-day equivalent of around $115 million), "the earnings doubled and the year after that, the earnings doubled again." While, in Hirschfield's words, "Jerry and Nesuhi were pretty happy" about the deal, "Ahmet never got over that he had sold the company too soon and I think he blamed me for it for years. Quite frankly, I think they didn't see what was happening as well as people like Clive Davis and Joe Smith and Mo Ostin and they sold themselves short. I think it was the confluence of the scandals and the problems they were having with the black acts but they sold for about as much money as they had. In net-out, it basically cost us nothing."

Telling a completely different version of his meeting with Sinatra in his autobiography, Wexler admitted that his never-ending anxiety about money was a major factor in bringing about the sale of Atlantic. After receiving his share of the purchase price, Wexler happily phoned an old friend from Washington Heights to inform him that Bennett Avenue "has its first millionaire." Conceding the label had been sold for far less than it was worth and that if the partners had waited a year, they could have asked for twice as much, Wexler added, "I have no regrets. The sale meant comfort and security for the rest of my life."

Sadly for Wexler, this did not turn out to be true. As he would say forty years later, "My end of the buyout was $4 million. A million of that went to taxes. So I had $3 million. I divorced my first wife. Half of it went to her plus a couple of houses. How the hell did I exist thereafter? Ahmet stayed the course and was probably worth more than a hundred million by being there when all the good stuff came down. The dollar options. The Time Warner deal and AOL and this and that. Just by staying there."

The year after the partners sold to Warner-Seven Arts, Atlantic grossed $45 million. Ahmet and Wexler offered the new owners $40 million to buy their label back only to be turned down. Although Ahmet and Jerry Wexler were still running the store at Atlantic, they no longer owned it. And while Ahmet would thrive in the corporate world that was now the order of the day in the record business, the same could not be said for the man who had pushed hardest for the sale of Atlantic in the first place.

FOURTEEN

# Helplessly Hoping

*"Jerry Wexler never liked Crosby, Stills & Nash because they wanted so much freaking artistic autonomy. While we were arguing about this, Wilson Pickett walks in the room and comes up to Jerry and says, 'Jerry,' and he goes, 'Wham!' And he puts a pistol on the table. He says, 'If that motherfucker Tom Dowd walks into where I'm recording, I'm going to shoot him. And if you walk in, I'm going to shoot you.' 'Oh,' Jerry said. 'That's okay, Wilson.' Then he walked out. So I said, 'You want to argue about artistic autonomy?'"*

—Ahmet Ertegun

## 1

In the spring of 1968, Stephen Stills, who was then keeping company with Judy Collins, for whom he had already written "Suite: Judy Blue Eyes," accompanied the folksinger to a recording session in Greenwich Village. When she left the studio to have dinner, Stills told the engineer, "Here's a hundred bucks. Will you just keep rolling? I've got these songs to put down." Thirty-four years later, three ten-inch boxes marked "Steve Stills" containing the original quarter-inch tapes that had been rescued from a Dumpster in the studio's parking lot found their way into Graham Nash's hands.

In Nash's words, "It was nineteen songs Stephen had written between the end of the Springfield in May 1968 and the beginning of Crosby, Stills & Nash in August. Stephen tunes up and goes, 'Helplessly Hoping.' He comes to the end. 'Change Partners.' Comes to the end, retunes, and starts 'Suite: Judy Blue Eyes,' which had never been put together and was still in three pieces. He did nineteen brilliant pieces of music that he'd written in four fucking months. That's how focused and creative he was at that point in his life. He had the music. In spades."

Intent on pursuing rock stardom despite the breakup of the Springfield, the band Stills formed with David Crosby and Graham Nash, two seasoned music business veterans who had also left their original groups for different reasons, soon attained the kind of rarefied status only great Hollywood movie stars had known. At a time when the postwar baby boom generation was coming of age and the counterculture was in full bloom, Crosby, Stills & Nash came to represent the social and political concerns their adoring fans held most dear. Their debut album would eventually sell more than three million copies.

A working-class boy from Blackpool, England, Graham Nash grew up in Manchester, where in 1963 he and his schoolmate Allan Clarke formed the Hollies. Named after Buddy Holly, the group had a series of harmony-driven pop hits in the United States. Nash had already begun looking to expand his musical horizons when he met the man who became his best friend and lifelong musical partner.

Unlike Nash, David Van Cortlandt Crosby was a child of privilege who could trace his family lineage back to a surgeon who had served on George Washington's staff during the Revolutionary War. His father, Floyd Crosby, was a brilliant cinematographer who won an Academy Award in 1931 for his work with documentary filmmaker Robert Flaherty on *Tabu* and later shot *High Noon*, Fred Zinnemann's 1952 multiple Academy Award-winning western drama starring Gary Cooper.

After graduating from the exclusive Cate School in Carpinteria, California, David Crosby dropped out of college to pursue a career in music and became a founding member of the Byrds with Jim McGuinn, Chris Hillman, and Gene Clark. The group had a number one hit in 1965 with its cover version of Bob Dylan's "Mr. Tambourine Man." Crosby then cowrote "Eight Miles High" with Clark and McGuinn.

At the Monterey Pop Festival in May 1967, Crosby angered McGuinn and Hillman by talking about politics between songs during the group's set and then obliging his good friend Stills by taking Neil Young's place in Buffalo Springfield when they performed. After

Crosby clashed with McGuinn and Hillman during a subsequent recording session, they dismissed him from the band.

A year later, Crosby and Stills sang with Nash for the first time at the singer Cass Elliot's house in Los Angeles. As Nash would later say, "We all knew. There was no fucking question. David and Stephen and I would sing almost that whole first album with one acoustic guitar and kill people. It was obvious that this was something really new and fresh and unheard of before." The producer Paul Rothchild then cut a two-song demo with the trio that he played for Ahmet. "In the middle of the first song," Rothchild recalled, "Ahmet takes out the checkbook and says, 'Fill in the number. I don't care—whatever it is doesn't matter.' "

While Stills would later say all three musicians "were morally committed to Ahmet from the start" and that he "was really like the Mother Superior of this group," the trio was not yet ready to sign a recording contract. Nonetheless, when Stills told Ahmet he wanted to go with Crosby to visit Nash in England so they could rehearse together but did not have the money to make the trip, Ahmet, in Nash's words, "reached in his desk and gave him two thousand dollars."

As neither the group nor Stills had a manager, Ahmet instructed Stills to contact Robert Stigwood while he was in London. The Australian-born rock impresario, who had begun his show business career as a theatrical agent, was then running his own label, RSO Records, while also managing Cream, a band that had broken big for Ahmet in America after recording the album *Disraeli Gears* in four days in May 1967 at Atlantic in New York. Two practical jokers who shared an affinity for the high life, Ahmet and Stigwood soon became close friends as well as business partners.

In Stigwood's words, "Ahmet was giving me Stephen Stills to manage. Stills flew in from New York and came to my office in Brook Street and I said, 'Nice to meet you. Let's have dinner or something.' And he said, 'On the way here, I saw a Rolls-Royce in the window of a car shop and I liked it. Can you have it delivered for me tomorrow?' I said, 'Well, I think we should talk about whether we're working together first.' He said, 'We've decided on you. Ahmet said Stiggy would be good.' I said, 'That's all well and good. But I'm not that good.' I already had enough to contend with. One visit to my office and that was it."

After Crosby, Stills & Nash returned from London where they had played a tape of their music for George Harrison with a view to being signed by Apple only to have him turn them down, they went looking for a manager before seeking a record contract. As a band, their situation was complicated by the fact that although Crosby was no longer in the Byrds, the group itself was still under contract to Columbia. As a member of the Hollies, Nash was signed to Epic, a label distributed in America by Columbia. Stills, who was contractually bound to Atlantic, had already gone to Ahmet for money but apparently felt no obligation to return the favor by bringing him the band. Instead, he urged his band mates to allow David Geffen and his partner Elliot Roberts, who then managed Neil Young and Joni Mitchell, to represent them. Although Crosby said he never thought Geffen "was that nice a guy, and I didn't trust him all the time," he acceded to Stills's wishes "because we were in the shark pool and we needed a *shark*."

Born in the Borough Park section of Brooklyn on February 21, 1943, David Geffen was seventeen years old when his father, a self-described Jewish intellectual who held a variety of jobs and became a Christian Scientist, died in Kings County Hospital. His mother, a Russian immigrant who had worked as a seamstress during the Depression, ran a bra and corset shop in Brooklyn and called her younger son "King David."

A starstruck kid who religiously went to neighborhood movie theaters and imagined himself onstage accepting an Academy Award while sitting in Radio City Music Hall, Geffen was a teenager when he read a biography of Louis B. Mayer. The storied head of MGM then became his idol. After graduating from New Utrecht High School, Geffen joined his older brother in Los Angeles. He then dropped out of Santa Monica City College, Brooklyn College, and the University of Texas before going to work as an usher at CBS Television City only to be fired for swinging at a man who cheered Art Linkletter's announcement that he was going to do his show on the day John F. Kennedy was assassinated in Dallas, Texas.

Determined to make a career in show business, Geffen passed himself off as a UCLA theater arts graduate and was hired to work in the mailroom of the William Morris Agency in New York. In a story that would become part of his show business legend, Geffen intercepted a letter from the university so his older brother could then write one attesting his résumé was accurate. In the mailroom, Geffen met his future partner Elliot Roberts, born Elliot Rabinowitz in the Bronx, and showed him how he had learned "the rudiments of deal making by studying memos and opening the mail."

Cutting corners and pulling moves that astonished even the most ambitious of his contemporaries, Geffen quickly rose through the ranks at William Morris and became a music agent, representing the Youngbloods and signing the Association. While managing the career of singer-songwriter Laura Nyro, he formed a close personal relationship with Clive Davis of Columbia, who became his first mentor in the record business. After Geffen played the Crosby, Stills and Nash demos for Davis, he assured Davis he would bring him the band as soon as he persuaded Atlantic to release Stills from his contract.

Not knowing whom else to contact at the label, Geffen made an appointment to see Jerry Wexler in his office at 1841 Broadway. Making his pitch, Geffen explained that since Buffalo Springfield had broken up, he was really not asking all that much by requesting Stills's release. While Wexler had never been a fan of the band's music and had little use for what he liked to call the long-haired "rockoids" of whom Ahmet was so fond, he liked agents even less. Exploding into one of his characteristic rages, Wexler barked, "Get the fuck outta here!" Picking up the much smaller Geffen, Wexler threw him out of his office. When Geffen returned to his Central Park apartment, where Stills was eagerly waiting to hear what had happened at Atlantic, Geffen told him, "My God, they're animals over there. We've got to get you out of there."

The next day, Wexler called Geffen to apologize for what he had done. Explaining he really had no right to be talking to him about this matter because Stills was Ahmet's artist, Wexler arranged for Geffen to meet with Ahmet. Having already invested money in the band, Ahmet should have been infuriated by Stills's decision to let Geffen go behind his back to try to sign them to another label. Far too skilled a diplomat to ever let his feelings interfere with what he already saw as a hugely profitable deal for Atlantic, Ahmet instead took a completely different tack.

In Geffen's words, their first meeting was "love at first sight . . . After an hour, he had me so completely charmed that there was nothing I wouldn't have done for him . . . Our relationship began with him courting me. It was a seduction. He was a genius at it and I went for it hook, line, and sinker. This guy was treating me like I was the most important person in the world to him at that moment. I just thought he was the greatest thing since chocolate chip cookies."

After Ahmet had convinced Geffen "he was the better person for CS&N," the manager hurried down to Black Rock, the CBS building on the corner of Sixth Avenue and 52nd Street, where he told Clive Davis he had changed his mind and asked him to release Crosby and Nash from their contracts. Upset that Geffen had reneged on his promise to bring him the group, Davis refused to let them go. In Geffen's words, "Clive said, 'Absolutely no. We'll have to work out some kind of compromise. For instance, I'll take the first record, and they can have the subsequent records.' I told Ahmet what Clive had proposed. Ahmet said, 'Listen, I wouldn't guarantee that these guys will be together to finish even a first record. Tell Clive I'll take the first record, and then he can have all the rest.' "

Even if Ahmet had not already wanted to sign Crosby, Stills & Nash, he now had yet another incentive to pursue the deal. As Bob Rolontz, the longtime head of publicity at Atlantic, would later say, "Ahmet knew how to play Clive. When he got an act that wasn't quite right, he would spread the word that it was a great band and Clive would sign them for big money." Adding fuel to the fire, the two men had by then already gone head to head for more than one act.

After Moby Grape had told Ahmet they would sign with Atlantic because he had promised to work closely with them on their album, one of the members of the group called to tell him that because Davis had offered them twice as much money, the band had signed with him instead. They had however inserted a clause into their contract that would permit Ahmet to come into the studio and work with them as much as he liked.

Knowing he had lost the band to Davis, Ahmet said he was very sorry to hear the news because he had intended to put out three singles at once when the album was released, something no record company had ever done before. A few months later, Ahmet was delighted to read in *Billboard* that the new Moby Grape album was coming out with three singles. As he would later say, "They made them do it. Which was one of the reasons that the record didn't make it."

At the Beverly Hills Hotel in Los Angeles, where the two record business moguls often found themselves watching one another as they did business from their respective poolside cabanas, Davis was talking to violinist David LaFlamme and two other members of the San Francisco band It's a Beautiful Day whom he had just auditioned. As Ahmet walked by, he said, "Look, I don't know who you are, but you are talking to the best in the business. You can't do any better than to entrust your musical lives to him." In his autobiography, Davis wrote, "The group was impressed and I was more than touched by this tribute." That Ahmet had no interest in the band and wanted Davis to sign them seems never to have occurred to him, either at the Beverly Hills Hotel pool or when he wrote his book.

In 1972 when Ahmet became convinced that Delaney Bramlett's drug problems would prevent Delaney & Bonnie from ever achieving widespread commercial success, he sold them to Davis at Columbia for $600,000. Jerry Wexler would later say earning this much money from an act without producing an album was even more creative than making records. The Delaney & Bonnie album on Columbia went nowhere.

Ahmet was now competing with Clive Davis not only for Crosby, Stills & Nash but David Geffen as well. Able to size up people in an instant and use that knowledge to his own advantage, Ahmet had immediately understood that Geffen's music business know-how, immense ambition, and deep-seated need for wealth and social prestige would make him an invaluable protégé. As Bob Rolontz would later say, "Ahmet stole Geffen away from Clive Davis."

Realizing Geffen had already decided to sign Crosby, Stills and Nash to Atlantic, Davis told him that in return for releasing Crosby and Nash from Columbia, he wanted Poco, a new band Atlantic had signed formed by Richie Furay of the Springfield and Jim Messina, the studio engineer who had replaced Bruce Palmer on bass. In itself, this demand was unprecedented in the record business. When Geffen relayed Davis's offer, Ahmet said, "That's pretty heavy," and turned him down. After Geffen pleaded with him by saying, "Ahmet, you must do this for me," he agreed to the deal.

While Stephen Stills would later claim he said, "Ahmet, you gotta think like you're a baseball team owner. We're going to trade Richie Furay for Graham Nash," the truth of the matter was that all on his own, Ahmet had won this one going away. In one fell swoop, he had swapped a band that would never make it as big for Crosby, Stills & Nash while also taking David Geffen away from Clive Davis. And while Geffen's idol as a teenager had been Louis B. Mayer, he had just unwittingly cast himself as Irving Thalberg, Mayer's second-in-command.

# 2

Marijuana smoke filled the air as Ahmet and Jerry Wexler walked into Wally Heider's Studio on Cahuenga Boulevard in Los Angeles where Crosby, Stills, and Nash had sometimes been doing as many as thirty takes of a song to get the vocals right while recording their debut album for Atlantic. As Phil Spector trailed in behind the partners, Stephen Stills immediately stopped what he was doing to greet Ahmet with a bear hug. "Yessir, we're working hard," David Crosby said. "At two bucks a minute, we can't afford to socialize. We may even bring this one in on time, Ahmet. That'll improve our reputation in the business a lot, right? 'Specially Stills."

As Stills guffawed, Ahmet affectionately ruffled the musician's hair. Making a joke of his own, Wexler suggested the band call their album *Music from Big Ego*. When the idea was flatly rejected, Wexler mumbled, "Guess they don't have the distance to appreciate it." After meeting Ahmet for the first time in the studio, Graham Nash would later say, "This guy could make wallpaper turn around and look at him. Every time he walked into a room, it didn't matter who else was there. Elvis could have been there and everyone would have been looking at Ahmet. It was very obvious when he walked into the room that this was a mighty, mighty presence."

After Ahmet, Wexler, and Spector left that night, the band spent nine hours cutting Crosby's "Long Time Coming." Everyone then went home except for Stills, who stayed behind until dawn working on a new arrangement that helped Crosby find himself as a lead vocalist. "At that point in his life," Nash recalled, "Stephen was an incredibly focused person. Without question, he was the leader of this band and there was a reason we called him 'Captain Many Hands.' He played everything on that first album except drums and the guitar I played on 'Lady of the Island' and the guitar Crosby played on 'Guinevere.' "

In the words of Ellen Sander, a rock critic who was present during many of those sessions, "Everybody is driven in a different way but with Stephen, it was really kind of obvious. He couldn't keep his hands off the board and he was driving the engineer crazy. He was just so consummately involved that he was with every single note every single minute. Stephen once said to me he realized what Buffalo Springfield had thrown away on the verge of what would have been an incredible run and he didn't want to see this venture go amiss."

While there had been nothing but sweetness and light between the band and the partners at Atlantic in the studio, a set-to that occurred before the album was released should have served as an early warning that the balance of power in the record business had shifted. Because Crosby, Stills, and Nash viewed themselves as artists with a capital "A," they would never be as easy to control as the acts with which the label had long since become accustomed to dealing.

"Did you know that Tommy Dowd remixed our first record?" Nash would later say. "It's not known and you know why? Because Crosby said, 'If you ever touch our fucking music again, I will cut off your arms.' I'm sure Ahmet must have had him do it but the point was— 'Don't fuck with our music without us.' " When David Geffen finally played the completed album for Ahmet in New York, he excitedly exclaimed, "They're going to be huge! They're going to be huge!" but then added, "They're not going to be as big as the Association."

After the Crosby, Stills & Nash album had been released to great critical acclaim and massive sales, the band was scheduled to perform in Chicago with Joni Mitchell opening for them and then at the Woodstock Arts and Music Festival. A protracted discussion soon began about finding another musician to join them onstage. "Absolutely, there was a conversation," Nash recalled. "We recognized Stephen needed some kind of impetus to push him into a different realm. He could play great lead guitar on his own. But it was obvious that when he was competitive with someone, it went to a higher level. We considered Stevie Winwood. And Jimi Hendrix. I'm not kidding. Now, that would have been a band."

As it turned out, neither Winwood, Hendrix, nor Mark Naftalin, the keyboard player in the Paul Butterfield Blues Band, was interested. David Geffen, Elliot Roberts, and Stills were having dinner with Ahmet in his Manhattan town house one night when he put on some old Buffalo Springfield albums and said, "We ought to add Neil to CSN. There's something about Neil Young that goes with this." Stills responded by saying, "But, Ahmet, he's already quit on me twice. What do you think's gonna happen this time?"

Nonetheless, Ahmet's idea made eminent sense to all concerned and when Roberts told Stills he would have to make the offer to Young himself, he did so. In Nash's words, "Neil and Stephen's relationship was pretty fiery at that point. They loved and hated each other. And they still do, to this day." In return for joining his former Buffalo Springfield band mate, Young wanted his name on the group as well as an equal share of the money. After his request was granted, the band began touring as Crosby, Stills, Nash & Young and their "concert price skyrocketed."

Before Atlantic issued *Déjà Vu,* the group's second album, a meeting concerning the cover took place in Ahmet's bungalow at the Beverly Hills Hotel. Inspired by Stills's great love for Civil War tintypes "and family journals of the 1860's," art director Gary Burden presented the partners with a cover featuring gold foil stamped lettering on "beautiful paper that was almost leather in feel and had a great bumped-up texture" made by "a family-operated paper mill in Georgia." The band loved it. To that point in time, album covers had cost about nineteen cents apiece to manufacture. The one Burden presented would have cost sixty-nine cents.

Emerging from the bathroom of the bungalow with his dark black hair bristling in every direction from his sleeveless undershirt, Jerry Wexler snapped, "Fucking artist appeasement! We could put it out in a brown paper bag and people would still buy it!" In the end, the band got its way and the cover was approved. Released in March 1970, *Déjà Vu* topped the charts and generated three hit singles.

On May 15, 1970, Ahmet was with the group at the Record Plant in Los Angeles when they recorded "Ohio," a song Neil Young had written after reading a *Life* magazine article about the killing of four Kent State students during an on-campus protest eleven days earlier. After taking the masters with him to New York, Ahmet released the song eight days later. Backed with Stills's "Find the Cost of Freedom," the record became a smash hit that overtook Nash's "Teach Your Children" on the charts.

As their fame mounted, the group became increasingly difficult to handle. When they played the Fillmore East in New York City in the spring of 1970, the playwright John Ford Noonan, then a member of the stage crew, called them "The Supremes." To get the group to do an encore for their fans, promoter Bill Graham had to shove hundred-dollar bills under their dressing room door. Bidding farewell to the audience by saying he would see them in the street, Stills would then walk each night to his waiting limo so he could be driven back to his hotel.

During their hugely successful 1970 summer tour, Stills so angered Neil Young at one show by hogging the spotlight that Young walked off stage and would not return for an encore. When the singer Rita Coolidge left Stills to be with Nash, the band broke up. At this point, even Ahmet believed Crosby, Stills, Nash, and Young were finally done.

At dinner one night in New York with rock critic Ellen Sander and Elektra Records founder Jac Holzman, Ahmet sorrowfully shook his head and said, "That group is gone. The only way they'll get back together again is for the others to go to Stills and ask him to come back and they'd never do it, they're too proud and too hurt." When Holzman suggested Ahmet could get someone just as famous and talented to replace Stills, Ahmet asked who that might be. "Paul McCartney," Holzman replied. Without missing a beat, Ahmet said, "That's a tremendous idea. Tremendous!" Lowering his voice, he added, "I wonder how much Apple would give me for the other three."

Once cocaine became the drug of choice in the rock scene, Stephen Stills became the subject of as many negative stories as have ever been told about any performer in the history of the music business. After CSNY's live album *4 Way Street* appeared in April 1971, David Geffen fired Stills as a client. Stills then printed bumper stickers that read, "Who is David Geffen and why is he saying those terrible things about me?"

Beginning a series of melodramatic breakups and reunions worthy of a Spanish telenovela, the individual members of the group made their own successful solo albums, tried to record together again, and then scrapped that project as well. Maintaining his relationship with all four artists, Ahmet released Crosby's solo album *If I Could Remember My Name*, Crosby and Nash's successful debut effort, and Nash's first two solo albums, *Songs for Beginners* and *Wild Tales*.

Coming off stage one night during his 1973 "Tonight's the Night" English tour, a "really drunk" Neil Young told Elliot Roberts that the set had gone so well he was going out for an encore. "Neil," Roberts said, "do an encore to who? There's no one here but Ahmet." "Ahmet's here?" Young asked. After being told he was sitting out front with a row of people, Young said, "All right! That's who was applauding." Walking back out onstage, Young did a three-song encore for him.

In Nash's words, "CSN signed with Atlantic for six albums. A record a year for six years. We've only *just* done six albums. My point is that Ahmet kept all those fuckers away from us. All those lawyers who said, 'Hey, the contract says . . .' And Ahmet would always be the one who said, 'Hey, leave them alone. Whatever they do, we will take.' No record guy ever got along better with his artists."

Which was not to say there were not also problems along the way. David Geffen was at a John Lennon recording session in Los Angeles in 1974 when he received an urgent call from Crosby. Screaming on the line, Crosby began calling his manager a crook and a thief and a motherfucker. Demanding to know how Crosby dared speak to him like that, Geffen hung up and then called Crosby's business manager to say he had just gotten a horrible call from the musician. Laughing, the business manager explained that he had just done an audit on Atlantic Records only to learn Ahmet had charged all the trips on which he had invited Geffen to accompany him to Crosby and Nash's joint royalty account. Calling Ahmet, Geffen, now furious himself, demanded to know how he could have done such a thing. Laughing, Ahmet replied, "What's the problem? They found it? We'll pay it."

Ahmet's long-standing relationship with Stills ended a year later. Unable to get the musician into the studio to record with Young, Tom Dowd scolded Stills who then called Ahmet with his own version of what had transpired. Calling Dowd at home that night, Ahmet gave him hell only to have Dowd tell him he had no idea how out of control the sessions had become. The next day Ahmet walked into the studio at five P.M. Young came in and began working. In no condition to do the same, Stills straggled in later that night. The two men spoke. A week later, Stills was on Columbia.

Twenty-two years later, during the week of the 1997 Grammy Awards in Los Angeles, Crosby, Stills, and Nash, who then still owed Atlantic two albums, met with Ahmet and Val Azzoli, then the co-chairman and co-CEO of the label, at the Peninsula Hotel in Beverly Hills. Telling Ahmet they "loved him to death" and had "always respected him," the musicians began, in Nash's words, "complaining bitterly that nobody at Atlantic knew who we were, they had no respect for us, they were not working our stuff, and we wanted out of there."

Trying to pacify Crosby, Azzoli told the musician how much he loved having him on Atlantic and that he was family. "You fucking asshole!" Crosby replied. "I haven't been on Atlantic Records for eight fucking years! Ahmet, are you fucking listening to this? This is what I fucking meant!" In Nash's words, "That was the end of Atlantic with CSN. Ahmet let us go that day. That's who he was."

# 3

During the two-year period after Atlantic had been sold, Ahmet and Wexler continued to run the label as partners while setting off in distinctly different directions to pursue their own interests in a record business that was expanding more rapidly than ever. Heading south to studios in Memphis and Muscle Shoals, Wexler returned to his roots and worked continuously, producing a variety of black artists whose music he loved and understood as well as anyone who ever lived.

Determined not to get fooled again by what became known as the second British invasion, during the late 1960s, Ahmet zeroed in on London as the place where he could find and sign new talent that had not yet broken in America. Setting up shop in the luxurious seventh-floor suite in the Dorchester Hotel on Park Lane designed by Oliver Messel where he always felt at home, Ahmet soon became a regular in the Scotch of St. James, the city's hippest private club.

His initial connection to the second flowering of the English music scene was Chris Blackwell. Born in London, Blackwell was a dedicated rhythm and blues devotee who had grown up in privileged circumstances in Jamaica before returning to England to attend the exclusive Harrow School. As a teenager, he would regularly come to New York to buy 78 RPM singles for 43 cents and then take them back to Jamaica, where he sold them for as much as £100 apiece to "the sound system" guys who played music and sold liquor at island parties.

As Blackwell would later say, "The key thing was for me that if I came across an Atlantic record, I would pick it and if there was one I didn't like, I would doubt my own taste because I had so much respect for the label because of the music they put out. That was something I wanted to emulate with Island Records. Where the label itself actually helped the act because if the act was on the label then the act must be interesting."

Twenty-two years old when he founded Island in Jamaica in 1959, Blackwell first met Ahmet a year later in New York. As Blackwell was trying to persuade Miriam Bienstock to allow him to distribute Atlantic records in Jamaica, Ahmet "popped his head in" to say he had already made such an arrangement with Byron Lee, who led the Dragonaires and owned the Dynamic Sound recording studio. Four years later when Little Millie Small had a smash hit for Island in England with "My Boy Lollipop," Blackwell did a deal for her next record "for no advance with Atlantic instead of Columbia for a $50,000 advance, something I never made the mistake of doing again."

Once Ahmet began making regular visits to London, he and Blackwell started to spend time together "because we were kind of kindred spirits. He was basically my hero and sort of a father figure to me. A mentor in a way. Somebody I looked up to in every respect. He clearly loved the music, he loved the people, he was not just one-dimensional, he was an extraordinary person. I knew him quite a long time before I ever did any record deals with him and we had a social relationship whenever he came to London because Ahmet wanted to make Atlantic a rock label."

While Little Millie Small never did much business for Atlantic in America, Blackwell "thought the Spencer Davis Group would definitely succeed because they were trying to make American black music. But it wasn't that successful. Atlantic had 'Keep on Runnin',' which was the first big hit in England, and then I gave them the second one and they didn't do that well with that one either."

Along with Charlie Greene and Brian Stone, Ahmet was sitting in the Scotch of St. James one night when "this little kid with red hair who looked about fourteen years old" took the stage with his group. In Stone's words, "Stevie Winwood started playing and Ahmet jumped up and said, 'Oh my God. Who is that, man?' And I said, 'Ahmet, you'll never believe this. It's your group.' He said, 'That's the best news I ever heard in my life.' "

A year after seeing Winwood for the first time, Ahmet threw a party at the Scotch of St. James for Wilson Pickett, who had just performed at the Astoria Theatre in Finsbury Park. Ahmet was standing at the bar in the club with his back to the stage when he heard someone playing guitar who "sounded like B. B. King." As "there was no one in England who could play like that," Ahmet looked over at Pickett and said, "Wilson, your guitarist sure can play the blues." Pickett said, "My guitarist is having a drink at the bar."

Turning to the stage, Ahmet saw "this kid with an angelic face and his eyes closed, just playing, and I said, 'My God, who is that?' And that was Eric Clapton." According to Ahmet, Robert Stigwood, who was standing next to him, said, "You really think he's great?" Ahmet replied, "He's fabulous. We have to sign him up right away." In Ahmet's words, "So Stigwood got with him, and that is how Cream was formed." In truth, as Stigwood would later say, "I took over Eric when Cream was formed. Jack Bruce and Ginger Baker had been in the Graham Bond Organisation and then they wanted to form Cream and as I was already managing them, I was asked to manage the group."

Then twenty-one years old, Clapton had already attained cult status in England for his lead guitar work with the Yardbirds but was virtually unknown in America. Stigwood then signed Cream to his own label, RSO Records. While Ahmet would later claim he always knew Cream would make it in America, Stigwood would later say, "He wanted the Bee Gees but he actually wasn't so keen on Cream. I played him their demo at Polydor in London and he said, 'Oh, fabulous, fabulous. But not very commercial.' That's from the horse's mouth and I don't say this in any negative way. Part of Ahmet's charm was that he was a great storyteller but he could really turn many corners in his story telling. I made him take Cream because I gave him the Bee Gees. And that is the absolute truth."

The Bee Gees were three teenage brothers from Australia who sounded so much like the Beatles that radio stations in America thought their first hit, "New York Mining Disaster 1941," had been made by the Fab Four. When they came to America for the first time and were staying with Stigwood at the Plaza Hotel, Ahmet showed up at the hotel where he "pretended he was the porter and took their luggage downstairs. He carried their bags to the elevator. They knew who he was of course." Stigwood returned the favor in London when Ahmet gave a party at the Dorchester to celebrate his new acts. "Just coincidentally," Stigwood would later say, "they were all white acts. And he said to me, 'You know, we've sort of become an all-white label.' I got someone to call him pretending to be a journalist and say, 'You're having a party to celebrate your becoming a white label.' He hardly ever forgave me."

While flying together to Paris, Stigwood and Ahmet's good friend Earl McGrath managed to get their hands on Ahmet's passport "and put an indecent photograph over his face and he presented it to customs." On a business trip to Tokyo where the three men shared a suite, Ahmet and McGrath came into Stigwood's bedroom and threw a bucket of water on him. Stark naked, Stigwood ran across the lounge only to be greeted by a delegation of Japanese senior management recording executives who had come to say goodbye to him. "It was all, 'Good morning, Mister Stigwood. Good morning.' They didn't really bat an eye lid." And then there was the evening in Los Angeles when Ahmet told Stigwood he was giving a black-tie party for him. Dressed to the nines, Ahmet had his driver take them both to a parking lot where he had paid a collection of seedy derelicts to greet them.

While Stigwood had a well-earned reputation as one of the hardest bargainers in the business, he and Ahmet recognized one another as fellow empire builders and never let their egos get in the way when working together to build an act or sell an album in which they both had a sizable financial stake. To promote "I Feel Free," Cream's first single on Atco in America, Ahmet persuaded Stigwood to fly the band to New York to appear at Murray the K's 1967 Easter show at the RKO Theater on 58th Street. Also featuring The Who, whose next appearance in America was at the Monterey Pop Festival, the show was headlined on alternate nights by Wilson Pickett and Mitch Ryder and the Detroit Wheels.

On the day after the 1967 Easter Sunday Be-In in Central Park, Eric Clapton went to the Atlantic studios, where he met Ahmet and Nesuhi for the first time and cut "Lawdy Mama," a song he had first heard Buddy Guy and Junior Wells do on *Hoodoo Man Blues.* In May, Cream flew back into New York on a Thursday night to record their second album. Before they arrived, Ahmet told Tom Dowd the band had to leave the country on a seven o'clock flight on Sunday night because that was when their visas would expire. In four days with Dowd at the board and Felix Pappalardi producing, Cream transformed "Lawdy Mama" into "Strange Brew." With lyrics by the English poet Pete Brown, *Disraeli Gears* (an English roadie's mistaken pronunciation of the derailleur gears on a racing bicycle that Clapton seized upon for the album title) also featured "Tales of Brave Ulysses" as well as the song that became the album's monster hit, "Sunshine of Your Love."

Photographer Don Paulsen, who was present during those sessions, would later say he was "utterly amazed at the degree of input" Ahmet had "in terms of choice of song, tempo, arrangement" with "musicians, who clearly had so much talent but who were equally so genuinely looking to him for guidance." Having already decided Cream should be Clapton's band, Ahmet pushed for him rather than Jack Bruce to do most of the singing only to relent when it became apparent to him the bass player was in fact the real leader of the group.

Unable to get Cream airplay in the U.K., Stigwood subsidized the group for a year until they finally broke big on the West Coast after a week-long engagement at the Fillmore Auditorium in San Francisco, where they were forced to begin improvising so they could expand their song list to fill two sets a night. While flying together to London, Ahmet, in Stigwood's words, "dropped a nugget of information to me that Cream and the Bee Gees were 50 percent of his album income at that time."

Unlike the Bee Gees, who would continue working together throughout their lives, Cream soon began to implode. "Basically, they didn't like each other," Stigwood explained. "On their third tour of America, there were rows and fighting every night. Ginger was going to murder Jack. Jack was going to commit suicide. And Eric was dying and saying, 'Get me out of here. I hate the two of them.' "

After Cream released *Wheels of Fire,* a double album with one live disc and the other a new studio recording that was roundly slammed by critics, Stigwood realized he could no longer keep the group together. Fed up with the drudgery of being out on the road with three musicians who drove audiences wild onstage but could not stand to be in the same room together, Stigwood came up with the idea for the band to do a 1968 farewell tour of the United States followed by two final concerts at the Royal Albert Hall in London.

"Cream was breaking up and Ahmet wanted one more album and they said we hate one another and did not want to do it," Phil Spector would later tell *Rolling Stone* magazine founder Jann Wenner, "and Ahmet said, 'Oh no, man, you have to do one more for me. Jerry Wexler has cancer, and he's dyin' and he wants to hear one more album from you.' They go in and make the album and Ahmet says, 'Jerry Wexler isn't dyin', he's much better, he's improved.'"

During their three years together as a band, Cream sold fifteen million records for Atlantic in America and Ahmet began what became his lifelong friendship with Clapton. After Tom Dowd expressed concern about how much heroin and cocaine the guitarist was using during the recording of *Layla* with Derek and the Dominos in 1970, Ahmet flew to Miami to see him. Taking Clapton aside, Ahmet talked about Ray Charles and how painful it had been for him to see Charles get caught up in the world of hard drugs. Becoming so emotional he began to cry at one point, Ahmet did all he could to persuade Clapton to deal with his problems but the guitarist continued his descent into hard-core addiction.

By then, Clapton had already formed and walked away from another short-lived supergroup. Just nine weeks after Cream had played its final shows at the end of 1968, the guitarist began jamming in the basement of his home in Surrey with his good friend Steve Winwood, who was then at loose ends during what proved to be a temporary breakup of Traffic, and the two decided to form a band. After Winwood persuaded Clapton to let Ginger Baker join them, they added Family bassist and violin player Ric Grech to the lineup.

With Robert Stigwood and Chris Blackwell working together to smooth out the contractual hassles, the new group made its debut on June 7, 1969, at a massive free concert in London's Hyde Park. In Stigwood's words, "We were going to do this free concert in Hyde Park and I was operating on blind faith and that was how they acquired the name. You had to get a council license to appear in Hyde Park and so I applied for 'Blind Faith.' I made the name up for the concert and that was it."

Five weeks later, Blind Faith began touring America in support of an album that would sell half a million copies in a few months. On July 12, as the band was performing at a sold-out Madison Square Garden in New York, Ahmet sat down for an extraordinary dinner meeting in a private room at "21" with Steve Ross and Ted Ashley, the cofounder of the Ashley-Famous Talent Agency. Born Theodore Assofsky in Brooklyn, Ashley had suggested that Ross acquire the Warner Brothers-Seven Arts corporation for $400 million. The deal, which gave Ross full control of Atlantic Records, had been announced just three days earlier.

Ross, whose birth name was Steven Jay Rechnitz, was the son of Jewish immigrants who settled in Brooklyn. After marrying the daughter of a Manhattan funeral parlor owner, he became the head of his father-in-law's company and used a bank loan to start a successful rental car agency, which he then merged with Kinney Garage, a firm that owned and operated parking lots, to form Kinney National. The company went public in 1962 with a market value of $12.5 million, and Ross then began acquiring a variety of other companies. After he purchased the Ashley-Famous agency for $13 million in November 1967, Ross and Ashley set their sights on a major show business acquisition. Their successful bid for Warner Brothers-Seven Arts was based primarily on the earnings of the company's very profitable record labels, Warner-Reprise and Atlantic.

When Ahmet learned of the acquisition, he let it be known he would be leaving Atlantic as soon as his two-year management contract ran out. To prevent this from happening, Ashley set up the dinner at "21" where the three men spent six hours discussing Ahmet's future at the label. At 12:45 in the morning, Ahmet tried to show Ross how little he really knew about the record business by saying, "Look, I've got a new group, Blind Faith . . ."

"You mean the guys from the Old Cream and Stevie Winwood, and they just sold out Madison Square Garden without selling a record?" Ross replied. As Ross would later tell the story, Ahmet excitedly leaped to his feet, said, "Yeah, man, you got it!" and then agreed to stay on at Atlantic. While Ross liked Crosby, Stills, Nash & Young, he had no idea "who or what Joni Mitchell was" and had been given this vital bit of information the day before by a friend who was a Wall Street entertainment analyst.

For Ahmet, the fact that Ross had gone to the trouble to find out about Blind Faith and then tried to impress him with the knowledge was what poker players call "a tell." It was a sign Ross knew he could never replace Ahmet and would allow him to continue running Atlantic Records on his own terms. For Ahmet, the truly decisive moment came when Ross pleaded, "Give us a chance," and then assured Ahmet he would do everything in his power to keep him happy. Ross himself would later call it one of the luckiest days of his life. And so it was that three superstar musicians who made only one record and were soon so at odds with one another that they began traveling to gigs in separate limousines helped shape the future not only of Atlantic but the entire record business as well.

By October 1969, Blind Faith was history. That Steve Ross could never have handled the rock 'n' roll histrionics Ahmet had already learned to deal with on a daily basis was best illustrated by a story Ahmet loved to tell about what happened after the end of the band's first and only tour of America. To recover from the grueling ordeal of being out on the road with Blind Faith, Ginger Baker decided to spend a month in Jamaica. Robert Stigwood called Ahmet from London to say that Baker, who owned an Aston Martin in England, wanted to rent one on the island.

Since no one in Jamaica, in Ahmet's words, "particularly knew what an Aston Martin was," Ahmet told Stigwood even he could not help him. Nonetheless, Ahmet got in touch with Chris Blackwell, whose cousin arranged for a friend who owned a Ferrari to let Baker drive the car for a month, provided Ahmet would pay for any damages, which he agreed to do. A few nights later, Ahmet "got a call in the middle of the night from Ginger Baker who was ranting and raving, screaming down the phone at me . . . 'I don't want a fucking wop car!' "

Politely, Ahmet explained there were no other cars of this kind to rent in Jamaica but "he just kept yelling and screaming at me down the phone." Calling Stigwood in London, Ahmet said they might as well ship Baker his car from London. "So they put the car on the plane and sent it to Jamaica but somehow the shipment got lost and then we had to trace it. It landed in Atlanta instead of Jamaica and finally the car got to Jamaica two days before he was leaving. He was furious."

The first time Ahmet had ever met the "hotheaded" drummer, Baker had told him, "I'm a communist. You understand? You keep that in mind, and you'll understand a lot about the way I behave." When Ahmet next saw Baker, the musician apologized for his behavior in Jamaica. "Well, that's okay," Ahmet said. "I kept one thing in mind that you told me some time ago and I didn't get angry." When Baker asked what that was, Ahmet replied, "Remember you told me you were a communist? I just kept that in mind."

While this was the punch line Ahmet always used when he told the story, Jac Holzman would later say the car Baker had wanted in Jamaica was in fact a Jensen Interceptor and that when Sheldon Vogel, who handled the finances at Atlantic, brought Ahmet a check for $10,000 to cover its shipping costs to Jamaica, Ahmet said, "Sheldon, just because I asked for the check doesn't mean you should bring it to me." As Holzman would later say, "That's the real end of the story. He didn't want to give the money to Ginger at all."

## 4

Despite Ahmet's deep connection to the music scene in London, it was Jerry Wexler who signed the English band that went on to sell the most records for Atlantic. Wexler had first met "Little" Jimmy Page when Bert Berns brought the guitarist to New York to play on R&B sessions. In the fall of 1968, along with Tom Dowd and the brilliant arranger Arif Mardin, Wexler was producing Dusty Springfield's iconic *Dusty in Memphis* album when the English pop singer told him Page was forming a band in London known as the New Yardbirds.

While Wexler remembered Page had "played his ass off" while recording for Berns and also knew John Bonham, another member of the new group, was "a hell of a drummer," he had never heard of lead singer Robert Plant. Based solely on Dusty Springfield's recommendation, Wexler decided to pursue them. That both Clive Davis and Mo

Ostin were also trying to sign the band only served to increase Wexler's interest and he arranged to meet with their manager in New York.

Bringing with him from London the tapes of what would become the band's first album, Peter Grant sat down with Wexler in his office at Atlantic. A hulking giant of a man who stood well over six feet tall and weighed more than 250 pounds, Grant sported a fierce horseshoe mustache that along with his prodigious gut made him look like the villainous professional wrestler he had once been. Stealing a beat on the competition, Wexler offered Grant a $75,000 advance as well as a five-year recording contract that the manager quickly accepted.

The band's American lawyer then called Wexler to say he could have the world rights for another $35,000. Asking the lawyer to let him think about it, Wexler offered the English rights to Roland Rennie, the head of Polydor Records, for $20,000 only to have him pass. In what turned out to be one of the best deals in the history of the record business, Wexler bought the world rights for $35,000.

Much like Ahmet, who no longer had to worry about how much it would cost to sign a new act, Wexler made the deal because the money was not coming out of his pocket. By then, Jimmy Page, John Bonham, John Paul Jones, and Robert Plant had decided to call themselves Led Zeppelin, a name Page had come up with while trying to persuade guitarist Jeff Beck as well as The Who's bassist John Entwhistle and drummer Keith Moon to join him only to have Entwhistle say the aggregation might go down like a "lead zeppelin," a term he used to describe a bad show. Grant then suggested Page omit the "a" in "Lead" so "thick Americans" would not pronounce it "Leed."

On November 23, 1968, Atlantic issued a press release announcing that while "the exact terms of the deal are secret," the label had signed "the hot new English group, Led Zeppelin" to "one of the most substantial deals Atlantic has ever made." As the release also noted, "Top English and American rock musicians who have heard the tracks have called Led Zeppelin the next group to reach heights achieved by Cream and Hendrix."

Unbeknownst to Wexler, Chris Blackwell had already "shaken hands with Peter Grant on Zeppelin for $25,000 an album for the world excluding America and Canada." As Blackwell recalled, "It was a handshake deal but I was dealing with Peter Grant and so it wasn't a deal until it really was a deal. And to tell you the truth, I'm glad I didn't get them because it wouldn't have worked for us at Island. Too dark. I couldn't have dealt with it."

At a time in the record business when every manager personified the act they represented, Grant had already acquired a reputation as a fearsome figure who would stop at nothing to protect his artists. "I signed Led Zeppelin," Wexler would later say, "and then I had nothing to do with them. Absolutely nothing. Ahmet took over their care and cleaning. I don't think I could have tolerated them. I got along fine with Peter Grant. But I knew he was an animal."

To say that Ahmet and Peter Grant had virtually nothing in common except for Led Zeppelin would be a major understatement. Before forsaking his studies at the age of thirteen to become a sheet metal worker, Grant had attended the Ingram Road School in southeast London. As Phil Carson, who played bass with Dusty Springfield before becoming Atlantic's label manager in England and then the manager of Yes, recalled, "I went to St. Joseph's College which was not five miles from the Ingram Road School where Peter Grant went. His school was real working-class and the Kray brothers [notorious English criminals] had gone there. Peter Grant was like them although he never did get involved in any crime."

When Carson was eleven years old, he witnessed a fight between the St. Joseph's College rugby team and "the Ingram Road boys. The entire first fifteen showed up, two or three years older than the nine or ten Ingram Road boys, and they got fucking slaughtered. Grant was in the fight and they came fully armed with sawed-off billiard cues which was not exactly the Queensbury rules and they just beat the shit out of the St. Joseph's college fifteen. It was incredible."

After doing his national service, Grant became a doorman and bouncer at a coffee bar where pop sensations Cliff Richard, Adam Faith, and Tommy Steele got their start. At the suggestion of the Australian-born professional wrestler who co-owned the coffee bar, Grant began wrestling on television in England and then became a bit-part actor, stuntman, and body double in movies and television. Turning his attention to the music business, Grant quickly became the most physically imposing and dangerously explosive manager in rock. After Grant had taken the Yardbirds on their final tour of America, Jimmy Page chose him to manage Zeppelin.

Fifteen days before their first album was released, the band was already on tour in the United States, making their American debut in Denver on December 26, 1968. A smash hit, *Led Zeppelin* soon hit the Top Ten, where it remained for the next seventy-three weeks, eventually selling eight million copies in America. Hailed as the inventors of heavy metal music, Zeppelin played electric blues infused with elements of folk and Celtic music in a manner no one had ever heard before.

As Bill Curbishley, The Who's long-term manager who also guided the solo careers of Page and Robert Plant, would later say, "Having worked with all these musicians, the difference between The Who and Led Zeppelin was that The Who never gave a bad show. They were always either good or absolutely amazing. Whereas Zeppelin were either awful or absolutely brilliantly amazing. There was no in-between. It had a lot to do with whatever condition they were in when they went onstage. It was also a different dynamic. Zeppelin was really about sex and The Who was more about intellectual frustration and aggression."

Once Zeppelin hit it big in America, Ahmet made it his business to form a close relationship with both Peter Grant and Jimmy Page. In the words of Lisa Robinson, the rock journalist who toured with Zeppelin throughout the 1970s, "Even though Robert Plant was the singer, the talker, the charmer, and more extroverted, it was initially Jimmy Page's band—he put it together with the help of Peter Grant. Ahmet always knew where the power was and so his focus was always slightly more on Peter and Jimmy than Robert."

Confirming that "in the beginning, it was all Jimmy," Curbishley would later say, "Then gradually Plant established himself in terms of writing songs, helping with the melodies, and writing all the lyrics, and it became more of a partnership and a democracy and nobody understood that better than Ahmet. He had this ability to deal with the pair of them but as time went by, the divisions became deeper and he was struggling a bit in terms of trying to get them to record."

At the start, in Phil Carson's words, "Zeppelin was all about boys having fun with no darkness to it whatever and Peter Grant in some ways the ringleader." The band soon acquired a reputation that became the gold standard for outrageous behavior on the road. Doing massive amounts of drugs and alcohol, the individual members of Led Zeppelin despoiled groupies as no band ever had before. In the words of

Mario Medious, who began his career at Atlantic as an accountant only to transform himself into "The Big M," a fast-talking FM promotion man, "Zeppelin had crazy hard-core groupies like the Plaster Casters who would give them head in a phone booth or at the dinner table. Guys in the band would say, 'I just got plated, man.' I didn't know what plated was. 'You were sitting at table, how could you get plated?' 'She plated me while I ate.' "

Becoming a devotee of Aleister Crowley, the occult philosopher, adventurer, and practitioner of black magic known as "the wickedest man in the world," Page dabbled in Satanism. Emulating the man he called "a misunderstood genius," the guitarist used some of his newfound wealth to purchase Boleskine House, Crowley's former estate near Loch Ness in Scotland.

At the end of Zeppelin's second American tour, drummer John Bonham, known for good reason as "The Beast," attacked rock journalist Ellen Sander in the band's dressing room and had to be pulled off her by Grant. In a backstage trailer at the Oakland Coliseum in 1977, Grant and the band's huge bodyguard beat one of Bill Graham's security guards so badly for supposedly having spoken rudely to Grant's son that the promoter had both men arrested.

As Mario Medious, who endured thirty-seven one-nighters with Zeppelin on the band's second American tour, would later say, "Ahmet and Peter Grant ended up being tight but they had fights all the time about money because Led Zeppelin innovated how bands got paid and controlled everything—what the album cover was like, everything. Grant was always complaining about something. That was why Atlantic sent me on the road with them. To cool him out."

Despite their differences, in Curbishley's words, "Ahmet had the talent to be able to talk to Peter Grant. He stood up to Peter and was not at all intimidated by him. Grant knew who Ahmet was and in the end, he owed Ahmet. It's okay to come in with a great album and all that but you cannot minimize what Ahmet put behind that band."

Whenever Led Zeppelin was on the road in America, Ahmet would appear in the band's dressing room before a show. Welcomed by one and all as an honored guest, he would partake happily of whatever was going around and then fly with the band on its private plane to the next gig. As Jerry Wexler would later say, "Ahmet was the guy who went to the concerts and dealt with the managers. He plunged into it heart and soul. He became their friend and it was those efforts that made Atlantic a monster company."

Spending little or no time with the band in the studio, neither Ahmet nor Wexler ever knew what kind of material Zeppelin was recording until the group actually submitted its new album. When the band delivered *Led Zeppelin II* in the fall of 1969, Wexler was forced to "throw out a hundred thousand dollars' worth of records because the bass was so heavy and overmodulated that the needle skipped. We had to have it redone so it was playable."

Two years after a shortened version of Zeppelin's only single, "Whole Lotta Love," became a Top Ten hit, the band released *Led Zeppelin IV*. Featuring "Stairway to Heaven," the most frequently played song in the history of FM classic rock radio, the album eventually sold 23 million copies. Over the course of its career, Led Zeppelin sold more than 110 million albums in America and at least twice that all over the world.

Eleven years after first playing together in the basement of a record store on Gerrard Street in London, Led Zeppelin's career came to an end. After consuming forty shots of vodka in a twenty-four-hour period, John Bonham asphyxiated on his own vomit and died in his sleep on September 25, 1980, at the age of thirty-two. "It all fell apart after Bonham died," Curbishley recalled, "because Robert Plant felt they shouldn't carry on. They tried with a couple of different drummers but it never really worked and so Robert went off to do a solo album." When Ahmet decided in 1984 to record a collection of his favorite songs from the 1950s, he coproduced the Honeydrippers album with Robert Plant, and the singer's version of Phil Phillips's 1959 hit "Sea of Love" became his biggest-selling single.

Despite Curbishley's continuing efforts to persuade Page and Plant to work together again, "Page was drinking a lot throughout that whole period and he used to close down. He was very insular. The bonding Plant was trying to achieve with him never really happened and it hasn't happened as of today. However much I still urge Page to call Robert, go have some lunch, just hang out, he can't do it. They're two different animals. Totally different animals."

The demise of Led Zeppelin also effectively ended Peter Grant's role as the most feared manager in rock. "When Grant was really in a bad state," Curbishley said, "Ahmet did a lot to shore him up and cover his ass. He went to see Grant in his house in England and sat down for twelve hours but Grant wouldn't come out of the bedroom. Towards the end, it was quite insane and Ahmet never got that far with him because it all spiraled into madness." Peter Grant died of a heart attack at the age of sixty on November 21, 1995. In Curbishley's words, "The lifestyle destroyed him."

Despite how much time he had spent on the road with Led Zeppelin and how close he had become with Grant, Ahmet never let himself be drawn into the vortex of madness that was the band's stock-in-trade. Recalling his initial meeting with Ahmet in 1969, Robert Plant would say, "Right in the middle of the eye of the storm was this absolutely elite gentleman, the master of serenity, as much at home with the backstage cavorting of Led Zeppelin as he was with the politesse of high society. We had some memorable nights together; I wish I could remember them. He was, to me, an oasis and a model—how to be settled in the midst of all this madness, how to know when to get excited and when not. Of course, he's been practicing for ages."

## FIFTEEN

# *Romancing the Stones*

*"It was '69 or '70, and I wasn't aware that the Rolling Stones contract with London Records was running out . . . One morning there's a knock on my bungalow door at the hotel where I'm staying, and it's a British roadie who tells me that Mick says it's OK if I want to come down to the studio where they are recording. I thank him very much, but I don't go because I have something else I have to do that night. The next morning a knock on my door again, same roadie, he says, 'Hey, listen, man. Mick wants you to come down,' and the next night, I did. They gave me a tremendous reception, all the guys in the band. I leave the studio, and I go out with Bill Drake, who was a very powerful man in radio. He liked me because I drank with him. Well that night we drank a couple of bottles of whiskey together. I tell him I've been to the studio where the Stones are recording, and Mick Jagger says he wants to talk to me, and I have a plan to meet him at the Whisky at midnight. Drake says, 'No kidding? Mick Jagger? Terrific.' By this time I'm getting very tired from the jet lag I had the day before and all the drinking. Anyway, we go to the Whisky. I've called ahead for a table, and Bill had a couple of girls, the four of us are sitting at the table, and I have another drink. Chuck Berry is onstage, and Mick arrives at twelve-thirty. I introduce him to Drake and the girls, and Mick sits down and starts telling me about their recording plans. He starts talking, and I doze off. I can remember this girl shaking me, going, 'Wake up, wake up. It's Mick Jagger. He's telling you something important.' Mick hates people who are into high pressure, but this was the opposite. Here he was telling me that the Rolling Stones have decided to sign with Atlantic, and I had fallen asleep."*

—Ahmet Ertegun

# 1

If only it had been this simple, Ahmet would not have spent the next eighteen months of his life working harder than he ever had before to convince Mick Jagger that the Rolling Stones did in fact belong on Atlantic Records. While the band would never earn nearly as much money for the label as Led Zeppelin, Ahmet saw the Stones as "the most desirable act in the business," the jewel in the crown that would confirm beyond all doubt that Atlantic was the number one record company in the world.

Ahmet had first met the band on October 23, 1964, at photographer Jerry Schatzberg's apartment at 333 Park Avenue South during a gala twenty-fourth birthday party for socialite Baby Jane Holzer. Two years later, Ahmet ran into Jagger again at a press party for Bobby Darin in London. In Ahmet's words, "We had a few laughs at that time but then I lost contact with him. Not for any specific reason but then Mick called me up when the Stones' contract with English Decca had about a year to go and they had decided to make a change."

The dark side of the original British Invasion, the Rolling Stones' distinctly dangerous onstage presence, sexually suggestive lyrics, and reputation for antisocial behavior caused them to be perceived in America as the antidote to the Beatles. It was not until "(I Can't Get No) Satisfaction" hit the top of the charts in 1965 that they achieved the superstar status in the U.S. they had already been accorded in England.

During the last week in October 1969 when Ahmet sat down with Jagger at the Whisky, the Stones were in Los Angeles preparing for their first American tour in three years. In July, Brian Jones, the founder of the group, had drowned in his swimming pool under mysterious circumstances shortly after having been asked to leave the band. The Stones had then performed with his replacement, ex-Bluesbreakers lead guitarist Mick Taylor, at a massive free concert in London's Hyde Park.

After being busted for drug possession at an LSD party at Keith Richards's country home in England in 1967, Jagger and Richards had been tried and convicted only to have their sentences overturned by a higher court. In the process, they had become counterculture heroes.

With the Beatles no longer touring, the Stones were about to stake their claim in America as the world's greatest rock 'n' roll band.

After completing a very successful three-week, fifteen-city tour that featured three sold-out shows at New York's Madison Square Garden, the Stones flew into Atlanta on December 2, 1969. The band then journeyed to Muscle Shoals, Alabama, where they recorded Mississippi Fred McDowell's "You Got to Move," "Brown Sugar," and "Wild Horses." Ahmet, who rarely spent time in what had become Jerry Wexler's home studio, was there to greet them.

Looking incredibly serious and focused in an immaculate dark suit, white shirt, and tie, Ahmet can be seen in a photograph talking intently to Jagger. In full hippie mode, shaggy-haired Jagger sports a studded leather horse collar around his neck. On his head, he wears a top hat fashioned from a Union Jack. While the pair seem like ambassadors from two different worlds, they spoke a common language based on more than their shared love of the blues.

Despite having released fourteen albums and twenty-nine singles in America and England, the Stones were still essentially broke because of the disastrous management deals they had signed first with Andrew Loog Oldham and Eric Easton and then Allen Klein. Jagger, who had attended the London School of Economics, was by then already on his way to becoming a consummate businessman who understood the inner workings of the record industry as well as Ahmet.

On December 6, 1969, as the Rolling Stones were performing at a huge free concert at the Altamont Speedway in northern California, members of the Hells Angels motorcycle gang who had been hired to provide security in return for cases of beer killed an eighteen-year-old black man named Meredith Hunter. Less than four months after the media had proclaimed the Woodstock Arts and Music Festival as the birth of the counterculture in America, the disastrous free concert at Altamont became its death knell. The event also served to increase the Stones' notoriety in America by geometric proportions.

"Ahmet got involved with the Stones right after Altamont," Peter Rudge, who managed the band's next tour of America, would later say. "That was a crossroads for the Stones. They could have gone any way after that point but Ahmet's courtship and signing of them took them from being one of the better rock bands to writing their own role in history. And Ahmet was embedded through all that behind the scenes."

Despite the role Ahmet would eventually play in the Stones' future, Mick Jagger was not about to allow the band to sign with Atlantic until he was certain no one could offer them a better deal. Bob Krasnow, the head of Blue Thumb Records in Los Angeles, was one of many record executives who did their best to convince Jagger that his label was the best fit for the Stones. As Krasnow would later say, "Mick and I were sitting in my office and I was pitching him like crazy and I said, 'Look, man, the world is changing and we need to stick together in America to make sure the world changes for the best.' I was probably stoned out of my mind and I got on one of my esoteric speeches and I fucked the whole thing up. I thought Mick had a social conscience. He said, 'Hey, I'm a tourist here, man,' and that was the last I ever heard from him."

Krasnow also tried to forge an alliance to sign the band with Marshall Chess, who had become president of the label founded by his father and uncle only to leave the company after it was acquired by a conglomerate. Deciding it would be better if they remained friends rather than try to work together, Chess asked Krasnow for permission to contact Jagger on his own and Krasnow gave him the singer's phone number in London.

Chess called Jagger in London and then flew there to meet with him only to be told the singer "was in Ireland writing when what he really had was some hot pussy there." A few days later, the two men sat down to talk in Jagger's living room. Jagger then took Chess to meet the rest of the Stones in their East London rehearsal room. Two weeks later, Chess received a telegram instructing him to come to London, where Prince Rupert Lowenstein, the merchant banker Jagger had asked to look into the band's tangled finances, authorized the twenty-seven-year-old son of Leonard Chess to begin formal negotiations for a new record deal with the understanding that once the Stones had their own label, Marshall Chess would run it for them.

As Chess, who had known Ahmet since he and Jerry Wexler had attended his bar mitzvah in 1955, would later say, "We talked about numerous labels but the Stones wanted to be on Atlantic. That was by far our first choice because Mick and Keith wanted it and I loved Ahmet. But we did negotiate with two or three other majors, including Chris

Blackwell at Island. But even before money was discussed, Atlantic was where they wanted to be."

By this point, Ahmet had been courting the Stones so ardently that Jerry Greenberg, who was then just beginning his career at Atlantic as a promotion man, recalled, "I used to ask Jerry, 'Where's Ahmet?' and he would always say, 'With Mick.' He followed Mick around for a year and maybe desperate is the wrong word but Ahmet wanted the Rolling Stones. Maybe because Jerry had signed Zeppelin. Maybe he wanted to have the biggest company in the world. Maybe because he loved Mick Jagger."

On July 31, 1970, the contract Allen Klein had negotiated for the Stones with Decca Records expired. Jagger was still considering his options a month later when Ahmet and Elektra Records founder Jac Holzman sat down together at nine in the morning in the Oliver Messel Suite of the Dorchester Hotel in London to discuss their plans to record the upcoming Isle of Wight Festival. Ahmet, who had been out so late with Jagger the night before that his driver was asleep at the wheel of the company Rolls-Royce parked outside the hotel, called the singer to say what a wonderful time they'd had together, a point with which Jagger readily agreed.

Having already spent an enormous amount of time and money courting Jagger while also cultivating a "marvelous relationship" with Prince Rupert Lowenstein, "a terrific person who quickly learned all the devious ways of the music business," Ahmet told Jagger the time had come for them all to sit down and make a deal. When Jagger said he would be happy to do so as soon as he had spoken with Clive Davis at Columbia, "all the color drained out of Ahmet's face" and the call came to an abrupt end. In Holzman's words, "Ahmet had this conversation with Mick and he was sort of bellying up to him about 'Wasn't that a wonderful time we had last night' and then Mick said, 'We'll talk to you as soon as we talk to Clive Davis,' and Ahmet was so obsessed he could not focus on our discussion."

Fighting to control his anger, Ahmet picked up the phone and "very deliberately" dialed Jagger's number. "Mick," he said. "I can understand you want to talk to Clive Davis, and you should. But I want you to know I can only make one Stones-sized deal this year, and it's either you"—and here Ahmet paused—"or Paul Revere and the Raiders." He then hung up the phone. Thirty seconds later, the phone rang. Ahmet did not pick it up. Nor did he bother doing so as the phone rang constantly for the next forty-five minutes.

As Holzman would later say, "I have no idea what Paul Revere and the Raiders were doing then but the point was that by picking them, he was fucking with Mick's head and yanking his chain. If he had picked a contemporary artist, Mick might have believed it." But then as Holzman would later write, "Ahmet was the greatest poker player in the business."

Rupert Lowenstein then contacted Clive Davis. When Davis spoke to Jagger over the phone, he told him his style was different from Ahmet's and that while he sometimes traveled, he could not spend a lot of time socializing with him. Jagger said his decision was strictly business and would not be based on social considerations. Because he knew "Columbia was the best company in the business" and was also well aware of Davis's reputation, Jagger encouraged Davis to make a bid for the Stones but told him to talk to Lowenstein about the actual numbers.

According to Davis, Lowenstein then told him the Stones wanted an advance of between $5 and $6 million (most likely over the length of a contract for five or six albums) as well as "a staggering royalty rate." As the band was then selling between 750,000 and a million units per album, less than half of what Columbia artists Chicago, Santana, and Blood, Sweat & Tears were selling and nowhere near Simon and Garfunkel's massive sales, Davis feared that if he paid the Stones what they were asking, it would cost him an unimaginable sum of money to retain his more successful acts when their contracts came up for renewal.

Deciding the stakes were too high for him, Davis opted not to meet the Stones' demands. Davis may have also known that with Ahmet in the game, he stood no real chance of signing the group but was only being used to help push up the final price. As Stones lead guitarist Keith Richards would later say, "I think we were fishing but at the same time, the idea of Atlantic Records loomed large on our English horizon. Just the idea of being on Atlantic blew us away. We'd already died and gone to heaven, man. I didn't really warm up to Clive too much but I was attracted to Atlantic because of their knowledge of black music and how they knew how to record. Ahmet was chasing

Mick but that was the obvious tail to chase, right? I was quite willing to let Mick carry on and do the main business but I think we were both saying, 'Atlantic Records sounds right to us.' "

Ahmet knew the band was leaning toward signing with him but Clive Davis's entry into the race only served to up the ante. As Ahmet would later say, "Whenever I saw Rupert or Mick with someone else, my heart sank. It was a painful, ecstatic courtship." Increasing his already dogged pursuit of the Stones, Ahmet arranged one of the more surreal high-level record business meetings of all time. Bringing Lowenstein and Marshall Chess together with Steve Ross at the Beverly Hills Hotel, Ahmet stood with them in the shallow end of the hotel pool explaining just how much he could do for the Stones with Ross's backing if the band signed with Atlantic.

Along with Atlantic lawyer Mike Mayer and Sheldon Vogel, the label's chief financial officer, Ahmet then sat down with Chess, Lowenstein, and their lawyer to hammer out the fine points of the deal in the conference room at the Atlantic Records office on 61st Street and Broadway in New York. As Chess would later say, "I felt I knew more than Ahmet about what it cost to press a record and how much profit was in it because we had pressed everything ourselves at Chess. We got a dollar an album from Atlantic which was the biggest deal ever at that time and a million-dollar advance. Which would be like five million today. Ahmet was patting his head with his white Sulka handkerchief because he was shvitzing when I said, 'It costs eighteen cents to press a record. Give me a fucking break.' It was not easy but the deal went down in two days and I was thrilled."

On April 1, 1971, a year and a half after Ahmet had fallen asleep on Mick Jagger in the Whisky, the Rolling Stones signed with Atlantic. The monster deal Marshall Chess had cut in New York led to the creation of Rolling Stones Records and guaranteed the band an advance of a million dollars per album for five albums against a royalty rate of more than 10 percent a record. As Ahmet would later say, "I think Jagger would have liked to be on a funky label. I think Jagger would have liked to be on Excello. We were the closest he could get to Excello and still get five million dollars." A huge deal by any standard that no other label was willing to match, it was also a contract Ahmet would have never signed if he had been spending his own money.

Quickly, Ahmet assumed the same role with the Stones he had already played over the years with other great Atlantic artists whose music he instinctively understood. Andy Johns, who was then twenty years old and just beginning his career as a recording engineer with the band, first met Ahmet at Olympic Studios in London. As Johns was mixing "Bitch," a track from the Stones' debut album on Atlantic, "a very suave old guy I didn't know came in. It was Ahmet, who had probably just had his hair cut in France and lunch in Budapest."

Sitting down at the back of the control room, Ahmet watched in silence for a while as Johns, in his words, "was struggling a bit with the mix. Then he said, 'Hey, kid! What you oughta do is add a little bottom to the guitars and turn the bass up.' He was a bit of an authority figure so I did what he said. *Bingo!* The thing jelled. He got up and wandered off and I said to Keith, 'Who the fuck is that?' Keith said, 'You don't know who that is? That's Ahmet Er-te-gun! And he's been making hit records since before you were born.' The reason the Stones signed with Atlantic was because they were so impressed with Ahmet. He could hang out with a prime minister in the morning and do blow with the fucking bass player in the evening."

Having grown up in England listening to Chuck Berry on Chess as well as Ray Charles and Ruth Brown on Atlantic, Mick Jagger and Keith Richards now had their own label headed by Leonard Chess's son that would be distributed by the man who had recorded so many of the artists they idolized. That the Stones had done the right thing by deciding to go with Atlantic was confirmed when Ahmet visited Jagger after the deal had finally been signed. As Jagger would later say, "It was in my house in London and he'd drunk so much bourbon that when we actually shook hands on the deal, the chair fell back and he fell on the floor." In what seemed to all concerned like a record business marriage made in heaven, the honeymoon was about to begin.

## 2

When it came to celebrating good fortune, most especially where his new darlings the Rolling Stones were concerned, no one could compare to Ahmet. Deciding to throw a gala party for the band on April 17,

1971, to announce the release of the first single from their debut album on Atlantic, he flew with a small group of traveling companions to the south of France, where the Stones were just beginning what would become their mad and calamitous year of living in tax exile.

In every sense, the trip marked the start of Ahmet's ascension to authentic full-blown rock royalty. As Stones tour manager Peter Rudge would later say, "During this period of his life, Ahmet was as high-profile as he had ever been and never, ever alone. I only ever saw him alone once at a meeting at Atlantic during one of those rare occasions when he was in the office. When he would travel, he was the first Puff Daddy. He always had a posse and you could see him coming from miles away."

As Ahmet boarded the 747 that would take him to France, he was accompanied by David Geffen, Stephen Stills, Jerry Greenberg, and the writer George Trow, who was then researching his profile of Ahmet, which would not appear in *The New Yorker* magazine for another seven years. Sipping a Chivas and soda on ice as he sat in the first-class cabin, Ahmet listened as Jerry Greenberg pitched him on signing a band called Pacific Gas & Electric, who were then on Columbia. When Greenberg told him how much the deal would cost, Ahmet said, "I don't think that figure appeals to me."

Knowing Trow was observing his every move and would be writing about him for a publication read by those whom he valued most, Ahmet promptly transformed himself into a rock 'n' roll version of Alexander Woollcott by telling the writer, "It is amusing, I think. For all their youthful charm, that group has as quotable a price as the utility for which they are whimsically named."

Having always brilliantly controlled his own image in the press, Ahmet then stage-managed the interview Trow did with David Geffen during the flight. In Geffen's words, "Ahmet said to me, 'Make sure you only say good things.' And I said, 'Well, what do you want me to tell him?' He said, 'I don't care. Make it up.' So I told him this story about how Ahmet had loaned me $50,000 and wouldn't let me pay it back. Anyone who knows Ahmet knows that's a made-up story. Later, Ahmet and I were having a big fight and he said to me, 'You've got a lot of fucking nerve! I gave you fifty thousand dollars.' I said, 'Ahmet, I made that story up for George Trow.' "

Much as he had done with Geffen, Ahmet had invited Greenberg on the trip for a specific reason. A former musician who as a promotion man based in New Haven, Connecticut, had demonstrated an incredible knack for breaking records in his local market, Greenberg had been hired at Atlantic by Jerry Wexler in 1967. He had made his bones at the label by persuading Wexler to pay $5,000 for a hit record that had come to him in the mail entitled "Tighten Up" by Archie Bell & the Drells.

Greenberg soon learned that Wexler, the toughest task master in the business, expected him to be available twenty-four hours a day, seven days a week. One year, Wexler ordered Greenberg into the office on Thanksgiving so he could do the mailing of a Wilson Pickett record being released the next day. In Greenberg's words, "Wexler was a maniac, but a *great* maniac. . . . Once he called my house on Yom Kippur, wanting to discuss an urgent business matter. My wife said I was in synagogue. 'What's the number there? I'll have him paged.' " As Greenberg recalled, "I was in B'nai Jacob in New Haven. It was a Conservative synogogue but they still wouldn't have taken the call. Working for Jerry Wexler was like going into the Marines. You either came out a sergeant or they found you dead in a fucking swamp."

While Greenberg's prior contact with Ahmet at the label had been so limited that he initially thought Ahmet ran Atco while Wexler was in charge of Atlantic, Ahmet had summoned Greenberg to his office some weeks earlier to say, "I'm signing the Rolling Stones, we're going to make the announcement next month in France, I want you to come with me, you're the only one I want Mick Jagger to talk to when I'm not here." When Ahmet learned Mica would be coming from Paris to join him in Cannes, he instructed Greenberg to bring his wife along and then took them both to Paris, where Greenberg had never been, for the weekend.

By taking Jerry Greenberg with him to the south of France, Ahmet effectively ended Greenberg's term of service as Wexler's second-in-command. From now on, Greenberg would be running the day-to-day operations at Atlantic, thereby allowing Ahmet to continue doing just as he pleased without having to worry about concerns that no longer really interested him.

Then twenty-eight years old and still functioning as Ahmet's eager and loyal protégé, David Geffen had come along so he could get the inside track on managing the Stones' next tour of America, a position coveted by a host of other music business heavies. By providing Geffen with unlimited access to Rupert Lowenstein and Mick Jagger during their visit, Ahmet was doing Geffen a favor that would also benefit him. At loose ends now that CSN&Y had broken up, Stephen Stills, whom Trow would later describe as "the odd man out" in the group, was there simply because he wanted to hang out with the Stones.

In the good old days when Ahmet and Jerry Wexler had set out on the road together in search of new talent and good times, the two men had been absolute peers united by their love for black roots music. Having ascended to brand-new heights by bringing the world's greatest rock 'n' roll band to Atlantic, Ahmet was now traveling like a potentate surrounded by courtiers whose music business survival depended in large part on his continuing favor. Nor was it an accident that Wexler himself was not around. For reasons best known only to himself, Ahmet had not invited him.

Although Geffen had already proven his own music business acumen by selling Tunafish Music, the publishing company he had formed for Laura Nyro, for $4 million, he was then still completely in thrall to Ahmet and happy just to spend time with him and Mica in the south of France. Nonetheless, Ahmet could not resist the urge to occasionally remind him of his proper place in the pecking order. When Geffen asked if there were any recording studios in France, Ahmet loftily replied, "France is like Brooklyn. They have everything." In Geffen's words, "It didn't feel like a put-down. The cutting remarks were part of Ahmet's sense of humor and not particular to me. He would also say things about Robert Stigwood, whom he considered a close friend and a very important manager. It was part of his nature and character. Ahmet was a complicated guy."

Nor could Ahmet contain himself as he and Mica sat down with Rupert Lowenstein and Geffen for dinner that evening in the Hotel Majestic on La Croisette in Cannes. When Lowenstein, a descendant of a royal family that traced its lineage back to the Holy Roman Empire, suggested it was time for them all to go to the party for the Stones, Ahmet said there was no need to do so yet because he and Lowenstein were the hosts. When Lowenstein told Ahmet that Jagger had recently given a big party in London only to arrive there four hours late, Ahmet told him, "You're not a rock-and-roll star, and the sooner you realize that, the happier you'll be."

By the time Ahmet arrived at the party at the Port Pierre Canto Club, for which Atlantic was footing the bill, Mick Jagger, Keith Richards, Charlie Watts, Bill Wyman, and Mick Taylor were already there with their wives and girlfriends. As Ahmet and Jagger embraced like the close friends and business associates they had now become, Ahmet said, "We have to do the whole thing, don't we?" Jagger replied, "If we had taps on our shoes, we could really do a number."

Both men knew the real purpose of the evening was to jump-start the sales of the Stones' new single as well as the album from which it came. While the party itself turned out to be a nonevent, even though Jagger did throw a glass of wine into the face of a photographer who had been bothering him all night, the English rock writer Nik Cohn accurately described what was really going on that evening by telling Trow, "Ahmet is the King of Rock and Roll. Ahmet is more important than Jagger . . . and more interesting. . . . Ahmet is really a figure, and Jagger is nothing more than a little rock-and-roll singer. And what is a rock-and-roll singer in the end?"

It was a question Keith Richards, Jagger's boon companion and songwriting partner, might have been hard pressed to answer. Having left the yacht club early in the evening to find his beloved dog Okie, Richards would later explain his sudden departure by saying, "That was my only friend at the party, man." Along with his companion, the Italian-born actress Anita Pallenberg, Richards then joined Ahmet, Stills, and Charlie Watts at bassist Bill Wyman's house in Grasse for the real party, which went on all night. As Ahmet was being driven back to the Hotel Majestic in his limousine at dawn, he leaned forward and with great aplomb told the driver, "We are very restless people. Please drive faster."

Ahmet's unwavering faith in the Rolling Stones was amply rewarded when their first single on Atlantic, "Brown Sugar," a song Jagger had originally wanted to call "Black Pussy" and which the band had first performed at Altamont, went to number one in America. The cover of *Sticky Fingers,* conceived by Andy Warhol for $30,000, featured a real zipper on a pair of very tight jeans worn by actor Joe Dallesandro. Because the zipper warped the first fifty thousand copies of the record when they were stacked, the zipper then had to be lowered to half-mast so the album could be shipped. The album became the Rolling Stones' biggest seller to this point in time.

On May 27, it replaced Crosby, Stills, Nash & Young's live *4 Way Street* double album as the number one album on the *Billboard* charts and stayed there for three weeks before eventually going triple platinum (selling three million copies). For the first time in the band's history, an album by the Rolling Stones topped both the British and American charts at the same time. Proving yet again how good he was at this business, Ahmet's daring gamble had paid off immediately. Atlantic easily recouped the million-dollar advance he had given the Stones for *Sticky Fingers*.

For Jagger and Richards, the bad news was that because they had written and recorded a good deal of the album while still under contract to Allen Klein, their former manager owned the copyrights to many of the songs and so they did not earn the far more generous royalties on this material they would have been paid by Atlantic. The obvious solution was for Jagger and Richards to begin writing and recording new material for what was now their eagerly awaited second album on Atlantic. As Ahmet soon learned, this was a problem not even he could solve.

### 3

Despite their shared history and how hard they had worked together to ensure the success of the band, Mick Jagger and Keith Richards had always been two birds of a completely different feather. While the ongoing tension between them had helped propel the band to superstar status, their widely divergent lifestyles now began taking precedence over their careers and the two found themselves at odds as never before. Ahmet did all he could to help speed the apparently endless process of recording their new album, but even he was forced to concede that in the Rolling Stones, he had finally met his match.

During the recording of *Sticky Fingers*, Keith Richards's drug problems had become so severe that he did not even attend the session during which "Moonlight Mile," the final track on the album, had been recorded. By the time the Stones found themselves living in luxury in the south of France in the spring of 1971, Richards and Anita Pallenberg, by now the parents of a young son, had both just managed to stop using heroin on a regular basis. Living like outlaws in a sumptuous villa overlooking the sea that soon became a riotous jet-set commune filled with a motley crew of beautiful people and high-born hangers-on, they had little use for the far more sedate manner in which Mick Jagger was now conducting himself and nothing at all in common with his new girlfriend, the Nicaraguan-born Bianca Pérez-Mora Macias.

Interceding in the life of the preeminent artist on his label in a manner no other record executive would have ever dared to do, Ahmet had actually helped bring the two together. Before the Stones decamped for the south of France, Ahmet had visited Jagger in the house he then shared with pop singer Marianne Faithfull on Cheyne Walk in London, where they had both been busted for possession of heroin, LSD, and marijuana on May 21, 1969.

Unbeknownst to either man, Faithfull had been upstairs listening as the two talked about her. Because she was heavily addicted to heroin, Ahmet urged Jagger to think seriously about the damage she could do to the band. "I know it's going to be tough on you," Ahmet said, "but she could jeopardize *everything*." When Jagger asked what he could do about it, Ahmet replied, "There's only one thing *to* do. I've seen a lot of heartbreak with junkies. Believe me, old friend, it wrecks the lives of everybody *around* them, as well. It's a bottomless pit, and she'll drag you into it unless you let her go." In light of all the money Atlantic was about to pay the Stones, Ahmet told Jagger he wanted "some guarantee that the whole deal isn't going to be blown because of Marianne. You can understand that, can't you?"

Shortly before Ahmet and Mica went to see the Stones perform the last of their three shows at the Palais des Sports in Paris some months later on September 23, 1970, Ahmet received a call from his old friend Eddie Barclay. A former jazz band leader born Edouard Ruault, he had founded Barclay Records, the premier label in France. A world-renowned playboy, Barclay would marry nine different women before his death at the age of eighty-four. As Mica would later say, "We brought Bianca to the show because she was living with Eddie Barclay and he came to Ahmet and said, 'You know, Bianca would love so much to go to the Stones.' So Ahmet arranged it and she spent the whole evening practically on the stage in her black cloak looking very beautiful and that was when it started."

A stunning dark-eyed beauty whose affection for high society mirrored Jagger's own long-standing fascination with upper-class life, the two soon became a couple. Unlike Faithfull, Bianca had little taste for the rock 'n' roll lifestyle and did not get along well with Pallenberg. A month after the band had settled into tax exile in France, Jagger stunned his fellow band mates by announcing he intended to marry Bianca, who was then four months pregnant with his child.

In light of his standing as a counterculture hero and his reputation as the greatest ladies' man of his generation, Jagger might as well have announced he had decided to enter the priesthood. Nonetheless, the two were wed on May 12, 1971, first by the mayor of St. Tropez at the town hall and then in church by a Catholic priest from whom Jagger had been taking religious instruction. Attended by a host of rock stars from England and a sizable percentage of the European press, the town hall ceremony became a major mob scene.

Leaving a record business convention in Las Vegas, Ahmet had flown to New York and then chartered a plane to France because, in his words, "I was a witness at the wedding. They have witnesses rather than best men." The actual best man at the wedding was Keith Richards. Wearing a pair of braided black tights and a long-sleeved white jersey under a green combat jacket, the guitarist arrived so late for the town hall ceremony that the local chief of police refused to allow him inside and both men were soon "standing there with their hands around each other's throats screaming in their respective languages." When Richards was finally granted entry, he chose for reasons known only to him to sit on the bride's side of the aisle.

As Ahmet would later tell Jason Flom, who began his career at Atlantic in 1979, "Keith was the best man and he was walking around with a bag full of coke, scooping it out with his hand and shoving it in his face. The chief of police came up to him and said in French, 'What is this powder?' Keith had this dumbfounded look on his face. Reaching into the bag, I grabbed some, started patting it on Keith's face, and said in French, 'You don't understand. They're not just musicians. They're also clowns. And this is their makeup.' "

Once Jagger and his new wife returned from their honeymoon, the Stones began recording in the basement of Richards's seaside villa. Richards, who now was again using heroin, would often go upstairs during sessions to put his young son to bed and never be seen again. As work on the new album slowed to a crawl, drug use in the house increased to unheard-of proportions and Jagger began spending more time in Paris, where Bianca gave birth to their daughter, Jade, in September. When the word came down at the end of November that the villa was about to be raided by the local gendarmes, the Stones were forced to leave France so quickly that Richards and Pallenberg left most of their personal possessions behind.

For the next six months as Jagger and Richards worked together in relative harmony in Los Angeles overdubbing and laboriously mixing and remixing what they had now decided would be the band's first double album, Ahmet made regular visits to the studio because, in bassist Bill Wyman's words, he "was keen to check on his investment." As Richards would later say, "We had a lot of tussles with Ahmet over *Exile on Main St.* We wanted a double album and he said, 'A double album doesn't sell as much as a single album.' We won. But as far as the sound and the material was concerned, his reaction was, 'That's what we need. They've gotta rock with this.' "

That a double album, especially one featuring a cover consisting of images shot by famed photographer Robert Frank as well as an insert of twelve perforated postcards by photographer Norman Seef, would also cost far more for Atlantic to manufacture was yet another factor in Ahmet's reluctance to issue *Exile on Main St.* as the Stones finally persuaded him to do. Six weeks before the album Mick Jagger had initially wanted to call *Tropical Disease* was to be released on May 7, 1972, with an extensive tour of North America by the Stones slated to begin on June 3 in Vancouver, Jagger and Richards were still trying to decide which mix of certain songs they liked best. Hand-carrying the masters with him, Marshall Chess flew to New York to deliver them personally to Ahmet so the record could be pressed at last.

Despite what the Rolling Stones had put him through while recording *Exile on Main St.*, Ahmet remained fiercely loyal to the band. Able to spin any story to his own advantage, he would later say, "I was with them a great deal in the south of France. I went down several times and it was a bit mad but it worked out all right. That madness and extravagance is part of their way. It's not related to the music and it is. To the average person in the street, their way of life is dramatic and everyone loves them for that. They enjoyed renting a castle in the south of France and having big parties with very good champagnes and Bordeaux wines and a great chef and all kinds of girls. The south of France was a great place for them. And while it lasted, it was great fun."

## 4

Had it not been for Ahmet, the Rolling Stones might never have even been allowed to enter America for what became to that point in time the highest grossing tour in rock 'n' roll history. While he would later deny he had done anything more than negotiate with the musicians' union so the band could perform in the United States, Ahmet used his extensive social and political connections to ensure that Mick Jagger would be granted an entry visa to America despite his 1969 drug bust in London.

Ahmet had first met Senator Jacob K. Javits, the very liberal Republican who sat on the Senate Foreign Relations Committee, through his considerably younger wife, Marion, a denizen of the New York art scene who was also a regular in the back room of Max's Kansas City, then the hippest downtown hangout in Manhattan. Happy to do a favor for a friend, her husband helped to resolve the problems the Stones might have faced if they had gone through ordinary channels.

As Peter Rudge, who planned and managed this tour, recalled, "It was all done correctly but everything is done on technicalities in that world. I think the Stones were let in because *Exile on Main St.* was about to be released and it was good for their record sales. It got smoothed over through personal connections. Because that's the way the system works, isn't it?"

In each of the thirty-one cities in the United States and Canada where the Stones performed on their tour, the band became front-page headline news. Selling out fifty-one shows in support of their new album, which quickly reached the top of both the American and British charts, the band grossed an unheard-of $3 million in ticket sales. In

1969, only *Ramparts* and *Rolling Stone* had covered the band's American tour. Three years later, the Stones' publicists had no trouble lining up major features in *Life, Time, Newsweek, Esquire,* and *Rolling Stone,* and the band found themselves traveling with their own press corps.

In light of all the excitement the Stones were generating on the road without him, it was not long before Ahmet joined the party and began showing up backstage at various shows, most often with two girls whose collective ages just about equaled his own. Flying into New Orleans on the Warner Bros. jet on June 26, Ahmet arrived about six hours before the Stones. Knowing "Mick and Keith and Bill Wyman and Charlie Watts wanted to hear some New Orleans music," Ahmet rented a studio in a warehouse at 748 Camp Street and hired "a good marching band and some of the blues guys like Professor Longhair to play for them."

In his words, "It's one thing to arrive in New Orleans like a tourist and walk around. You'll luck into some music and might hear some band playing a bar. You might hear Raymond Burke or some of the old guys but what the Stones dig is black blues music and it's not easy to find that in one evening. If they wanted to hear Longhair, he might be playing in Algiers and it would have taken them two hours to get there."

Ahmet arranged for Roosevelt Sykes, a sixty-six-year-old Chicago-based boogie-woogie piano player known as "The Honeydripper," Snooks Eaglin, a blind guitarist, and the fabled Longhair, whom Ahmet and Herb Abramson had first seen on their field trip down south in 1948, to perform with a New Orleans street marching band at what became the first great party Ahmet threw for the Stones on the tour.

In a huge room with bare beams, a dusty floor, and a single fan whirring overhead—the temperature soon hit a hundred degrees—Ahmet was in his element. By midnight, as Longhair began ripping through "Stagger Lee," people were sniffing cocaine off the back of their hands as they danced and sweated to the music. By the time Jagger and Richards swept into the party, the joint was jumping and the music was going round and round.

When the street band Ahmet hired began strutting across the floor led by a magnificent old black man in a black hat and white gloves with a starred white sash across his chest and a stuffed pigeon dangling off one shoulder, everyone began walking behind them in time to the second line while waving white handkerchiefs in the air. The munificent patron who had made it all happen, Ahmet sat beaming in a corner of the room writing checks he handed to each musician after their set was done. As he did so, one old musician asked him, "Mick Jagger? Which one is he?"

The party in New Orleans was the kind of gift only Ahmet could have given the Stones and no one enjoyed it more than him. Aside from the overwhelming amount of money and the maddening artistic freedom the band had demanded in return for signing with Atlantic, this was the real reason the Stones had decided to record for the label. Three decades after Ahmet had first come to New Orleans, he was still the vital link between the music now topping the charts and all that had come before.

Ahmet also loved being out on the road with the Stones because it allowed him to indulge in his always unbridled sexual appetites. In the tightly closed community that surrounded the band on tour, stories about Ahmet's nocturnal activities were often exchanged even as he stood in the dressing room talking to Jagger and Richards before a show.

The single most scurrilous tale concerned an elaborate practical joke Mick Jagger played on Ahmet by respectfully requesting he have dinner with a very proper young woman who planned to enter the diplomatic corps and wanted to discuss her career plans with him. Taking great care to underline the point so Ahmet would behave himself, Jagger stressed that the girl was the daughter of a high-born family who only wanted his sage advice. At some point during the evening, Ahmet found himself lying beneath a glass coffee table in a hotel room as the girl, a high-priced hooker whom Jagger had hired for the night, did unspeakable things on the other side of the glass.

As Peter Rudge would later say, "Ahmet brought so much of the glamour and glitz and sex to that tour because I think he saw it as an opportunity. For Ahmet, Mick was a prize and a capture. Ahmet could read Mick perfectly and he knew exactly what buttons to press with him. I can't believe any record executive ever had a relationship with an artist like Ahmet did with Mick. There were also other moments with Ahmet that were horrendous. He was a tough negotiator. In the 1970s, Mick was really the manager and we were all de facto managers. So Mick would have me working Ahmet on an angle, he'd have Marshall Chess working Ahmet on an angle, he'd have Rupert Lowenstein working Ahmet on an angle, he'd have someone talking to Jerry Greenberg, someone talking to Nesuhi, and someone taking Jerry Wexler out to dinner. That was how Mick was."

When the Stones finally hit New York during the third week in July, with their final show at Madison Square Garden scheduled for Jagger's twenty-ninth birthday, Ahmet pulled out all the stops. In his words, "There were three days of concerts in New York and it was a nightmare because of the number of people who wanted to come. Originally, I was just going to give one party but then I made it two. The first was supposed to be a general reception for the Stones and the official people on the tour and the other was a personal thing I wanted to do for the Stones for being on Atlantic for the first time but it grew out of all proportions because the same people wanted to go to both parties."

On Monday night, June 24, 1972, six hundred people, David Geffen and Andy Warhol among them, crowded into two large banquet rooms at the exclusive Four Seasons restaurant on East 52nd Street. The party quickly became a zoo scene. As the burnt carbolic smell of amyl nitrate poppers filled the air, the Stones themselves seemed bewildered by the insanity.

As a very weary Richards sank into a chair to avoid being run over by those who wanted to get close to him, he noted, "Right now is when you realize you're a product." To the sound of a low grumbling roar from the other side of the room, Mick and Bianca Jagger made their grand entrance as a bevy of photographers walked backward in front of them popping flashbulbs in their faces. Moving steadily, Jagger just kept going until he was out a side door and riding back downstairs in an elevator, leaving the party before most people even knew he had arrived.

Two days later, Ahmet and Mica arrived late for the Stones' last show at Madison Square Garden only to find their seats had already been taken by people who had no business being there. Making no attempt to evict them, Ahmet spread his white handkerchief on the concrete step beside the seats so that Mica, looking very fashionable as always in a black dress accented by an ivory bracelet trimmed with gold, could sit down. When someone handed Ahmet a joint, he passed it on.

Backstage at the Garden that night, chaos reigned. As Dick Cavett nervously interviewed Jagger for his late night network talk show, Andy Warhol and Truman Capote sat side by side taking it all in like a pair of elder vampires. After appearing with Johnny Carson on *The To-night Show* to discuss a band he repeatedly called "The Beatles," Capote would say his "intuition told him the Rolling Stones would never tour this country again" and "would not even exist in three years time" because "they were evanescent people who were not at all important."

Six years earlier, Capote had invited five hundred of his best friends to his masked Black and White Ball at the Plaza Hotel. The guest list that night included Senator Jacob and Marion Javits, Mr. and Mrs. Henry Ford, Senator Robert Kennedy and his wife, Ethel, Jacqueline Kennedy, Greta Garbo, Mr. and Mrs. John Steinbeck, Frank Sinatra, Harper Lee, Henry and Clare Booth Luce, Stavros Niarchos, Prince Stanislaus and Lee Radziwill, William Styron, Norman Mailer, Diana Vreeland, Penelope Tree, Tennessee Williams, Edward Albee, Andy Warhol, Governor Nelson Rockefeller and his wife, Happy, as well as assorted Astors, Vanderbilts, Hearsts, Rothschilds, and Whitneys.

The event of the season, if not the era, the party brought together luminaries from the disparate worlds in which Capote felt very much at home. It also set the gold standard for all New York City high society gatherings until Ahmet and Mica decided to throw an intimate little bash for their friends and the Rolling Stones on the Starlight Roof of the St. Regis Hotel on 55th Street just east of Fifth Avenue. Although Capote would later say, "Ahmet and Mica Ertegun are simply two people on the make. Their party was an Ertegun affair and had little relationship to the Stones," he was there as well.

By the time Ahmet and Mica arrived at the St. Regis, the lobby was already jammed by drag queens with white paint on their faces, who "lolled in gilt chairs, desperate for an invitation." Before being allowed entry to the inner sanctum, those who had actually been invited to the party had to be carefully vetted by secretaries with private security guards by their side. As many as a hundred people still managed to crash the event.

One of them was Zsa Zsa Gabor, the Hungarian-born actress and socialite whom Ahmet's father had helped bring to America with her husband, a left-wing Turkish journalist, before World War II. Then seventeen years old, Ahmet had turned Gabor on to marijuana for the first time by passing her a joint. As he would later say, "She never got very high."

In her tie-dyed evening gown, Gabor began working the party as if her life depended on it. Although she had no idea who Bob Dylan was until her escort, A&P heir Huntington Hartford, informed her he was the most famous rock star in the world, Gabor said, "Oh well, then. I luhv him!" At Dylan's request, she had her photograph taken with him while saying, "Dollink, ven you're hot, you're hot." As Ahmet would later add, "And when you're not, you're not."

Clad in a straw hat, a flannel shirt, and dark shades, Dylan described the party to a *New York Times* reporter by saying, "It's encompassing ... it's the beginning of cosmic consciousness." Calling the party "a Felliniesque finale to the Stones tour," the reporter noted that the guest list read "like a Who's Who of guest lists." Working together, Mica and Mick Jagger had come up with a once-in-a-lifetime collection of people who represented both the high and the low life Ahmet had always loved, as well as all the disparate worlds in which he felt very much at home.

Gianni Bulgari, Andrea de Portago, Oscar and Françoise de la Renta, Graziella Lobo, Count Vega del Ren, Ceezee and Winston Guest, Caterine Milinaire, Lady "Slim" Keith, Lord Hesketh of Easton Neston Castle, Diana Vreeland, Bill Blass, Bill and Chessy Rayner, Bobby Short, Kenneth Jay Lane, Kitty Hawks, Freddie and Isabel Eberstadt, and Clyde and Maggie Newhouse were there, as were Woody Allen, Carly Simon, Dick Cavett, George Plimpton, Jerry Wexler, Bill Graham, and Tennessee Williams.

As Mario Medious, who snuck Peter Wolf and the J. Geils Band in through the kitchen by having them pretend to be roadies carrying Muddy Waters's amps, would later say, "It was an unbelievable society trip because Ahmet was into that. Ahmet had to do that because Ahmet is the man. Ahmet is *The Man*, you dig? People stepped back when he walked in. When I walked in, I was just another motherfucker."

At three in the morning as Count Basie and his band played, one of Andy Warhol's female superstars popped out of Mick Jagger's five-foot-high birthday cake wearing nothing but a pair of minuscule black pasties on her breasts and a garter on her right leg. A group of old black tap dancers in white pants, boaters, and white four-in-hand ties carrying white canes led by Sandman Sims then performed. They were followed by Muddy Waters, who had written the song from which the Stones had taken their name.

Some of those who had spent six weeks on the road working day and night to ensure the tour would be a success were not amused. "It's a travesty; well, it's ironic," Peter Rudge said. "I wonder how many of them bought tickets. This has been a rock 'n' roll tour for the kids and a social tour for everybody else." In Bill Wyman's words, "Society finally accepted us on that tour. I couldn't care less. I'm not very interested in society. If they want to make out they like us, it's okay with me. But I'm not playing music for society."

As people partied until five in the morning on the Starlight Roof of the St. Regis that night, one era was most definitely ending as another began. Through the force of his personality and the wide-ranging connections he and Mica had made in high society, Ahmet had brought the Rolling Stones into a brand-new universe even they did not yet fully understand. As Peter Rudge recalled, "Ahmet and Mick crossed rock 'n' roll over into mainstream culture. They had the same agenda. They truly, truly did."

While the party had none of the authentic soul of the truly joyous celebration Ahmet had put on for the Stones in New Orleans, it did serve to elevate his own standing. No longer just a legend within the record business, Ahmet had now transformed himself into as great a star as any artist who had ever recorded for his label.

## 5

Though no one knew it at the time, the Rolling Stones had hit their creative peak while recording *Exile on Main St.* Their next three albums on Atlantic, *Goats Head Soup, It's Only Rock 'n' Roll,* and *Black and Blue,* spawned hit singles and sold more than enough copies to justify the label's continuing investment in the band. But critics complained the Stones had lost their way and were now following musical trends rather than setting them as they had once done.

Continuing to do just as he pleased in the studio, Mick Jagger gave Ahmet fits by writing a song for *Goats Head Soup* entitled "Starfucker" that contained sexually suggestive lyrics referring to movie star Steve McQueen. Fearing a lawsuit, the label's attorneys urged Ahmet to remove the song from the album. Knowing the title would guarantee the song would never be played on the radio in the United States or England and many American outlets would refuse even to distribute an album with visible profanity on the back over, Ahmet used all his powers of persuasion to convince Jagger to change the name of the song to "Star Star."

When the band's five-year contract with Atlantic expired in 1976, the Rolling Stones were once again free to sign with another label. Because Ahmet considered Jagger "a very close personal friend . . . I told him the Stones should make a killing on this contract, because, to be realistic by the time of the next contract they'll be near forty, and one can't be sure what will happen then. So I advised him."

When Robert Stigwood began trying to persuade the Stones to sign with RSO Records and Polygram, Ahmet was forced to compete for the band. From his suite at the Plaza-Athenée Hotel in Paris, Stigwood conducted negotiations by phone with Jagger, who was staying at the equally posh Georges V. Writing down Stigwood's latest offer, Jagger would then relay the terms to Rupert Lowenstein in Beverly Hills so he could use them to leverage more money from Atlantic.

Despite his long-standing relationship with Jagger, Ahmet had to come up with a $7 million advance for the band's next five albums to keep the Stones on his label. On February 16, 1977, the Rolling Stones signed a new five-year deal with Atlantic to distribute their records in America while selling the rights outside the U.S. to EMI. As Ahmet would later say, "And what happened was that they got so much for the European rights, and so forth, that they could stay with Atlantic in America."

A year later thanks to Jagger, Ahmet found himself embroiled in a very public controversy that threatened to destroy his reputation as a champion of black music. In June 1978, the Stones released *Some Girls*.

With Ronnie Wood of the Faces having replaced Mick Taylor on lead guitar and Jagger now playing guitar as well, the album fused elements of punk rock and disco and sold more than six million copies in the United States, making it the band's most successful album in America.

Viewed by many as the aging dinosaurs of rock, the Stones had proved once again they had not yet lost their edge. When Keith Richards was asked why the Stones had chosen to call the album *Some Girls*, he replied, "Because we couldn't remember their fucking names." Although "Miss You," the first single from the album, became the last Stones' song to reach number one in America, Ahmet's problems began as soon as the album was released.

The cover featured cut-out photographs of the Stones in drag along with a variety of female celebrities. Lucille Ball, Farrah Fawcett, Raquel Welch, Marilyn Monroe's estate, and Liza Minnelli, representing her mother, Judy Garland, all objected to being portrayed in such a manner and threatened legal action. At great expense to both Atlantic and Rolling Stones Records, the cover was withdrawn and the album had to be reissued.

While that brouhaha cost everyone money, it was small potatoes compared to the controversy stirred up by the lyrics of the title track, which included the line, "Black girls just wanna get fucked all night." As Jagger would later say, "I suppose we ask for it if we record things like that. Christ, I don't do these things intentionally. I just wrote it . . . That's real, and if girls can do that, I can certainly write about it, because it's what I see."

When Ahmet asked Jagger "to please change the lyrics," he replied the song was about "a stupid guy talking" and was "supposed to be a satire." In Ahmet's words, "I said, 'I don't think people are going to understand that when they hear *"black girls like to fuck all night."*' It came to a point where I couldn't get him to change the lyrics, so I knew that trouble was going to come. But if I hadn't put out the record the way it was, the Stones could have left the label. Our contract was set so that he had the right to put whatever he wanted in the records, as long as it wasn't illegal—and it wasn't illegal to say that."

To Ahmet's amazement, the album received excellent reviews and sold like crazy without anyone objecting to the lyrics. In his words, "I thought, 'Jesus, we've gotten away with this,'" while also proving the

Stones "had no black following." Ahmet then got a call from his old friend Hal Jackson, the former deejay who, after cofounding the Inner City Broadcasting Corporation with Manhattan borough president Percy Sutton, had purchased WLIB, the first African American owned radio station in New York City, and then WBLS.

"Ahmet," Jackson said, "I hate to tell you this, I've been deluged with complaints about this record. You've got to take it off the market." After Ahmet explained that his contract with the Rolling Stones made it impossible for him to do so, Jackson told him he had received a letter of complaint signed by fifteen associations of Baptist women who considered Jagger's lyrics offensve.

The issue ratcheted up to another level when the Reverend Jesse Jackson, who had marched from Selma to Montgomery with Dr. Martin Luther King and then founded Operation PUSH (People United to Save Humanity), called to say, "Ahmet, you're in a world of trouble." Quickly going public with the issue, Jackson described the song as "vulgar and obscene" and "an insult to colored people." Announcing he would soon be meeting with Mick Jagger and representatives of Atlantic Records about his complaint, Jackson added, "We do not want to act like censors but we feel that Mick Jagger has a social responsibility."

Within a week of Hal Jackson's initial call, Atlantic's offices in Midtown Manhattan were being picketed by what Ahmet would later call "everybody you could possibly think of . . . even the Abyssinian Church." Marching up and down the street with signs, the protesters urged everyone to boycott the label's records.

On every level imaginable, Ahmet's worst nightmare had now come real. Having built his label on music made by black artists for a black audience, he was now being confronted on a daily basis by black protesters demanding no one buy his records because a white band that had begun its career playing black rhythm and blues had insulted black womanhood. In practical terms, as Peter Rudge would later say, "Ahmet was stuck between a rock and a hard place. He could either piss off Mick or piss off the entire ethos on which Atlantic Records had been founded. Ahmet was consistent in that he didn't want to take on Jesse Jackson or the black coalition because he would have had to answer to too many great Atlantic artists. That was not something Ahmet could live with and so he chose in my opinion to piss off Mick."

Over the years, Atlantic had demonstrated its own sense of social responsibility by regularly contributing money to Jackson's organization. In Jerry Wexler's words, "He used to come up to my office for his taste and I would throw a check at him like a Hungarian cavalry officer throwing a bag of gold at his tailor. Ahmet and I had separate offices and I would call Ahmet on the intercom, and say, 'Ahmet, he's coming down. Don't give. I gave already.' While every social and political stance of his is good and admirable, he tried to subvert our artists and turn Wilson Pickett and Otis Redding against me so he could set up a picket line and get more money from me."

According to Ahmet, who had always maintained a far better personal relationship with Jackson than Wexler did, it was Jackson who came up with a plan to solve Atlantic's problem by advising Ahmet to come to Chicago to meet with the groups who had initiated the boycott. Ahmet brought with him his longtime assistant Noreen Woods, a black woman who was "like my guardian angel" as well as "a great friend" of Jesse Jackson. Before the meeting began, Jackson warned Ahmet that even though he was about to really light into him and curse him "and say horrible things," Ahmet was to "just go ahead and calmly explain what this is about."

"Scared to death" as he walked into the meeting to be confronted by "a sea of black faces—there must have been a hundred people there, all filled up with anger," Ahmet would later say, "I thought I was going to be lynched. I was the only white person in the hall—and it was very scary." Ahmet then began explaining he had no control over what the Rolling Stones recorded and that Mick Jagger was not a racist but "quite to the contrary: he has a black child."

Playing his part to perfection, Jackson said, "Oh man, are you kidding me? . . . You go there, take advantage of black people, and on top of that, you take their money selling records . . . then you turn around and insult them like this. This is black womanhood you're insulting." In Ahmet's words, Jackson then "started to insult me irrationally, and to such an extent that the crowd suddenly began to react against him— because I was calmly continuing on, while he was ranting and raving." As the crowd began turning toward Ahmet, Jackson shifted gears and said, "On the other hand, Ahmet, you've done so much for so many black artists . . . you can't control what this musician has done. I guess

Jagger didn't mean to say that . . . It might not be clear on the record, because you can hardly understand the lyrics." In Ahmet's words, "And suddenly, the whole thing had come to an end."

Once everyone sat down to have lunch, people began coming over to ask Ahmet questions about Wilson Pickett and LaVern Baker, and "we all left as happy and contented as can be. Jesse is a genius, you know, because he had orchestrated this whole thing knowing that I had tried not to put out the record with that lyric. That man saved my life."

Ahmet still had to pacify Hal Jackson, who said he would be willing to forget the entire incident if Jagger presented the award at Jackson's 1979 Talented Teens International pageant in Los Angeles. Breaking his own rule of never being "pushy" with Jagger, Ahmet persuaded him to appear at the event and then flew to Los Angeles, where he called Jagger the day before his scheduled appearance to remind him about it.

Ahmet was about to have lunch with the socialite author Brooke Hayward when he received a frantic call from Hal Jackson saying he was at Jagger's hotel but the singer could not be awakened. Ahmet rushed over to the hotel only to be told Jagger had been up all night partying and had only gone to bed an hour earlier. "I shouted at him," Ahmet said. "I threw water at him, but nothing would wake him up."

Furiously, Hal Jackson demanded that Ahmet come up with another celebrity to present the award or there would be "big trouble." As he and Brooke Hayward had not yet had lunch, Ahmet directed his driver to take them to the Cocoanut Grove, where he persuaded Hayward to deliver an off-the-cuff speech to "a thousand expectant black teenage girls waiting for Mick Jagger." Ahmet then had Noreen Woods talk about how she had worked her way up through the ranks at Atlantic and everyone went home happy.

Shortly before his death, Jerry Wexler would explain the real nature of the elaborate charade with Jesse Jackson in Chicago by saying, "Ahmet had to pay a million dollars to them. Ahmet told me he had to make a public mea culpa and then Jesse turned it around and defended him. The contribution had already been agreed upon and the deal was down. Jesse first had to kick Ahmet's ass and then redeem him."

Fulfilling their contract, the Stones went on to record *Emotional Rescue, Tattoo You,* and *Undercover* for Atlantic. By the time their second five-year deal with the label expired in 1983, in the words of

Rupert Lowenstein, "I don't think Atlantic was all that enchanted with the next contract, and I don't think the Rolling Stones were all that enchanted with Ahmet. Familiarity breeds contempt. The excitement had gone."

While Ahmet did fly to London to push the bidding higher, the Stones signed with CBS, a label headed by the explosive Walter Yetnikoff, a record executive whose penchant for screaming tirades and foul-mouthed invective made Jerry Wexler seem like a Boy Scout. In what was then the richest deal in the history of rock, the Stones received a $6 million advance for each of their next four albums as well as $4 million for publicity. In order for CBS to recoup its advance, each new album by the Stones would have to sell three million copies.

As Peter Rudge would later say, "It always shocked me Mick went there but Columbia and CBS were more powerful then than they had ever been before or afterwards. They were the big red Formula One machine, the one to get on, and Mick wanted to make money. When we signed with Atlantic, it was Ahmet's record company. By 1984, it wasn't anymore. Atlantic had served their purpose. Ahmet had served his purpose. The legacy of the Stones was secure. Then you cash in, don't you?"

Unlike Yetnikoff, with whom the band would part company once their contract with CBS was done, Jagger and Ahmet remained close long after their business relationship was over. In Rudge's words, "Mick is one of those people who doesn't look back when he moves on. He's not sentimental. The greatest tribute to Ahmet was that he and Mick remained lifelong friends."

## SIXTEEN

# *The Boy Wonder*

*"I was sitting in Ahmet's office and I said to him, 'How do you make a lot of money in the music business?' and he looked at me and said, 'You wanna know how?' and he got up from his desk wearing his very elegant handmade shoes, his Turnbull & Asser shirt, and a Hermès tie looking like a banker and he hunched over with his head down and sort of rumbled across the floor. I said, 'What the fuck is that?' He said, 'That's how you make a lot of money in the music business.' I said, 'I don't get it.' He said, 'I'm gonna do it one more time, watch.' So he did the same thing again and I said to him, 'I still don't get it.' He said, 'Schmuck, this is it. One more time. Take notes.' And he did exactly the same thing so I said, 'I don't get it.' He said, 'If you're lucky, you bump into a genius and that makes you rich in the music business!' Which is the truth and he bumped into a lot of geniuses."*

—David Geffen

## 1

Most of those who heard this oft-repeated story about Ahmet assumed he had been talking about bumping into musical geniuses like Ray Charles, Jerry Leiber and Mike Stoller, or Mick Jagger and Keith Richards. As Doug Morris, who worked alongside Ahmet for nearly twenty years at Atlantic, would say, "It's about bumping into people like Phil Spector, Jerry Wexler, and David Geffen who were talented and really had a connection to the culture. It's more than ears. There's a certain kind of intuitiveness about these people who really get it. It's this understanding, this bilingual kind of thing, this talent. And some of it is inexplicable."

Recognizing just how well David Geffen fit this particular job description, Ahmet brought him into the record business in 1970 by suggesting he form his own label that Atlantic would then distribute. A deal that at first blush seemed too good to believe for all concerned, the arrangement eventually helped put an end to the greatest partnership in the history of the record business.

Unlike Jerry Wexler, who had also begun his career at Atlantic as Ahmet's eager and willing student, David Geffen was twenty years younger than Ahmet when he went into business with him. While the two men had much in common, their relationship was always fraught with far more emotion than Ahmet and Wexler had ever allowed themselves to express to one another.

Having begun his career as an agent and then a manager, Geffen truly loved his artists. Willing to go to any length to protect them, he soon earned a reputation as a fierce negotiator who would stop at nothing to get the best deal for his clients. As Paul Rothchild, the producer whom Geffen helped edge out of the mix before signing Crosby, Stills, Nash and Young to Atlantic, would later say, "He plays hardball with a smaller, harder ball than anyone else."

David Geffen's road to success as an authentic record business mogul began in 1970 after he had thrown away a demo submitted to him by the singer-songwriter Jackson Browne only to have his secretary find some eight-by-ten photographs of the performer in the trash, thereby prompting her to urge Geffen to listen to his music. Twenty-two years old, Browne had already written "These Days" and "Colors of the Sun" while under contract to Elektra, only to be dropped by the label after folksinger Tom Rush had recorded the songs.

Convinced Browne was going to become a star, Geffen flew with him to New York so the singer could audition for Clive Davis. As Browne was performing, Davis politely explained he had to leave the room to take a call from Goddard Lieberson, the former head of Columbia Records. Incensed, Geffen ordered Browne to pack up his guitar and they walked out of Davis's office. Geffen then offered Browne's services to Atlantic.

"I'm telling you, this guy is good," Geffen told Ahmet. "I'm the guy who brought you Crosby, Stills, and Nash. I'm doing you a favor. You gotta sign him, he's gonna be a big star. You'll make a lot of money, Ahmet." In Geffen's words, "Ahmet looked at me, rubbed his bald head, and said, 'You know what, David? I have a lot of money. Why don't you start a record company and then you can have a lot of money too.' I thought, 'Fuck him. I will start a record company.'"

After deciding to call his new label Shelter Records, Geffen learned that Denny Cordell, a British record producer who had made big hits with the Moody Blues and Procol Harum, already owned the name. Consulting a thesaurus, Geffen came up with Asylum as the perfect name for a company he intended to be a safe haven for a brand-new generation of singer-songwriters who were not only skilled musicians but also poets creating work that was uniquely their own. In his or her own way, each was also somewhat mad.

In return for a 50 percent stake in the new label, Atlantic agreed to manufacture, distribute, and promote Asylum's records for three years with all costs to be charged against the joint venture and all profits to be split equally between the two companies. Ahmet then introduced Geffen to Steve Ross, whom Geffen would later call "kind of a father figure." Ross gave the arrangement his blessing and Asylum was in business.

A year passed before Asylum released any product but by then Geffen and his partner Elliot Roberts had signed twelve artists to the label, among them Jackson Browne, Joni Mitchell, Linda Ronstadt, J. D. Souther, and the Eagles. Because Geffen and Roberts also managed those who recorded for them, they effectively put an end to the Hollywood studio paradigm on which Atlantic had been founded.

After Jackson Browne had opened for Joni Mitchell at Carnegie Hall on February 23, 1972, Ahmet hosted a gala midnight supper to celebrate the launch of Asylum Records at the Sky Garden Roof atop the St. Moritz Hotel overlooking Central Park. Grateful for all Ahmet had done for him, Geffen told him, "We're going to be partners in everything forever."

Certain the Eagles would become even bigger than CSN&Y, Geffen spent $125,000 to record the band's debut album at Olympic Studios in London. Ahmet did not share his enthusiasm for the group until he heard their version of Jackson Browne's "Take It Easy." Instructing the

Atlantic promotion department to work the record as hard as possible, Ahmet told *Record World* magazine on May 6 that the song would "be number one in six weeks." By midsummer, the single had risen to number twelve on the charts.

Thanks to Ahmet, Geffen had now become someone Joni Mitchell would describe in her 1974 song "Free Man in Paris" as the man who was "stoking the star making machinery behind the popular song." In Geffen's words, "Ahmet was involved in the most important transforming moment of my early career and from that point on, he and I became inseparable friends. We went everywhere together. He took me on my first trip to Paris. He introduced me to collecting art. Ahmet was the first person to tell me you had to have Louis Vuitton luggage and Turnbull & Asser shirts and Hermès ties. He was a great storyteller and one of the most entertaining people you could ever meet. The one word you'd inevitably have to come up with for Ahmet was fun. Ahmet was a lot of fun."

Which was not to say the two men were not also often at odds with one another. As Geffen later said, "Ahmet was unbelievably complicated and he had a lot of demons. We were once having a big fight about something and I said to him, 'You know, the problem with you, Ahmet, is that everybody loves you. But do you love anybody?' " It was a question Jerry Wexler would never have asked.

When Steve Ross approached Geffen about selling Asylum in 1972, Geffen asked for $7 million. Ross agreed to pay it if Geffen quit the management business and signed a long-term employment contract with Warner Communications, the parent company that owned Atlantic. In return for selling his half-interest in the label, Geffen received $400,000 in cash, $1.6 million in promissory notes convertible into WCI common stock, 121,952 shares of Warner common stock then worth $4.7 million, and a yearly salary of $150,000 to run Asylum as a subsidiary of Atlantic.

While Asylum continued issuing one Top Ten album after another that generated huge profits, Warner's ill-advised purchase of the computer game company Atari cost a billion dollars. Six months after Geffen had sold his label, the value of his common stock plummeted to $800,000. Understandably unhappy with this turn of events, Geffen went to Ross to renegotiate the deal. Eager to keep Geffen happy, Ross came up with a plan to merge Asylum with another label Ahmet had helped him acquire.

In 1969, Ahmet had introduced his fellow St. John's College alumnus Jac Holzman, the founder of Elektra Records, to Ross and Ted Ashley, who asked Holzman if he would be interested in selling his label to them. Holzman was agreeable to an acquisition deal, but he feared the merger might cause antitrust problems. The deal went nowhere until Ahmet met with Holzman in June 1970 to negotiate a price for Elektra. When Holzman said he wanted $10 million, Ahmet offered $8 million. After an hour and a half of "very congenial" negotiations in which the price kept rising in half-million-dollar increments, Ahmet bumped the offer to $9.5 million only to have Holzman insist he would not sell for less than $10 million.

As Holzman would later say, "In many ways, Ahmet was a rug merchant. He loved to *hondle*. It was not Ahmet's money. It was the game. And when you know it's the game, you just keep saying no. If you ever watched Ahmet play backgammon on the Warner jet with Steve Ross, these were two guys who went at it. It wasn't for blood but they had a lot invested. Ahmet would go off and sleep for fifteen minutes and wake up totally refreshed and continue the game. I don't know if they played for money but they both had to win and Ross was better at numbers than Ahmet."

A day after Ahmet and Holzman had sat down together, the deal was done for $10 million, with Holzman agreeing to stay on as the head of Elektra for three years. In Ahmet's words, "We bought Elektra and then Jac Holzman wanted to quit so they put him in charge of quadraphonic sound or something that didn't happen. There was nobody to run Elektra so I told Steve Ross, 'Let David Geffen run it. He can run Elektra.' So he took Asylum Records, the label I started with him, to Elektra to try to build it up like a third big label which it never quite became. It was like a poor third of the three Warner labels. He did pretty well with Elektra but he didn't stay there very long."

To persuade Geffen to revitalize Elektra, Ross offered him a yearly salary of a million dollars while also promising to pay him the difference in cash each year between the current Warner stock price and what it had been worth when Geffen had sold Asylum. In August 1973, Geffen became the chairman of Elektra-Asylum. Promptly remaking the new label, he dropped twenty-five of Elektra's thirty-five acts and fired the art director along with the entire promotion, publicity, and production staffs.

Stealing a beat on the competition, Geffen then made front-page news in the trades by convincing Bob Dylan, who had spent his entire career on Columbia, to form his own label, Ashes and Sand, that would be distributed by Elektra-Asylum. After recording *Planet Waves* in three days in Los Angeles, Dylan set off on a six-week, twenty-one-city nationwide tour, on which he played forty sold-out shows.

Unfortunately, one of those who had also been bidding for Dylan's services was Jerry Wexler. In 1971, Wexler, then fifty-four years old, had also fallen in love with Geffen's twenty-four-year-old assistant. The two were married in 1973 but Wexler knew Geffen had tried to persuade her to stop dating a man old enough to be her father. With all this as backstory, the stage was now set for the heated confrontation that would spell the beginning of the end of Jerry Wexler's brilliant career at Atlantic.

## 2

A Yale graduate with a penchant for one-liners who regularly served as toastmaster general at various music industry fundraising affairs, Joe Smith had begun his career in the record business as a disc jockey in Boston during the mid-1950s. After Atlantic's local distributor had laid some cash on Smith so he would play the label's new releases, Ahmet, Nesuhi, and Wexler would always make a point of having dinner with the man they "regarded as the intellectual deejay" whenever they visited the city. They soon all became good friends.

A one-of-a-kind record executive who could crunch numbers with corporate accountants while also dealing with the Grateful Dead, Smith had risen steadily through the ranks to become the president of Warner Brothers Records. Because Smith was also known throughout the industry as a genial host, Steve Ross decided to bring his top music division executives together in Smith's well-appointed home on Roxbury Drive in Beverly Hills so they could all discuss how best to move forward as a team.

The day itself began innocently enough with a photo shoot of the reigning monarchs of the record business out by Smith's pool. As Smith would later say, "They lined all of us up on the diving board for the picture. Jerry Wexler, the two Erteguns, Mo Ostin, myself, and David Geffen. Steve Ross was sitting on the lawn and I said, 'Steve, if this diving board goes, there's your music division.' He jumped up and said, 'Get 'em down. You can take this picture on the ground. You don't have to send them up there.' "

As they were all being photographed, Geffen said something to Wexler about having just signed Bob Dylan. "OK, David," Wexler replied. "You've got Dylan. Now just let's forget the whole thing." Everyone then repaired to the large screening room off the garage, where Ross began the meeting by reminding his executives that while labels within the company were allowed to compete with each other for an artist, they could not do so by offering more money. Wexler, whose long-standing dislike for Geffen had just been reignited, said, "Well, if we're going to follow some kind of rules, let's talk about who's fucking up the rules here." Referring to Bob Dylan, Wexler pointed at Geffen and said, "You stole an artist that we had!" Doing his best to look unconcerned, Geffen replied, "You're an old washed-up music man, what the fuck do you know?"

Completely losing control of himself as he had done so many times before, most often in the privacy of his office or in a recording studio where the only witnesses were musicians who worked for him, Wexler rose from his chair. Red-faced, the veins bulging in his neck, he lunged at Geffen while screaming, "You agent! You'd jump in a pool of pus to come up with a nickel between your teeth!"

Leaping from his seat, Joe Smith grabbed Wexler before he could throw a punch at Geffen. In a matter of moments, Wexler's "enormous temper" had transformed a conclave of the most powerful men in the record business into a potential Pier Six brawl. "We can't have this!" Steve Ross yelled. "We can't have this!" Getting to his feet, Mo Ostin said, "I'm outta here. I won't sit through this." As Geffen would later say, "I couldn't believe it. No one could. Jerry's face turned red. The veins on his neck looked like they were going to pop. I thought he was either going to have a heart attack or put a knife through my heart. He yelled at the top of his lungs with such violence and vitriol everyone stopped what they were doing and just held their breath."

As Smith recalled, "I had to jump on Jerry's back. Geffen was sitting on a couch with this little grin after he had just zinged Jerry about why Dylan would want to sign with an old man like him and Wexler had yelled that he was an agent who would dive in a pool of pus. The next subject was supposed to be distribution and manufacturing and as Jac Holzman, who could put a nation to sleep, was getting down to details, I said, 'We're not going to get anywhere with this. Let's have lunch.' "

Everyone then adjourned to the dining room, where they took their seats at the table by the name cards Smith's wife had made for them. Unaware of what had just happened in the screening room, she thought the distinctly uneasy atmosphere that prevailed during the meal was caused by her guests' dislike of her cheese soufflés. As Smith would later say, "What happened at my house became a legendary story. It was also absolutely the beginning of the end for Jerry in terms of how Steve Ross looked at him as well as that Ahmet sided with Geffen. We'd never had turmoil in the executive ranks of the record companies but Geffen was a master planner and his middle name was turmoil. He was the best at it."

In Geffen's words, "Jerry was furious I had gotten Dylan because he was very competitive with me and Ahmet loved me and Ahmet had at that point started to lose faith in Jerry. And all of that combined into an outburst that was really unpleasant, to say the least. I wasn't goading him. Jerry Wexler had an opinion about agents in general. I thought it was incredibly embarrassing behavior and purely jealousy but I never held it against him and I forgave him." As David Horowitz, whom Steve Ross had just hired to oversee his record companies, would later say, "I was there when it happened and it was certainly ill considered. This was a diatribe against agents and Ted Ashley was more than just a very well known former agent, he was one of the senior management team."

Six months later, after Bob Dylan had returned to his record business roots by signing a long-term deal with Columbia, Geffen approached Ahmet with a plan to merge Elektra/Asylum and Atlantic. In Ahmet's words, "David said, 'Let's put Atlantic and Elektra/Asylum together and you and I will become cochairmen.' And he was right. It was a good idea because we could save $25 million a year by not having five different lawyers, different accountants, different this, different that. Instead, we'd have it all in one."

With Ahmet and Geffen as cochairmen and Wexler as vice chairman, the merger of Atlantic/Elektra/Asylum was formally announced in a press release on June 28, 1974, that stated, "We have contemplated merging our two divisions for some time now in order to achieve more efficient operations for both companies. We believe that the combined Atlantic, Elektra and Asylum labels now have the best line-up of talent of any firm in our industry."

Basing his account on an interview with Ahmet, Geffen biographer Tom King wrote that Ahmet had "been frightened to share" this information with "Jerry Wexler and his other lieutenants" before the press release appeared and so "mutiny was declared at Atlantic Records on the day plans of the merger made the papers." Both Jerry Greenberg and Sheldon Vogel threatened to quit if the merger went through. Tracking down Ahmet while he was on a business trip in Europe, Wexler told him point-blank he would never report to Geffen. Shifting into full Old Testament mode during their conversation, he also said, "One day, you'll cry tears of blood from this wonder boy of yours." Supposedly it was then Ahmet decided he could not go ahead with his decision.

According to King, when Ahmet told Geffen the merger was not going to happen, Geffen angrily demanded, "How can you do this to me?" Ahmet replied, "Now come on, David. I'm sorry it is not going to work, but you need to understand. I'm trying to hold this company together, and I have to protect Jerry and everybody else." Geffen then said, "This is between us! You know this is the best thing for the company."

In truth, the merger fell apart because much like Louis B. Mayer at MGM, Ahmet was not about to relinquish his power to anyone. For Ahmet, the real key to the deal was that if he merged Atlantic with Elektra/Asylum, the resulting label would have, in Jerry Greenberg's words, done "much more business than Warners Brothers Records and be much bigger than them. That was why Ahmet had agreed to it." To iron out the details, Ahmet had sent Greenberg to meet with Mel Posner, the president of Elektra/Asylum. Posner began running through a list of changes that would take place at the new label.

In Greenberg's words, "Mel goes, 'Okay, we're keeping our sales guy. Your sales guy is going. We're doing this. That's going to change.'

These were David Geffen's marching orders. Then he says, 'You know the Rolls-Royce?' Ahmet had a Rolls-Royce in California that sat there with a driver so he could use it when he came to Los Angeles. So Mel says, 'The Rolls-Royce has got to go. David says we don't need it.' I said, 'Ahmet's Rolls-Royce has gotta go? We don't need it?' He goes, 'Yeah.' "

Having carefully written everything down, Greenberg told Posner he would relay what they had discussed to Ahmet. As Greenberg put it, "I don't walk back. I run back and bust into Ahmet's office and I say, 'Ahmet, David's already got a whole list of who's staying and who's going but I want to start with the most important thing just to show you where all this is going. They want to get rid of your Rolls-Royce. David doesn't think you need it out there full-time anymore and I just wanted you to know. But it's your call.' "

Telling Greenberg to hang on, Ahmet picked up the phone and called Steve Ross. With the deal having already been announced in the trades, Ahmet told Ross, "Steve, I've been giving this merger a lot of thought. Asylum has a certain image and a certain way of attracting artists and we have our own image. If you put the two together, it's not going to work. We'll be much more successful keeping them separate." In Greenberg's words, "The next thing I know, the merger's undone."

As Ahmet explained, "So then I kind of postponed it, and David got very upset, and the whole thing fell apart. I think David was quite hurt. But I think everyone thought he would come on too strong, and be too disruptive." Even in a tempestuous business where long-term relationships between the rulers of record labels could fall apart during a single phone call only to then be put back together before the end of the day, Ahmet's decision to reverse a merger that had been front-page news in all the trades was extraordinary.

While no one ever loved the perks that came along with running Atlantic more than Ahmet, he did not cancel the deal simply because David Geffen wanted to take away his Rolls-Royce in Los Angeles. In what must have come as a truly great shock, Ahmet suddenly realized that in Geffen he had found a student who in time would outdo his master. To protect himself and his position, Ahmet had to ensure Geffen was not given the opportunity to do so at Atlantic.

Understandably upset by this bizarre turn of events, Geffen would later say, "Ahmet never cared about upsetting Jerry Wexler. Jerry was never a consideration. Ahmet is a big boy, and Ahmet does what he wants, and Ahmet is not that considerate of his employees. They don't have that big a vote. Ahmet's a little bit like the gorilla—he sits where he wants . . . Ahmet and I agreed on a merger but he got very upset because friends of his were calling him up to find out if it was a demotion for him." Geffen would also note, "By the way, it wasn't a rupture in our relationship."

While Ahmet's decision to kill the merger was the first in what would become a long series of rifts, slights, snubs, perceived offenses, and misunderstandings between the two men, Ahmet and Geffen continued to consider one another friends. But even when they saw one another socially, Ahmet could not keep from doing everything he could to keep Geffen in what he still perceived as his proper place.

At some point after the merger had failed, Ahmet found himself in Los Angeles without any plans for the evening. As this in itself was a unique event, Ahmet suggested to Tom Dowd, who was also in L.A., that he meet him and Bianca Jagger for dinner in a restaurant at nine that evening. Arriving with her and "another lady—some countess" at ten-thirty, Ahmet began ordering champagne before sitting down to a meal that did not end until one in the morning.

By then, Mick Jagger had joined the group, prompting Ahmet to say, "There's got to be a party somewhere." Instructing a waiter to bring a phone to his table, Ahmet called singer Bette Midler to ask what she was doing. He then told her there was a party at Cher's house and he would pick her up on his way there. Despite the fact it was now nearly two A.M., Ahmet then phoned Cher to tell her he was coming over with Dowd, Mick and Bianca, the countess, and Midler "for a nightcap."

Having long since parted company with Sonny, Cher was then living with David Geffen. When Ahmet and his group arrived at their home that night, Cher looked "beautiful in this gold lamé dress." Everyone then went into the living room, where Jagger sat down at the piano as Cher began singing. Clad in a pair of tennis shoes and shorts, Geffen took it all in. "Look at that creep," Ahmet confided to Dowd. "How can he dress like that?" Addressing Geffen, Ahmet said, "David, what a lovely outfit!" Ahmet then asked Cher if everyone could have some champagne. "Of course," she told him, "we always have some chilled." When Geffen asked her where the champagne was, Ahmet looked at him and said, "We never had that problem when Sonny was here."

"That was Ahmet," Dowd said, "pulling people's strings. Ahmet has a great deal of respect for Geffen but he doesn't like him as a human being. He has no allegiance to him—because David has no allegiance to anything except for dollar signs. And Ahmet will not renege on a human being, like David would." Loyal to a fault, Dowd would spend his entire career at Atlantic without ever being paid royalties for the many hit albums he produced for the label before dying at the age of seventy-seven in 2002.

After Geffen's relationship with Cher ended, he began losing interest in the music business and fulfilled his childhood dream of running a movie studio by becoming the vice chairman of Warner Brothers in 1975. Two years later, he was mistakenly diagnosed with transitional cell carcinoma and retired from show business to teach a course on the music industry and artist management at Yale.

Eventually given a clean bill of health, Geffen decided to return to the record business in 1980 and asked Steve Ross for $25 million to start a new label called Geffen Records in return for a 50 percent stake in the company. A decade later, Geffen would sell his label to MCA for $550 million in stock, thereby making him, as *The New York Times* reported, "one of the nation's richest individuals."

In Geffen's words, "When I came back into the record business in 1980, Ahmet wanted me to come to Atlantic Records and I said, 'Not a chance. I'm going to sign with Mo Ostin.' And he said, 'Why with Mo?' I said, 'Because for all these years I was retired, he never stopped calling me and telling me how much he wanted me.' And Ahmet said to me, 'You'll never have a laugh.' The truth of the matter was that Ahmet was an awful lot of fun. But you had to pay big time to be in his company."

When the two men saw one another for the first time after Geffen had decided to go into business with Ostin and Ahmet asked why Geffen had not returned to Atlantic, Geffen responded, "Are you kidding? You're out of it. Without Jerry Greenberg, Atlantic is nothing! Atlantic is finished!"

In time, Geffen's own business acumen would far outstrip that of his mentor, resulting in a personal fortune of more than a billion dollars. Staying with what he knew best, Ahmet would spend seven decades as the chairman of Atlantic Records. It was a position he feared he would never have held on to for that long had he made David Geffen his partner.

## 3

Like a long-distance marriage that existed in name only, so long as Ahmet and Jerry Wexler were operating from different geographic locations, they could maintain the appearance that they were still partners. Although Wexler had continued to function as a skilled producer and a capable record executive, he and Ahmet had long since parted ways.

When Wexler began coming into work on a daily basis to Atlantic's plush new offices at the Warner Communications headquarters at 75 Rockefeller Plaza, he soon realized he had been excluded from the day-to-day operations of the label. With both the promotion and marketing departments now reporting to Jerry Greenberg, who had also signed many of Atlantic's new acts, Wexler, in Greenberg's words, "couldn't slip back into what he used to do." Unable to tolerate the situation, Wexler soon confronted Ahmet by pointing out he had specifically agreed Wexler would be included in all decisions made at the label. Telling his longtime partner he worked far too spontaneously to ever be part of such an arrangement, Ahmet also informed Wexler that those who now worked at Atlantic no longer felt the need to report to him.

As always, Wexler's personality was at the heart of the matter. Within the new corporate structure at Atlantic, Ahmet told Wexler he was "viewed as abrasive, derisive, and cynical, a maverick at meetings, a flaunter of my quick sales of option stock, an undiplomatic critic." When Wexler had first begun working at Atlantic, nearly every independent record label had been run by men who shared these same traits.

In the very corporate world the record business had now become, where everyone was expected to be a team player while understanding precisely which rung he or she occupied on the executive ladder, Wexler simply no longer fit. Unlike Ahmet, a natural-born diplomat who could handle any situation with consummate ease and so was flourishing at Warner Communications, Wexler could not tailor his personality to suit his new environment. Ahmet also felt that Wexler had no real interest in the company itself but only really cared about his own artists.

Wexler then demanded to know if Ahmet had now become his boss. Ahmet replied by saying that because of the position he occupied in the corporate structure, the final decision in all such matters belonged to him. As Wexler would later write, "For me it was parity or nothing. No parity, no Wexler."

"The problem," Joe Smith said, "was that when Jerry came back to New York, he would fight off everything and deride anything that came down from Warner Communications, the parent company. Ahmet knew how to play the game very well. He had tickets to everything and tables at all the right restaurants and the corporate guys would run around with Ahmet while Wexler was being cantankerous."

Wexler wrote Ahmet a letter on May 3, 1975, in which he stated, "Under no circumstances, Ahmet, can I be your employee. That's the bottom line." Ahmet's response was "Man, you can't quit! It's unthinkable." Once he realized Wexler had made his decision and would not change his mind, Ahmet did all he could to ensure his longtime partner would get what he was due. As David Horowitz recalled, "One of my first assignments was to work out a parting deal with Jerry. We were prepared to be more than reasonable because the man had made a huge contribution to Warner's, and Ahmet certainly didn't bear him any ill will. I can't say for sure but I think Jerry wanted out."

On July 17, Jerry Wexler formally announced his resignation as vice chairman of Atlantic Records effective August 1. As he would later say, "When I walked out, I didn't know what I was going to do for a living or how I was going to survive. But I couldn't abide the situation. Which was me becoming junior to Ahmet." While the parting itself was amicable, the long friendship between Ahmet and Wexler ended when he left Atlantic.

In the ensuing years, the two men had no contact at all with one another because, in Wexler's words, "Ahmet sees only two kinds of people—social people and morons. And I ain't either one." Cuttingly, Wexler also suggested the words on Ahmet's tombstone should read, "He Meant It When He Said It." Wexler recalled, "There was a big draft between us for years. A big draft. But we very much came together again towards the end."

Two years after Wexler left Atlantic, he was hired by Mo Ostin to head the New York A&R department of Warner Brothers Records. After leaving the label, he produced albums by Dire Straits, Bob Dylan, and Carlos Santana. Nearly a decade passed before Ahmet and Jerry Wexler saw one another again as members of the nominating committee of the newly created Rock and Roll Hall of Fame in New York.

As Suzan Hochberg, the director of the institution, recalled, "Jerry called me the day before the nominating committee's first meeting and he was very nervous and apprehensive about coming. 'You don't understand,' he said. 'I haven't seen Ahmet in a long time and there was some friction when we parted. Is he really going to be there?' When he walked in, Ahmet and Jerry saw one another and they hugged each other and that was it. The hatchet was buried." Ahmet and Wexler were inducted into the Rock and Roll Hall of Fame in 1987.

By then, both men realized that the astonishing body of work they had done together during their twenty-two-year partnership at Atlantic would never be equaled. In every way possible, Wexler had given his life to the label. Working at a feverish pace, he had come into the office early, stayed late, and then spent his weekends at home calling distributors on one of the first multi-line push-button phones to let them know that, in his son's words, if "they didn't pay for the hit that was out right now by Solomon Burke, they would not get Ben E. King's next record."

In the Atlantic office at 234 West 56th Street, where their desks had faced one another, the two men had staged elaborate charades whenever a manager would come in with an act they wanted to sign. Debating how big a royalty they could afford to pay without bankrupting the label, the partners would go back and forth with one another before finally reaching the figure they had both agreed upon beforehand. As the manager and the artist watched, they would then shake each other's hands on the deal right in front of them.

Functioning more powerfully as a unit than either could ever have done on his own, they had cajoled great artists into recording material they instinctively knew would be commercially successful. On the road, they had kibitzed and caroused together, goofed on everyone they had met like a pair of hip comics, and even shared a single bed. In the studio, they had clapped their hands in time to the beat while singing backup as Joe Turner cut "Shake, Rattle and Roll."

On the day Jerry Wexler left 75 Rockefeller Plaza for the final time, he took with him something no one would ever replace at Atlantic. Except for Nesuhi, Ahmet had now lost his last real peer in the record business. As never before, Ahmet was now truly on his own at the company he had founded.

# SEVENTEEN

# *The Years with Ross*

*"At the moment when I met Ahmet, at the beginning of this decade, it was assumed that the style of the years to come would derive from the principal styles of the nineteen-sixties ... but then as I saw Ahmet together with important custodians of the style of the nineteen-sixties and noted his greater power and presence, I began to understand that it would be* his *style (eclectic, reminiscent, fickle, perverse) that would be the distinctive style of the first years of the new decade, that Ahmet would achieve this new importance as exemplar precisely because he lacked the inflexible center I had confusedly looked for, and that he would achieve it through his intuitive, obsessive mastery of the modes of infatuation."*

—George W. S. Trow Jr.

## 1

Much like the subject of what many still consider to be the greatest profile ever to appear in *The New Yorker* magazine, George William Swift Trow Jr. was a child of wealth and privilege who adored black music, amassed an astonishing record collection featuring old 45s by Little Willie John, and regularly attended shows at the Apollo Theater. Born into "an extremely venerable family in the history of New York City" whose "style was that of the brownstone elite," Trow was the son of the night editor of the *New York Post* and the great-great-grandson of the prominent New York printer whose city directory "was the precursor of the telephone book."

Educated at Phillips Exeter Academy and Harvard University, where he became president of the *Lampoon* and cowrote the 1964 *Hasty Pudding Show,* Trow joined *The New Yorker* two years later and began writing unsigned pieces for "The Talk of the Town" section of the magazine that were "jazzy, telegraphic, *emphatic.*" Due in no small part to his family background and social connections, Trow became good friends with Jacqueline Onassis and Diana Vreeland. In 1970, he helped found *National Lampoon.* A year later, Trow began working on the two-part profile of Ahmet that would establish him, in the words of *New Yorker* staff writer Hendrik Hertzberg, "as a cultural critic of the first rank."

A social equal who was on a first-name basis with many of the wealthy and fashionable people Ahmet and Mica were seeing on a nightly basis, Trow had little trouble persuading Ahmet to grant him unlimited access. In the words of Ian Frazier, Trow's good friend and fellow *New Yorker* staff writer, "George went everywhere with Ahmet, he hung out with Mica, and he had Ahmet to his club. A much much classier club than the Harvard Club, the Knickerbocker Club. It was not like he showed up, did the profile, and moved on. He became part of that group of people."

In May 1971, Trow had flown to the south of France to celebrate the release of the Rolling Stones' debut album on Atlantic. On June 27, Trow accompanied Ahmet and Mica to the final concert at Bill Graham's Fillmore East on Second Avenue and Sixth Street. In a story Graham loved to tell, Ahmet had walked into his office on the night the J. Geils Band performed at the theater for the first time. Wearing a "blue suit, white-on-white shirt, blue-on-blue tie," Ahmet "looked like he had just won the dance contest somewhere." Not realizing the manager of the J. Geils Band was also there, Ahmet asked Graham how the group had done. Cutting off the promoter before he could answer, Ahmet said, "I *knew* it! They *sucked*! I knew I shouldn't have signed them. *Terrible,* huh?" Graham then said, "Ahmet, may I introduce you to the *manager* of the J. Geils Band?"

Without missing a beat, Ahmet called the manager by his first name, which he had only just learned, and then told him this was a game he and Graham often played. When the manager asked if he actually had seen the band's set, Ahmet said, "I would miss their set? I wouldn't miss the *J. Geils* set." People began laughing so hard that they had to leave the room.

Having already earned a well-deserved reputation in the music business as a fearsome screamer and shouter whom no one could control, Bill Graham was also the nominal head of a label called San Francisco Records, distributed by Atlantic. Although Fillmore Records, the label the promoter had set up with Clive Davis at CBS, was far more successful, Ahmet and Graham never exchanged a harsh word.

The same could not be said for Graham and Jerry Wexler. Graham once so infuriated Wexler by screaming at him over the phone that Wexler promptly ordered the promoter to get into a cab and come to his office so he could "beat the shit" out of him. Unlike Wexler, Ahmet always knew exactly how to handle Graham and once made him wait so long on the phone as he dictated two long and incredibly complicated letters to a nonexistent secretary that when Ahmet finally got back to him, Graham had completely forgotten what he had called to complain about.

When Graham pointed out one day that he could not discuss business with Ahmet because there was so much else going on in his office at Atlantic, Ahmet promptly walked the promoter downstairs and instructed his driver to take them to an old office building on Broadway and 48th Street. Walking past a sign that read "Tango Palace," Ahmet escorted Graham to the seedy dime-a-dance hall on the second floor, where both men were immediately approached by "five or six very sexy looking girls wearing dresses with their boobs popping out."

Handing a befuddled Graham $20, Ahmet told him to pick out a girl and start dancing with her. At three in the afternoon in the otherwise deserted dance hall, Ahmet "took one girl and he took another. The music was playing and we were dancing and I said, 'Okay. Now we can talk. What do you want to talk about?' "

On the night Bill Graham essentially ended the psychedelic music era in New York City by closing the Fillmore East, Ahmet appeared for the final show in a blue blazer, white pants, a yellow polo shirt, and yellow socks with a matching yellow handkerchief in the breast pocket of his jacket. When a "minor record company executive" asked Mica, attired in "a striking black dress," if she liked the Allman Brothers, who were on the bill that night and whose records Atlantic distributed, she said, "Yah. They are divine, no?"

When Mica asked Ahmet if they could get a drink, he explained to her that Second Avenue was crowded with people who did not have tickets and it would not be easy to find a place to go in a neighborhood then largely populated by working-class Ukrainian immigrants, hippie dope dealers, and the New York chapter of the Hells Angels. "But I think there must be hundreds of places to drink here, no?" she said.

On the same block where he had seen Bunk Johnson, Louis Armstrong's trumpet teacher, when the musician first came to play in New York at the Stuyvesant Casino in June 1946, Ahmet led Mica outside. Crossing the street, they walked into a dive where anyone else who looked like them would have been immediately relieved of all their valuables. In a dire joint where six men sat at the bar drinking whiskey with beer chasers, Ahmet coolly ordered Mica a glass of white wine.

Trow also accompanied Ahmet as he discussed deals with Steve Ross, Sheldon Vogel, and Jerry Greenberg while flying to Los Angeles on the Warner jet. He dined with him at Martoni's, the hip L.A. music business hangout, and then rode with Ahmet in a limo to a recording session where David Crosby and Graham Nash supplied Ahmet with the harmony vocals for a track they had just cut by singing them for him, "one at each ear."

Trow went with Ahmet, Mica, and seven friends, among them Bill and Chessy Rayner, Mica's partner in a design firm Ahmet had suggested they name MAC II, to the Rainbow Grill atop 30 Rockefeller Plaza, where Duke Ellington and his band were performing. Nearly forty years after he had first seen Ellington at the Palladium in London, Ahmet listened far more intently to the music than any of his guests.

When the once handsome but still elegant Ellington, who in Trow's words "looked ravaged," came over to pay his respects to Ahmet after his first set, the two men kissed one another and Ellington said, "Such a wonderful party. I was wondering who was supplying that wonderful *pastel* quality." Before the band leader began his second set, most of Ahmet's guests left. Ordering a series of vodka stingers, Ahmet discussed Ellington's "Black and Tan Fantasy" as "a burlesque song" and then told Trow, "A lot of my friends are very nice jerks, if you know what I mean. They're very nice, but they're jerks . . . They don't deserve to have Duke Ellington play for them."

On May 2, 1977, Trow ran into Ahmet in Studio 54. Jerry Greenberg, who by then had signed Chic and the Trammps to Atlantic and was a good friend of Studio 54 cofounder Steve Rubell, had asked

Ahmet if he wanted to invest in the disco only to have him reply, "What do we know about that? No. Stay away." In light of the drug and tax evasion problems that would eventually send Rubell and his partner, Ian Schrager, to jail, Ahmet's decision proved wise. He did however become a regular at the club and in a photograph taken a year later can be seen sitting along the wall with Elton John, Andy Warhol, Jerry Hall, who in time would marry Mick Jagger, and the socialite Barbara Allen, who lovingly caresses Ahmet's face with one hand while holding a cigarette in the other.

Along with the fashion designer Halston, Diana Vreeland, and Mick Jagger and a host of others that night in 1977, Ahmet watched Bianca Jagger celebrate her thirty-second birthday by riding across the floor of Studio 54 on a white horse led by a young man and woman with circus costumes painted on their naked bodies. As if to proclaim the dawning of yet another brand-new era in the city, the famous scrim of the man in the moon with a cocaine spoon to his nose then came down across the stage.

Precisely why it took Trow seven years to write his profile of Ahmet, no one knows for certain but at some point Ahmet may have asked him to hold off on publishing it because of the delicate nature of his relationship with the Rolling Stones. After Trow finally submitted the piece to William Shawn, the legendary editor of *The New Yorker,* the writer was talking with Ian Frazier in his office at the magazine. In Frazier's words, "There was a knock on the door and it was Mr. Shawn, which in itself was a thing of enormous significance. He said, 'Oh, Mr. Trow, I was looking for you.'" The two men then stepped out in the hall to talk. Five minutes later, Trow walked back in "and closed the door and his face was tomato red. I said, 'Well, what did he say?' And George said, 'Shawn said this piece is Proust.'"

Written in the dense and sometimes impenetrable style of a Victorian novel, the piece ran on sixty pages in two consecutive issues of the magazine. In a world not yet as media-saturated as it has since become, Trow's massive and detailed profile of Ahmet was an immediate sensation. Becoming the cornerstone of his legend outside the record business, it also served as the template for everything that would be written about him afterward.

"Ahmet had not yet become a cultural icon," Jamaica Kincaid, a staff writer at the magazine who was also close to Trow, would later say, "and that piece placed him. George really gave the lifestyle the legitimacy it might not have had and a kind of grandeur because Ahmet was part of a social upheaval that really changed everything. The Ertegun profile was unequaled in my time at *The New Yorker*. It had an indelible taste. You could read it and taste something you had never tasted before and haven't since. It was so good that it made me lose interest in writing profiles. You just read it and wiped your brow and knew there would never be anything like it again."

While both Mica and David Geffen would later say Trow seemed to be in love with Ahmet, in Kincaid's words, "I wouldn't say George was obsessed with Ahmet any more than anything he was writing about. He was obsessed with his subject as any good writer would be. For George, Ahmet's clothes were the details. Every detail for him was a revelation and an opportunity to describe."

After the profile appeared, Ahmet and Trow lost contact. "When it was done," Kincaid would later say, "George didn't ever really quite know what to do with himself again. It just really changed everything and changed his relationship with Ahmet and Mrs. Ertegun. George was very much a part of their social circle to that point and I think it was a complimentary profile but the sharpness and magical-ness of George's writing must have been searing to them in some way because there was never the same kind of intimacy after that. I think the piece stung both the subject and the author and they sort of drifted apart. It was the end of the marriage and the breach had a bit of the postcoital irritation about it."

Nor was this the only breach the piece caused. As David Geffen was looking through *The New York Times* on May 25, 1978, he came across a full-page ad taken out by *The New Yorker* to announce the publication of Trow's profile. Four days later, after reading what Ahmet had said about him in it, Geffen ran to the bathroom and threw up. Having been portrayed in unflattering terms, Geffen had good reason to be upset. As Ian Frazier would later say, "First and foremost, the piece is about Ahmet. It's also a great portrait of David Geffen and the difference between him and Ahmet as well as being really prophetic in terms of what Geffen would later become."

In one of the many interchanges between the two that Trow

described, Geffen was waiting to talk to Ahmet in his bungalow at the Beverly Hills Hotel when he received a call from Joni Mitchell. As Geffen spoke to the singer-songwriter, with whom he had once shared a house, Ahmet told Trow, "He must be talking to an artist, He's got his soulful look on. He's trying to purge at this moment all traces of his eager greed."

Trow also recounted an incident in which Geffen tried to persuade Ahmet to pay him an advance of $50,000 to cover the studio costs for Crosby and Nash's first album, even though they had already negotiated a deal providing $5,000 in reimbursement for every $100,000 worth of albums sold. "We'll give you ten thousand dollars," Ahmet told Geffen, "and you can go to Santa Monica Boulevard and watch a couple of movies, or whatever you do all day."

Pointing out it was "sound business practice, and besides, I want it," Geffen said, "Why don't you concede for once? Why not make a gesture of good will, taking into account the entire relationship? Why not give the fifty thousand dollars?" Telling Geffen he needed the money to run his company, Ahmet finally settled on an advance of $35,000. "If you're in that kind of trouble," Geffen responded, "I'm selling my stock." After the two men had bantered about which one of them was "chintzy," Ahmet said, "You know, a soldier is sometimes too good a soldier. Whatever happens, I'm your friend and I love you, but don't squeeze the juice out of every situation." Trow also managed to dismiss the future billionaire by writing, "There was a brief vogue for David Geffen."

After reading the first installment of the profile, Geffen called Ahmet and yelled, "You're responsible for this outrage! George wrote those things about me because you told him to!" Coolly, Ahmet said, "Don't be ridiculous, David. I don't have any control over what this man writes." In the words of biographer Tom King, Geffen then decided he would never work with Ahmet again.

By this time, Ahmet and Geffen had already fallen out with one another after an incident on a plane when Ahmet had continued flicking ashes from his cigarette onto Geffen's head as he sat in front of him. Geffen warned Ahmet that if he did not stop, he would pour a glass of water on his head. In Geffen's words, "And he didn't stop it and I did it and he went mad and then we didn't speak for a while."

After patching up their differences, the two men were flying on the Warner jet to Barbados when Geffen began talking about how much money he had only to have Ahmet tell him, "Oh, David, people who have any class or taste don't talk about money." Ahmet, "who liked pushing buttons," then proceeded to get Geffen so "wound up and flipped out and angry" that they "had a huge fight when the plane landed and nobody who was staying at David's house was allowed to go over to have dinner with the Erteguns next door."

They reconciled only to fall out with one another yet again when Ahmet told Geffen's authorized biographer that Geffen had been spreading rumors throughout the record industry that Ahmet was anti-Semitic. In light of all the years Ahmet had spent in a business largely dominated by Jewish executives and how closely he had worked with Herb and Miriam Abramson, Jerry Wexler, Jerry Greenberg, Doug Morris, and a host of others at Atlantic, the charge would have seemed laughable to anyone familiar with his history.

Nonetheless, when Geffen learned what Ahmet had said about him to his biographer, the two men had a heated conversation over the phone and then did not speak to one another for years. In Geffen's words, "He said it because he was jealous. He couldn't stand that I had become so successful and so wealthy. It burned his ass."

When both men found themselves at Barry Diller's Academy Awards party in Los Angeles on March 25, 2001, Geffen angrily confronted Ahmet about his statement. Having been asked by Mica not to make a scene, Geffen decided to "simply get over it because what was the point? Ahmet was an old man and I thought, 'Give this up.' There was nothing he did that could have stopped me from loving him. But it sure was exasperating."

## 2

For most of those who lived in Manhattan during the 1970s, the city had become, in the words of *Vanity Fair* columnist James Wolcott, "a metropolis on the verge of a nervous breakdown with a side order of panic in needle park" where "the tourists looked scared" and "getting back to the hotel alive was one of the main items on their checklists."

Despite how dire life had become for some in the city, Ahmet had only to look out his office window at 75 Rockefeller Plaza to know just how well he was doing.

Befitting his status as the head of a record label that earned $75 million in 1973 while boasting an industry-high 25 percent profit margin before taxes, Ahmet's well-appointed second-floor office, designed for him by Mica, overlooked "21," thereby allowing him to watch the city's most important power brokers step from their limousines each day so they could do business with one another inside the restaurant. As he would later say, "I like the view out the window. It's a terrific way to keep track of who's lunching with whom."

In what was a banner year for the record business, the four labels that comprised the Warner Music Group, Atlantic, Elektra, Asylum, and Warner Brothers Records, sold a quarter of a billion dollars' worth of records and tapes worldwide. While David Geffen, Joe Smith, and Mo Ostin all held positions of great power within Warner Communications, David Horowitz, who oversaw the group's financial operations, would later say, "Ahmet was first among equals because he was a legendary guy. He was our superman." As chairman of the committee that coordinated the distribution system shared by all four labels, Ahmet now had nearly a thousand employees reporting indirectly to him. By any standard, he had finally reached the very top of the mountain in an industry that continued expanding beyond anyone's wildest expectations.

To celebrate Atlantic's twenty-fifth anniversary in April 1973, Ahmet chartered an Air India 747 and took two hundred people to Paris for a gala four-day sales meeting. As soon as the plane was airborne, everyone on board "started lighting joints, snorting coke, and partying seriously." After Jerry Wexler had fallen asleep on the plane, Ahmet took his passport and replaced his photograph with that of a woman having sex with a donkey. When Wexler presented his passport at the airport in Paris, the gendarme looked at the photo and then at Wexler and then back at the photo again. Trying to be helpful, Wexler said, "I used to have a beard" as Ahmet collapsed with laughter. The fun continued after the group had checked into a luxury hotel and gone out for "a ten-course gourmet meal at a five-star Parisian restaurant," where the bar bill alone came to $16,860.

Born with "an apparently boundless appetite for the good life," Ahmet continued buying his custom-made suits and jackets at Huntsman at 11 Savile Row in London. His handmade shoes came from John Lobb in Paris. The proud owner of a 1934 Bentley, a 1957 Sunbeam, and a 1965 Rolls-Royce, he was driven around the city in two Cadillac Fleetwoods, one green and one blue, by two chauffeurs, one white, the other black. Ahmet's extensive art collection now included works by Jasper Johns, Robert Rauschenberg, Ellsworth Kelly, and Larry Rivers, as well as a recently acquired painting by his "favorite artist, Henri Matisse."

In their elegant five-floor town house on East 81st Street, which had been featured in *House and Garden*, Ahmet and Mica continued hosting lavish dinner parties while spending their weekends on Long Island in their equally fashionable retreat on Shinnecock Bay in Southampton. When Ahmet first saw the plans for a house Mica had modeled on a Russian dacha, he asked "Where do you put the orchestra?" and then had the living room enlarged. In accordance with Oscar Wilde's dictum that three addresses always inspired confidence, Ahmet and Mica had also purchased and were reconstructing their summer home in Bodrum, then an undiscovered village on the Aegean Sea in southern Turkey. In time, they would acquire a luxurious apartment in Paris.

During a conversation Ahmet had with his assistant Jenni Trent Hughes about the trappings of success, she asked him how someone would know when he or she had finally arrived. "And he said, 'When you have no keys. If you've arrived, there's always someone there to open the door for you. When I go home in New York, Armenia opens the door. If I go home in London, Aurelia opens the door. If I get on the plane, Guy Salvador opens the door. If I go downstairs to the car, Ray opens the door.' And he was right. The fewer keys you have in your life, the more you know you've arrived."

As Ahmet grew older, his social standing became increasingly important to him. When the socialite author Barbara Howar accompanied him to a gala event thrown by a very wealthy A-list couple, Ahmet made it plain that, in her words, "He was not happy he had been seated with me. He didn't even bother to pretend. He was just in such a snit, I cannot tell you. I found it amusing because I just didn't care. But he thought he deserved better and was being wasted with people who already knew him."

Over the years, Ahmet also became more politically conservative, making a generous donation to *National Review* magazine, for which William F. Buckley then thanked him with a handwritten note. Befriending Donald Rumsfeld, who had served as chief of staff under President Gerald Ford, Ahmet staunchly defended him and the war in Iraq when Rumsfeld assumed the position of secretary of defense in George W. Bush's administration. As Howar would later say, "For Ahmet, the lid came off everything when Ronald Reagan became president. Everything was deregulated, everybody was on Wall Street, and this was the time of Ahmet's real ascendancy when he made the counterculture chic."

While Ahmet had always traveled in a wide variety of different social circles, the music he was now releasing on Atlantic no longer interested him nearly as much as the lifestyle it afforded him. After Wexler had left the label, Ahmet said, "He is sad because he sees the music to which he gave his life is no longer important. It is a mistake to invest the music we recorded with too much importance. It isn't classical music, and it cannot be interpreted in the same way. It's more like old Fred Astaire movies. They're fun, but they're not great art. And they shouldn't be seen as great art."

Ahmet owed much of his newfound wealth to the apparently endless largesse of Steve Ross. As David Horowitz recalled, "Clever as he was, Steve was very vulnerable to certain people and it was like that with Ahmet." In the words of Jay Emmett, Ross's longtime friend who ran the movie and publishing divisions at Warner Communications, "Steve had a great philosophy when it came to our employees. He paid Ahmet, Nesuhi Ertegun, Joe Smith, and Mo Ostin absolutely outrageous salaries with bonuses and options. It was far more than they could have gotten anywhere else. Steve was super-generous with Ahmet but Ahmet never really truly trusted or liked Steve."

Fixated on flying everywhere he went on the Warner Gulfstream II corporate jet, Ahmet came to Emmett one day to say he needed the plane to go to Turkey. In Emmett's words, "So I looked at him and said, 'Business or pleasure?' And he said, 'Jay, I swear, it's business.' He was going to Bodrum where he had a house. I said, 'Ahmet, let me tell you about our plane.' 'Yes?' 'It can only be used for pleasure.' "

On another occasion after Ross had given options to Ted Ashley, Frank Wells, and John Calley in the movie division, enabling each of them to buy a hundred thousand shares of WCI stock at a very favorable price, Horowitz told Emmett that Ahmet was unhappy with the arrangement because he had "no shares." Saying he found this hard to believe, Emmett learned that Ahmet had already sold his hundred-thousand-share option "at a very high price" and "made a lot of money." When Horowitz informed him Ahmet wanted another hundred-thousand-share option, Emmett said, "Talk to Steve, don't talk to me." As Horowitz would later say, "Ahmet wanted the options and I was horrified but he hit Steve up for them. Steve had no intention of giving him more because this was like duplicating them. And he said yes. He was defenseless. I thought he might have waited a year but no."

In Emmett's words, "Steve gave him another hundred thousand shares because Ahmet had sold his and was running around saying, 'What a cheap company. I don't have any shares. What is that all about?' Ahmet always pushed Steve for more of everything and Steve gave in each time." Just as Ahmet had proven when he and Ross had sat down for their first marathon negotiating session at "21," Ahmet always seemed to know just how to get what he needed from him. He also knew how to keep Ross happy by letting him know how profitable Atlantic had become.

Jerry Greenberg, who by now had become the president of Atlantic Records, recalled, "Ahmet would come in at four in the afternoon and call me in at six. 'What's going on?' And I'd say, 'Ahmet, we're going to have a fucking big band. I just signed this group Genesis. They're going to break. It's going to be unbelievable.' And verbatim, he would pick up the phone and call Steve Ross while I was sitting there and say, 'Steve! We're going to have a big fucking band from England called Genesis and they're going to be . . .' That was Ahmet. It didn't bother me at all. I loved Ahmet."

Making deals Ahmet would have never considered, Greenberg paid a $50,000 advance and a 12 percent royalty for a comedy album by the cast of Norman Lear's hit television show *All in the Family*. It sold 750,000 records. He signed John Belushi and Dan Aykroyd to the label in their *Saturday Night Live* incarnation as the Blues Brothers and then shook hands with their manager, Bernie Brillstein, on a quarter-of-a-million-dollar advance for the soundtrack to *The Muppet Movie*.

In Greenberg's words, "I said to Ahmet, 'I just made this fucking great deal with Bernie Brillstein.' 'What is it?' 'Heard of *The Muppets*?' 'No.' I told him it was a big TV show. He said, 'Nothing from TV sells. Look what happened to Sonny and Cher and Tony Orlando.' I said, 'This is different. A bunch of puppets.' 'What the fuck are puppets going to do?' I said, 'Kermit the Frog has this great fucking song, "Rainbow Connection."'" Ahmet dropped his glasses, looked in my eyes, and said, 'Okay. If you say so.' He thought I had lost my fucking mind. Sold a million albums."

By then, Greenberg, who also signed Foreigner, had become Robert Stigwood's go-to guy at Atlantic. Intent on bringing Greenberg to RSO Records, Stigwood offered him "a major part of the company, the film company, the whole nine yards. I said, 'I'll only go if I can take Sheldon Vogel with me.' I went to Vogel and he saw the deal memo and he said, 'I think I'm in.'"

Calling Ahmet while he was on vacation in the south of France, Greenberg said he was leaving the company to go work for Stigwood. "He said, 'You're leaving? You can't leave. You have to come over here and talk to me.' I said, 'Sheldon's coming too.' '*Sheldon's going too? What are you, fucking crazy? Get on a fucking plane and get over here right now!*'" After Greenberg and Vogel had flown to see him in Europe, Ahmet "called Steve Ross right in front of us and said, 'They can't take these guys. These are my guys. You gotta give them this, you gotta give them that.' And they worked out a new deal for us."

In a business where successful record executives had now become more important than rock stars and were constantly looking for an opportunity to earn more money than they were already making, everyone was in play. After Greenberg had passed on the opportunity to join David Geffen at Asylum, he asked for his own label at Atlantic only to have Ahmet refuse. Telling him to forget the label, David Horowitz offered Greenberg more stock in the company and then asked, "Is Ahmet a problem for you?"

In Greenberg's words, "I said, 'No, he's not.' I was not leaving because I wanted Ahmet's gig. If I had wanted, I could have said, 'Well, Ahmet never shows up and he doesn't do this or that,' but I didn't because I loved Ahmet. He had built the company and I would have kept him there no matter what." Twenty-four hours after Greenberg had informed Sheldon Vogel that Alan Hirschfield, who had negotiated the sale of Atlantic to Warner, had offered him his own label at Twentieth Century Fox, Greenberg was given a deal to start Mirage Records at Atlantic. By then, "the record business had taken a real dump" and five years later, Greenberg left to form United Artists Records with Jerry Weintraub.

As Greenberg said, "Sheldon Vogel was the unsung hero there. Ahmet used him as the bad cop. He was the money guy but it was Ahmet who watched every dime. We didn't have a great year and Sheldon told me Ahmet and Mica were going somewhere and flying coach. Ahmet used to use the Warner jet like a taxi cab. All of a sudden, he called me into his office and said, 'We can't use the jet anymore.' 'Why not?' 'They're charging us. They've broken it down. Take the plane and it's three thousand an hour.' "

Greenberg would also sit with Ahmet each year as he went through the list of Christmas bonuses for Atlantic's employees. "It would be, 'Cut him. Cut him. Don't give him anything.' I'd go, 'Ahmet, you're not here all year. I'm here. I know what this guy did.' Sheldon Vogel will tell you I had to fight to get a guy an extra $3,000. I don't want to call Ahmet cheap, but he was cheap with some things, extravagant with others."

In a business where boosting profits each year was now what mattered most, record executives had also become as fungible as artists had once been. In the spring of 1984, rumors began flying that Steve Ross was thinking of replacing Ahmet at Atlantic with Walter Yetnikoff, the tempestuous head of CBS Records, who was then on a hot streak.

In his strange and often fanciful autobiography, Yetnikoff would later write that Ross saw Ahmet as a snob who looked down on him and so offered Yetnikoff Ahmet's job. According to Yetnikoff, Ross said he would pay him $8 million up front to become part of the Warner Music Group. After the two men shook hands on the deal, Yetnikoff sent his lawyer Allen Grubman to work out the details with Ross. As Grubman would later say, "It wasn't to replace Ahmet per se. I started having some meetings with Steve Ross and he was saying, 'I want to bring Walter into the record company.' There was no specific job he was going to be jumping into. Ross was going to bring him over and put him in an enormously powerful position and then figure it out."

Described by David Geffen as "a brilliant guy who knew how to deal with everybody," Ross was so good at the game that, in Geffen's words, "If you liked a particular kind of jam at his table for breakfast, the next day a case of it would come to your house. He would open the door for you, he would carry your bags, he would light your cigarette, and it would end up costing you a fortune. He was a very unique guy."

Ross's real genius was the art of the deal. After working out precisely how much he was prepared to pay for a new acquisition, Ross would explain the offer to Jay Emmett and then ask him to repeat it. In Emmett's words, "I'm not a financial brain but I could remember what he'd said two minutes ago. After I'd repeated it, he would rip up the paper he had written the numbers on and say, 'No. If you understand this, they're going to understand it.' And then he would come back with a more convoluted deal. Steve was the smartest deal maker in the world and if he was acquiring something he really wanted, he would pay anything for it."

As he proved one day at a meeting in his apartment with Allen Grubman, Ross also understood the art of war. When the lawyer asked why he was so interested in bringing Yetnikoff into his company, Ross instructed his butler to bring him a pitcher of water and two empty glasses. Taking the pitcher, Ross filled each glass halfway. "This is Warner's," he said, pointing to one glass. "And this is CBS. Now, watch this, Allen." Taking the CBS glass, Ross emptied it into the Warner's glass and said, "Now, do you see what I've done? Not only have I doubled the amount of water in the Warner's glass, I've emptied the CBS glass."

As Grubman would later say, "In those days, Walter was so identified with CBS, people believed that if he wasn't there, it would have a dramatic effect. And maybe it would have. But unfortunately after the deal was basically made, there was a reversal because of the crash of the Atari stock and it didn't happen." Yetnikoff would later say that he saw taking over Atlantic, a single label in the Warner Music Group, as a comedown from CBS, where he was running all the labels, both international and domestic. Perhaps because of the money involved, Ross told Yetnikoff the board at Warner Communications would not approve the deal and so it never happened.

Despite Ahmet's love for the life that his lofty position within the Warner corporate structure had provided him, he could have never spent a day working under Walter Yetnikoff. Nor would the two men have lasted much longer as associates. Having managed to survive this particular crisis, Ahmet went right on doing business as he always had at Atlantic by replacing Jerry Greenberg with Doug Morris as his new right-hand man.

Although Ross never completely lost interest in the music group at Warner's, he soon turned his primary attention to the movie business, which had always been his first love. By leaving them to their own devices, Ross did, however, manage to keep some of the greatest record men who ever lived working together in comparative harmony longer than anyone else could have. In the process, he also created what has now become yet another standard feature of corporate life in America.

In the words of one music industry insider, "What Steve Ross was really good at was making it possible for all these guys who worked for him to make a lot of money. He would elevate the compensation of all those under him and then go to the board of directors because it would create a rationale for the board to give him more money as well. By any standard, he was one of the pioneers of monster executive compensation."

## 3

Ever since Ahmet and Nesuhi had kicked a ball around the grounds of the Turkish embassy as boys, both brothers had been mad about soccer. Not long after Steve Ross acquired Atlantic, he learned Nesuhi was thinking of leaving the label. When Ross asked what it would take to make him stay, Nesuhi said, "I want a professional soccer team." With Ross's enthusiastic backing, Ahmet and Nesuhi then created the social and cultural phenomenon known as the New York Cosmos.

While attending the 1970 World Cup in Mexico City, Ahmet threw a party at which he persuaded eight other Warner executives to join him and Nesuhi in putting up $35,000 apiece to launch the Gotham Soccer Club, Inc. in the fledgling North American Soccer League. A year later when Nesuhi took Ross and Jay Emmett to watch the team play in St. Louis, there were 340 people in the stands. An ardent sports fan who had tried to buy the New York Jets, Ross soon became obsessed with the Cosmos and transferred ownership of the team to Warner Communications.

Two years later, Ross moved the Cosmos to shabby, run-down Downing Stadium on Randall's Island in New York, where the team regularly drew fewer than five thousand spectators to their games. Seeking a superstar who would bring people into the stands, Nesuhi persuaded Ross to accompany him to Brazil, where the game's greatest player, Edison Arantes do Nascimento, better known as Pelé, had only recently retired at the age of thirty-four.

Acting on a recommendation from Nelson Rockefeller, former New York governor and now the vice president of the United States, Ross brought in Henry Kissinger to persuade the Brazilian government to allow a player who had become a national treasure to join an American team. Having first fallen in love with the sport as a boy growing up in Germany, Kissinger was such a diehard soccer fan that he had continued attending his hometown team's games even after the Nazis had made it dangerous "for anybody of Jewish origin to go to any crowded place."

At a chaotic press conference at "21" on June 10, 1975, the Cosmos announced they had signed the world's greatest soccer superstar to a three-year contract for an unheard-of $4.5 million. Ahmet also signed Pelé to a recording contract at Atlantic. Two years later, the brilliant striker performed two songs on the soundtrack album from a movie about him that was released by the label.

When Pelé made his American debut on Randall's Island, more than three hundred journalists attended the game. In a country where only ethnic minorities then understood and appreciated the sport, Pelé proved to be so popular that the stadium gates had to be locked to keep people out after the stands were filled. The Cosmos soon became what Jay Emmett would later call "a big ego thing for the Erteguns and for Steve" but the team was not profitable. When Ross was asked by a woman at the annual stockholder meeting how much money the company was spending on the Cosmos, in Emmett's words, "Steve told her, 'Five million dollars a year.' Then he looked at her and said, 'Three cents a share,' and the whole place cheered. And they were losing five million dollars a year on them."

Although Emmett would later say Nesuhi had far more to do with running the team, Ahmet became the public face of the organization. As the president of the Cosmos, he was "completely hands-on in wooing the succession of aging international stars who came to play for the team," among them the flamboyant Italian striker Giorgio Chinaglia, who soon became a cult figure in New York. A year after Pelé had joined the Cosmos, Ahmet helped engineer the signing of Franz Beckenbauer, the legendary German sweeper known as "Der Kaiser."

Giving Beckenbauer the full rock star treatment, Ahmet took him to dinner one night at Elaine's, the Upper East Side literary hangout that was then the hippest spot in the city. Spying Woody Allen at a neighboring table, Beckenbauer asked Ahmet if he could meet him. Violating the unwritten rule that no one ever spoke to the reclusive comedian and filmmaker while he was dining in the restaurant, Ahmet began leading the soccer star toward his table only to have Allen turn around and say, "My God, Franz Beckenbauer!" Regularly, Ahmet also took members of the Cosmos to Studio 54 to join the bevy of stoned-out superstars, social climbers, and various girls of the moment who comprised what then passed for café society in New York.

Obsessed with the team's fortunes, Ahmet and Nesuhi made certain that a piece of paper with the lineup they thought should be on the field was given to the coach before each game. For obvious reasons, their lineup always included the Turkish goalkeeper Erol Yasin. When David Hirshey wrote a story in the New York *Daily News* quoting Shep Messing, the regular keeper, as saying he had been benched because he had the wrong passport, Ahmet called up Hirshey and berated him for being anti-Turkish. The sportswriter replied that he was "anticorporate interference."

Thanks in great part to Ahmet's unceasing promotion of the team, the Cosmos became the hottest ticket in town. Ross persuaded celebrities with ties to Warner Communications to attend Cosmos games, and the team began drawing massive crowds to Giants Stadium in New Jersey, their new home playing field. On August 14, 1977, 77,691 people attended a playoff game between the Cosmos and the Fort Lauderdale Strikers. Among them was Ross, who would become so excited when his team played that he had installed a seat belt at his regular spot in the upper deck to keep him from falling over the edge during the game.

After Giorgio Chinaglia had scored three goals to lead the Cosmos to an 8–3 victory over their opponents, Robert Redford, Henry Kissinger, and Mick Jagger made their way through the locker room to offer their congratulations "with the Erteguns following them around like puppies, stopping only to massage Pelé's feet or rub Beckenbauer's shoulders."

In a series of photographs taken in the locker room that day by Ahmet's good friend Jean Pigozzi, Ahmet can be seen in a soaking-wet white shirt with his pants down around his ankles swilling from a bottle of celebratory champagne alongside Cosmos coach Eddie Firmani and a player who wears nothing but a towel. As the defender Werner Roth, who had grown up in Queens and attended Brooklyn Technical High School, recalled, "Ahmet brought everyone into that locker room and every arrogant rock 'n' roller turned into a pontificating little boy in front of Pelé."

Two months later, Ahmet journeyed to Beijing with the team. As he would later tell *The New York Times*, the team's eventual goal was to become the best in the world "and the way to get there is to play anywhere against the best at any time. We've never shied away from anyone." Because of the unlikely marriage Ahmet had brokered between the sport and rock 'n' roll, an ownership group composed of Peter Frampton; Rick Wakeman, the keyboardist of Yes; Paul Simon; Frank Barsalona of Premier Talent; rock manager Dee Anthony; and Terry Ellis and Chris Wright of Chrysalis Records was awarded the franchise for the Philadelphia Fury.

The calamitous collapse of the Atari game corporation in 1983 caused Warner Communications to report a post-tax loss of $418 million after twelve consecutive profitable years. As part of his plan to rebuild the Cosmos so he could sell it, Ross persuaded Ahmet and Nesuhi to resign their positions with a club that by now was no longer attracting rock stars and celebrities to its games. By 1985, Warner Communications had sold or closed ten separate ventures. A year later, the Cosmos folded.

While Ahmet had managed to have as much fun as possible with the Cosmos, he had also popularized a sport that youngsters all over America would eventually play, helping to pave the way for the United States to host the World Cup for the first time in 1994. In record business terms, Ahmet had helped break soccer in America.

# EIGHTEEN

# The Rock and Roll Hall of Fame

*"I knew John Hammond, Jerry Wexler, and Sam Phillips and I'm here to tell you Ahmet was the greatest record executive who ever lived. He was more creative, he had wider taste, he kept himself in the game longer, he had the greatest rapport with the artists, and he made a market again and again and kept it. He did R&B, free jazz, hard rock, soul music, psychedelic rock, disco, and all that stuff in the 1980s and 1990s. He also happened to be kinky in a bunch of different ways, one of which was that he wasn't particularly dedicated to what you and I know as the truth. The other was that he was comfortable playing the rogue in a world where economic justice wasn't even a consideration."*

—Dave Marsh

## 1

With Atlantic making more money than ever and Doug Morris handling the day-to-day operations as president of the label while Sheldon Vogel oversaw financial matters as vice chairman, Ahmet's "real job" at the company during the 1980s had become, in the words of writer Eric Poole, "to play the role of Ahmet Ertegun: taking calls from top agents and managers, stroking the important acts, showing up at the shows, flying to New Orleans for a party for Robert Plant." As Ahmet also told Poole, "There's a lot of work to do around here. Fortunately, I have people to do it for me."

While many employees at the label no longer saw Ahmet on a regular basis in the office, he still "set the tone for all operations" and remained the man in charge. Having reached an age when most men begin thinking seriously about retirement, he showed no signs of slowing down and could still stay out until four in the morning only to appear at a company meeting five hours later looking fresh and alert and then astound all those present by coming up with the breakthrough idea.

With artists like Foreigner, AC/DC, Twisted Sister, Yes, White Lion, INXS, Genesis, and Debbie Gibson forming the mainstay of the Atlantic roster during this decade, the label bore little resemblance to what it had been back when Ahmet was still going into the studio on a regular basis to record the music he loved. Admitting the company had "slipped badly in jazz and rhythm and blues" but that he was working as hard as he could to rectify the problem, Ahmet had developed a completely different set of ears for the music Atlantic needed to keep releasing to continue earning huge profits. In his words, "I listen to some current things but mostly I play people like Pee Wee Russell and Bud Freeman and always, Jelly Roll Morton's 'Shreveport Stomp.' In my opinion, that's the hottest record ever made."

Having risen to a position of overwhelming power in a business that no longer interested or challenged him, Ahmet seized upon an idea for an annual pay-per-view cable television awards show and transformed it into an institution to which he began devoting nearly as much time and energy as he had put into building Atlantic Records. The original concept for the Rock and Roll Hall of Fame Foundation had come from a producer named Bruce Brandwein, who wanted to use the organization to lend credibility to a yearly awards ceremony at which the greatest names in rock would be honored and then perform, thereby creating a must-see television event for their fans.

Along with music business attorney David Braun and Suzan Hochberg Evans, who had just graduated from Brooklyn Law School after having majored in communications and journalism at Boston University, Brandwein met with Ahmet to pitch him on the concept in the winter of 1983. After the meeting, Ahmet called Evans to say he was interested in the idea and wanted to discuss it again but only with her. As they were talking about the project in his home one night, Ahmet said, "Why should I do this if it will be a profitable organization for someone else but a charity for me? If this is going to be a well-respected organization the artists are going to buy into and I can put my stamp on, it has to be not-for-profit. It can't be an excuse to do a television show."

After naming a few people he thought should get involved to start the ball rolling, Ahmet picked up the phone, called Noreen Woods, and said, "Noreen, what's the name of that kid who runs Sire Records?" He then sent Evans, who was twenty-four years old, to see forty-one-year-old Seymour Stein.

Instructing Evans to send informational packets about the project to Stein, Allen Grubman, and *Rolling Stone* magazine founder Jann Wenner, Ahmet invited them all to lunch at Pearl's Chinese restaurant. In Grubman's words, "I was sitting there eating one spare rib after another as Ahmet began talking about a baseball hall of fame and this hall of fame and all these halls of fame. And then after a few years, it grew into something enormous. Out of a simple lunch of Chinese food. It was unbelievable."

On April 20, 1983, the four men formed the Rock and Roll Hall of Fame Foundation. Selecting Evans as the foundation's executive director, Ahmet installed her in an office three doors down from him at Atlantic and began soliciting contributions from other record companies to fund the project. As she would later say, "Atlantic Records made a contribution and I drew my salary out of that account so Ahmet really did bankroll us in the beginning." In Jann Wenner's words, "You couldn't really have an institution driven by the TV show. It had to be the other way around because in order to make it work, it had to be nonprofit. Breaking the deal with the TV producer took a year or a year and a half with depositions and everything but I just said we were not going to do it that way. And then the real struggle was to figure out what it would be and where it would be located."

Before the board could begin searching for a physical location, it had to incorporate the foundation, formulate the rules for induction, and create a nominating committee. As Evans recalled, "When we had the early meetings with Ahmet and Jann and Seymour and Allen Grubman, Ahmet used to say, 'What kind of board meeting is this? This is like a *Saturday Night Live* writers meeting. We have to get serious.' Allen Grubman used to look around and say, 'Ahmet, the five of us, this is the Rock and Roll Hall of Fame? Is this going to take off, or are we it?'"

Within a year, Bob Krasnow, the head of Elektra, and Jon Landau, the former music writer who managed Bruce Springsteen, had been brought into the mix but in Evans's words, "We were really concentrating on the rules for induction and election so we could start honoring artists. That was phase one. We always thought we would eventually purchase a brownstone in New York City and have a few pieces of memorabilia or an actual hall of fame with plaques but that was down the line."

Shortly before the Rock and Roll Hall of Fame held its first induction ceremony in 1986, Cleveland disc jockey Norm Knight contacted the board about his city's interest in becoming the institution's permanent home. Knight then came to New York with a delegation of business leaders and Cleveland mayor George Voinovich for what everyone thought would be, in Evans's words, "A courtesy meeting but they made such an impressive presentation that Noreen Woods passed me a note that said, 'Pack your bags.' Then Ahmet said, 'If Cleveland is doing this, do we have a fiduciary duty to investigate other possible sites?' "

Once people learned about the project, the board was "approached and pitched by Philadelphia, Memphis, New Orleans, Chicago, Los Angeles, and New York, and this went on for many months." When Harold Washington, the first black mayor of Chicago, made his pitch, in Evans's words, "He said, 'You know, I really love Bruce Springheim.' We all looked at each other and said, 'All right, we're not going to Chicago.' "

After 600,000 fans had signed a petition favoring Cleveland as the site for the institution and the city had pledged to provide public funds to pay for construction costs, the board decided, as Evans would later say, "if the Rock and Roll Hall of Fame was going to be a success, Cleveland was the place to do it because they were serious about it, they were very energetic, they really wanted it, and they really needed it. It was definitely the best deal."

The news that Cleveland had been selected as the home for the Rock and Roll Hall of Fame was announced at the institution's first awards dinner in the Grand Ballroom of the Waldorf-Astoria in 1986. With twelve hundred people in attendance, Chuck Berry, James Brown, Ray Charles, Sam Cooke, Fats Domino, the Everly Brothers,

Buddy Holly, Jerry Lee Lewis, Elvis Presley, Jimmie Rodgers, Jimmy Yancey, Robert Johnson, John Hammond, Alan Freed, and Sam Phillips were named as the institution's first honorees.

Right from the start, Ahmet insisted the only person who should design the building that would house the institution was I. M. Pei, the world-famous sixty-six-year-old Chinese-born architect whom Jacqueline Kennedy had selected to create the John F. Kennedy Presidential Library and Museum in Cambridge. The winner of the prestigious Pritzker Architecture Prize, Pei had also designed the John Hancock Tower in Boston, the East Building of the National Gallery of Art in Washington, the Jacob K. Javits Convention Center in New York City, and the glass and steel pyramid at the Louvre in Paris.

After Ahmet had called Pei to say, "We want you to do this," the architect contacted Evans a few days later and said he had told his daughter Ahmet had asked him to design the Rock and Roll Hall of Fame. She said, "But you're an old man. What do you know about rock and roll?" Pei told Evans, "Suzan, those are fighting words. I'm going to do it." Because Pei "really didn't know anything about rock 'n' roll," Ahmet, Wenner, Stein, and Evans took him to concerts in New York and sent him books about rock 'n' roll. They then escorted the architect on a weekend trip to Graceland.

After arriving in Memphis, Ahmet learned that the Louis Vuitton case specially made to hold his shoes had been lost in transit. So obsessed with everything made by the designer that when a friend facetiously inquired if he owned a Vuitton toothbrush, his immediate reply was to ask if they made them, Ahmet was beside himself. As Jann Wenner would later say, "Ahmet was so panicked that he had Suzan Evans order our chauffeur to wait for fourteen hours at the airport at who knows what cost to recover it."

After touring Graceland, everyone continued on to New Orleans, where they spent the night visiting Tipitina's and Cosmo's Factory. A couple of days later, Pei called Evans and said, "I've got it. I get what rock 'n' roll is. It's about energy and that's what my building is going to reflect. Energy."

While the original budget Cleveland had proposed in 1985 was $26 million, the sum quickly rose to $40 million. Financed through a combination of public funds, a bond issue that was repaid through hotel taxes, and "a lot of private donations," the final cost of constructing the Rock and Roll Hall of Fame reached $100 million. Situated on the shores of Lake Erie, the building Pei designed features a slanting glass wall not unlike the one he had constructed at the Louvre.

Coated in white metal, the seven-level main structure is connected by a walkway to an adjoining circular performance space mounted on a pillar. Employing "the forms of shopping mall architecture," Pei used "large walkways and escalators" to allow visitors to "travel from exhibition gallery to gallery effortlessly." By combining "off-centered wraparounds and angled walls," the architect hoped to provide what he called "a sense of tumultuous youthful energy, rebelling, flailing about."

On September 2, 1995, the Rock and Roll Hall of Fame opened its doors with a ribbon-cutting ceremony attended by Yoko Ono and Little Richard, followed by a seven-hour outdoor concert broadcast live by HBO from nearby Cleveland Browns stadium. Ahmet and Mica attended the event with their good friends Renaldo and Caroline Herrera and Sid and Mercedes Bass. As Evans would later say, "Ahmet was delighted that weekend because it would never have happened without him. He was so revered and so highly respected that everyone wanted to work with him on it and he was really the force behind this. He was always on the phone with any problems we were having and he put his stamp of approval on everything. Ahmet got the whole music industry actively involved."

In Jann Wenner's words, "Ahmet was the guiding moral and aesthetic sensibility and consciousness. All along the way, decisions had to be made on every level. How do you reconcile the formality and elegance of a museum with the rudeness and street stuff of an art form like this? Without getting so precious? Throughout all of this, Ahmet was the lodestone about what would be appropriate and what would be in good taste and what would not. In the end, it was always, 'What does Ahmet think?' Because Ahmet had the vision."

In much the same way Herb Abramson, Jerry Wexler, and Jerry Greenberg had taken care of the day-to-day business at Atlantic, Wenner "deputized" himself to Ahmet by saying, "Okay, I'll be the guy who gets it all organized. I'll be the hit man." As he would add, "In the record business, marketing was always about how to get your records played on the air for free. Therefore, what the record business guys knew about marketing was cash and cocaine. Because of their huge success over the years, they all thought they were experts at this. They were just experts at payola. These people were now on the board of the Rock and Roll Hall of Fame trying to build a hundred-million-dollar building and they just did not have a clue."

Nonetheless, in the house Ahmet had built, Wenner decided to surprise the man who had made the Rock and Roll Hall of Fame a reality by naming the main exhibition hall after him. While Ahmet seemed "nonplussed" by the honor, no one took more pleasure when it came to inducting new honorees. Tinged with humor and his own brand of erudite music scholarship, the speeches Ahmet carefully wrote by hand on lined yellow notepaper and then delivered in his characteristic hipster drawl reflected his deep, abiding love for a particularly American art form he believed "had changed history and popular culture" and so deserved to be preserved for future generations.

The annual induction ceremony also soon became noteworthy for the incredible collection of rock superstars who would perform at the end of the dinner. In Wenner's words, "Some years, you had these fantastic jam sessions with Keith Richards, Mick Jagger, Tina Turner, and Bruce Springsteen all playing together onstage. When those jams took place, it was the best show of the year and I felt it had to be shared with a larger audience."

Although Ahmet initially "mightily resisted" televising the event, Wenner insisted "it was wrong to be that elitist about it. The nature and character of the dinner wouldn't change so long as we didn't make it into a live show. We could tape it." In typical fashion, Ahmet finally conceded by saying "I don't think the issue is whether or not we're whores. I think what we're discussing is how much we charge." In 2008, the Rock and Roll Hall of Fame's nonperformer award was renamed the Ahmet Ertegun Award.

While some questioned the basic notion of enshrining an anti-establishment art form like rock 'n' roll in such a formal setting and there were continuing controversies concerning the nominating and selection process, those who had labored to bring about the creation of the Rock and Roll Hall of Fame did not let it affect the way they did business with one another. Even as he and Ahmet were collaborating to form the institution in 1984, Bob Krasnow of Elektra was doing all he could to sign a band whose last album had sold only twenty thousand copies. As he would later say, "Ahmet wanted Metallica in the worst way and we weren't supposed to outbid each other inside the Warner Music Group. They were at half a million for the advance and I said, 'Fuck it,' and I went to a million. Doug Morris went crazy and went to Ahmet and he called me one night just as I got home."

As Krasnow recalled, "I get on the phone and Ahmet says, 'I was in this limo the other night and they told me you were in this limo with those guys from Metallica and you told them we were a piece of shit and I'm going to fuck you up and you're going to pay for this.' It was just outrageous but I couldn't answer because he wouldn't let me. Not yelling but forceful and swearing like crazy and Ahmet didn't swear that much. But he was pissed."

Thinking Ahmet was going to get him fired for what he had done, Krasnow hung up. The next day, he called Steve Ross to let him know he intended to do whatever he could to sign the band. "And Ross said, 'I'm not getting involved.' That was his brilliance. We sold only 200,000 copies of the first album and Ahmet was kind of happy that nothing really happened and the next album sold twenty million worldwide. I hated competing with Ahmet. But when I did beat him, I loved it."

## 2

Nearly forty years after Ruth Brown had become his label's first big star, Ahmet found himself doing battle with her in what soon became a very public controversy. The issue was money owed to the singer as well as many of the other pioneering black rhythm and blues artists who had helped give Atlantic its start. While some viewed the bitter five-year legal struggle that followed as simply a case of chickens coming home to roost, the real reason Ahmet became the poster boy for the issue was his enduring success.

By the mid-1980s, Ahmet was the last formerly independent record label owner still in the business. As Howell Begle, the lawyer who represented Brown and many other black artists in their campaign to be paid what they were owed, would later say, "Ahmet was still around. Of all the people from that era, he was the only guy left so he couldn't say he didn't remember or didn't know because there was no place for him to hide. He was still there and he still had the same people like Fran Wakschal working for him."

Over the years, Ahmet had always made a point of stressing that, unlike its competitors, Atlantic had paid its artists the royalties they were due. As Begle would learn during his long pro bono stint as Brown's attorney, this was true only up to a certain point in time. "A big fan of early rock 'n' roll and R&B" who had first seen Ruth Brown perform on Alan Freed's television show, Howell Begle had graduated from Sewanee University and then attended the University of Michigan Law School. After being drafted into the army during the Vietnam War, he served for three years as a captain charged with military prosecutions on Okinawa. Returning to civilian life, Begle spent the next decade in Washington representing high-profile clients like Senators George Mitchell of Maine and Bob Dole of Kansas, Governor Ann Richards of Texas, and CBS newscaster Roger Mudd.

Asked by a friend to meet Brown as she was performing at Ford's Theatre in Washington in 1982, Begle brought along several of the singer's albums, which he asked her to autograph. When Brown asked where he had gotten them, Begle said he had paid dearly for the albums only to be told by the singer that she herself had not received any royalties from Atlantic since leaving the label in 1961.

In dire need of money to pay her bills two years later, Brown had written a ten-page letter to Ahmet in which she had "laid herself naked." Although he then sent her a check for a thousand dollars, the singer remained convinced she was "entitled to more than crumbs from the rich man's label." At some point, Brown had also gone to see Ahmet at Atlantic to ask for another loan only to be told to take a seat and wait. Four hours later, she was still sitting there.

After being forced to work as a bus driver and a nurse's aide to support herself, Brown had resuscitated her show business career in the 1970s when Norman Lear cast her in several episodes of his hit television series *The Jeffersons*. When Brown began seeing European reissues of albums she had recorded for Atlantic, the singer contacted three different attorneys only to have each of them drop her case after being informed by Atlantic that she was in debt to the label for a very considerable sum and should not pursue the issue lest they come after her for the money. Brown was also told the statute of limitations on collecting royalties had run out.

The actual two-page contract Brown signed with Atlantic in 1952 had guaranteed her a $200 payment for each side she recorded for the label. By 1958, her fee had risen to $325 a side. Brown was also to receive a 5 percent royalty rate but only after Atlantic's production costs had been recouped. In accordance with what was then standard industry practice, Brown was charged for all musicians' fees and arrangements. She received no royalties on promotional copies of her records and Atlantic withheld a 10 percent allowance for breakage. If only one out of three sides she had cut was released, recording expenses for all her sessions were attached to it.

In a business where disputes over money were always personal, Ruth Brown was ideally suited by both temperament and personality to take on a record industry colossus like Ahmet Ertegun. Begle said, "I truly believed in Ruth because this woman was tough as nails. I knew I could trust her and I believe Atlantic knew she was not going to be bought off. And she had a loud mouth. Ruth would just bash these people from the stage and tell her story of how this whole generation of artists was being beaten down."

After Begle had procured copies of Brown's original contracts with Atlantic from the American Federation of Television and Radio Artists in 1984, he learned the label was legally obligated to provide her with regular statements showing whether or not she had earned any royalties. In Begle's words, "So I said, 'I bet these guys don't know what she's earned,' and if I can get them to start issuing statements to her and other people, they're going to possibly commit mail fraud," an offense for which Begle knew Atlantic could be prosecuted under the RICO act. Begle then began pestering the label for Brown's royalty statements. In his words, "I was in there screaming at them all the time, 'Don't you have royalty statements? Don't you have copies of anything?' But who in their right mind would have copies of royalty statements twenty-five to thirty years later? Out of frustration one day, Fran Wakschal said, 'Okay. It's in that box over there.' "

In the box, Begle found Brown's royalty statements from May 15,

1955, through 1964. The statements revealed that at the end of her career at Atlantic, Brown owed the label $25,830.83. The box also contained three memos that comprised what Begle called "the smoking gun." Dated June 8, 1983, one memo read, "We did not pick up royalties earned foreign from 4/1/60 to 9/30/71."

In Begle's words, "What they were basically admitting in the memo was that when all these artists finished their careers in the 1960s and they all had these large debit balances, the company decided there was no way in hell these people were ever going to work their way out so let's don't even bother to go through the exercise of even posting what they earned. All of Atlantic's royalty statements were fraudulent because they knew they were missing eleven years' worth of data in those that had debit balances. Every statement they had sent out after that was just another nail in their coffin under RICO."

Deciding it would be futile to sue Atlantic because "these people were going to drain all our financial resources in discovery" and because he knew most of his other clients would have been willing to accept any settlement offer the label made them, Begle decided to try his case in the court of public opinion.

With Brown, Begle appeared on the CBS newsmagazine show *West 57th*. While being interviewed by Meredith Vieira, Begle told a national television audience that Big Joe Turner had actually worked his way out of his unrecouped balance until Atlantic decided to release a fourteen-volume retrospective package of its early hits to coincide with the fortieth anniversary of the label and then charged him for all the remastering costs.

Then seventy-four years old, Turner was, in Begle's words, in "awful, terrible shape. He weighed 450 pounds and all he wanted to do was eat crabs. His diabetes was really killing him." Two months after the television segment aired, Turner, "The Boss of the Blues," died of a heart attack on November 24, 1985. Doc Pomus, the legendary songwriter who had first worked for Atlantic during the label's earliest days in the Hotel Jefferson, had by then already called Ahmet to let him know Turner was dying and that Pomus was doing a benefit show for him at the Lone Star Cafe.

As Pomus recalled, "I'd spoken to Ahmet maybe twice in fifteen years and it sure wasn't because Henry Kissinger had invited us to the same party. But Ahmet and Mica came to the benefit, hanging out all night in this funky joint eating chili. She was like something from another planet but Ahmet paid for Joe's funeral and the mortgage on Joe's house, without telling anyone. That was righteous, that was noble, and I knew then that Ahmet, in a certain way, was the same guy I knew forty years ago." In Begle's view, "Ahmet loved to be the good guy. He didn't pay these people anything in the sense of what they were owed but he was happy to have them come to him and say, 'I'm down on my luck, I need help with making my house payments.' "

In July 1986, with the help of Congressman Mickey Leland of Texas, Begle arranged for Ruth Brown to testify at a congressional hearing chaired by Representative John Conyers of Michigan concerning pending legislation to limit the filing of civil suits under the RICO act. Jesse Jackson also attended the hearing and the story about Brown's appearance before the committee appeared in newspapers all over America. Shortly before the hearing, Begle received a royalty statement from Atlantic covering her earnings from June 1, 1960, to May 31, 1980. The singer's total royalties came to $354 for domestic earnings and $431 in foreign sales.

Three months later, Leland arranged for Begle to sit down with Jesse Jackson, who was scheduled to meet with Steve Ross the next day. Flying to New York, Begle spent the night explaining to Jackson how artists like Brook Benton, Solomon Burke, Ruth Brown, the Chords, the Clovers, the Coasters, the Drifters, Clyde McPhatter, Sam and Dave, Chuck Willis, Ivory Joe Hunter, Rufus and Carla Thomas, Booker T. and the MG's, Eddie Floyd, Chris Kenner, Willis Jackson, the Marquees, William Bell, and Doris Troy had been deprived of their royalties.

After Jackson told Ross, his general counsel, and Bob Morgado, whom Ross had brought in to oversee the Warner Music Group, of his concerns about the scarcity of black executives in record industry management positions as well as Warner's business dealings in South Africa, Begle talked for thirty minutes. Jackson then informed Ross that he and Begle were on their way to a black radio programmers' convention in Houston. In Begle's words, "We went down there together and Jesse signed up 150 radio stations who agreed to refuse to report their airplay of Atlantic artists to *Billboard*."

In March 1987, Australian journalist Claudia Wright wrote an article in *The Washington Post* entitled, "Ahmet Ertegun: The Skeletons in the Closet Sing Rock 'n' Roll" in which she noted that Atlantic had reported earnings of over $200 million in 1985. In light of Ahmet's position as the chairman of the board of the American Turkish Society and a member of the National Committee on American Foreign Policy, along with David Rockefeller and Henry Kissinger, Wright called him the most important political asset Turkey had in America and said the potential lawsuit over delinquent royalties could only serve to embarrass Turkey and its friends in the United States.

For the next fourteen months, Begle met with Warner executives as well as Leland and Jackson to resolve the issue. Leland pushed for the creation of the Rhythm & Blues Foundation to aid and represent pioneering black artists. After the Warner Music Group offered to contribute $150,000 to establish the foundation, Leland's representative held out for a $1.5 million donation because, in Begle's words, "It was all going to charity so it didn't really matter to them."

The final agreement stipulated that Ahmet would pick thirty-five artists whose royalty accounts would be reopened. Only actual session costs and advances would be deducted from their royalties and all un-recouped balances would be wiped out back to 1970, the year Atlantic had stopped keeping track of their earnings. The Warner Music Group agreed to donate $1.5 million to create the Rhythm & Blues Foundation and also established a royalty payment fund of $250,000 from which Ruth Brown received $30,000 and groups like the Coasters and the Drifters were given $50,000 payments.

Three days before Atlantic's gala fortieth anniversary celebration at Madison Square Garden on May 14, 1988, Begle received a check for $1.5 million. As he would later say, "The gala made them settle. The check was written out of the proceeds of the Madison Square Garden concert, which were going to charity anyway. No letter. No press release on the deal. Just a note that said, 'Don't cash till Monday.' No agreement, nothing. Just, 'Here's the money, you sonsabitches.' " During the show, however, Bob Morgado pledged to come up with another $450,000 over the next three years to cover the new foundation's operating expenses.

As Dave Marsh recalled, "Ahmet could have worked with any

entertainment lawyer and it could have all been settled on the q.t. but Howell was from another solar system so it couldn't have been, 'I'll take care of you when I sign the new kid.' For Ahmet, it involved admitting the story wasn't true. It blew his cover. It never had anything to do with dollars because the dollars were not that many and they weren't coming out of his pocket."

With comedian Dan Aykroyd, the former Blues Brother who had performed with Sam Moore of Sam and Dave at the gala, Doc Pomus, Bonnie Raitt, Dave Marsh, Mickey Leland, Jesse Jackson, and Howell Begle as members of the board, and Ahmet in attendance, the directors of the Rhythm & Blues Foundation met for the first time in September 1988. Ahmet and Begle, who was then still "pushing to get the royalty rates up" had "a really intense argument."

"In a real fit of anger," Begle said, "Ahmet basically told me he was receiving all of Joe Turner's royalties. Sort of like, 'You stupid ass guy, you think you're doing something good. You know who's getting this money? Me.' I had been getting copies of Joe's royalty statements and I could never figure out who was the other person who was being copied on them but then it made complete sense. So if Ahmet paid off the mortgage, he did it in return for asking for Joe's royalties. Because Ahmet didn't need that embarrassment, the next thing I saw on Joe's royalty statement was the Atlantic Foundation so Ahmet had changed it. He corrected the situation and gave the money to charity."

Expecting the rest of the industry to follow Warner's lead, Begle and Marsh then went to the heads of other record labels only to learn they had no intention of doing so. Irving Azoff, who was about to leave MCA, did agree to void all the contracts the label had acquired from Chess and Checker, wipe out all unrecouped balances for those artists, and offer them a 10 percent royalty rate. Eventually, both Capitol/EMI and Sony also agreed to raise their payments to that level.

"We were in a Rhythm & Blues Foundation meeting one day," Marsh recalled, "and I said, 'I don't ever want to go through this again. That's why I'm here.' And Ahmet said, 'That was never going to happen. There never was a problem.' I looked at Doc Pomus as we were walking out of the room and Doc said, 'It don't matter because these guys are never going to care about it the way we do. And they're basically going to get to write the history.' And I thought, 'Not on your life.' "

In her autobiography, Ruth Brown wrote about a conversation Marsh had with Pomus before his death in 1991 in which the songwriter told him, "The guys at Atlantic were not like the rest of them. They were better." When Marsh asked if they were better enough, Pomus said no but that "Ahmet was not Morris Levy." In response to Marsh's question as to whether the partners at Atlantic had stuck "to what the letter of their artists' contracts said," Pomus replied, "No, they did not."

While many of those who ran independent record labels in the early days of the business regularly put their names on songs they had not written, Ahmet and Jerry Wexler had always maintained they had taken songwriting credit only for work they had actually done. But as Solomon Burke pointed out, "Jerry claimed he and Bert Berns wrote 'Everybody Needs Somebody to Love,' which they did not. I wrote the song and Jerry suggested I had to put his and Bert Berns's name on the song so somebody would play it. We bickered constantly over the fact he wouldn't give back the writing and publishing and that carried on until his demise. They're still credited and they're getting 75 percent because Jerry escalated the ownership once the record took off and groups like the Rolling Stones recorded it."

Shortly before Ben E. King was asked to leave the Drifters in 1961, the singer had written "Stand by Me" with the group in mind and then rehearsed the song with them. After King finished a solo session with Mike Stoller and Jerry Leiber, they asked if he had anything else to record. According to King, "I showed them this song. They gathered around and did a head arrangement real quick and that was how the song came out. But all of a sudden, I adopted two writers. They put their names on it." Leiber and Stoller tell a completely different version of the story.

King then came up with "Don't Play That Song (You Lied)," a soundalike hit on which songwriting credit was shared by Ahmet and Betty Nelson. In King's words, "Ahmet had the ability to write a song and he might have changed a word here and there. I wasn't upset his name was on it. That meant they were going to push it because they got a part of the pie." It was precisely because of such practices that Begle and Marsh had worked so hard to create the Rhythm & Blues Foundation.

In 1991, Marsh resigned in protest from the board when Time Warner reneged on its payment of the final third of the $450,000 Morgado had pledged to cover operating expenses until EMI also agreed to offer financial support. Marsh questioned whether this was a result of Time Warner's "failed stock offering" or, as he wrote in his *Rock & Roll Confidential* newsletter, "Is it just a reassertion of the record industry's plantation mentality, in which music makers are treated like sharecroppers, to be paid what the companies want, when they get around to it? Either way, it's intolerable."

By then, Ruth Brown had become a member of the board of the Rhythm & Blues Foundation. After having been nominated for induction into the Rock and Roll Hall of Fame for five consecutive years, the singer was dropped from the list of potential honorees in 1990 and 1991. In her autobiography, Brown wrote she had been told this was Ahmet being "vicious and vindictive. This is his retribution. He'll never forgive you for getting the better of him."

As Jon Landau, a member of the nominating committee since its inception, explained, "There is no truth to the story that Ahmet tried to keep Ruth Brown out of the Rock and Roll Hall of Fame because that's not the way it works. The nominating committee includes more than thirty members and is really independent. Ahmet was certainly on the committee but I never perceived him as having a negative attitude towards Ruth nor pressuring anyone in any way. The fact that someone appears as a nominee one year and not another is a commonplace happening and so I would not attach any great weight to it. In other words, there was no conspiracy."

When Brown was finally inducted in 1993, Ahmet introduced her. As she accepted her award, Brown said, "I really don't think there's much more to say at this point . . . except where's my gold record, Ahmet?" The singer then thanked him for the gift he had brought her after her automobile accident in 1949. Saying this award was also a gift, she added, "The only thing left for me to do now is record for Atlantic again."

As Brown wrote in her autobiography, "Many tried their darndest to conjure up where I had this hatred going for Ahmet Ertegun. I told them that was not and never had been the case. Anger and resentment, undoubtedly, and a burning sense of injustice. For every Picasso he had hanging on his wall, I had a damp patch on mine. But hatred? Never." While Begle described the two as "good-natured ex-combatants," this was before Brown learned from Dave Marsh that Ahmet and Herb Abramson had been partners with her manager, Dorothy Calloway.

In Jerry Wexler's view, "It was not as if Ruth Brown did not have a point to make about the royalties but you must remember that her career went into decline and she wound up in the red because there were always these 'twos and fews' she would come in for. She kept coming in for a little taste. 'Can I get twenty-five hundred? Can you give me a thousand?' The money went on the record. It was a charge against royalties. And she is such a little hypocrite. When she would see Ahmet, it was, 'Oh, Ahmet, how are you, darling?' It was just horrible."

In Begle's words, "Ruth was difficult. Absolutely. And a diva of major proportions, yes." In 1987 before the royalty dispute had been resolved, Brown was appearing in "a little off-Broadway show called *Staggerlee.*" As the singer was sitting in her dressing room after a performance, she was told a man from the record company was there to see her. Brown asked who it was and what record company he was from only to hear her visitor answer, "It's Ahmet from Atlantic."

In Brown's words, "I just looked at him, he looked at me, and I think his eyes got watery, and I got watery. Before I knew it, the tears were running. And he just walked over to me, and I embraced him, and he said in my ear, 'Let's don't talk now, but everything's going to be all right. I'd never let anything happen to you.' " As he turned away, Ahmet said, "You know, Ruth, you got a good lawyer." Insofar as Ahmet and his first great star were concerned, it was *Rashomon* right to the bitter end.

## 3

Like Topsy, the event Ahmet had originally planned to hold at Radio City Music Hall on May 14, 1988, to celebrate his label's fortieth anniversary grew and grew until it became an extravaganza that began in Madison Square Garden at one-thirty in the afternoon and did not end until twelve hours later when Led Zeppelin performed live for the first time since the death of drummer John Bonham. Officially entitled "Atlantic Records Fortieth Anniversary: It's Only Rock & Roll," the marathon concert was broadcast live overseas on HBO, while in America, ABC aired highlights of the show.

With tickets priced at $50 to $100 and Coca-Cola having provided $3 million for corporate sponsorship rights as well as a guarantee of another $2 million in merchandising, the show raised more than $10 million for charities ranging from Amnesty International to the fledgling Rhythm & Blues Foundation. In the course of a single day, the concert also provided Ahmet with the opportunity to demonstrate the unique position he held in the history of what had now become the most popular form of music in the world.

The show began with the Coasters doing "That Is Rock 'n' Roll," followed by Stephen Stills and Graham Nash performing "Southern Cross" to a nearly empty arena without band mate David Crosby, who lay sick in his hotel bed. At one-forty-five in the afternoon, Phil Collins, who had begun his career as the drummer in Genesis, took the stage to perform "In the Air Tonight."

In 1980, Collins had played Ahmet a final mix of the song only to have him ask where the downbeat was. After Collins pointed it out to him, Ahmet said, "You know that, I know that, but the kids listening on the radio won't know that." Returning to London, Collins added drums to his two-track mix and the song became a huge hit that established his solo career. Collins explained, "Ahmet was not only musical, but he also knew the audience's shortcomings—no point in being hip if they miss it." The two became such close friends that, in Collins's words, "On more than the odd occasion, he referred to me as 'the son he never had.' "

Among the show's many highlights were LaVern Baker giving her first performance in America in two decades, Ben E. King doing a medley of Drifters' songs, guitarist Steve Cropper leading a tribute to Otis Redding, and Foreigner doing "I Want to Know What Love Is" with Stills, Collins, and Roberta Flack. Sam Moore and Dan Aykroyd appeared as the Blues Brothers, the Rascals played together for the first time in seventeen years, the Bee Gees performed after a nine-year hiatus, and Rufus Thomas, then seventy-one years old, did "Walking the Dog" in shorts and platform boots.

The list of those who did not appear at the show was equally impressive. Mick Jagger and Keith Richards had said they would be there but did not appear. Nor did Neil Young or Eric Clapton, "who did not want to be railroaded into a Cream reunion." Pete Townshend of The Who, whom Doug Morris had signed to Atco as a solo act, was also not there. Nor were INXS, the J. Geils Band, Bette Midler, or Chic. Aretha Franklin did not appear because her fear of flying had kept her in Detroit. The most significant no-show was Ray Charles, who did not perform because he was appearing across town with Peter Martins and the New York City Ballet at Lincoln Center, a gig Ahmet had persuaded him to play with Fathead Newman, Phil Guilbeau, and Hank Crawford from his original band.

Having been left behind by the rock market, the artist Ahmet had respected above all others had re-signed with Atlantic in 1977. Eager to make hits with Charles for a new audience, Jerry Wexler had offered to take the artist to record in Muscle Shoals only to have him say, "I got my own ideas, cousin," and then insist he would only deal with Ahmet. The two clashed over the material Charles had chosen to record and after Charles refused to work with any of the producers Ahmet suggested, he was forced to release an album by Charles that went nowhere. By 1980, both men were ready to call it quits and Charles went his own way again, this time for good.

After Ahmet had spent some time backstage at Madison Square Garden reminiscing about the old days with Ruth Brown and Fathead Newman, the tenor sax player told him he had to go join Charles at Lincoln Center. Saying "Tell Ray I said hello," Ahmet moved off only to have Newman turn to Ruth Brown and say, "I won't tell Ahmet what Ray really told me to tell him." "Don't," she replied. "It's been a good evening so far."

Escorted by their bodyguards, Henry Kissinger and his wife, Nancy, arrived at the show at five P.M. as a rejuvenated Crosby, along with Stills and Nash, were playing "Wooden Ships." Finding Mica, who was wearing an Atlantic Records warmup jacket and a strand of enormous pearls, the Kissingers made their way past Bill and Chessy Rayner, Sid Bass, Mercedes Kellogg, and Jerry Zipkin to greet Ahmet. As a cloud of marijuana smoke drifted their way from an adjoining section, Ahmet kissed the Kissingers on both cheeks, introduced them to Steve Ross, and then escorted the couple backstage.

In the years since Kissinger had helped bring Pelé to the Cosmos, he and Ahmet had become good friends who often traveled together with their wives. In 1974 while Kissinger was still serving as secretary of state, Ahmet had traveled with him to Turkey. With Turkish troops having occupied Cyprus and peace talks to resolve the future of the island under way in Geneva, Kissinger told Ahmet he did not want to give any interviews during his visit. Nonetheless, there were headlines about him in the Turkish newspapers every day. As Kissinger would later say of their visit, "Ahmet had appointed himself as my press secretary and held interviews about my thoughts, which made me wildly popular in Turkey. Even when he was driving you mad, you couldn't really be angry at Ahmet."

After a military coup took place in Turkey in 1980 and there was no contact between the American government and the new regime, Ahmet invited Kissinger to stay at his summer home in Bodrum and then arranged a trip to Ankara, where they met with the new president and the defense and foreign ministers. In Ahmet's words, "It was important for America and Turkey and it was a pleasure for me."

Five years later, Ahmet and Mica and the Kissingers visited China. In Kissinger's words, "I tried to explain to Ahmet that the Chinese take everything that is said in my presence seriously because I have a certain status there. Ahmet might have been willing to accept that if I had not made the mistake of telling a Chinese leader that Turks have no sense of humor. This obliged Ahmet to tell a joke every time we met a Chinese official. Some of them, I'm sure, they had never heard before."

At a formal dinner one night, Ahmet told a joke about a Chinese rabbi who had gone to services at Temple Emanu-El in New York. Asked about the experience, the rabbi said he had loved the service and the synagogue was beautiful but, "I didn't see anyone who looked Jewish." Because the hosts did not get the punch line, Kissinger was forced to explain it to them.

While Kissinger knew nothing about the world of rock 'n' roll and "had no connection whatsoever with that kind of music," he was comfortable with fellow celebrities like Michael Douglas, Bill Murray, and Bianca Jagger, all of whom were backstage that night at Madison Square Garden. Introducing Kissinger to someone he had never met, Ahmet said, "Henry, this is my friend Wilson Pickett."

Known for good reason as "The Wicked Mr. Pickett," the legendary soul singer had recorded classics like "In the Midnight Hour" and "Mustang Sally" for Jerry Wexler and then gotten them both banned from the Stax studios in Memphis after starting a fistfight with soul singer Percy Sledge. When he was asked to record a cover version of the Beatles' "Hey Jude," Pickett insisted Jerry Wexler would never release a song called "Hey Jew." Short-tempered and physically explosive, Pickett regularly carried a gun. In May 1988, he was still on probation for having brought a loaded shotgun to a bar fight in New Jersey.

Delighted to be meeting the former secretary of state, Pickett said, "Henry Kissinger, my man!" and then gave him a big hug. Beaming, Kissinger replied, "Mr. Pickett, a pleasure." It was a moment only Ahmet could have engineered. The point was underlined when Phil Collins walked up and introduced himself by saying, "How do you do, Dr. Kissinger? I'm Otis Redding." Courteously, Kissinger, who had never lost his thick German accent, replied, "I luff your music, Otis." Without missing a beat, Ahmet then dragged Kissinger off down the hall.

At midnight, Led Zeppelin finally took the stage for their long-awaited reunion performance. After flying in from London on the Concorde, Jimmy Page had spent six minutes rehearsing with his former band mates and John Bonham's son and then insisted Atlantic rent the hotel suite next to his so he would not be disturbed by the telephone. Opening their thirty-one-minute set with "Kashmir," the band also performed "Whole Lotta Love" and "Stairway to Heaven." The celebration continued after the show at a party where at five in the morning Ahmet said, "I'm a happy man."

Some days later, Ahmet sent Jerry Wexler a form letter on Atlantic Records Fortieth Anniversary stationery in which he wrote, "Dear Jerry, Thank you for being involved in the fortieth anniversary of Atlantic Records. Having so many members of the Atlantic family under one roof was a thrill that I do not expect to ever be repeated in my lifetime. I want you to know that your participation had very special meaning for me and I will always remember it. With warmest personal regards and much love, Sincerely, Ahmet."

Unfortunately, as Wexler would later say, "I declined to appear at

Atlantic's fortieth anniversary. Because of the way it was being produced for television, they were going to drag me out like a wooden Indian and use me as a prop. It was all Ahmet and there was no sense of collegiality. So I didn't go." When Wexler received Ahmet's letter, in the words of Jerry Greenberg, "He went crazy."

# NINETEEN

# Clash of the Titans

*"You get to be a certain age and these things happen and you say, 'Look, this is not a fight for me to start at my age.' Right now, I have a very, very comfortable job. Most people my age have been retired for years. I have the luxury of picking what I do and doing whatever I like with very few obligations and a lot of perks. Why would I now upset the apple cart? Because it is not something I can control."*

—Ahmet Ertegun

## 1

In the spring of 1983, the Atari Corporation, which had accounted for a third of Warner's annual income and been one of the fastest growing companies in United States history, suffered a precipitous $500 million loss that caused the price of Warner's common stock to plummet from $60 to $20 a share. In the new regime Steve Ross instituted to save his company from ruin, Ahmet was forced to use all his considerable diplomatic skills in order to survive.

Intent on spinning off Atari as he had done with other ventures once they had proved to be no longer profitable, Ross authorized Warner executive Bob Morgado to do "all the cost cutting" for him so he could restore Warner Communications to its former lucrative position. After Morgado had "let over a thousand employees in the corporation go," he turned his attention with Ross's blessing to the music division. As Joe Smith explained, "The music division was bloated and not doing well and Steve couldn't fire anybody so he brought in Morgado. He was not a real likable guy and didn't fit with the music guys."

As chief of staff for Governor Hugh Carey of New York, Morgado had worked with Wall Street banker Felix Rohatyn to help create the MAC bonds that bailed New York City out of its financial difficulties in the 1970s. He had also been instrumental in planning and constructing the World Financial Center and the Javits Convention Center in Manhattan. Just before Carey left office in 1982, Steve Ross made Morgado his special assistant and then put him in charge of the record companies at Warner Communications.

Accurately, Morgado saw Atlantic, Warner Brothers, and Elektra as three separate labels that were being run "imperially" by Ahmet, Mo Ostin, and Bob Krasnow. Unable to change the structure at Atlantic because "Ahmet stood there, blocking the doorway," Morgado decided instead to start with what he called his "area of greatest opportunity." In the words of Warner's label executive and author Stan Cornyn, this was also "a euphemism for 'least-defended fortress'—WEA International," a division then being run by Nesuhi.

Linda Moran, who worked for thirty-five years at Atlantic and then at the Warner Music Group, said, "Nesuhi put Warner Music International together. He handpicked the head of every country. It was his idea to create it." Nonetheless, Morgado felt the division was, in Cornyn's words, "loose, undirected, and indifferent." Yet another issue was that none of the label heads, Ahmet among them, was pleased with the man Nesuhi had chosen to succeed him as the head of the division.

In May 1985, Morgado brought in Castilian-born Ramón López, the former head of Polygram Records in the United Kingdom, on an equal footing with Nesuhi as the vice chairman of Warner International. Refusing to concede power to López, Nesuhi continued running the division as he always had. In response to Morgado's urging, the label heads, Mo Ostin and Ahmet among them, decided less than a year later to cancel Nesuhi's contract and replace him with López.

While Ahmet and Nesuhi had over the years begun leading increasingly separate lives, the bond between them was still so strong that Ahmet could not bring himself to tell his brother the bad news. In part this was because Ahmet would have been unable, in Cornyn's words, to answer the question, "With all your power, you couldn't stop this?" According to Cornyn, Ahmet then asked Ostin to inform his brother of the decision. Ostin explained, "I don't think Ahmet could have stopped it. It was a situation which had steam-rollered to the point where there was no turning back. It wasn't anything Ahmet instigated. I think he just recognized this was going on and also felt there was no way he could prevent it." David Horowitz was the one who actually told Nesuhi of the decision.

Moving to an office next to the one occupied by Morgado on the twenty-ninth floor of 75 Rockefeller Plaza, Nesuhi began recording jazz for East/West, a label Atlantic had once distributed that Ahmet reactivated for his brother to run. He also led the fight by the International Federation of Phonograph Industries to stamp out record piracy in Hong Kong, Singapore, Egypt, Turkey, and South Korea.

On March 20, 1989, Nesuhi wrote a long letter to his old friend Jerry Wexler. Going into detail about his recent medical history, Nesuhi noted he had begun experiencing stomach pains more than a year earlier only to be misdiagnosed by a doctor in London. After seeing a physician in New York who suspected he was suffering from ulcers, Nesuhi had learned he was suffering from large cell lymphoma in his stomach.

After having an ulcer and part of his stomach removed and losing thirty pounds, Nesuhi was now about to begin undergoing chemotherapy and expected to "be fully fit and well again after six treatments." Staying in Ahmet's house so he could get "some peace and quiet" while his daughter Leyla and his son Rustem from his fourth marriage were home, Nesuhi urged Wexler to begin writing his book. "Frankly," he confessed, "I am also thinking seriously of starting a book of my own; the trouble is, I can't write English half as well as you can."

Two months later, Nesuhi was admitted to Mount Sinai Hospital in Manhattan. On July 15, 1989, at the age of seventy-one, he died from complications following cancer surgery. In his obituary in *The New York Times* the next day, Susan Heller Anderson wrote, "Elegant and dapper, Mr. Ertegun spoke several languages—all of them quietly. He was a reticent person in a flamboyant industry, and had two passions outside music—soccer and art."

Delivering a formal eulogy for his brother at a celebration of his life, Ahmet described him as his "mother's favorite child" and "a natural musician who could play many instruments by ear and also sing beautifully." Calling him "a loner" and "a perfectionist" who let "very few, if any people into his inner sanctum," Ahmet concluded by saying, "Nesuhi was my inspiration. Everything I did in my life, I did with the hope that I would get his nod of approval. He is no longer here for me to get that nod but I will continue to try to live by his standards. I miss him very much."

Six weeks later, on August 29, 1989, Waxie Maxie Silverman, in whose Quality Music Shop both brothers had searched for old 78s while growing up in Washington, died at the age of seventy-nine. At a time when it would have been impossible for him to ignore his own mortality, Ahmet was told by Morgado he would now have to share the job of chairman and CEO of Atlantic with Doug Morris.

Morris had begun his career in the music industry as a songwriter. In 1966, he cowrote "Sweet Talkin' Guy," a hit for the Chiffons, as well as what he would later call "the most embarrassing song I ever wrote." Entitled "Moulty," the song was a minor hit on which Victor "Moulty" Moulton, the drummer of the Boston garage band the Barbarians, who had lost his left hand at the age of fourteen while holding a homemade pipe bomb that exploded, narrated the story of his life while also singing lead.

In 1970, Morris founded Big Tree Records. He first met Ahmet a year later when he bought the rights to a record by an English pop group called the Magic Lanterns only to have Ahmet call to inform him he had put the record out some years before and it still belonged to him. After Morris produced "Smokin' in the Boys Room," a hit for Brownsville Station on Big Tree, he sold his label to Atlantic in 1974 and began working there.

Four years later, Morris became president of Atco. Although Pete Townshend was being offered more money by Jerry Moss at A&M, Mo Ostin at Warner Brothers, and Walter Yetnikoff at CBS, Morris persuaded Townshend to sign as a solo act with Atco. Two years later, Morris signed Stevie Nicks of Fleetwood Mac and brought in Jimmy Iovine to produce a series of big solo hits for her. In a substantive shift in style that accurately reflected the changing nature of the record business, Morris succeeded Jerry Greenberg as the president of Atlantic Records in 1980.

As Greenberg would later say, "I'm the guy who bought Big Tree Records. I brought Doug in and I made him president of Atco because

Ahmet wasn't around and I needed help. And when I left, I said, 'Make Doug president and I'm here as a consultant and don't worry about it, it'll run fine' and Ahmet got another nice Jewish boy to run his company for him. Doug is a good guy but more corporate and political than I ever was."

Like all those who had preceded him, Morris was also willing to study at the feet of the master. In Morris's words, "I learned a lot from Ahmet. I'd had my own successful record company so I knew how to promote records and I had an intuitive feeling for what would sell, or not. More than anything else, I learned about the art of the business from Ahmet. I learned how to talk to people."

After an "amazing" first year on the job during which Atlantic released five of the Top Ten selling records of 1980, Morris learned how generous Ahmet could be to those who enabled him to continue running the label in his own unique manner. When Ahmet gave Morris, who was then earning $250,000 a year, a year-end bonus of $750,000, Morris said to his wife, "Wow, what did we do? Win the Lotto?" As Morris recalled, "Ahmet then gave me another check for $250,000 of his own bonus money and said, 'This is a much better number.' So I got a million. And I was bought lock, stock, and barrel that day for life."

Morris also saw firsthand how Ahmet dealt with situations that would have driven another man in his position to distraction. After Atari had gone down and threatened to take Warner Communications with it, Steve Ross called Morris and Ahmet to a meeting because, in Morris's words, "They had to get more serious with the record business so it would become a cash cow again and they wanted to know our strategy and tactics for the coming year." As he left the office that day at five o'clock, Ahmet told Morris he would take care of everything at the meeting. In Morris's words, "I said, 'No preparations?' And he said, 'Don't worry about it.' " Wearing a tan suit and a yellow tie, Ahmet then walked out the door.

The next morning, Morris showed up at the meeting fifteen minutes before it was scheduled to begin at nine A.M. Ahmet was nowhere to be seen. At nine-fifteen, he strolled into the room and, in Morris's words, "So help me, he had the same suit on and the same tie, except it looked like he had spilled a drink on himself."

As Morris sat there thinking, "Oh, here's where we get fired," Ross asked both men to outline their detailed plans to increase Atlantic's profits for the coming year. Without missing a beat, Ahmet said, "Doug and I are going to have more hits." In Morris's words, "There was a slight smattering of applause and everyone said, 'Thank you. That's a good strategy.' And we left. By the way, the next year we had a lot more hits."

Under increasing pressure from Morgado, who saw Morris as the key to Atlantic's future success, Ahmet informed Sheldon Vogel in 1989 that he would now have to report to Morris. Although Vogel had always been Ahmet's most loyal supporter as well as his trusted financial adviser in all his business concerns, both personal and corporate, Ahmet told Vogel, "If you want to stay, you're on your own. I can't support you."

"Like all of us," Vogel would later tell Stan Cornyn, "Ahmet was looking for his future." Better than anyone else at the label, Vogel understood that despite all the money Ahmet had earned, his position at Atlantic was what mattered most to him. Vogel also recognized Ahmet's "genius for staying in the middle so he doesn't get on anyone's side. He doesn't get in anybody's way . . . he's never on the wrong side of anybody."

After Morris had chosen Mel Lewinter to serve as his chief financial officer, Morgado gave Vogel a new two-year contract and elevated him to the corporate level, where as a member of Morgado's staff, he occupied a prized corner office. When the label failed to meet Morgado's financial expectations in 1989, Morgado bluntly told Ahmet "Atlantic isn't cutting it," and insisted he share his chairman/CEO position with Morris. As Morgado would later tell Cornyn, "I felt that it couldn't work at Atlantic unless it worked *with* Ahmet. It had to be somebody Ahmet would accept."

By keeping Ahmet on as the titular head of the label, Morgado persuaded him to name Doug Morris as his successor. In Linda Moran's words, "Ahmet worked for several years without a contract. He was never going to leave because it was his company and Sheldon Vogel used to say, 'You have to have some pride. You have to force them to give you a contract.' But he would not do it. He just stayed there and no one knew he was working without a contract."

In 1991 when Morgado finally did offer Ahmet a contract for a five-year term as cochairman of Atlantic, the terms were more than generous. Guaranteed an annual salary of $600,000 for the first three years and $750,000 for each of the final two years, Ahmet was also given a signing bonus of $2.5 million in addition to a lucrative annual bonus to be approved by Morgado. Having already been granted an option to purchase fifty thousand shares of stock, Ahmet was given the right to purchase another 115,000 shares over the next five years with the company guaranteeing he would earn at least $11.5 million from the investment.

The company also agreed to take out a million-dollar life insurance policy on him while absorbing the $970,000 mortgage loan Ahmet had been given in 1979 on his town house, the full principal of which was still outstanding. The agreement further stipulated that the company would pay all of Ahmet's business expenses. After the contract expired, Ahmet would be paid one half of his base compensation for another five years in return for the exclusive use of his advisory services on music recording, video, and music publishing.

Then sixty-eight years old, Ahmet had been given what to those on the corporate level must have seemed like a lifetime deal. While the timing may have been sheer coincidence, it seems reasonable to assume Ahmet had been given this deal as a quid pro quo for accepting Morgado's demand that Doug Morris be allowed to formally assume command of Atlantic.

Now free to do as he liked at the label, Morris brought in Val Azzoli, who had managed Rush, to help him change the corporate structure at Atlantic. He named Sylvia Rhone, who had developed acts like En Vogue and Pantera, to head East/West Records. At a later date, he brought in Danny Goldberg, who had managed Nirvana, to run Atlantic's West Coast office. With Morgado providing the money, Morris also acquired 25 percent of Jimmy Iovine and Ted Field's Interscope label, which would now be distributed by WEA.

On March 4, 1989, Steve Ross made a bold move to solve his financial problems by engineering a merger between Warner Communications and Time Inc. that resulted in the creation of the largest media company in the world with assets of more than $20 billion. David Geffen was so upset Ross had not told him of his plans that he then sold Geffen Records to MCA for $545 million.

Despite his lucrative contract, Ahmet continued pushing Steve Ross for added compensation. After learning from Mo Ostin in 1992 that executives in the movie division had been given large grants of company stock, Ahmet told Doug Morris, "Okay. We gotta go up and get ours." Although Morris still considered himself "the junior partner" and "not at all like these guys," he accompanied Ahmet to a meeting at which Ahmet told Morgado they wanted the same stock options that other top executives had already been given.

Ross, who was then sixty-five years old and suffering from prostate cancer, was at his Long Island estate and so Morgado said he would have to call him to ask about it. After Morgado told Ross what Ahmet and Morris were asking for, both men could hear Ross screaming over the phone, "Tell them they're fired and to get the fuck out of the office!" After leaving Morgado's office, Morris asked Ahmet what they were going to do now. "What do we do?" Ahmet said. "Well, we'll go around to Sony and we're gonna start a label."

The two men were in a car on their way to Sony headquarters in the CBS building at 51 West 52nd Street when the phone rang and Morgado informed them Ross had called back and okayed the deal. In Morris's words, "In the beginning, if Ahmet had gone upstairs to Ross and said, 'Look what I've built for you, I'm only getting a dollar a year, I want a dollar and a quarter a year,' I believe Ross would have said, 'You want to know something? I'm going to give you a dollar fifty a year.' "

After checking himself into a Los Angeles hospital as "George Bailey," the hero of Frank Capra's *It's a Wonderful Life* with whom he had always identified, Steve Ross died of prostate cancer on December 20, 1992. Less than a month later, Gerald Levin, an attorney who had begun his career as a programming executive at HBO before becoming CEO of Time Inc., assumed control of Time Warner and gave Morgado "his full backing" to run the music division as he saw fit.

Levin "appeared to have taken a liking to Morgado" and his decision also made eminent financial sense. In 1985, the combined gross revenues of the Warner Music Group labels had been around $900 million. By 1993, the figure had risen to $3.3 billion. The group's earnings of $296 million were greater than any other division at Time Warner except for cable television. Their combined market share was 22.2 percent, with Sony Music next at 15.3 percent.

Much of the revenue had actually been generated by the introduction of the compact disc to replace the 33⅓ long-playing album that had for so long been the mainstay of the industry. In vast numbers, record buyers had then begun purchasing albums they already owned on vinyl in what was widely promoted as a vastly superior sonic format.

While it would later be reported Ahmet had opposed the conversion from vinyl to CD, he had, as Morris would later say, "questioned it like everyone else because we didn't know anything about it." In the words of David Horowitz, who along with Jac Holzman was the leading proponent of the new compact disc format within the division and "actually made the decision to go full steam ahead" with the conversion, "the label heads were always fighting new technology. They didn't get MTV. Ahmet pooh-poohed it. Nobody on the staff except for Doug Morris saw MTV as an opportunity rather than a threat. They were still record people and this was another medium. The creative aspect of their business was to find talent and the technology was fixed."

Despite the increased profits generated by the Warner Music Group, the death of Steve Ross ended a wildly extravagant era in which the heads of his record labels had run their companies like feudal lords. It also set the stage for what would become known in the media as "The Clash of the Titans" and "The Showdown at the Hit Factory," the day when those whom Ross had left behind would finally confront one another over the issue of who would run the huge moneymaking concern the division had become. As always, Ahmet was right in the eye of the storm.

## 2

On October 27, 1994, Ahmet got into the backseat of his chauffeured Mercedes and told his driver to take him to an apartment on Central Park West where he joined seven other colleagues, all of whom were prepared to leave their jobs, thereby creating what one newspaper account of the struggle called "an unprecedented palace revolt that could paralyze the world's largest record company."

Still physically strong, Ahmet was now using a cane to help him get around after having shattered his pelvis by falling down in his town house eight months earlier. In Mica's words, "We have two houses joined together and to get from his dressing room to the bed, he had to go down four steps. He had probably had a few drinks and he missed the steps and crashed and broke his pelvis."

Having already had a hip replacement, which, in Mica's words, "was then more of a production than it is now," Ahmet had been scheduled to have his hip repaired and underwent "a surgery of nine or ten hours in which every bone was put together so they were all hanging on a chain and it looked like an Egyptian band around your neck. And then a year later something was rubbing against something else so they had to go back in and fix it. The hip replacements were nothing but the pelvis was serious."

Making his way to the apartment where Stuart Hersch, who ran Atlantic's video division, lived, Ahmet joined Danny Goldberg, who by now had become president of Atlantic, and five other Atlantic executives. Clutching cell phones, they spent the next three hours anxiously awaiting the outcome of a showdown between Doug Morris and Bob Morgado. The issue that had brought them together was Morgado's decision to bring in Rob Dickins, the chairman of Warner Music in the United Kingdom, who had "a reputation for being one of the most arrogant and imperious people in the music business," to replace the recently departed Mo Ostin as the head of Warner Brothers Records.

During a series of phone conversations with Morgado the night before, an utterly frustrated Morris, who viewed the move as a sign he had no real authority as head of the Warner U.S. Music Group, had offered to return to his old position as chairman of Atlantic. Morgado accepted his offer. Morris had then contacted all those at Atlantic who were loyal to him and asked them to meet in Hersch's apartment the following morning while he sat down with Morgado in his office at Rockefeller Center.

After his meeting with Morgado was over, Morris arrived at the apartment around noon convinced that Dickins's appointment had already been announced. Ahmet called Morgado to express his concern about the decision, and Morgado asked him and Morris to come meet with him. Not knowing what the outcome would be, the entire team returned to work. At two in the afternoon, Ahmet and Morris sat down with Morgado for a three-hour meeting at which Morgado acquiesced to all of Morris's demands. Morris told Morgado he wanted to appoint Danny Goldberg to succeed Ostin and Morgado agreed to do so.

Morgado then issued a four-paragraph statement in which he said his dispute with Morris had been "blown way out of proportion" and that rumors of problems between them were "merely speculation" and "without merit." He also referred to Morris, who had previously been named as the president of the Warner U.S. Music Group as its "chairman and CEO," thereby giving him a de facto promotion.

As Fredric Dannen would later write in *The New Yorker*, "Morgado had caved in, and Morris and his loyalists are not sure to this day why, but some of them suspect that Gerald Levin had made good on his threat to intervene." In truth, after one of Morris's loyalists called Edgar Bronfman Jr. from Hersch's apartment, the heir to the Seagram fortune, who owned 15 percent of Warner's stock, had made it plain he was siding with Morris, thereby forcing Morgado to reverse his decision.

Four days later, Danny Goldberg, who had only recently moved with his family from Los Angeles to New York, was officially appointed to replace Mo Ostin as the chairman of Warner Brothers Records. He then returned to the West Coast. Val Azzoli became the president of Atlantic, thereby making Ahmet once again the sole chairman of the label he had founded. Ahmet responded to the changes by saying, "This isn't the first time in the history of the music business that executives have argued in the back room. In moments of emotional outburst, people can say all kinds of silly things to each other that they wish they hadn't said afterward. The important thing is that the music division is now united and moving forward."

On May 3, 1995, seven months after he had placated Doug Morris and his fellow executives by giving into all their demands, Morgado was fired by Levin. Bypassing Morris, Levin then appointed Michael Fuchs to head the Warner Music Group. A forty-nine-year-old entertainment lawyer who had once represented Carly Simon, Fuchs had joined HBO in 1976 and become its chairman in 1984. Having established a reputation as a brilliant television executive, Fuchs would now be running both the cable network and the music division.

As he was about to assume his new position, Fuchs ran into Joe Smith, the executive vice-president of Warner Brothers Records, at a party and told him, "We're coming in there and you bandits won't be able to operate like you used to anymore." In a remark to which Fuchs apparently paid little heed, Smith replied, "Us bandits made the company you're coming into."

## 3

On June 21, 1995, seven weeks after assuming control of the Warner Music Group, Michael Fuchs called Doug Morris to his office at HBO. Expecting to be told he was finally being promoted to run the music division, Morris learned how mistaken he had been when Fuchs handed him a press release that read, "DOUG MORRIS RELIEVED OF ALL RESPONSIBILITIES AT WARNER MUSIC GROUP." Followed to his office by security guards who watched as he packed up his personal belongings, Morris was then summarily escorted from the building.

Fearing Morris and his loyalists were planning a coup backed by Edgar Bronfman to take the division away from him, Fuchs had persuaded Levin that Morris had to be let go. On November 16, just 195 days after he had assumed control of the Warner Music Group, Fuchs himself was fired by Levin. Like Bob Morgado before him, Fuchs received a $60 million golden parachute to ease his departure from the company.

In time, Doug Morris would go on to become the chairman of Universal Music. However, his sudden departure from the Warner Music Group ruptured his relationship with Ahmet. As Morris would later say, "I was very unhappy Ahmet did not stick up for me when that happened. He sort of went to Turkey and tried to avoid the flak. It was very disappointing to me. I wasn't let go. I was brutally fired and I don't think there was anything he could have done about it but he didn't get on the phone and say this was a terrible injustice to the press and I guess I expected him to do that. I think he knew I was very angry at him."

During all the years they had worked together at Atlantic, Ahmet had done nothing but praise Morris to anyone who would listen. "Of all the people I've worked with," Ahmet told Fredric Dannen, "he's the straightest person I've ever known. . . . It's incredible but in all the years I've been with Doug we have never had an argument and we have never left the office without hugging one another."

By then, Ahmet had already distanced himself from Morris during the power struggle for control of the music division. Ahmet's new view of Morris was summed up by Jac Holzman. "When Morgado was tossing out Doug Morris, Ahmet was telling a small circle of people including me and a few others that he hardly knew Doug Morris and had never had him over to his house. This was about not going underwater with a guy who was being tossed overboard even though he would have been in the water for a very short period of time."

Recalling the day when he and Ahmet had gone to Sony after they had both been briefly fired over the phone by Steve Ross, Morris assumed Ahmet would now join him. In Linda Moran's words, "Doug wanted Ahmet to leave the company and go with him. To walk out the door and quit. He assumed Ahmet was loyal to him. First of all, Ahmet was loyal to no one. Only to himself."

The parting between the two men was so bitter they did not talk to one another for five years. On October 15, 1998, Morris was invited to speak at a gala United Jewish Appeal benefit dinner chaired by David Geffen at Pier Sixty on the Hudson River honoring Ahmet on his fiftieth anniversary in the record business. After Geffen had told his "bumping into geniuses" story, Morris stood up and "I talked about how for fifteen years, every morning it was a high five and every night it was a hug good night and how it was fifteen years of real fun. I really told the truth about those years which were incredible and it was a very emotional thing."

The next day, Ahmet sent Morris a letter saying he had made "the most lovely speech of the evening and the reason I was able to do it was because I knew him the best of everyone and he really appreciated it and everything was okay after that. Every time I would meet him, he would say to me, 'I miss you.' " Just like Herb Abramson, Jerry Wexler, David Geffen, and Jerry Greenberg, Doug Morris was now someone with whom Ahmet had once worked at Atlantic. They were now all gone, but he was still there. In the end, this was always what Ahmet had cared about most.

# TWENTY

# *Bawitdaba in Bodrum*

*"I'm not really interested in business as such. I'm interested in doing a lot of things that are pleasing to me and that I can afford. So over the last twenty-five years or so, I haven't put myself into group discussions about sales methods or meetings on merchandising. I've stayed out of all that and left it to the younger people I've brought in to run those parts of the company because they don't interest me."*

—Ahmet Ertegun

## 1

In large part, Ahmet was able to withstand the corporate battles at Time Warner because he was now devoting so much of his time and energy to pursuits that had nothing to do with the record business. Foremost among them was his interest in art. As his longtime assistant Jenni Trent Hughes would later say, "Ahmet was an artist and he lived art. It was the Oscar Wilde thing—buy art, create art, or be art. And he did all three."

Long "before the market for the work began to skyrocket," Ahmet had begun collecting early American avant-garde art in the late 1970s. In the words of Elizabeth Moore, an art dealer at the Terry Dintenfass Gallery in New York, "Ahmet had this real talent for discovering the unknown, whether it was in music or art. I think that the chase itself gave him tremendous pleasure. Ahmet was always on the hunt . . . He loved to discover things, and I think that the art collection had something to do with that. It was the unknown, the thing that no one else was looking at, in which he could see the potential."

In addition to his collection of Russian avant-garde Suprematist and Constructivist works as well as several paintings by René Magritte that Nesuhi had bought in Europe shortly after the artist's death in 1967, Ahmet assembled a collection of 280 modern American paintings and works on paper done by eighty artists during the first half of the twentieth century. As Mica would later say, "When Ahmet got an idea in his head, nobody could stop him. He read a book about the American painters in Paris during the period when Gertrude Stein and Stanton Macdonald-Wright were there and started buying paintings and all of a sudden we had three hundred paintings and then he asked his friends if they also wanted to invest in this with him."

Although the collection was, in the words of art historian Avis Berman, "corporate in its impetus and formation," Ahmet did all the buying and so the works "reflect his eye and are conditioned by his comprehension of and intuitiveness about music. Ertegun embraced the modernist tradition in the arts, whether he found it in classic jazz or the rhythms and patterns of such painters as Arthur Dove, Oscar Bluemner, Burgoyne Diller, Werner Drewes, Morgan Russell, Paul Kelpe, Morris Kantor, or Fredrick Whiteman."

In 1986, about eight years after Ahmet had begun the collection, the group he had formed decided to sell some of its holdings. Early modernist works by Georgia O'Keeffe, Marsden Hartley, Arthur Dove, and Max Weber were snapped up, but there was little interest in the American Abstract Artists group. That part of the collection was eventually sold to the Naples Museum of Art in Florida in 1999 for about a tenth of what it is now worth.

Having always expressed his fixation with his own appearance by filling the closets at his various residences with more elegant suits and expensive pairs of handmade shoes than he could ever wear, Ahmet purchased paintings in much the same manner. In Berman's words, "If Ertegun spotted merit in art, he was not content with one or two examples of his or her work; often he bought in bulk from the galleries, and sometimes his purchases were redundant."

By doing so, Ahmet was able "to assemble a large collection of esthetically and historically valuable paintings by this coalition of artists in a relatively short time." Not surprisingly, many of the artists whose works Ahmet collected had also been inspired by jazz and "he enjoyed discussing the association he discerned between jazz and their grammar of seeing." His preference for paintings "with strong, even flamboyant color" was also "compatible with the jazz esthetic."

In the soundproof room in his Manhattan town house, where Ahmet listened to music, a David Hockney painting of a Picasso mural hung over the fireplace. Although his personal collection constantly changed as he loaned pieces to museums all over the world, the room at one point also contained works by Jasper Johns, Le Corbusier, and Picasso. Having filled all his homes with art, Ahmet eventually had to keep some four hundred paintings in storage because he had no place to put them.

The great love for beauty Ahmet and Mica shared could also be seen in their summer home. While on a motor trip through Turkey in 1971, they had come upon a ruined house known as Aga Konak in Bodrum, a then undiscovered village on the tip of a peninsula in the Aegean near the Greek islands of Kos and Patmos. Known in ancient times as Halicarnassus, it was the site of the 140-foot-high tomb Queen Artemisia had built in 353 B.C. in memory of her late husband and brother, King Mausolus. The tomb became one of the Seven Wonders of the World.

After Ahmet bought the ruin from the fifty-four heirs of the original Ottoman owners, Mica set about restoring it with stones from the ancient Mausoleum. Situated on the water, the compound eventually comprised two houses joined together by a one-story kitchen beside a garden of mimosa, lime, orange, and pomegranate trees. At the bottom of the garden, there was an old well, a fountain, staff quarters, and a guesthouse.

The whitewashed walls of the main residence featured a collection of Arabic calligraphy as well as drawings and paintings of Turkish scenes. In rooms filled with furniture from the Ottoman Empire, brown wooden shutters kept out the blazing midday heat. An invitation to spend time with Ahmet and Mica in Bodrum in July soon became what *Vanity Fair* magazine called "the hottest ticket in town."

Over the years, luminaries such as Princess Margaret, Princess Olga of Greece, Mick Jagger, Rudolf Nureyev, Oscar de la Renta, Pat Buckley, Irving "Swifty" Lazar, and a host of others came to stay with Ahmet and Mica in Bodrum. Each day began with a breakfast of "bread, honey, rose petal jam, yoghurt, and fresh ripe figs, apricots, and peaches." After a short ride into town, where camel herds still wandered along the main street, to pick up the newspapers, Ahmet and Mica and their guests would visit tailors who made shirts and pants to order overnight and shop for kilim rugs and bolts of cotton cloth.

At noon, they would all board *Miss Leyla*, the traditional hundred-foot-long Turkish vessel known as a gulet named after Nesuhi's daughter, for a leisurely sail to, in Ahmet's words, "one of several hundred coves that surround us. After a swim in the clearest water to be found anywhere in the Mediterranean, we have a lunch of fish and local specialities." Returning home "later in the afternoon for a quick siesta," everyone then met for drinks and dinner in the courtyard of the house.

"After dinner," Ahmet would later say, "we may go out to a few clubs and discotheques. At the end of a very late evening, we observe an old custom and serve the traditional Turkish tripe soup which is supposed to ward off hangovers." In one of the most beautiful spots in the world where the staff was so dedicated to everyone's well-being that Jenni Trent Hughes once came upon a young Turkish girl happily cleaning the stones in the courtyard with a toothbrush, the leisurely routine then began all over again the next day.

Even in Bodrum, Ahmet sometimes played the role of benevolent host to women with whom he had more than a platonic relationship. One of them was a striking thirty-four-year-old blond French dermatologist named Veronique Simon, who was often a guest at Bodrum and then became a friend with whom Ahmet traveled. As she would later say, "Ahmet was the last sultan of Turkey. It was the Ottoman blood in his body. A man of this dimension will never stay with one woman. In the East, you love only one woman but you have the woman who is the mother of your children, the favorite, the courtesan, and each woman has her place in the heart and brain of this kind of man. Ahmet was an Oriental man with the totality of the Oriental way. And in another way, he was an American man as well."

Over the years, music business insiders delighted in trading stories about Ahmet's latest indiscretions. As David Geffen would later say, "Cher loved Ahmet. He used to grab her breasts and she would say, 'Oh, Ahmet.' He liked to do that." However, even in a business where the one-night stand was standard practice, many women were offended by Ahmet's behavior. "He was a misogynist," said Susan Joseph, who managed singer Laura Branigan while she recorded for Atlantic. "A guy who pinched your ass. I was in a hotel room with him and Laura, and he tried to put his hand up my skirt. I actually had to smack his hand. He didn't have a lot of respect for women. He was sleeping with every artist he could, including Laura."

By the end of his life, the list of women Ahmet had touched in social situations had reached epic proportions. Nor did Ahmet seem particularly discriminating when it came to the women he pursued. "His thing wasn't just good-looking women," Dorothy Carvello, one of his assistants at Atlantic, said. "Don't think they were all off the pages of *Penthouse* and *Playboy*. It was equal opportunity and there were some you couldn't believe. You would be scratching your head. That filter in his brain didn't exist. Whatever felt good, he would go for. The guy always did whatever he wanted to do. He was free. He didn't have to answer to anyone." Nor could Carvello understand Ahmet's attachment to a woman in the music business with whom he carried on a long-running affair.

Jenni Trent Hughes, who also worked for Ahmet but never found his behavior offensive, was once riding with him in a car through the oil fields in Turkey when "the local mayor showed up with his wife and she was gorgeous and Ahmet went, 'Oh, look at that one.' And I said, 'You know, it's a shame you can't find oil the way you find women. Because we'd be the richest people in the world.' He laughed himself silly."

Having grown up with servants who had catered to his every need, Ahmet expected his female assistants to deal with the consequences of his lifestyle. For many years, Noreen Woods, who eventually became a vice president at Atlantic, served as what someone would later call his "cleaner." In Ahmet's words, she was, "The only person I trusted totally with everything. If my wife was away and would be returning on a certain day and I was out at night in somebody's house having drunk a lot or done some drug and holed up with two chicks somewhere, the chauffeur would call her and she would come in with him and defy the ladies keeping me there and grab me and put my clothes on and bring me home so I would be there when my wife returned. I mean, it was service beyond any expectation."

As David Geffen saw it, "I don't think any of these women were a threat to Mica. Ahmet came from a culture where people had many wives and Mica knew who she had married. His friends would find it intolerable for her but she was always patient. Mica is really an extraordinary person and she loved Ahmet."

In Mica's words, "Ahmet had tons of women before I met him and he probably had a whole slew while I was married to him. Not probably. I know it's true. But I never knew their names. I couldn't have cared less. I never felt threatened for one minute. When I was there, he was always there. If I traveled or he went to California and he had some chicks there, who the hell cares? I have a totally different outlook about this and I think that's why our marriage was so good. Because we respected one another and gave ourselves freedom. He liked to have a good time and I'm sure he did a lot of naughty things."

## 2

In 1998 at the age of seventy-five, Ahmet fell head over heels in love with a musician he called his "young Elvis." Following in the footsteps of Ray Charles, Bobby Darin, Stephen Stills, and Mick Jagger, Kid Rock became the last in a long line of artists upon whom Ahmet lavished so much of his time and attention that it sometimes seemed he cared far more about their personal relationship than the business they had in common.

The son of a wealthy car dealer who grew up on an apple farm in Romeo, Michigan, Robert James Ritchie had acquired his stage name as a teenage deejay working basement parties for $30 a night where patrons enjoyed watching "that white kid rock." At the age of seventeen, he signed with Jive Records but was dropped by the label after his first album, *Grits Sandwiches for Breakfast*, was banned by the FCC from radio play for its sexually explicit lyrics.

After cutting two more albums for another label that then also dropped him, Kid Rock went to work as a janitor in a studio in Detroit so he could afford to record his fourth album there. A popular live act in his home state, he performed at a small club in Cleveland where Andy Karp, an A&R man for Lava Records, saw him. Karp then brought Jason Flom, the head of the label, to a special showcase performance at which they were the only record executives present.

Beginning his career at Atlantic in 1979 at the age of eighteen by putting up posters for the label in record shops for $4 an hour, Flom had risen through the ranks to become the head of A&R by signing Twisted Sister, Fiona, White Lion, and Skid Row. As Flom would later say, "When Twisted Sister became big, someone played Ahmet something and asked what he thought and he said, 'I don't like it but what the fuck do I know? I haven't had a hit in seven years.' "

Flom went on to sign a variety of successful acts like Hootie and the Blowfish, who sold an astonishing twenty million records for Atlantic, as well as Jewel, Tori Amos, and the Southern rock band Collective Soul. When Doug Morris offered Flom the chance to revamp Atco, he decided instead to start his own label and formed Lava Records, which was distributed by Atlantic. With acts like Matchbox 20, Uncle Kracker, Sugar Ray, Trans-Siberian Orchestra, the Corrs, and Evelyn King, Lava sold ninety million records over the next eight years and Atlantic bought the label outright in 2002.

After seeing Kid Rock perform at the showcase, Flom signed him for $100,000 and released *Devil Without a Cause*, his debut album on Lava, on August 18, 1998. In Flom's words, "It was one of the incredible albums of all time but nobody else liked it. The people at Atlantic thought it was a joke, the industry thought it was a joke, radio hated it, press hated it, MTV, nothing was going." The album languished on the charts for months until Flom arranged for Kid Rock to perform at an industry party in Los Angeles. "I dragged Ahmet to the show and the room must have had fifty people in it. During the set, Ahmet turned to me and said, 'You know you found Elvis.' I said, 'Yeah, I know but I need someone else to help.' "

The next day, Kid Rock came to the Peninsula Hotel, where he, Flom, and Ahmet "all sat around the pool in bathrobes and the two of them became thick as thieves. It was a perfect match. Ahmet was as happy hanging out with Kid Rock as Mick Jagger or the dauphin of France. He got it and he never wavered. For a few years, I was so close to Kid Rock that he used to introduce me as his dad and then it changed. Ahmet supplanted me as the father figure."

As Kid Rock, whose friends refer to him as "Kid," "Rock," or

"Bob," would later say, "We did this show in L.A. Some celebrity shin-dig. Name 'em and they were there. Who's Who. I was onstage playing and no one gives a shit. Everyone's talking. Whatever. Got their noses up each other's asses. And there was this old dude standing there with a cane staring at us. Watched the whole show. And the next day I get this call. 'This is Ahmet Ertegun. I just want to know how's my young Elvis doing?' That was pretty much the first thing he ever said to me."

After Lava released "Bawitdaba" as a single in May 1999, Kid Rock "proceeded to blow up overnight." With a chorus that sampled Sugar Hill Gang's classic "Rapper's Delight" and a title that came from Love-bug Starski's "Live at the Fever," the song began with Kid Rock repeat-ing the lyrics, "Bawitdaba da bang/a dang diggy diggy diggy/said the boogy/said up jump the boogy" six times before howling out his name. Repeating the introductory line four more times, he then went into his own wild, twisted version of an old-school rap over a thrashing, convul-sive, head-banging heavy metal backing track.

A month after the song was released, Kid Rock's debut album on Lava went platinum. After he performed the song at the 1999 Woodstock Festival, the album went double platinum and eventually sold seven million copies. In 2000, "Bawitdaba" was nominated for a Grammy Award in both the Best New Artist and Best Hard Rock Per-formance categories.

With his long unkempt blond hair flying in his face as he performed bare-chested in shades and a white panama hat or his trademark red fedora, Kid Rock was a natural-born hell-raiser who fused elements of rap, heavy metal, and country and western music while projecting an irresistibly authentic white working-class persona that immediately crossed him over into the mainstream pop market. Although Ahmet was old enough to be his grandfather when they met, the two men soon became close friends.

While working on his second album, Kid Rock invited Ahmet to come to Detroit with him to hear some of his new material. After tak-ing Jason Flom and Ahmet to a little café "he fell in love with" where they ate barbecue pork sandwiches, the three men went into the studio together. As Kid Rock recalled, "I'll never forget that day. I get into the studio, I'm a wreck, I've slept maybe an hour. We're discussing me being a wreck and Jason Flom said, 'You gotta slow down, Rock. You're going to kill yourself.' Blah blah blah blah. Ahmet leaned over and said, 'You know what, man? Some of the best rock 'n' roll records ever made were made on drugs.' I don't think he meant it like don't stop. He was just being honest. He was always a very honest person."

Ahmet and Kid Rock then began hanging out together on a fairly regular basis. Scheduled to have lunch with Ahmet at his weekend home in Southampton one day, Rock called to say he couldn't make it only to have Ahmet say, " 'I don't care what shape you're in. Get over here.' I go over there, he goes, 'What's the matter, man?' I go, 'I been up all night. I haven't been doing good things. I'm having girl trouble.' I'm waiting to hear this fucking wisdom from this man who has seen and done it all and he's like, 'You want a Baby Ruth, man? A Baby Ruth will make you feel better.' So here comes James with a fucking tray of Butterfingers and Baby Ruths and I had a Baby Ruth. Then Ahmet got on the phone with my girlfriend and straightened everything out."

Rock then went to visit Ahmet and Mica in Bodrum. In his words, "I had never seen anything like that house. Unbelievable. I said to Ahmet, 'What's this?' Ahmet goes, 'That stone's from the Mausoleum. Leave it alone.' I was putting out cigars on it. I hadn't met Mica yet so I put on a suit and tie. I just thought it was the right thing to do. Ahmet's always sharp so I dressed up."

As Mica would later say, "I arrived from Paris and I saw this man in this blasting heat in this navy blue suit with a tie on and I said, 'What happened? Are you crazy?' And he said, 'Well, I knew you were coming and I thought I would get dressed up.' Kid Rock is very smart and well educated and he's crazy. He came and stayed with us in Turkey twice."

At a dinner party in New York one night, Ahmet was busily talking to people at his table when Rock came over and asked his permission to ask Mica to dance with him. In the words of Erith Landeau, Ahmet and Mica's longtime friend, "Ahmet sort of looked at him like, 'What the hell do you want from me? If she wants to dance, go dance with her.' He invited Mica to dance and he was holding her like she was made of Chinese porcelain. He was so careful not to hold her too tight and crease her dress. It was so cute and so touching."

In the summer of 2000, Ahmet went to Detroit to record a young jazz saxophone player named James Carter whom Atlantic had signed. Jason Fine, who would go on to become executive editor of *Rolling*

*Stone* magazine but was then a staff writer who had been assigned to interview Ahmet would later say, "They wanted to make a record in Detroit where James Carter is from in a club so it would have the feeling of an old jazz record and Ahmet loved the idea so they went to Baker's Keyboard Lounge, the oldest continuously running jazz club in the country. A tiny funky old place where maybe fifty people could sit in vinyl booths and at an old bar."

The club was so small that Ahmet had to set up a mobile recording studio in an RV parked outside. Seventy-seven years old and wearing a long wool sport coat, a crisp white shirt with an open collar, and pressed light tan pants, Ahmet was using a bamboo cane to get around but spent the entire night "running back and forth between the mobile studio and the club."

Because Aretha Franklin was scheduled to sing and could not abide air conditioning, Fine recalled, "It was a hundred and ten degrees in the club. When you ordered a drink, the ice had melted by the time it came from the bar to the table. I was sweating like a pig but Ahmet looked as cool as he could be. He had an incredible multigenerational array of sax players onstage and was telling Aretha he wanted her to sing the blues on this one, calling out the songs, working up the arrangements, and running the session. It was unbelievable."

After the session ended, Fine, who was then thirty-four years old, sat around drinking and talking with Ahmet until nearly three A.M. At eleven the next morning, Ahmet's driver came to take Fine to lunch with Ahmet at "an incredible house in Bloomfield Hills designed by one of Frank Lloyd Wright's students that was owned by Ahmet's old friend Alfred Taubman," a well-known real estate developer and philanthropist who had pioneered the modern shopping mall.

In Fine's words, "There was an absurd amount of art all over the house. Picassos next to Egon Schiele etchings and Lichtenstein and Degas. The walls were covered with this stuff." Still hungover from the night before, Fine was escorted by the butler to the dining room table, where Ahmet was sitting with the multiple Grammy Award-winning singer Anita Baker, Kid Rock, and the current love of Rock's life, Pamela Anderson, the buxom blond model, actress, and *Playboy* Playmate who had formerly been married to Tommy Lee, the drummer in Mötley Crüe.

"Kid was wearing long red shorts, a white shirt, and a white bowler hat with a red bandanna on it," Fine recalled. "Pam was wearing a purple miniskirt and a white tank top out of which she was exploding. At one point, we walked to the bathroom at the same time and she stopped in front of this Lichtenstein and said, 'This is so Pop.' And I thought to myself, '*You* are so Pop.' She looked just like the Pop Art on the walls."

At the table, Ahmet presided over a discussion about the best jazz singers as well as the early days of *Rolling Stone* magazine and his relationship with Jann Wenner. At one point, he asked, "Ya boys want hot dogs?" Ringing a bell, he told a servant, "Hot dogs, please," and they were then served on silver trays accompanied by silver bowls filled with condiments. After everyone had drunk a good deal of wine, Fine did a short interview with Ahmet. When the meal ended around four o'clock, a still "wiped out" Fine thought he would return to his hotel room for a nap.

Taking him right back to the club, Ahmet ran "another amazing session, saying things like, 'The organ's a little loud. Maybe we should change drummers on this song.' He had unbelievable control of everything and Kid Rock and Pamela Anderson and Natalie Cole came down. All the generations of music Ahmet had been involved with were in this funky little club in Detroit—jazz and soul, Aretha and James Carter and Kid Rock." According to Rock, "I never saw that kind of energy in a guy that age. He could keep up with me and anybody can tell you, I can go. But Ahmet would keep up with me."

During the second week in January two years later, Rock was celebrating his thirty-first birthday with Anderson in a luxury villa with a swimming pool in Careyes, Mexico. "We're by ourselves and after about two days, I go, 'I love you but I got nothing else to say to you. I'm out of things to talk about. Can't fuck anymore. We've done that. What are we going to do here for the next seven days?' She says, 'Why don't you invite some of your friends?' I'm like, 'I don't have friends with private jets and shit.' And I go, 'Yeah, wait a minute.' So I called the town house looking for Ahmet and Mica answered. She goes, 'He's in L.A. I'm sure he'd love to come.' I call Ahmet. Foop! He was there the next day."

Flying to Mexico in a private plane with Veronique Simon and a couple who were Rock's friends, Ahmet and his traveling companions arrived at the villa after a long drive. In Simon's words, "The villa was fine but there was nothing to do and Kid Rock was absolutely drunk all the time. Pamela didn't eat and she didn't drink because she wanted to stay as she was and I started to build a relationship with her and Ahmet was in the middle of nowhere with Kid Rock and he was younger than all these people who were drunk with nothing to say." Going into business with Simon, Anderson then became the spokeswoman for the Simon Solution Two-Step System for Fuller Plumper Lips, also known as the Pamela Anderson Lip Plumper.

"Ahmet hung out with us for five days," Kid Rock said. "It was great because we had a Mexican chef who went to school in France and all we could say was fucking huevos rancheros and guacamole and chips. So all we did was drink Coronas and eat that shit for like two, three days. But when Ahmet finally got there, he would order for us in French. We also had a mariachi band and I got up and I was trying to jam with them and I was shit-faced and Ahmet was like, 'Sit down. You're drunk!'"

Later that year, Ahmet invited Rock to join him at a dinner after the New York premiere of the HBO movie *The Gathering Storm,* in which Albert Finney and Vanessa Redgrave portrayed Winston and Clementine Churchill. As Rock recalled, "Winston Churchill's grandson was there and all the New York elite, and I'm like, 'Ahmet, I got on a wife beater and cowboy boots.' 'No, don't worry. Nobody's dressed up. Come on over.' Sure enough, I walk in there and you could hear a pin drop. I sit down next to him and go, 'You motherfucker.' And he's like, 'You look good, man.'"

In a photograph taken by Bill Cunningham that appeared in the Sunday *New York Times* on October 27, 2002, Ahmet and Kid Rock can be seen decked out in matching red fedoras looking very much like two high school buddies dressed up for the prom in clothes they just stole from a secondhand store. "Bette Midler does this thing for the parks in New York City," Rock would later say. "So I'm like, 'Let's get sharp and wear identical suits and hats,' Ahmet's like, 'That's awesome. Let's do it!' Full matching black suits, red ties, and red hats."

Ahmet had first seen Bette Midler perform for "a convention of hairdressers" in 1972 at the Upstairs at the Downstairs, a hip bistro on West 56th Street. Having already made a name for herself by appearing with her pianist Barry Manilow at the Continental Baths at Broadway and 74th Street where the audience was almost entirely male and usually attired only in bath towels, Midler knocked Ahmet out that night with her snappy patter, great pipes, and unmistakable style. Saying "I've never been so stunned by a performer," he signed her to Atlantic and then co-produced *The Divine Miss M*, her first album for the label. Even after the singer had left Atlantic in 1995 to record for Mo Ostin at Warner Brothers Records, she and Ahmet remained good friends.

Recalling Ahmet and Kid Rock's appearance at her benefit gala, Midler said, "It was hilarious, It was the best costume ever. I think the theme was, 'Come as You Wish You Were.' They were wearing matching red fedoras but when Ahmet took his off, he had a toupee under it. I laughed and laughed. Kid Rock liked to have a good time and had access to Pam Anderson so why wouldn't Ahmet like to hang out with him? There was no Pam Anderson around Mick Jagger." In the words of Lisa Robinson, a contributing editor of *Vanity Fair* magazine, "Ahmet always seemed as delighted to be around Kid Rock as he was around Mick Jagger. He really got a kick out of him. It was a very mutually affectionate relationship."

Rock was with Ahmet one night "at this big party uptown" during one of the Rock and Roll Hall of Fame induction weeks in New York City "and everybody was there. Everyone. From Springsteen on down. Me and Ahmet are sitting there chilling and Mick Jagger walks in. And he recognizes me and comes over and says, 'Hey, Bobby, how you doing?' Gives me a kiss. Gives Ahmet a kiss. Walks around the room and walks out. And Ahmet goes, 'You make him nervous, man!' "

### 3

On May 29, 2000, during the Memorial Day weekend, Ahmet suffered what Mica would later call "a pretty serious stroke" at their home in Southampton. Although he did not lose consciousness, Ahmet was rushed to a local hospital. By the time he was transferred to Mount Sinai Hospital in Manhattan, it was too late for doctors, in Mica's words, "to puncture the retina of his eye to release the pressure" and he lost the sight in his right eye.

Continuing to maintain a schedule that would have daunted a man half his age, Ahmet never spoke publicly about being unable to see out of his right eye and many who were closest to him, Kid Rock among them, never knew he was partially blind. When Dave Marsh saw Ahmet using a cane at a Rock and Roll Hall of Fame meeting, he asked him if it was his knees or his hips that were bothering him. Without going into further detail, Ahmet said, "It's my stroke." By then, he had begun taking anticoagulants to prevent blood clots from forming in his circulatory system.

A year later at the age of seventy-eight, Ahmet underwent triple by-pass and aortic valve repair surgery at New York-Presbyterian Hospital. As Mica would later say, "Ahmet wanted to go to the Cleveland Clinic to have it done but they told him they had the best person, Dr. Mehmet Oz, to do it. Ahmet said, 'I don't want to be operated on by a Turk' but then he gave in." Oz, who would become a media celebrity, was, in Mica's words, "brilliant and he did a fabulous job. Ahmet recovered fairly quickly from that and he had no pain or shortness of breath."

While Ahmet was supposed to be sleeping one night in the hospital, he overheard two doctors discussing whether he would survive the procedure. "Up to that point," he would later say, "I was taking everything very lightly. I thought, 'As soon as I get out of here, I'll start drinking again. Booze. Smoking. Everything, right?' But when I heard that, I said, 'Oh.'"

One of the doctors then gave Ahmet a detailed analysis of the wear and tear that his tumultuous lifestyle had wreaked upon him. When Ahmet asked how he knew all this, the doctor replied, "I know because I've seen what it's done to your body. Don't think all that's just gone by." Having smoked cigarettes for years, Ahmet promptly quit cold turkey with "no withdrawal symptoms at all" and regularly began doing physical rehabilitation exercises. As his old friend Julio Mario Santo Domingo said of Ahmet in 2002, "He must be the strongest man in the world, like a Turkish wrestler. The abuse he has subjected his body to is not to be believed—he must have very special genes."

Ahmet proved this point yet again by surviving a protracted bout with listeria, a rare but potentially lethal bacterial infection he may have contracted from eating unpasteurized cheese. Symptoms tradi-tionally associated with listeria include fever, muscle aches, and nausea or diarrhea. If the infection spreads to the nervous system, it can cause convulsions and lead to meningitis and so is usually treated in a hospital with intravenous doses of antibiotics.

Mica at first thought Ahmet had "wisteria" and could not understand how a flower could make him so ill. After she understood the real nature of his illness, she said, "It was a very, very serious thing, and he had to spend two months in the hospital and was now a little more debilitated." From his bed at New York-Presbyterian, Ahmet continued working with Frances Chantly, who had become his assistant in 2000 and always referred to him as "Mr. Ertegun." In her words, "He said I was helping keep him alive by making him work."

While Ahmet was still the patriarch at Atlantic and continued coming to work on a daily basis after being released from the hospital, his role at the label had become largely ceremonial. Jason Flom and Craig Kallman were now responsible for overseeing the music released by the company. A lifelong record fanatic who by the age of thirteen had already begun amassing the 350,000 LPs that would eventually comprise the largest vinyl collection in the world, Kallman had begun his career in the music business as a teenage deejay playing disco, punk, rock, reggae, New Wave, alternative, and electronic music in clubs like Danceteria, Area, the Palladium, and the Tunnel.

After graduating from Brown University, Kallman started his own record label, Big Beat, and released a series of hits that convinced Doug Morris to bring him in at Atlantic in 1991. "To me," Kallman said, "Atlantic was the iconic label because Zeppelin had been my favorite band. I loved the Stones and Ray Charles and Aretha and when I walked into the building the first day, it was like walking into the sacred halls." After Morris persuaded Kallman to sell Big Beat Records to Atlantic and join the company, Ahmet personally anointed Kallman as the last in a long line of his direct successors by telling the twenty-six-year-old entrepreneur, "We're going to develop you to be president of Atlantic one day."

Kallman's eventual accession in 2002 was made more difficult by the digital revolution that had by then effectively destroyed the business Ahmet had spent his entire life building. In June 1999, Shawn Fanning, an eighteen-year-old student at Northeastern University in Boston, came up with a program that allowed people to share MP3 music files over the Internet for free.

Calling the program Napster after the nickname he had been given for his "nappy haircut," Fanning made his online music file sharing service available free to all who wanted to use it. Napster soon attracted hordes of college students who began downloading music without paying for it. At its peak, the service was used by more than sixty million people who downloaded 2.79 billion songs—on which record companies did not collect a penny.

Rather than try to acquire the technology so they could use it themselves, the Recording Industry Association of America filed a federal lawsuit for copyright infringement against Napster in December 1999. Two years later, the file sharing service was shut down by order of a U.S. district court judge. By then, the damage had already been done. As Bill Curbishley would note, "It was like the record companies lived in this illusory world where they had built this castle on a mountain with a moat around it that was impregnable and no one was ever going to get in. And then lo and behold, someone dropped in by parachute. It was as simple as that. They shot themselves in the head. None of them paid any attention to the new technology and the Internet until it was much too late."

In 2000, the record industry sold 785 million albums on CD and vinyl. Over the next eight years, sales fell 45 percent. As one industry analyst noted, "The *Titanic* that is physical media started slowly sinking in 2000. Certainly this is a traumatic event for those who worked there, but it's an expected product of the digital transformation."

That anyone could now download a single track from any album also put an end to the product that for the past four decades had been the mainstay of the industry. As David Geffen described the new reality: "What made the record business was that when the LP came out, it went from being a singles business to an album business. And now it's turned it back into a singles business and that's a miserable business. There's still musical talent and there always will be and music is more a part of people's lives than it has ever been before but unfortunately, it's free. Try and compete with free. There will always be a record business and there will always be people paying for music but as long as it's convenient to steal it, why not steal it?"

Two years after Steve Jobs of Apple announced the creation of iTunes on January 9, 2001, the iTunes store began selling individual tracks online for 99 cents (a dime more than the price of a single during the era of independent record labels). No longer able to earn a living from record sales, musicians began relying on revenue from live performances as well as the direct sale of CDs in order to survive. With consumers now able to view and listen to music for free on YouTube, Myspace, and Facebook, artists trying to break into the business no longer needed to audition for record company executives because they could sell their music directly online.

While rock superstars like U2, Radiohead, and Pearl Jam were still able to market albums in a variety of new ways, their sales were a fraction of what they had once been. In the words of one management executive, "There's a prevailing wisdom that many established acts don't need a record label anymore. This is the new frontier. This is the beginning of a new era for the music business."

Although the digital revolution did not affect Ahmet personally, it did wreak havoc at the Warner Music Group. In desperate need of cash to pay off corporate debt incurred by its disastrous merger with AOL in 2000 and fearing the record industry would never return to the levels of profitability it had once generated, Time Warner sold the division for $2.6 billion in 2003 to a private investment group headed by Edgar Bronfman Jr.

Bronfman then persuaded Lyor Cohen, the forty-four-year-old head of the Island Def Jam Music Group to run the division. As Cohen would later say, "The basic architecture and plans of Def Jam were really written by Ahmet and Jerry Wexler. We started out as a rap label and through that, we attracted a lot of rock 'n' roll artists. Which is similar to Atlantic because jazz had been the rap music of that moment in time."

The son of Israeli immigrants, Cohen had been born in New York and then grew up in the Los Feliz section of Los Angeles. After graduating from the University of Miami, where he studied global marketing, Cohen began promoting shows in Los Angeles featuring rap artists and bands like the Red Hot Chili Peppers. He then began working for Russell Simmons in New York and soon made a reputation for himself as a white man who could handle himself in a black world as the road manager for Run-DMC.

Nicknamed "Little Lansky" by rap producer Irv Gotti, Cohen became the president of Def Jam Records in 1988. When Doug Morris

happened?' I say, 'If that were what happened, it would be called a documentary and neither you nor I would have seen it.'"

Four days later, Ahmet, who earlier in the month had been honored with the first Grammy Industry Icon Award, told a reporter from the online magazine *Slate* that while he liked the actor who had portrayed him in *Ray* and thought director Taylor Hackford had "made a terrific movie, you must realize that I'm not the kind of shy little guy as portrayed in the movie. I don't care what the man looks like or anything but it should have been somebody hip."

Ahmet's initial reaction to his portrayal by actor Curtis Armstrong, whose big break had come in *Revenge of the Nerds*, had been far more visceral. After Mica and Barbara Howar had accompanied Ahmet to a special screening of *Ray* arranged for him by Hackford in Los Angeles, Ahmet was, in Howar's words, "absolutely crazed. We couldn't shut him up. He was like, 'I have never worn clothes like that! I've never worn a double-breasted suit! Two-toned shoes!' Mica was going, 'Ahmet! Ahmet! Ahmet!' He was crazed and he stayed crazed and angry the entire night."

As they walked into a restaurant in West Hollywood after the screening to have dinner with Hackford, "Mica said to me, 'You keep Taylor occupied and I'll try to keep Ahmet quiet.' Mica and I were like two colonels keeping Ahmet separated from Taylor." As Jerry Wexler, portrayed in the film by Richard Schiff, who had played presidential assistant Toby Ziegler in the long-running NBC series *The West Wing*, said, "*Ray* was terrible. I felt the same way about it as Ahmet. We were stick figures. Just a couple of suits."

Having spent years working on the project before filming began, Taylor Hackford had spent countless hours interviewing Ahmet about the early days at Atlantic and had become part of Ahmet and Mica's social circle. As the director noted, "The best time to talk to Ahmet was at two in the morning after he'd had many vodkas and the stories came out." Acknowledging that Ahmet did not like the way he was portrayed in the movie, in which Ray Charles called him "Omelet," as Otis Redding had actually done, Hackford said, "Eventually, Ahmet hosted a screening in New York and once people began recognizing him in airports after the movie became a hit, he got into it."

Though far fewer people saw it, Ahmet had also been portrayed in *Beyond the Sea*, the 2004 Bobby Darin biopic written and directed by Academy Award–winning actor Kevin Spacey, who also played the lead role. For reasons known only to him, Spacey chose a forty-six-year-old Turkish actor named Tayfun Bademsoy to play Ahmet. With a full head of dark hair and the wrong kind of goatee, Bademsoy bore no resemblance to the way Ahmet had looked in 1958.

The single funniest cinematic moment in which Ahmet was involved occurs in Frank Zappa's 1971 movie *200 Motels*. Zappa, who was so fond of Ahmet that he named one of his sons after him, had asked Ahmet to play the part of a business executive in the film but when he was unable to do so, Zappa worked him into the script by having one of his leading characters say, "Ahmet Ertegun used this towel as a bathmat six weeks ago at a rancid motel in Orlando, Florida . . . It's still damp. What an aroma!" Snorting it, the character then got stoned out of his mind.

# TWENTY-ONE

# *"The Encore Was Heaven"*

*"When Ahmet dies, he will have squeezed the tube of life completely*
*dry. And they'll have to bury him facedown or he'll dig his way out."*

—Doug Morris

## 1

In November 2005, Ahmet joined about eighty people who had worked
at Atlantic Records over the years for a reunion in Las Vegas. Ahmet
was busily trading stories with Jerry Greenberg about the good old days
when Susan Joseph, Laura Branigan's former manager, who had won a
judgment against the artist for $600,000 and then forced Ahmet to pay
her the money out of the singer's royalties, sat down at his table. In Joseph's words, "He was an old man and I wanted to be polite and I went
to sit with Jerry Greenberg and Ahmet said, 'I'd like you to leave my
table,' and I said, 'No problem.'"

The following summer, Ahmet was honored at the opening night
concert of the Montreux Jazz Festival in Switzerland, which he and
Nesuhi had helped Claude Nobs found in 1967. As Kid Rock would
later say, "It was like a tribute to Ahmet and he invited all the people
he wanted to sing over there. Robert Plant. Stevie Nicks. Me. George
Duke. Stevie Winwood. Chic." After throwing a party "in this mackin'
suite Ahmet got me overlooking the lake," Rock was arrested by Swiss
police, who mistakenly believed he had stabbed an intruder who had
broken into singer Chaka Khan's suite only to have her beat him up
with an umbrella.

When Ahmet, who himself was out after every show in Montreux eating dinner long past midnight, called the next morning to invite Kid Rock to his suite to watch a soccer game, Rock told him he had just gotten out of jail. "I've never heard someone cuss people out in so many different languages. He was laughing but he was upset. Once we had lunch, he called Claude Nobs. 'The show's fucking canceled! Who the fuck takes my artist to jail? There'll be no Robert Plant tonight! No anybody!' Then he's calling someone in French, cussing them out, and I'm like, 'Yeah.' Turned out the mayor sent me a free watch for my trouble. A Swiss watch. Ahmet thought that was the funniest thing ever."

Before a marathon show that also featured Paolo Nutini—the Scottish singer who was "the last new Atlantic artist Ahmet really embraced and took under his wing"—performing with Ben E. King, Ahmet attended the sound check that afternoon. In the words of longtime Atlantic publicist Bob Kaus, "Ahmet didn't like the way it was sounding and he kept telling the bass player to turn down. Finally, he walked back to the board and basically mixed the live sound himself. He was yelling at the sound guy, 'This sounds terrible! You need more guitar! The bass is too boomy! We have to fix this. I have unhappy artists here.' And he made it right and the show was phenomenal. It was as if he was sitting in the studio listening to every detail and making a great record."

On Saturday night, August 1, clad in a houndstooth sport jacket, a white shirt, white linen pants, and brown shoes, Ahmet got onstage with his cane in hand to sing with Stevie Nicks, Robert Plant, and Nile Rodgers of Chic during the finale. After Stevie Winwood performed a moving solo rendition of Ray Charles's "Georgia" and Ahmet came onstage to acknowledge his award, his hand kept shaking as he held the microphone.

Two months later, on October 9, Ahmet sat down in his Manhattan town house with the English singer James Blunt, who "at that moment was Atlantic's biggest star," for his final interview with Susan Steinberg, the director who for the past three years had been working on a documentary entitled *Atlantic Records: The House That Ahmet Built* for the American Masters series on PBS.

Steinberg, who had been an editor and assistant on *Gimme Shelter, Woodstock,* and *Cocksucker Blues,* structured the film around conversations between Ahmet and Robert Plant, Jimmy Page, Aretha Franklin,

Eric Clapton, Mick Jagger, David Geffen, Lyor Cohen, Chris Black-well, Phil Collins, Wynton Marsalis, Ben E. King, and Ray Charles, who died shortly after his segment was shot. Narrated by Bette Midler, the project was produced by Ahmet's old friend Phil Carson, who had previously produced the Sun Records documentary, *Good Rockin' Tonight*, for the American Masters series.

After Blunt left Ahmet's town house that day, Steinberg said, "Ahmet, we would love some shots of you just listening to music." As Bob Kaus would later say, "They put on a Louis Armstrong CD and without looking at the liner notes, Ahmet identified when it was recorded and who was playing every instrument. He closed his eyes and was completely transported. All of a sudden, it was as if there were no cameras there. Ahmet was completely in another time and space."

Three days later, Ahmet flew to the Bilbao Museum in Spain for the opening of a show of his good friend Jean Pigozzi's collection of African art. Unable to accompany him because she had just returned from an extended business trip to Rio de Janeiro, Mica said, "I knew I couldn't let him go alone because he wasn't walking well and I didn't want to send him with a nurse." In the end, Veronique Simon went with him. In Pigozzi's words, "Ahmet was not very well. He was a bit tired and he was in a wheelchair and I had never seen him go around in a wheelchair before."

In Simon's words, "We spent three days in Bilbao and Ahmet was in a bad mood and very tired. It was the first time in my life I ever saw him tired and he was a little afraid of traveling. When we arrived in Bilbao, he was afraid his suitcase would not arrive at the airport. He was very quiet and I had the feeling it was the end and I would never see him again." Pigozzi, who had spent many wild nights with Ahmet, then arranged for him to fly back to New York on real estate developer and philanthropist Eli Broad's Gulfstream IV.

On Wednesday, October 25, a week after he had sat in at a rehearsal for the Genesis reunion tour at a small studio in Chelsea, Ahmet addressed a company breakfast for Atlantic department heads and senior executives in a restaurant in Rockefeller Center. In Bob Kaus's words, "Ahmet came and spoke and it was deeply moving. In essence, he said, 'Atlantic is in better shape now than it has been in years and I'm very happy with the job that everyone is doing to continue the company's legacy.' In retrospect, I had this sense he was saying, 'It's all okay now. My company is fine and I'm leaving it in good hands.' " Craig Kallman recalled, "Ahmet was pretty frail but it was an amazing speech. I had been with him a month before at the Peninsula Hotel in L.A. and it was like one in the morning and toothpicks couldn't keep my eyes open and he was like, 'C'mon, we're going somewhere else.' I said, 'I can't do it. I'm crashing. Ahmet, it's all you.' "

For Ahmet, the definition of hell had always been having to go home early. Recalling a night she had spent with him in New York when "we were all much younger," his friend Erith Landeau described being with Ahmet on their way home after dinner when he suggested they head to a jazz bar on the West Side for a drink. "I said, 'Fine.' And we walked in and it was sort of a long room, very dark and smoky, and the minute we got in, the word was rolling from the door to the back— 'Ahmet Ertegun is here. Ahmet Ertegun is here. Ahmet Ertegun is here.'

"All the musicians who had either worked for him or knew him or played for him grabbed him and within two minutes I nearly lost him. I don't know if you ever saw Ahmet when he was listening and really concentrating on the music. He would close his eyes three-quarters and listen and he would get the rhythm and he would move his foot. He went into a trance. It was magical. And all the musicians looked to see what he was doing and they sang to him and for him."

## 2

Ahmet was scheduled to fly with Mica on Saturday, October 28, 2006, to Michigan in a small chartered plane so they could attend Kid Rock's "hometown wedding" to Pamela Anderson. Having already tied the knot in St. Tropez, Beverly Hills, and Nashville, the couple intended to marry yet again, this time with Ahmet as the best man. After a powerful storm caused extensive travel delays at all the New York City airports, Ahmet called Rock from his town house to say, "I'm so fucking pissed off. We're sitting here, Mica's got her cowboy boots on and we can't fly out. They won't let us off the ground."

Later that day, Craig Kallman called Ahmet to update him on a project they had first discussed some months earlier. Inspired by *The Sopranos* and *Entourage*, Kallman had pitched Ahmet on the idea of creating "a well-done dramatic series about the music business" that would deal with "sex, drugs, rock 'n' roll, the Mafia, and every figure in the business" with Ahmet as the central character. Confident he "could get the show on the air" if it was done right, Kallman then contacted Taylor Hackford, who had already pitched HBO on a miniseries about Atlantic Records only to decide he could not do justice to the material in so limited a format. The two decided to become producing partners in "a full-blown dramatic hour-long scripted cable show" that would run over seven seasons and cover Ahmet's entire career. Informed of Hackford's involvement, Ahmet joked, "Make sure you do a better job on me than *Ray*."

When Kallman spoke to Ahmet that afternoon, he told him of his most recent conversations with Hackford and then said, " 'Listen, we've just been getting into how much poetic license we have.' He said, 'Craig, you can make up whatever you want. I'll say it's true.' It was so Ahmet. I was laughing and we had a great conversation."

After Kallman told Ahmet about a new band he was interested in signing, he said, "Hey, Ahmet, I may need you to come to London with me. 'No problem. Tell me when you want to go.' It was the fastest tell-me-when-you-want-to-go ever and I'm sure he was thinking, 'Which girls am I calling? And what clubs am I going to?' His energy level was unreal. He was absolutely ready to jump on a plane and go."

The next morning, Ahmet and Mica went to Woodlawn Cemetery in the Bronx to attend the unveiling of the gravestone of Joyce Wein, the wife and business partner of George Wein, the founder of the Newport Jazz Festival. "The chosen burial ground for New Yorkers of African American and Afro Caribbean descent," the cemetery is the final resting place for Miles Davis, Duke Ellington, Lionel Hampton, W. C. Handy, Coleman Hawkins, Milt Jackson, Illinois Jacquet, Jackie McLean, King Oliver, Max Roach, and Cootie Williams, among others.

As Ahmet walked with Mica past the graves, many of them marked by large, elaborate headstones, he noted that so many of the artists he had once known and worked with were now gone, while he was still around. Always so busy living that he seemed to give little thought to his own mortality, Ahmet did have a clear view of death. Two years earlier as he had sat listening to a minister talk about where people went after they died at the funeral service for soul singer Doris Troy at the Williams Institutional CME Church in Harlem, Ahmet had turned to his assistant Frances Chantly and, in her words, "made this motion with his hand as though to indicate that when we die, it's over. There is nothing afterwards."

When they sat together at the end of the day at Atlantic, Ahmet and Doug Morris would, in his words, "talk about death all the time. He once said to me, 'When I die, I'm going to be buzzing around this building making sure who came to the funeral.' He also said, 'When I die, I don't care what happens. Because I'm going to be dead.' "

After Ahmet and Mica left Woodlawn Cemetery that day, he told her, "Well, we should go to the Stones." As she would later say, "Because we were rested, you know? If we had gone to Kid Rock's wedding, we probably wouldn't have gone to the Stones." That night, Ahmet and Mica went to the Beacon Theatre, an aging three-thousand-seat venue on Broadway at 74th Street, to attend a benefit concert by the Rolling Stones for the William J. Clinton Foundation in honor of the former president's sixtieth birthday. The show was filmed by Martin Scorsese for a documentary entitled *Shine a Light*, which was dedicated to Ahmet.

Wearing a midnight blue blazer lined with red silk, a thickly knotted white woolen tie, a white-collared blue shirt, gray suspenders, and gray pants, Ahmet entered the crumbling seventy-six-year-old former movie theater through the stage door and was sitting in the very funky downstairs lounge when Jane Rose, Keith Richards's longtime manager, caught sight of him. As she would later say, "Ahmet was family. Whenever he showed up, everyone was happy to see him. I was thrilled he was there and I said, 'You've got to say hello to Keith and the guys' and everyone said, 'No, he can't walk.' But he wanted to see the band so I took him up to the dressing rooms in the elevator."

Rose escorted Ahmet to Richards's tiny dressing room, where drummer Charlie Watts joined them. The three men began talking and, as Rose recalled, "I was sitting in Ahmet's lap because the dressing rooms at the Beacon are so small. Ahmet was always Ahmet, grabbing me whenever he saw me or he'd look at my boobs, smile, and go, 'Hey,

Jane.' That was Ahmet. It was more affectionate and hilarious than any kind of sexual pass." Rose then began taking photos of Ahmet, Richards, and Watts.

After having fallen while on holiday in Fiji six months earlier, Richards had suffered a subdural hematoma and then undergone surgery to relieve pressure on his brain. When Ahmet asked the guitarist how he was doing, Richards replied, "Feel the bumps, baby," and let Ahmet run his hand over the places where six pins had been inserted into his skull. "He asked me how my head was after the bang. I said, 'Have a feel.' Because I have a big dent on the left side, front lobe. He was rubbing it and we were laughing our heads off about it."

Returning to the downstairs lounge, Ahmet was having a drink with Mica and Rupert and Josephine Lowenstein when the wife of the Stones' former business manager said she was going to the bathroom. In Mica's words, "Ahmet said, 'I'll go too.' And I said, 'I'll come and help you' and he said, 'No.' The bathroom was two yards from where we were sitting and then Josephine came back and said, 'Ahmet fell. You had better go there.' The light wasn't working in the bathroom and Ahmet pushed the door open with his back to leave and it wasn't a step, it was just about ten inches of clearance, and with his legs like that, he fell backwards and hit the back of his head."

Alan Dunn, who spent more than thirty-five years working for Mick Jagger and had flown with Ahmet on his private plane when he attended the Atlantic reunion in Las Vegas, recalled, "Ahmet was trying to get out of the bathroom and the door jammed and he pushed on it and he came flying out and the girl who had taken him there tried to catch him but he came out too fast. As he went down on the floor, he flipped over because the cut was on the back of his head and there was a good deal of blood on the floor and he kept saying, 'Mica, Mica, where are my glasses? I can't see out of my right eye.' And she said to him, 'You haven't been able to see out of your right eye for the past five years.' "

After an ambulance had been called, Ahmet was put on a stretcher and taken by order of the Stones' attending physician to New York-Presbyterian. In the words of Shelley Lazar, who was handling VIP tickets for the Stones that night, "Alan Dunn and I were standing there with tears in our eyes. It was quite emotional for me to see this powerhouse of a man totally helpless with a bloody bandage around his head strapped to a stretcher."

"When I saw them take him out on a stretcher," Jane Rose said, "I went to a bad place because of what had happened to Keith. I had a really bad feeling about it." Never losing consciousness, Ahmet continued talking to Mica in the ambulance and then at the hospital. Because he was still bleeding and needed surgery, Ahmet was taken off blood thinners by his doctors. "A few hours after the operation was finished," Mica would later say, "he talked and he was in a good mood and feeling good and then the strokes started because the blood thinners had been preventing the strokes."

In the words of Jann Wenner, who had also been at the Stones' show but had no idea Ahmet had fallen backstage, "The doctors told me he seemed to be okay when he arrived in the hospital. He was still conscious but he had swelling in the brain so they took him off the blood thinners and drained the blood from his head. After two or three days, he had regained consciousness and seemed to be making a recovery. He was talking and responsive and then he suffered a series of small strokes, possibly because they had taken him off the blood thinners. A series of small blood clots went to his brain and the cumulative effect was a huge stroke. And he never regained consciousness."

Lapsing into a coma, Ahmet became the center of an extraordinary scene that went on for weeks as those who loved him tried to rouse him back to life. In Wenner's words, "Mica came night and day, and Nesuhi's wife and their kids were there, and they waited to see if he would improve and kept monitoring him, but it was pretty clear after the first couple weeks he was not going to improve. They had a boom box in his room playing jazz, and he actually looked calm and very healthy."

"We tried everything to get him to wake up," Erith Landeau said. "I was there with him alone one evening and I took his arm and I was so mad he wouldn't talk, I shook his arm and said, 'Ahmet! Kid Rock and Pamela are already divorced and you are still not up! Wake up! Wake up!' I looked at myself and said, 'What are you doing?' I was just trying to help. Everyone did. They brought music. They spoke Turkish to him. Nothing worked."

The first time Jann Wenner came to visit Ahmet in the hospital, he broke down and sobbed in Landeau's arms. In Landeau's words, "The way Jann spoke to Ahmet in the hospital was unbelievable. 'You are bigger than life. You can't do this. You can't leave. I need you. We need you. There is so much more to be done.' It was really wonderful."

On November 15, Jane Rose sent the photos she had taken of Ahmet, Keith Richards, and Charlie Watts backstage at the Beacon to him along with a note wishing him a speedy recovery. On the back of one photo was a handwritten note that read, "Dear Ahmet, Get well. I'll see you soon. C.R. Watts, drummer, the Rolling Stones." Believing the sequence of events backstage at the Beacon that night had been "ghostly," Keith Richards had written, "Ahmet, never touch my head again. One love, Keith."

On the day before Thanksgiving, Frances Chantly went to see her "beloved boss" and "was alone with him and I began talking to him and really pouring my heart out to him. I played some jazz music for him and said if he could hear me, he should move his eyebrows. His eyebrows were twitching like crazy and I knew he understood what I was saying and he could hear me. That was like my goodbye to him and when I saw him again, he was unconscious and there were no signs of life. For a long time, I blamed the Rolling Stones even though I knew it was not their fault."

Six weeks after the accident, Ahmet's family and his doctors reached what Wenner would later call "a kind of a unanimous decision they should not prolong it further. They didn't exactly stop life support but they let him die. He had left a living will and after six weeks, his wishes were finally honored and he died peacefully with Mica and his family there."

On Thursday, December 14, 2006, Ahmet Munir Ertegun, the greatest record man who ever lived, died at the age of eighty-three in the Weill Cornell Medical Center of New York-Presbyterian Hospital on East 68th Street in Manhattan. A year earlier, Ahmet had told an interviewer how he would like to be remembered by saying, "I did a little bit to raise the dignity and recognition of the greatness of African-American music."

Having always lived to the beat of his own drummer, Ahmet had died doing what he liked best—waiting to listen to music made by artists he loved at a funky joint in New York City. And while the way in which this happened was so perfect that no self-respecting Hollywood screenwriter would have ever tried to sell it as the final scene in the movie of Ahmet Ertegun's long and eventful life, Neil Young, an artist whom Ahmet had always revered, put it best by saying, "It's suitable his last conscious moments were at a concert because that was the way he lived. It's too bad he had to go. But I'm glad he didn't have to go with some debilitating disease where we had to sit and wait. He went to a show. And the encore was heaven."

### 3

As he had sat having lunch with Lyor Cohen at Atlantic, Ahmet had, in Cohen's words, "described some of the key points of his passing and what he expected from that and I basically executed his wishes. Because he said he didn't want it to be a memorial, he wanted it to be a celebration." Cohen then promised Mica he would see to it that Ahmet's body would be taken back to Turkey in a manner befitting the way he had lived.

In Cohen's words, "What I had not realized is you cannot rent a Gulfstream because to transport a coffin, it has to be encased in zinc and the zinc casing is too large to make it into a Gulfstream so I had to get a huge plane. I called all my friends who have huge planes and the only one whose plane was not in the shop was Donald Trump. He said yes without hesitation but we would have had to make two stops for gas and suddenly Paul Allen lent me the plane he uses for the Seattle Seahawks."

After loading Ahmet's coffin on to Allen's 757 on Friday, December 15, 2006, Cohen, Jann Wenner, Jean Pigozzi, Chris Blackwell, Earl McGrath, Craig Kallman, Kid Rock, Frances Chantly, Bob Kaus, Erith Landeau, and others accompanied Mica and Nesuhi's wife and her two children to London, where the plane refueled for the final leg of the journey. As Cohen described it, "We stopped in London to pick up friends and I think there were like forty-three people on the plane. We were all basically numb. You know what it's like to fly overnight. You kind of not sleep, you're groggy, and it was completely surreal, like a Fassbinder film." Arriving in Istanbul the night before the funeral, the group went to a hotel for dinner and then to a little jazz club to attend a tribute for Ahmet, where Kid Rock joined an impromptu jam session by performing "Bad, Bad Leroy Brown."

On Monday, December 18, everyone attended a service at Marmara University's Religious Studies Department's mosque on the Asian side of the city. Along with the captain of Ahmet's sailing boat, most of the staff from Ahmet and Mica's home in Bodrum were there. Accompanied by a good deal of security, the foreign minister of Turkey spoke.

As Jann Wenner recalled, "The Islamic tradition is that anyone can come to the service. The mosque was so mobbed that you could get a little scared and Ahmet's Western friends kind of hung off to the side. We all had laminated paper photographs of Ahmet pinned to our lapels, which is another tradition they have. It was extremely chaotic, which sort of seemed inappropriate to the dignity of the individual being buried but it was also somehow symbolic of Ahmet's return to the land of his father and the Turkey he loved so much."

In accordance with Muslim law, the burial ceremony was then held outdoors in the small Ertegun family plot, where Ahmet's father and mother had been interred in an old cemetery on a hill overlooking the Bosporus in Uskudar, the section of the city where Ahmet had been born. As Lyor Cohen would later say, "Muslims believe the community buries people. The community believes they are supposed to come to an open burial ceremony so everyone was invited. So it was full of pandemonium and emotion and very physical." Just getting to the actual gravesite was difficult because a couple of hundred people had jammed themselves into the narrow alleyway leading to the cemetery. In Wenner's words, "It was the chaos of Turkey but you started to get the sense Ahmet was back among his people."

In Mica's words, "The chauffeur missed the way to the cemetery and in the Moslem religion, the minute the body comes, they put it in the ground. They don't wait and when I arrived with my niece, the body was already in the ground and she began screaming and yelling. The current prime minister of Turkey, who was then the foreign minister, put me next to the grave during the ceremony and it is not usual to do that." As Jann Wenner would later say, "Mica was incredibly stoic throughout the entire thing and then she would break down. But she was so involved in making sure everyone else was getting through it and so into decorum and handling things right that she was almost preoccupied with making other people feel comfortable."

Wrapped in the traditional Muslim burial shroud made of clean white cloth known as a kefen, Ahmet's body was lowered into the ground without a coffin. After placing a bouquet of white roses on the grave, Mica stood there for a long time staring at the photograph of Ahmet beside the grave. She then crossed herself, lifted some dirt, and scattered it into the grave. All those who had come to pay their last respects to Ahmet, including the gardener from his home in Bodrum, then followed suit.

As Erith Landeau described the scene, "When Ahmet was put into the ground, they were praying and there was a fence around the family plot and Lyor Cohen was holding the fence and crying like a child. Not sobbing but crying. I could see he really, really loved Ahmet. And then he told me, 'When I came to Atlantic and they told me I would have to share a floor with Ahmet, I thought, 'What do I need this old guy for? He's eighty-something. What is he going to teach me?' He said, 'Erith, he taught me everything. In the end, he would sit in my office because I wanted him to be with me. I wanted to be next to him all the time.' "

After the burial service was over, everyone went to the house in which Ahmet had been born for lunch and another prayer service. At eleven o'clock that night, the plane that had brought Ahmet and his friends and family to Turkey returned to New York. Mica flew to Paris. After a life that had taken him around the world and back again so many times that every page of his passports was completely covered with entry and exit stamps, all of Ahmet's rambling was finally done.

Ahmet Ertegun at the Lenox Lounge in Harlem, 1997.

# *Acknowledgments*

First and foremost, I would like to thank Mica Ertegun for making it possible for me to write this book by giving me her unending cooperation and support. Without the help of Ahmet's sister, Selma Goksel, who sent me countless e-mails from Turkey, I could never have reconstructed Mehmet Ertegun's role in the formation of the Turkish republic or the childhood she shared with Ahmet and Nesuhi in Turkey, Switzerland, France, England, and Washington, D.C.

I will also be eternally grateful to Craig Inciardi, curator of the Rock and Roll Hall of Fame, who opened the vault in New York for me so I could spend four days wearing white gloves as I examined the sixty boxes of Ahmet's personal papers that now comprise the Ahmet Ertegun Archive at the Hall of Fame Library in Cleveland. Never failing to respond to my endless requests for more material, Craig also provided me with DVDs and videotapes I could never have found without him. Performing tasks above and beyond the call of duty, the inimitable Jesse Reiswig served as my research assistant in New York. I can never thank him enough for patiently reading Ahmet's oral history interviews into a tape recorder so I could then transcribe them for this book.

Having worked for and with Jann Wenner of *Rolling Stone* for the past forty years, I owe him a debt of gratitude for unearthing sources for me and for his continuing concern that I get everything right about Ahmet. I also want to thank his assistant Ally Lewis for her help. Merci beaucoup aussi to Mica's assistant Monique Mirouze for putting up with all of my requests for information and for sending me digital copies of letters Ahmet had written that were not among his personal papers.

Had Will Dana, the managing editor of *Rolling Stone,* not asked me to write the tribute to Ahmet that appeared in the magazine shortly after his death, I would never have been able to write this book. I would like to extend my heartfelt thanks to Jason Fine, who was then the executive editor of *Rolling Stone*, who made that piece better than it would have been without him. He also arranged an invitation to Ahmet's tribute at Lincoln Center, bought me lunch at Patsy's so we could gaze at the hallowed doorway at 234 West 56th Street through which Ahmet, Jerry Wexler, and Ray Charles had once walked, and took me to dinner at the Waverly Inn, where I accosted Lyor Cohen for an interview. My thanks as well to Nicole Frehsee for all her help.

David Brendel provided me with valuable information. Richard Havers in England graciously sent me priceless material concerning Duke Ellington's appearance at the Palladium in London. Catherine Tackley also provided me with information about this event. My thanks to Linda Moran for responding to questions no one else could have answered.

My thanks as well to Paul Wexler for the CD of the original version of "Drinkin' Wine Spo-Dee-O-Dee." I would like to thank Brian Higgins for providing me with material from the Lefsetz blog about Ahmet and patiently explaining the mathematics of publishing and songwriting royalties. Thanks to John Thompson for the Buffalo Springfield boxed set and for singing their songs with me on the streets of Rome that day. Thanks to Bonnie Simmons for the CD of Ahmet instructing Ray Charles how to sing "Mess Around." My gratitude to Chris d'E. Vallencey in England for providing me with information about the cost of an Aston Martin in the mid-1950s. Thanks as well to Frances Chantly for graciously providing me with an actual ticket to the tribute to Ahmet at Lincoln Center.

My thanks to Paul Bresnick, who came up with the idea for this book, and then placed it with Simon & Schuster, where I have had the great good fortune of working with Bob Bender, who has been as patient and gracious throughout this long process as anyone I have ever known. Thanks as well to Johanna Li for all her aid. The always brilliant Josh Maurer helped me find the title for this book, which comes from a remark Veronique Simon made when I interviewed her.

Thanks to Craig Kallman for the guided tour of Ahmet's office at Atlantic, to Bob Kaus for supplying the photos from the Atlantic

Records Archive, and to Grayson Dantzic for all his help in locating and identifying them. Thanks as well to Ahmet's good friend Jean Pigozzi for making his extensive collection of photographs of Ahmet available to me, and to Tasha Seren for all her help in compiling them.

Thanks to the Rock and Roll Hall of Fame for allowing me to use the photographs of Ahmet from their collection and to Jodi Peckman at *Rolling Stone*, who compiled the wonderful tribute book for Ahmet that was distributed at Lincoln Center and then uploaded all those images for me. My thanks to Michael Randolph for providing me with his father's astonishing photographs of the golden days at Atlantic. Thanks to Brian Lipson, Bryan Besser, and the very erudite Eric Reid for all their help and sage advice. My thanks to Hendrik Hertzberg at *The New Yorker* for helping me locate those who worked alongside George Trow at the magazine.

After seeing Ahmet in action during the Rolling Stones' tour of America in 1972, I interviewed him for the first time while researching my book *S.T.P.: A Journey Through America with the Rolling Stones*. I then spoke to him again for *Bill Graham Presents: My Life Inside Rock and Out*. I was also fortunate enough to have spent many hours on the phone with Jerry Wexler and then wrote the tribute to him in *Rolling Stone* following his death in 2008. Barbara Abramson was a great source of information and also sent me to the documentary *Atlantic: Hip to the Tip* as well as the Atlantic press release announcing Herb Abramson's return to the label. Miriam Bienstock was also unfailingly gracious in responding to my many questions. I would also like to thank the late Charlie Gillett, who died shortly after I spoke to him, for having written *Making Tracks*, his book on Atlantic Records. Much like Ahmet, Charlie also truly loved the music. To the great Solomon Burke who passed on in 2010, rest in peace, rest in peace.

Closer to home, my thanks to Jeff Greenberg for bringing me *The WPA Guide to Washington, D.C.* and Ray Charles's autobiography, *Brother Ray*. A true artist, Michele Frantz performed Photoshop wonders for me. Thanks to Kevin Daly for the unbelievable rock 'n' roll golf tournament hookup and to all the boys at Monterey International for hanging out with me. Thanks to Bill Sagan, Nathan Nishiguchi, and Katherine York for providing me with a copy of my long-lost 1988 interview with Ahmet.

I would like to thank Donna for the author photograph and for putting up with the impossible work schedule I kept while writing this book. After all is said and done, she is the one with the gold record. As always, I send all my love and best wishes to Sandy and Anna.

Robert Greenfield

May 16, 2011

# Notes

*Unless otherwise indicated, all quotations are from interviews conducted by the author.*

*AE = Ahmet Ertegun*

## EPIGRAPHS

PAGE

xi   *"He was"*: Atlantic: *Hip to the Tip.*

xi   *"Ahmet had"*: Wexler and Ritz, *Rhythm and Blues.*

xi   *"Ahmet was"*: Kissinger, Author Interview.

## PROLOGUE: A DAY OF TRIBUTE IN NEW YORK

PAGE

xvii   *"the little Turkish prince"*: Burke, AE Tribute.

xvii   *"I loved"*: Clapton, AE Tribute.

xvii   *"a ducker and"*: Hackford, AE Tribute.

xvii   *"irony and"*: Wexler, AE Tribute.

xvii   *"Hey, homes"*: Ibid.

xvii   *"had no"*: Ibid.

xvii   *"Ahmet, thank you"*: Ibid.

xviii   *"Well, he hasn't"*: Wenner, AE Tribute.

xviii   *"Ahmet was"*: Jagger, AE Tribute.

xviii   *"a diverse"*: Ibid.

xviii   *"Here's our"*: Nash, AE Tribute.

xviii   *"Here's something"*: Ibid.

xix   *"entertaining"*: Clapton, *Clapton.*

xix   *"I still felt"*: Ibid.

## ONE: COMING TO AMERICA

PAGE

1   *"The older I get"*: Wade and Picardie, *Music Man.*

2   *David Geffen first heard*: Geffen, Author Interview, 6/10/09.

2   *posted on a well-read music blog*: lefsetz.com/wordpress.

2   *"a bit Barnum and Bailey"*: Curbishley.

2   *"Do you know why"*: Ibid.

2   *Trinity College*: Motion, *The Lamberts.*

2 *had been commissioned:* en.wikipedia.org/wiki/Kit_Lambert.

3 *"feel snubbed by":* Trow, "Profiles."

3 *"Ahmet, don't go":* Howar.

3 *"Boys":* Rudge.

3 *was shocked to see:* AE, Columbia University Oral History Research Office, AE Archive.

3 *"the Turk":* Kinzer, *Crescent and Star.*

3 *"Europeans came to perceive":* Ibid.

3 *"The Turks are":* Ibid.

3 *"I shall always":* Ibid.

4 *was present when the Treaty of Lausanne:* Selma Goksel e-mail, February 12, 2009.

4 *"in a house on the rocky hills":* AE, AE Archive.

4 *a truly primitive land:* Kinzer, *Crescent and Star.*

4 *the grandson of a Sufi sheik:* Selma Goksel e-mail, March 23, 2009.

4 *Ozbeker Tekkesi:* Selma Goksel e-mail, October 7, 2010.

4 *Exempt from military service by imperial decree:* Hanioglu.

4 *short-lived first marriage:* Selma Goksel e-mail, April 13, 2009.

5 *"probably would have become a singing star":* AE, Columbia University Oral History Research Office, November 13, 2002, AE Archive.

5 *Bespectacled, with a thick mustache:* Photo, www.londra.be.mfa.gov.tr.

5 *piercing blue eyes:* Kinzer.

6 *they were now being held as hostages:* Hanioglu.

6 *soul searching:* Selma Goksel e-mail, February 12, 2009.

6 *chief legal adviser:* Official Document, Department of State, Division of International Conferences and Protocol, June 25, 1934, AE Archive.

6 *a handwritten document:* Selma Goksel e-mail, March 23, 2009.

6 *she was furious:* Selma Goksel e-mail, February 12, 2009.

7 *"I have no religion":* Mango, *Ataturk.*

7 *"Although my father was basically a timid man":* AE, undated autobiographical fragment, AE Archive.

7 *"left behind the teeming hodgepodge":* Ibid.

7 *"the clean quiet serenity":* Ibid.

7 *"this bland beautiful sterile country":* Ibid.

8 *18 Kalcheggweg:* Selma Goksel e-mail, May 13, 2009.

8 *"a mixture of Turkish":* AE, undated autobiographical fragment, AE Archive.

8 *eight days:* Selma Goksel e-mail, February 15, 2009.

8 *"Hanimefendi":* Selma Goksel e-mail, July 3, 2009.

8 *A short, stout:* Photo, AE, *"What'd I Say."*

8 *"the sad haunting Oriental":* AE, undated autobiographical fragment, AE Archive.

8 *"would never participate":* Ibid.

9 *"a beloved distant":* Selma Goksel e-mail, February 2, 2008.

9  *"a miserable-looking beggar"*: Selma Goksel e-mail, February 8, 2009.

9  *"perhaps a bit spoiled"*: Ibid.

9  *"He was like a hero"*: AE, undated autobiographical fragment, AE Archive.

9  *In a photograph from this period*: Photo, AE, *"What'd I Say."*

9  *"was always a bloody"*: AE, undated autobiographical fragment, AE Archive.

10  *33 rue de Villejust*: Selma Goksel e-mail, May 13, 2009.

10  *"I don't like this"*: Selma Goksel e-mail, February 7, 2008.

10  *broomstick as a mast*: Selma Goksel e-mail, February 2, 2008.

10  *Stephan Mallarmé, the actor Jean Gabin*: www.forum.prepas.org.

10  *Josephine Baker, the Mills Brothers*: Gross, "The Real Sultan of Swing."

10  *"It's nothing"*: AE, undated autobiographical fragment, AE Archive.

11  *a street full of holes*: Mica Ertegun, 4/25/09.

11  *"Mother, what happened"*: AE, Columbia University Oral History Research Office, 11/13/02, AE Archive.

11  *At his own request*: Official Document, Department of State, Division of International Conferences and Protocol, June 25, 1934, AE Archive.

11  *"a couple of ruffians who"*: AE, Columbia University Oral History Research Office, January 23, 2003, AE Archive.

11  *his mother panicked*: Selma Goksel e-mail, February 7, 2008.

11  *July 23, 1932*: Selma Goksel e-mail, April 5, 2009.

11  *invited to dine*: Selma Goksel e-mail, April 2, 2009.

11  *practiced her curtsy*: Ibid.

12  *"they hardly ever saw"*: Selma Goksel e-mail, February 7, 2008.

12  *"was very British and very strict"*: Ibid.

12  *"We wore our party"*: Ibid.

12  *"was interested in women"*: Goksel.

12  *"Ahmet just sort of left"*: Ibid.

12  *"the King of Jazz"*: Newspaper clip, source unknown, Richard Havers e-mail, July 2, 2009.

12  *"His Famous Orchestra"*: Newspaper ad, source unknown, Richard Havers e-mail, July 2, 2009.

12  *The grandson of a former slave*: en.wikipedia.org/wiki/Ellington_Duke.

13  *"typically expected of black artists"*: Harvey G. Cohen, "Dawn of the Jazz Age."

13  *"the primitive, discordant, rule-breaking"*: Ibid.

13  *three huge cardboard cutouts*: Photo, ibid.

13  *pearl gray*: Lawrence, *Duke Ellington and His World*.

13  *nearly four thousand*: Ibid.

13  *9 pence*: Newspaper ad, source unknown, Richard Havers e-mail, July 2, 2009.

13  *the kind of extended ovation*: Harvey G. Cohen, "Dawn of the Jazz Age."

13  *three trumpet players*: Photo, ibid.

13  *"a display of neat and fast footwork"*: Newspaper clip, source unknown, Richard Havers e-mail, July 2, 2009.

13  *"the original snake hips girl"*: Lawrence, *Duke Ellington and His World*.

13 *"the program to a happy conclusion"*: Ibid.

13 *"scores of smartly dressed young English people"*: Ibid.

13 *"hundreds in the hinterlands"*: Ibid.

13 *"a small army of"*: Ibid.

13 *"besieged the Duke"*: Ibid.

13 *"a precursor to Beatlemania"*: Harvey G. Cohen, "Dawn of the Jazz Age."

14 *"It was nothing like"*: AE, Columbia University Oral History Research Office, January 23, 2003, AE Archive.

14 *to see Cab Calloway*: Gross, "The Real Sultan of Swing."

14 *"I was twelve"*: AE, Columbia University Oral History Research Office, November 13, 2002, AE Archive.

15 *"there were very many cowboys there"*: AE letter, October 21, 1934, AE Archive.

15 *"I kiss you"*: Ibid.

15 *"making the trip"*: AE, Columbia University Oral History Research Office, November 13, 2002, AE Archive.

15 *four days, thirteen hours, and fifty-eight minutes*: en.wikipedia.org/SSRex.

15 *"a rung above the first-class cabins"*: Selma Goksel e-mail, November 20, 2009.

15 *"But when the sea"*: AE, Columbia University Oral History Research Office, November 13, 2002, AE Archive.

16 *"There were only"*: Selma Goksel e-mail, March 27, 2009.

16 *"enjoyed roaming around"*: Selma Goksel e-mail, November 20, 2009.

16 *"thousands of dollars"*: AE, Columbia University Oral History Research Office, November 13, 2002, AE Archive.

16 *"We arrived in"*: Ibid.

16 *"the black Pullman"*: Ibid.

16 *"very strict"*: Ibid.

16 *"Americans were savages"*: Ibid.

17 *"a shameful act"*: Akcam, *A Shameful Act*.

17 *"outlawed ethnic and minority"*: Balakian, Author Interview.

17 *"earnestly hoped"*: Minassian, *Musa Dagh*.

18 *"utterly negative"*: Ibid.

18 *"If the movie is made"*: Ibid.

18 *"Munir Ertegun became"*: Balakian, 2/16/09.

18 *"My personal view"*: Selma Goksel e-mail, 2/8/09.

18 *donated $3.5 million*: Draft of press release, August 26, 1994/For release September 12, 1994, AE Archive.

18 *"There are different"*: Bennetts, "Devil in a Bespoke Suit."

19 *"made it clear"*: Sassounian, "Ahmet Ertegun Knew What's Good for Turkey."

19 *"a shame that the"*: Ibid.

19 *"I could not write"*: Ibid.

## TWO: THE NATION'S CAPITAL

PAGE

20 *"When I was just"*: AE, Columbia University Oral History Research Office, April 22, 2003, AE Archive.

20 *"seat and center of domestic"*: Federal Writers Project, *The WPA Guide to Washington, D.C.*

21 *"John Law"*: Ibid.

21 *"rows of small squalid houses"*: Selma Goksel e-mail, January 26, 2008.

21 *"to spend and to dream"*: Scott, "Turkish Delight."

21 *"architectural elements of"*: www.Turkeyembassy.com.

21 *a huge ballroom*: Photo, Scott, "Turkish Delight."

21 *cost $400,000*: Scott, "Turkish Delight."

21 *"So we wound up"*: AE, Columbia University Oral History Research Office, January 23, 2003, AE Archive.

22 *one of the first things*: Ibid.

22 *"I first found myself"*: AE, Columbia University Oral History Research Office, January 23, 2003, AE Archive.

22 *"unfortunately mentioned"*: Ibid.

22 *"excused from both chapel"*: Letter from the Reverend Albert H. Lucas, April 13, 1935, AE Archive.

22 *"glad indeed to"*: Ibid.

22 *"Your Excellency"*: Ibid.

22 *"learned to regard"*: Ibid.

22 *"sympathy with"*: Ibid.

22 *"Mr. Headmaster"*: Letter from Mehmet Munir to the Reverend A. H. Lucas, April 16, 1935, AE Archive.

22 *"My father took me"*: AE, Columbia University Oral History Research Office, January 23, 2003, AE Archive.

23 *"at least three times"*: Selma Goksel e-mail, February 2, 2008.

23 *"imitation black speech"*: AE, Columbia University Oral History Research Office, January 30, 2003, AE Archive.

23 *"Washington was like"*: AE, Columbia University Oral History Research Office, January 23, 2003, AE Archive.

23 *"a dime apiece"*: AE, "What'd I Say."

24 *"things that others"*: Poole, "Lush Life."

24 *"a habitué of"*: AE, Columbia University Oral History Research Office, January 23, 2003, AE Archive.

24 *"shilled for a while"*: Ibid.

24 *"was really just colored water"*: Ibid.

24 *"greasy place"*: Ibid.

24 *"all the strippers"*: Ibid.

24 *"Eastern European Gypsy"*: Ibid.

24 *"beer joints where"*: Ibid.

24  *"Black Broadway"*: Virtual Tour of Shaw, www.pbs.org/ellingtonsdc/vtVenues .htm.

24  *"the Washington equivalent of"*: AE, Columbia University Oral History Research Office, January 23, 2003, AE Archive.

24  *"everything clicked"*: Ibid.

25  *"a lot of the teachers"*: AE, *Landon Magazine.*

25  *"school's more traditionalist"*: Ibid.

25  *"We were always"*: AE, Columbia University Oral History Research Office, January 23, 2003, AE Archive.

25  *"a long list of names"*: Selma Goksel e-mail, January 9, 2009.

25  *"is a made-up word"*: Ibid.

25  *"waited till the"*: Wade and Picardie, *Music Man.*

26  *"Satchelmouth Swing"*: Weeks, interview, www.allaboutjazz.com.

26  *"Lips Page's special"*: Ibid.

26  *"started collecting very seriously"*: AE, Columbia University Oral History Research Office, January 23, 2003, AE Archive.

26  *"Collecting Hot"*: AE, Columbia University Oral History Research Office, January 30, 2003, AE Archive.

26  *"a big head"*: Wade and Picardie, *Music Man.*

26  *"didn't have Communist tendencies"*: Ibid.

27  *"European"*: Ibid.

27  *"including my parents"*: Selma Goksel e-mail, January 22, 2009.

27  *"disgraceful episode"*: Ibid.

27  *"My first meeting"*: Document, AE Archive.

28  *zoot suit:* Selma Goksel e-mail, February 8, 2009.

28  *"not well known"*: Holzman, Author Interview.

29  *"You started out"*: Ibid.

29  *"jewel of the program"*: Ibid.

29  *"My first question"*: Ibid.

29  *Ralph Waldo Emerson:* Documents, AE Archive.

29  *Because she had cared:* Selma Goksel e-mail, January 31, 2008.

30  *"an intellectual bookshop"*: Columbia University Oral History Research Office, January 23, 2003, AE Archive.

30  *"said was a"*: Ibid.

30  *"a mixed crowd"*: Ibid.

30  *"very unusual"*: Ibid.

30  *"a young guy"*: AE, *"What'd I Say."*

30  *"We've been reading"*: Gottlieb.

30  *waiters in white jackets:* Bill Gottlieb photo.

30  *huge bust of Kemal Ataturk:* Selma Goksel e-mail, November 23, 2009.

31  *the only restaurant:* AE, *"What'd I Say."*

31  *"quite possibly the hippest"*: *Rolling Stone* magazine as quoted by Katz, "Lester Young Turns 100."

31 *"bread"*: Ibid.

31 *"That's cool"*: Ibid.

31 *"You dig?"*: Ibid.

31 *"I feel a draft"*: Ibid.

31 *"bells"*: Ibid.

31 *"to be"*: Mezzrow and Wolfe, *Really the Blues.*

32 *"outraged Southern senator"*: AE, *"What'd I Say."*

32 *"It has been brought"*: Ibid.

32 *"that God had created"*: Selma Goksel e-mail, January 28, 2009.

32 *"errand boy"*: AE, Columbia University Oral History Research Office, January 30, 2003, AE Archive.

32 *"When we gave"*: Ibid.

32 *"advertised in the white"*: Ibid.

32 *"little flyers"*: Ibid.

32 *"didn't know it"*: Ibid.

32 *"make a big scene"*: Ibid.

32 *"Swingtime in the Capital"*: AE, *"What'd I Say."*

32 *"Man, you gotta give"*: Ibid.

33 *"The Turkish Ambassador came"*: Memorandum to the President from Adolph Berle, Assistant Secretary of the Department of State, April 6, 1940, AE Archive.

33 *"There is a"*: Ibid.

33 *"My father"*: AE, Columbia University Oral History Research Office, November 13, 2002, AE Archive.

33 *life in the nation's capital*: Conant, *The Irregulars.*

34 *"the star"*: Goksel.

34 *"Listen, you return that"*: AE, Columbia University Oral History Research Office, November 13, 2002, AE Archive.

34 *"I don't know"*: Ibid.

35 *"heart used to sink"*: Ibid.

35 *"stand at attention"*: Ibid.

35 *"At which point"*: Ibid.

35 *"difficult, if not impossible"*: Selma Goksel e-mail, April 1, 2009.

35 *On March 14, 1944*: St. John's College Commencement Exercises Booklet, AE Archive.

35 *medieval philosophy*: Weiner, "Ahmet Ertegun."

35 *"whole embassy was astir"*: Selma Goksel e-mail, June 19, 2008.

35 *In a photograph*: Photo, George Skadding, http://google.com/hosted/life.

36 *"I am deeply grieved"*: Statement by the President of the United States, November 11, 1944, AE Archive.

36 *On January 25, 1946*: Memorandum for the President, original signed and returned to Dean Acheson on January 25, 1946, AE Archive.

36 *"the battleship on which"*: AE, *"What'd I Say."*

36 *"Although we felt"*: Selma Goksel e-mail, June 19, 2008.

## THREE: MAKING RECORDS

PAGE

37  "After the Second": AE, Author Interview, 3/11/88.

38  "visited by close friends": Selma Goksel e-mail, December 16, 2009.

38  some of her personal belongings: Selma Goksel e-mail, May 14, 2009.

38  $100: Ibid.

38  $5 to $25: Gillett, Making Tracks.

38  "I get more than": AE, Columbia University Oral History Research Office, January 23, 2003, AE Archive.

38  turned down offers: Ibid.

38  "working hard": AE, Letter to Selma Goksel, July 3, 1947, AE Archive.

38  "didn't feel like": AE, Columbia University Oral History Research Office, January 23, 2003, AE Archive.

38  even to speak out against: http://en.wikipedia.org/Conscription_in_Turkey.

38  a very attractive young: Selma Goksel e-mail, June 29, 2009.

39  send Ahmet $30: Selma Goksel e-mail, June 23, 2009.

39  "Ahmet had some": Selma Goksel e-mail, February 8, 2009.

39  "I have not found": Undated letter to Selma Goksel, AE Archive.

39  want ads: AE, Columbia University Oral History Research Office, January 23, 2003, AE Archive.

39  "a bunch of crooks": Ibid.

39  "After that": Ibid.

39  "he could memorize": Selma Goksel e-mail, June 21, 2008.

39  "a cheap recording studio": AE, Unidentified video interview, AE Archive.

40  "could sing the blues": Ibid.

40  "all these guys who": AE, Columbia University Oral History Research Office, January 23, 2003, AE Archive.

40  "knew what black life": Atlantic: Hip to the Tip.

40  "around to thinking": Gillett, Making Tracks.

40  "breezed in": AE, "What'd I Say."

40  "I'd like one of": AE, Columbia University Oral History Research Office, January 30, 2003, AE Archive.

41  "made a lot of money": Ibid.

41  "Oh, I've got money": Ibid.

41  "a rich friend": Letter to Selma Goksel, August 22, 1947, AE Archive.

41  "who had an avant-garde": AE, "What'd I Say."

41  "I'm not interested": AE, Columbia University Oral History Research Office, January 30, 2003, AE Archive.

41  "in the Forest Hotel": Ibid.

42  "a very tough lady": Ibid.

42  "the star dressing room": Ibid.

42  "with the big star": Ibid.

42  "It quickly became": Ibid.

42 *"best friends for"*: AE, Unidentified video interview, AE Archive.
42 *"We didn't have"*: AE, Columbia University Oral History Research Office, January 30, 2003, AE Archive.
42 *Born in Brooklyn*: White, "Herb Abramson."
43 *published a small newspaper*: Abramson.
43 *Erasmus Hall High School*: Erasmus Hall High School records.
43 *"the poor man's Harvard"*: www.barrypopik.com.
43 *"he could find"*: Abramson.
43 *"he was a Jew"*: Ibid.
43 *"a lot of very"*: Bienstock.
43 *"tried desperately to"*: Bienstock.
43 *"I already lost"*: Abramson.
43 *"ran five miles"*: Ibid.
44 *"very late in"*: Bienstock.
44 *"did a lot of things"*: Ibid.
44 *Abramson's two biggest hits*: Kramer, "Atlantic and R&B Trend Developed Side by Side."
44 *"He didn't like"*: Abramson.
44 *"a different kind of mind"*: Bienstock.
44 *"The reason"*: Abramson.
44 *"his heart was"*: Ibid.
45 *"Atlantic was formed"*: Ibid.
45 *"knew all"*: AE, "What'd I Say."
45 *"where to get pressings"*: AE, Author Interview, 3/11/88.
45 *"Ahmet was such a"*: Sander, *Trips*.
45 *"They all knew"*: AE, "What'd I Say."
45 *"We all went"*: Goksel.
46 *"thought he was"*: Ibid.
46 *"Over a two-and-a-half"*: Abramson.
46 *"Dr. Sabit hasn't been"*: AE, Letter to Selma Goksel, Selma Goksel e-mail, June 24, 2009.
46 *a contract consisting*: Document, AE Archive.
46 *"The name Atlantic"*: AE, "What'd I Say."
47 *"active in promotional"*: Ibid.
47 *"We were grabbing at"*: Ibid.
47 *"We must have"*: AE, Columbia University Oral History Research Office, May 1, 2003, AE Archive.
48 *"the major companies"*: Ibid.
48 *"just thrown in the garbage"*: Ibid.
48 *$60 a week*: Gillett, *Making Tracks*.
48 *"The name sounds good"*: Letter to AE from Nesuhi Ertegun, January 22, 1948, AE Archive.
49 *"time to be properly"*: Ibid.

49  *"Received press release"*: Ibid.
49  *"By the way"*: Ibid.
49  *"Nobody believes"*: Bienstock.
49  *"Ahmet was still very"*: Gottlieb.
50  *"He didn't have"*: Ibid.
50  *"Ahmet had"*: Bienstock.
50  went to number twelve: AE, *"What'd I Say."*
50  *"selling most of the"*: Selma Goksel e-mail, April 2, 2009.
50  *"I only hope"*: Letter from Selma Goksel, May 13, 1948, AE Archive.
50  *"very sweet"*: Bienstock.
51  *"He could do"*: Ibid.
51  *"We were very"*: AE, *"What'd I Say."*
51  *"It was a funky"*: Wakschal.
51  *"dozens of small"*: Jackson, *Big Beat Heat.*
51  *"the Street of Hope"*: Ibid.
52  *"Dearest sweetest darling"*: Letter from AE to Selma Goksel, January 28, 1949, AE Archive.
52  *"patent development"*: Ibid.
52  *"sixty odd"*: Ibid.
52  *"working very hard"*: Ibid.
52  *"getting the patents"*: Ibid.
52  *"usually had quite"*: Ibid.
52  *"The record company"*: Ibid.
53  *"and this figure"*: Ibid.
53  *"26 distributors"*: Ibid.
53  *"$90.00 to"*: Ibid.
53  *"tremendous master"*: Ibid.
53  *"elderly couple"*: Ibid.
53  *"extremely nice"*: Ibid.
53  *"absolutely schmaltz"*: Bienstock.
53  it would *"make"*: Ibid.
53  *"either Montgomery Clift"*: Letter from AE to Selma Goksel, January 28, 1949, AE Archive.
54  *"We made a recording"*: AE, Columbia University Oral History Research Office, January 23, 2003, AE Archive.
54  *"did not sell"*: Bienstock.
54  *"Dear Ahmedakis"*: Undated letter to AE from Vernon Duke, AE Archive.
54  *"in Variety, Newsweek"*: Ibid.
54  *"a series of"*: AE, Columbia University Oral History Research Office, January 23, 2003, AE Archive.
54  *"the music of"*: Ibid.
54  *"of course a mistake"*: Ibid.
55  *"Can't you push"*: AE, *"What'd I Say."*

55 *while pushing around:* en.wikipedia.org/wiki/mcghee_stick.

55 *In a photograph:* Photo, Frank Driggs Collection; in AE, *"What'd I Say."*

55 *"Drinkin' wine":* Tosches, *Unsung Heroes of Rock 'n' Roll.*

56 *"The only blues singers":* AE, *"What'd I Say."*

56 *"That's my brother's":* Ibid.

56 *"No man":* Ibid.

56 *Wilbert "Big Chief" Ellis:* the houndog.blogspot.com.

56 *"sometimes sing 13 bars":* AE, *"What'd I Say."*

57 *"gave us confidence":* Gillett, *Making Tracks.*

57 *"a stack of":* Ibid.

57 *"the police couldn't have":* Ibid.

## FOUR: THE HOUSE THAT RUTH BUILT

PAGE

58 *"Ahmet was eyeing":* Evans, *Ray Charles.*

59 *"and from then":* Ruth Brown with Yule, *Miss Rhythm.*

59 *describe the relationship:* Trow, "Profiles."

59 *"I hired a singer":* Deffaa, *Blue Rhythms.*

60 *"got a job":* Smith, *Off the Record: An Oral History of Popular Music.*

60 *"Washington's elite would":* http:culturemob.com.

60 *A curving replica:* www.pbs.org/ellingtonsde.

60 *elegantly dressed guests:* www.gwu.edu.

60 *"Rendezvous of the":* Ruth Brown with Yule, *Miss Rhythm.*

60 *"a gorgeous lady":* Ibid.

60 *"high energy performance":* nfo.net/usa.

60 *offered the singer:* Deffaa, *Blue Rhythms.*

60 *sent a telegram:* Bienstock.

60 *"There is a girl":* Ibid.

60 *"She was":* Deffaa, *Blue Rhythms.*

61 *"Ruth Brown was":* AE, Columbia University Oral History Research Office, January 23, 2003, AE Archive.

61 *Her biggest number:* Trow, "Profiles."

61 *"Ruth Brown wanted":* Atlantic: Hip to the Tip.

61 *"Capitol also":* Gillett, *Making Tracks.*

61 *Waxie Maxie Silverman:* AE, *"What'd I Say."*

61 *"The well-established":* Ruth Brown with Yule, *Miss Rhythm.*

62 *" 'manager'—in quotes":* Deffaa, *Blue Rhythms.*

62 *Billie Holiday:* Ruth Brown with Yule, *Miss Rhythm.*

62 *"in her powder-blue":* Ibid.

62 *"on which to scribble":* Ibid.

62 *$1,000:* Deffaa, *Blue Rhythms.*

62 *"love of Ahmet":* Ibid.

62 *"already in":* Ibid.

62  *John Hammond:* Marsh.

62  *"what I would":* Ruth Brown with Yule, *Miss Rhythm.*

63  *"Ruth Brown wanted":* Gillett, *Making Tracks.*

63  *"I said, 'Let's sing' ":* "The World of Soul," *Billboard.*

63  *"For us":* AE, *"What'd I Say."*

63  *"He said, 'Yeah. But' ":* Ibid.

63  *"went nowhere":* Ruth Brown with Yule, *Miss Rhythm.*

63  *"I had tasted":* Ibid.

64  *"loved and respected":* Ibid.

64  *"the more forceful":* Ibid.

64  *"made many of the":* Ibid.

64  *composed "especially":* Ibid.

64  *seven-inch 45 RPM:* Ibid.

64  *"They were charging":* Ruth Brown with Yule, *Miss Rhythm.*

64  *"Calloway Assoc. Formed":* The *Billboard,* July 30, 1949.

65  *"I actually called Ruth":* Marsh.

65  *"What did it mean?":* Ruth Brown with Yule, *Miss Rhythm.*

65  *"Blanche Calloway diplomatically":* Deffaa, *Blue Rhythms.*

66  *"I was Ruth's manager":* Bienstock.

66  *"The whole thing":* Ibid.

66  *315-pound:* en.wikipedia.org/wiki/John_Lomax.

66  *first field trip down:* AE, *"What'd I Say."*

66  *"any real funky blues":* Ibid.

67  *"Unfortunately":* AE, Keynote address to Music Row Industry Summit, un-dated, AE Archive.

67  *"Herb and I":* Gillett, *Making Tracks.*

67  *"the most incredible":* AE, *"What'd I Say."*

67  *"playing incredible":* Ibid.

67  *"could tell it":* Ibid.

67  *"Have you":* Ibid.

67  *"Man, I am":* Ibid.

67  *Lomax had recorded:* en.wikipedia.org/Blind_Willie_McTell.

67  *"No man":* AE, *"What'd I Say."*

67  *"made himself":* Wilentz, *Bob Dylan in America.*

68  *"a musical magician":* AE, *"What'd I say."*

68  *"I ain't going":* Ibid.

68  *muddy field:* AE, Author Interview, 11/72.

68  *"the rhythm":* AE, *"What'd I Say."*

68  *"or rather":* Ibid.

68  *"like an animated":* Ibid.

68  *"there had never been":* Trow, "Profiles."

68  *"We're from":* AE, *"What'd I Say."*

68  *"Just put":* Ibid.

68 *"because they figured"*: Ibid.

69 *"creating these weird"*: Ibid.

69 *"singing in the"*: Ibid.

69 *"My God!"*: Ibid.

69 *"I'm terribly"*: Ibid.

69 *same studio in Atlanta:* www.jazzdisco.org.

70 *Star Records:* en.Wikipedia.org/Professor_Longhair.

70 *and His New Orleans Boys:* www.jazzdisco.org.

70 *Roy Byrd:* encyclopedia.stateuniversity.com.

70 *Selective Service Act:* en.Wikipedia.org/wiki/Selective_Training_and_Service _Act_of_1940.

71 *"male alien who"*: Letter from Welsh to AE, November 22, 1948, AE Archive.

71 *three more letters:* Letter from Welsh to AE, February 23, 1949, AE Archive.

71 *"not now entitled"*: Letter from Welsh to AE, March 29, 1949, AE Archive.

71 *"that is, your"*: Ibid.

71 *"draft holiday"*: www.history.com—Peacetime Conscription.

71 *"continue my studies"*: AE, Undated letter, AE Archive.

72 *his political views:* en.Wikipedia.org/wiki/Eduard_Heimann.

72 *"Dr. E. Heimann"*: Examination Booklet, January 30, 1951, AE Archive.

72 *"Please explain"*: Letter to AE from Nesuhi Ertegun, November 21, 1952, AE Archive.

72 *"preference immigrant"*: Undated letter to Sadi Koylan from M. M. Notkins, Levitt, Rosenberg, Stone, and Notkins, AE Archive.

72 *On June 8, 1953:* Letter to AE from United States Department of Justice, Immigration and Naturalization Service, June 8, 1953, AE Archive.

## FIVE: MESS AROUND

PAGE

73 *"Although Ray"*: AE, *"What'd I Say."*

73 *"I remember when"*: AE, Columbia University Oral History Research Office, April 22, 2003, AE Archive.

73 *$4,880:* AE, Withholding Statement, W-2 Form, 1950, AE Archive.

73 *"one dollar and"*: AE, Document, July 10, 1950, AE Archive.

74 *fathered twelve children:* en.Wikipedia.org/wiki/Ray_Charles.

74 *first began using:* Charles and Ritz, *Brother Ray.*

74 *"in a style modeled"*: Gillett, *Making Tracks.*

74 *the Lotus Club:* AE, Columbia University Oral History Research Office, January 23, 2003, AE Archive.

74 *"I want a"*: Lydon, *Ray Charles.*

74 *"I guarantee"*: Evans, *Ray Charles.*

75 *"Done deal"*: Ibid.

75 *"Ray Charles, Blind Pianist"*: Lydon, *Ray Charles.*

75 *no hurry:* Ibid.

75 *"Ray Charles!"*: AE, *The Charlie Rose Show,* 2/21/05, AE Archive.

75 *"produced four jazz-influenced"*: Gillett, *Making Tracks.*

75 *New York musicians:* Lydon, *Ray Charles.*

75 *"very temperamental"*: Gillett, *Making Tracks.*

75 *spent a week:* Lydon, *Ray Charles.*

76 *"such a small"*: Kornbluth, "Ahmet Ertegun."

76 *"I Know"*: Standard Uniform Popular Songwriter's Contract Agreement, December 14, 1950, AE Archive.

76 *capital letters:* Document, AE Archive.

76 *"a flimsy vinyl"*: AE, *"What'd I Say."*

76 *"an eccentric"*: Gillett, *Making Tracks.*

76 *"Some people"*: AE, *"What'd I Say."*

76 *"had a great"*: Poole, "Lush Life."

76 *"We'd get"*: Kornbluth, "Ahmet Ertegun."

77 *"I wrote teenage"*: Poole, "Lush Life."

77 *setting the tempo:* Lydon, *Ray Charles.*

77 *died three months:* en.Wikipeida.org./wiki/Pinetop_Smith.

78 *"Whereas we thought"*: AE, Speech for Ray Charles, AE Archive.

78 *Nesuhi called:* Gottlieb.

78 *"a very attractive"*: AE, Columbia University Oral History Research Office, March 14, 2003, AE Archive.

78 *Carl Enstam:* AE, Marriage License, January 28, 1953, AE Archive.

78 *a minister:* Gross, "The Real Sultan of Swing."

78 *eight different movies:* www.imdb.com.

78 *"glamour girls"*: cgi.ebay.co.uk/Glamour-cigarette-cards-Actresses-Showgirls.

78 *married once before:* AE, Marriage License, January 28, 1953, AE Archive.

78 *After studying drama:* http://library.uncg.edu/Women'sVeteransHistoricalColl ection, Oral History Interview with Coralee Burson Davis.

78 *mental cruelty:* AE, Marriage License, January 28, 1953, AE Archive.

79 *Hodgkin's disease:* http://library.uncg.edu/Women'sVeteransHistoricalCollec tion, Coralee Burson Davis Collection.

79 *Hartford Agency composite:* Document, AE Archive.

79 *in a photograph:* Photo, Wexler and Ritz, *Rhythm and the Blues.*

79 *"did stage sets"*: AE, Columbia University Oral History Research Office, March 14, 2003, AE Archive.

79 *"a nice apartment"*: AE, Columbia University Oral History Research Office, April 22, 2003, AE Archive.

79 *"When they"*: AE, Columbia University Oral History Research Office, March 14, 2003, AE Archive.

79 *"artist"*: AE, Marriage License, January 28, 1953, AE Archive.

79 *Sadi Koylan:* Marriage Certificate, February 6, 1953.

79 *Charles Addams:* AE, Columbia University Oral History Research Office, March 14, 2003.

79 *"finally found an"*: Ibid.

79 *"She then became"*: Ibid.

80 *"They got married"*: Bienstock.

80 *"getting very tan"*: Letter to AE from Jan Holm, July 23, 1954, AE Archive.

80 *"He used to be"*: Hughes.

80 *"When I was"*: AE, Columbia University Oral History Research Office, March 14, 2003, AE Archive.

81 *"He told me then"*: Goksel.

81 *"It was difficult"*: AE, Columbia University Oral History Research Office, March 14, 2003, AE Archive.

81 *"decided to separate"*: Ibid.

81 *"She said"*: Ibid.

81 *"a good friend"*: Bienstock.

81 *"I was very"*: AE, Columbia University Oral History Research Office, March 14, 2003, AE Archive.

81 *"After Jan and I"*: AE, Columbia University Oral History Research Office, April 22, 2003, AE Archive.

82 *"who had"*: Mica Ertegun.

82 *Ray Charles would: Atlantic: Hip to the Tip.*

83 *"Are you coming"*: Wade and Picardie, *Music Man.*

83 *"What are"*: AE, Columbia University Oral History Research Office, January 23, 2003, AE Archive.

83 *"Tokyo Rose"*: Wade and Picardie, *Music Man.*

83 *"If the distributors"*: Bienstock.

83 *"as coldly neutral"*: Lydon, *Ray Charles.*

83 *"Herr Doktor"*: AE, Columbia University Oral History Research Office, March 14, 2003, AE Archive.

83 *"Nein, nein"*: Ibid.

83 *" 'Oh, this' "*: Ibid.

84 *opera singer*: en.wikipedia.org/wiki/Tom_Dowd.

84 *"He was"*: Bienstock.

84 *"In those days"*: Kornbluth, "Ahmet Ertegun."

85 *"What tools"*: Tosches, *Unsung Heroes of Rock 'n' Roll.*

85 *"Hell, if you're"*: Ibid.

85 *"began to approach"*: Ibid.

85 *"Jesse Stone"*: Gillett, *Making Tracks.*

86 *"like people"*: Ibid.

86 *"In half an"*: Ibid.

86 *"I listened"*: Tosches, *Unsung Heroes of Rock 'n' Roll.*

86 *"based on"*: Gillett, *Making Tracks.*

87 *"was all wrong"*: AE, "What'd I Say."

## SIX: SHAKE, RATTLE AND ROLL

PAGE

88  *"With Jerry"*: Smith, *Off the Record.*

88  *"When I left"*: Wade and Picardie, *Music Man.*

88  *"Everyone was worried"*: AE, Columbia University Oral History Research Office, January 30, 2003, AE Archive.

89  *"considered them"*: Wexler and Ritz, *Rhythm and the Blues.*

89  *"Being your"*: Ibid.

89  *"guru"*: Ibid.

89  *"Ackerman said"*: Stein.

90  *"an ecstatic Marxist"*: Jerry Wexler, Author Interview.

90  *"always a flaming"*: Ibid.

90  *"Gerald is"*: Wexler and Ritz, *Rhythm and the Blues.*

91  *"I've never"*: Ibid.

91  *"oedipal implications"*: Ibid.

91  *"Freud, shmeud"*: Ibid.

91  *"an affinity for"*: Ibid.

91  *"I was the only"*: Holland, "I Met Everybody in the Business."

91  *"Rhythm and blues is"*: Wexler, Interview by McFarland and Titus, KKSU.

91  *"because she"*: Wexler and Ritz, *Rhythm and the Blues.*

91  *"fell into"*: Ibid.

92  *"about our craft"*: Wexler, Speech for Jesse Stone, Urban League Dinner, Orlando, Florida, 1996.

92  *"always looked on"*: Jerry Wexler, Author Interview.

92  *"If I was"*: Wexler and Ritz, *Rhythm and the Blues.*

92  *"ravening fear"*: Wade and Picardie, *Music Man.*

93  *"We were very similar"*: Jerry Wexler, Author Interview.

93  *"little playlets"*: Ibid.

94  *"two 'Miss Fines' "*: Wexler and Ritz, *Rhythm and the Blues.*

94  *"The road trips"*: Jerry Wexler, Author Interview.

94  *"do you no good"*: Cohodas, *Spinning Blues into Gold.*

95  *"He was like"*: Chess.

95  *"the New York Jews"*: Ibid.

95  *"poured them out"*: Jerry Wexler, Author Interview.

95  "chaya": Ibid.

95  *"The Chess brothers"*: Ibid.

95  " *'Listen, motherfucker' "*: Gillett, *Making Tracks.*

96  *"Ahmet used to"*: Jerry Wexler, Author Interview.

96  *"I can't bother"*: Cohodas, *Spinning Blues into Gold.*

96  *"If his records"*: Wexler and Ritz, *Rhythm and the Blues.*

96  *"was a good friend"*: AE, Columbia University Oral History Research Office, January 30, 2003, AE Archive.

96  *"I liked Leonard"*: Jerry Wexler, Author Interview.

97 *"Get the fuck"*: Cohodas, *Spinning Blues into Gold.*
97 *"a steady"*: Ibid.
97 *"Motherfucker"*: Ibid.
97 *"It's fashionable to"*: Jerry Wexler, Author Interview.
98 *"We weren't"*: Wexler and Ritz, *Rhythm and the Blues.*
99 *"The Basie Band"*: AE, *"What'd I Say."*
99 *"the toughest"*: Ibid.
99 *"shouldn't be"*: Ibid.
99 *"Okay, if you"*: Cornyn with Scanlon, *Exploding.*
99 *"For four"*: Ibid.
99 *"All right, cuz"*: Gillett, *Making Tracks.*
99 *"I threw a"*: Tosches, *Unsung Heroes of Rock 'n' Roll.*
100 *"the perfect record"*: Ibid.
100 *"a story of"*: Marcus, "Atlantic Records 1947–54," quoted in *"What'd I Say."*
100 *"a great actor"*: Ibid.
100 *"their heads off"*: Ibid.
100 *"a flashy"*: Ibid.
100 *"still sounds"*: Ibid.
101 *"These guys"*: Paul Wexler.
101 *"very inexpensive motel"*: AE, *"What'd I Say."*
101 *"I've got something"*: Ibid.
101 *"stunned"*: Lydon, *Ray Charles.*
101 *"an amazing succession"*: Ibid.
102 *"anxious stream"*: Ibid.
102 *"had found"*: Ibid.
102 *"The record blended"*: Ibid.
102 *"a sing-along"*: Ibid.
102 *"It was a real"*: Ibid.
102 *"quick mimic"*: Ibid.
102 *"played a"*: Ibid.
102 *"Totally focused"*: Ibid.
102 *"followed the news"*: Ibid.

## SEVEN: BROTHERS IN ARMS

PAGE
104 *"Ahmet looked upon"*: Wexler and Ritz, *Rhythm and the Blues.*
104 *"Herb's Back"*: *News from Atlantic* press release, April 25, 1955.
105 *"the bobby soxers"*: Cohen, *Machers and Rockers.*
105 *"Up-to-date"*: Ibid.
106 *"You can't"*: AE, Unidentified video interview, AE Archive.
106 *"So, foolish"*: Wade and Picardie, *Music Man.*
106 *"exasperation and exacerbation"*: Wexler and Ritz, *Rhythm and the Blues.*
106 *"Nesuhi was the"*: Hentoff, quoted in AE, *"What'd I Say."*

107  *"let us decide"*: Ibid.

107  *"they knew Nesuhi"*: Ibid.

107  *"There was also"*: Ibid.

107  *"moldy fig"*: Wade and Picardie, *Music Man.*

107  *"That was"*: Ibid.

107  *"When Herb"*: Bienstock.

108  *"Herb came"*: Jerry Wexler, Author Interview.

108  *"an absolutely"*: Wade and Picardie, *Music Man.*

108  *"He fancied himself"*: Ibid.

108  *"Herb lost"*: Bienstock.

108  *"I think Herb"*: Gottlieb.

108  *"never knew"*: Abramson.

108  *"Herb was"*: Confidential Author Interview.

109  *"He came back"*: Jerry Wexler, Author Interview.

109  *"She was very"*: Bienstock.

109  *"To this point"*: Ibid.

109  *"to prove that"*: Gillett, *Making Tracks.*

109  *"It behooved us"*: Jerry Wexler, Author Interview.

110  *"The Ahmet Ertigons"*: Louis Sobol, "New York Cavalcade," *New York Journal-American*, November 20, 1957.

110  *"the muse for"*: Bienstock.

110  *"the cool all-American"*: *Time*, December 22, 1961.

111  *"The girls I was"*: AE, Columbia University Oral History Research Office, March 14, 2003, AE Archive.

111  *"Ahmet and I"*: Julio Mario Santo Domingo.

111  *"Welcome home"*: Confidential Author Interview.

111  *"In those days"*: AE, Columbia University Oral History Research Office, April 22, 2003, AE Archive.

111  *"Aston Martin"*: Gross, "The Real Sultan of Swing."

111  *"I think I was"*: AE, Columbia University Oral History Research Office, April 22, 2003, AE Archive.

112  *"I made a"*: Ibid.

112  *"and a band"*: Gross, "The Real Sultan of Swing."

112  *"Of course"*: Ibid.

113  *"No future history"*: Herb Abramson, *Cash Box,* July 28, 1956.

114  *"shout incessantly"*: Jackson, *Big Beat Heat.*

115  *"The baksheesh"*: Wexler and Ritz, *Rhythm and the Blues.*

115  *"good enough"*: Jackson, *Big Beat Heat.*

115  *"doing dives"*: Abramson.

115  *"a beautiful $80"*: Ibid.

116  *"with this beguiling"*: Ibid.

116  *"was missing"*: Ibid.

116  *"the boys down"*: Ibid.

116 *"Principals of Atlantic"*: Memorandum from Paul G. Marshall, Marshall & Ziffer, February 11, 1958, AE Archive.

116 *"take place"*: Ibid.

116 *"Mr. Youngstein"*: Ibid.

117 *"I am"*: Marshall.

117 *"Max Youngstein"*: Ibid.

117 *"Herb always"*: Abramson.

117 *"Jerry was"*: Marshall.

117 *"the United Artists"*: Ibid.

117 *"Herb didn't"*: Abramson.

117 *"It was"*: Ibid.

118 *"Let me tell"*: Jerry Wexler, Author Interview.

118 *"Herb insisted"*: Wade and Picardie, *Music Man*.

118 *"I had"*: Ibid.

118 *"Herb tried to"*: AE, Columbia University Oral History Research Office, March 14, 2003, AE Archive.

118 *"was not for"*: Ibid.

119 *"lost all his money"*: Ibid.

119 *"I sometimes look"*: Wade and Picardie, *Music Man*.

119 *"Herb was"*: Letter from Jerry Wexler to Barbara Abramson.

## EIGHT: SPLISH SPLASH

PAGE

121 *"better material"*: www.bobbydarin.net.

121 *"shooting the"*: Clark and Robinson, *Rock, Roll and Remember*.

121 *"Bobby Darin"*: AE, Unidentified video interview, AE Archive.

122 *"Can you"*: Jerry Wexler, Author Interview.

122 *"creating a"*: AE, Unidentified video interview, AE Archive.

122 *"he needed"*: Ibid.

122 *"a little"*: Ibid.

122 *"because that"*: Ibid.

122 *"eights"*: www.bobbydarin.net.

122 *"When I cut"*: Darin and Paetro, *Dream Lovers*.

122 *"I thought"*: Jerry Wexler, Author Interview.

122 *"It was"*: AE, *"What'd I Say."*

123 *"Bobby Darin"*: Marshall.

123 *"took a very"*: Ibid.

123 *"I wish"*: Ibid.

124 *"Well, maybe"*: AE, Unidentified video interview, AE Archive.

124 *"I know"*: Ibid.

124 *"a teen idol"*: Darin and Paetro, *Dream Lovers*.

124 *"What are"*: Ibid.

124 *"he was going"*: Clark and Robinson, *Rock, Roll and Remember*.

124 *"As we were"*: Ibid.

125 *"Two records"*: Wexler and Ritz, *Rhythm and the Blues.*

125 *"Each sold"*: Ibid.

125 *"during one"*: Billboard, 1/13/58.

126 *"Atlantic's 'Money' "*: Ibid.

126 *"We started"*: Ibid.

126 *"alive and healthy"*: Ibid.

126 *"Our pleasant"*: Ibid.

127 *"FOR DEEJAYS"*: Dannen, *Hit Men.*

127 *"a lavish"*: Barlow, *Voice Over.*

127 *"around-the-clock"*: Ibid.

127 *"play money"*: *Time*, 1/8/59.

127 *"liquid refreshments"*: Ibid.

127 *"I was"*: Smith, Author Interview.

127 *"They were"*: Chess.

127 *"one of"*: Barlow, *Voice Over.*

128 *"I remember"*: Chess.

128 *"Ahmet hired"*: Marshall.

128 *"in the mob"*: Ibid.

128 *"a great breakfast"*: Ibid.

128 *"Remember"*: Ibid.

128 *"media frenzy"*: Barlow, *Voice Over.*

129 *"When I"*: Krasnow.

129 *"Tom Donahue"*: Ibid.

129 *"When I read"*: Marshall.

130 *"Therefore the"*: Ibid.

130 *"a very"*: Ibid.

130 *"the crime"*: Ibid.

130 *"people had"*: Ibid.

130 *"never talk"*: Ibid.

130 *"In the"*: AE, Columbia University Oral History Research Office, January 30, 2003, AE Archive.

131 *"Immediately a"*: Lydon, *Ray Charles.*

131 *"the grunts"*: Ibid.

132 *"dance-craze"*: Ibid.

132 *"unwanted choruses"*: Ibid.

132 *"they had"*: Ibid.

132 *"the dance"*: Ibid.

132 *"the life"*: Ibid.

132 *chills*: Ibid.

132 *"a fortune"*: Ibid.

132 *"the label's"*: Ibid.

132 *"a singer"*: AE, *"What'd I Say."*

133 *"stuck in"*: Lydon, *Ray Charles.*
135 *"soulless corporation"*: Ibid.
135 *"exceptional"*: Ibid.
135 *"emotionally"*: Ibid.
135 *"We felt"*: Evans, *Ray Charles.*
135 *"the guy"*: AE, Columbia University Oral History Research Office, January 30, 2003, AE Archive.
136 *"I would"*: Lydon, *Ray Charles.*
136 *"Seventy-five cents"*: Ibid.
136 *"Afterwards"*: Evans, *Ray Charles.*
136 *"I worked"*: Paul Wexler.
136 *"He was"*: Babitz.

## NINE: LOVE AND MARRIAGE

PAGE
137 *"I fell in love"*: AE, Columbia University Oral History Research Office, March 14, 2003, AE Archive.
138 *"find his way"*: Mick Brown, *Tearing Down the Wall of Sound.*
138 *"a natural gift"*: Ibid.
138 *"terrific fear"*: Leiber and Stoller with Ritz, *Hound Dog.*
138 *"was frightened"*: Ibid.
138 *"I'd never"*: Mick Brown, *Tearing Down the Wall of Sound.*
138 *"one hundred"*: Ibid.
139 *"a natural hit"*: Wexler and Ritz, *Rhythm and the Blues.*
139 *"going to come"*: Mick Brown, *Tearing Down the Wall of Sound.*
139 *"I don't know"*: Marshall.
139 *"Phil went"*: Ibid.
139 *"We got"*: Ibid.
139 *"Let me"*: AE, *"What'd I Say."*
140 *"That's terrific"*: Mick Brown, *Tearing Down the Wall of Sound.*
140 *"fabulous"*: Ibid.
140 *"Are you"*: Ibid.
140 *"some new"*: AE, *"What'd I Say."*
140 *"That's the"*: Ibid.
140 *"succumbed to"*: Ibid.
141 *"Ahmet loved"*: Wenner, Author Interview.
141 *"Even in those"*: AE, Columbia University Oral History Research Office, January 30, 2003, AE Archive.
141 *"Ahmet brought"*: Richards, Author Interview.
142 *"a natural"*: Bennetts, "Devil in a Bespoke Suit."
142 *"so sad"*: Mica Ertegun.
142 *"At the end"*: Poole, "Lush Life."
142 *"the little"*: Mica Ertegun.

143  *"very caring"*: Ibid.

143  *"very busy"*: Ibid.

143  *"pathological"*: Turda, "To End the Degeneration of a Nation."

143  *"Of course"*: Mica Ertegun.

143  *"was shoved"*: Ibid.

144  *"the Dolder"*: Ibid.

144  *"we wouldn't"*: Ibid.

144  *"tried to"*: Ibid.

144  *"I put"*: Ibid.

144  *"very rich"*: Ibid.

144  *"some money"*: Ibid.

144  *"We had"*: Ibid.

144  *"it was"*: Ibid.

144  *"I was"*: Ibid.

145  *"If you"*: AE, Columbia University Oral History Research Office, March 14, 2003, AE Archive.

145  *"nearly split"*: Mica Ertegun.

145  *"Ahmet adored"*: Ibid.

145  *"was against"*: Ibid.

145  *"I do not"*: Undated letter from Mica Ertegun to AE, AE Archive.

145  *"Mica is"*: Gross, "The Real Sultan of Swing."

146  *"We began"*: AE, Columbia University Oral History Research Office, March 14, 2003, AE Archive.

146  *"he was"*: Bennetts, "Devil in a Bespoke Suit."

146  *"I really"*: Pigozzi.

146  *"a dance floor"*: Wolfe, *The Kandy-Kolored Tangerine-Flake Streamline Baby.*

146  *"laying fives"*: Ibid.

146  *"a few socialites"*: Ibid.

147  *"sailors, leather-jacketed"*: Gelb, "Habitues of Meyer Davis Land Dance the Twist."

147  *"fund-raising"*: Ibid.

147  *"a hundred"*: Wolfe, *The Kandy-Kolored Tangerine-Flake Streamline Baby.*

147  *"and I remember"*: Mica Ertegun.

147  *"Café society"*: Gelb, "Habitues of Meyer Davis Land Dance the Twist."

147  *"a dance crowd"*: AE, *"What'd I Say."*

147  *"had never"*: Ibid.

148  *"She did"*: AE, Columbia University Oral History Research Office, March 14, 2003, AE Archive.

148  *"When Jerry"*: Ibid.

148  *"begun moving"*: Wexler and Ritz, *Rhythm and the Blues.*

148  *"the business"*: Ibid.

## TEN: THE OAK ROOM

PAGE

150 *"If you didn't"*: Wade and Picardie, *Music Man.*

150 *"Ahmet and I"*: Marshall.

151 *"began laughing"*: Ibid.

151 *"The first"*: Ibid.

151 *"if someone"*: Ibid.

151 *"A couple"*: Ibid.

151 *"I was not"*: Jerry Wexler, Author Interview.

152 *"In the"*: Stoller, *RS* staff interview.

154 *"automatically started"*: AE, *"What'd I Say."*

154 *"hit a"*: Ibid.

154 *"Smash!"*: Leiber, *RS* staff interview.

155 *"At that"*: Wade and Picardie, *Music Man.*

155 *"Mr. Lust"*: Ibid.

155 *"Mr. Disorderly"*: Wexler and Ritz, *Rhythm and the Blues.*

155 *"relaxed and friendly"*: Wade and Picardie, *Music Man.*

155 *"Fine"*: Ibid.

155 *"the big falling"*: Ibid.

155 *"took offense"*: Ibid.

156 *"George was"*: Stein.

156 *"his destructive"*: Wade and Picardie, *Music Man.*

156 *"out of"*: Leiber and Stoller with Ritz, *Hound Dog.*

156 *"Red Bird was"*: Ibid.

156 *"who would"*: Ibid.

157 *"Can you"*: Stein.

157 *"Who needs"*: Leiber and Stoller with Ritz, *Hound Dog.*

157 *"We're hardly"*: Ibid.

157 *"With the"*: Ibid.

157 *"it was"*: Ibid.

157 *"I didn't"*: Ibid.

157 *"Him and"*: Ibid.

157 *"Can you"*: Wade and Picardie, *Music Man.*

158 *"There was"*: Ibid.

158 *"truly upset"*: Mica Ertegun.

158 *"That was"*: Wade and Picardie, *Music Man.*

158 *"mishandled"*: Ibid.

158 *"There are"*: Ibid.

158 *"It is"*: Leiber and Stoller with Ritz, *Hound Dog.*

159 *"The Mafia"*: Wade and Picardie, *Music Man.*

159 *"Morris looked"*: Marshall.

159 *"He invited"*: Mica Ertegun.

159 *"I brought"*: Krasnow.

160 *"silent partners"*: Wade and Picardie, *Music Man.*

160 *"a favor"*: Ibid.

160 *"We were"*: Ibid.

160 *"Bert knew"*: Marshall.

161 *"amateur"*: Ibid.

161 *"they had"*: Ibid.

161 *"enormous respect"*: Ibid.

161 *"of any"*: Ibid.

161 *"I didn't"*: Ibid.

161 *"set up"*: Author Interview.

161 *"some mobsters"*: Ibid.

161 *"orchestrated"*: Ibid.

161 *"obsession with"*: Wexler and Ritz, *Rhythm and the Blues.*

161 *"The breach"*: Marshall.

162 *"When the"*: Author interview with anonymous.

162 *"I know"*: Douglass.

162 *"I think"*: Mica Ertegun.

## ELEVEN: I GOT YOU BABE

PAGE

163 *"After Sonny"*: AE, Columbia University Oral History Research Office, March 14, 2003, AE Archive.

164 *"Dedicated to"*: George Frazier, "The Art of Wearing Clothes."

164 *"buys ready-made"*: Ibid.

164 *"somehow came"*: Ibid.

164 *"he promptly"*: Ibid.

164 *"Ahmet and"*: Bienstock.

164 *"the man"*: Richards, Author Interview.

165 *"There were"*: Stone.

165 *"Greene and Stone wore"*: Goodman, *The Mansion on the Hill.*

165 *"Greene and Stone were"*: McDonough, *Shakey.*

165 *"around Manhattan"*: Goodman, *The Mansion on the Hill.*

165 *"short and"*: Stone.

166 *"living with"*: Ibid.

166 *"wrote this"*: Ibid.

166 *"just wanted"*: Ibid.

166 *"We play"*: Ibid.

167 *"were five"*: Ibid.

167 *"with the radio"*: AE, Unidentified video interview, AE Archive.

167 *"How can"*: Ibid.

167 *"and he"*: Ibid.

167 *"young man"*: Ibid.

167 *"came up"*: Stone.

167 *"We said"*: Ibid.

168 *"No problem"*: Ibid.

168 *"Doesn't bother"*: Ibid.

168 *"So we"*: Ibid.

168 *"Ahmet had"*: Ibid.

168 *"Charlie and"*: Ibid.

169 *"had great"*: Ibid.

169 *"He said"*: Ibid.

169 *"the greatest act"*: Ibid.

169 *"Only two"*: Ibid.

169 *"We told"*: Ibid.

169 *"They saw"*: Ibid.

169 *"Ahmet, Jerry"*: Ibid.

170 *"a giant party"*: Ibid.

170 *"play at this"*: Ibid.

170 *"It was"*: Stone.

171 *"rather Shakespearean"*: Altham, "Sonny and Cher Get Even."

171 *"My dear"*: Schmidt, "Cher's Fashion History."

171 *"And the"*: Ibid.

171 *"very tall"*: AE, "What'd I Say."

171 *"looked as"*: Ibid.

171 *"Oh"*: Ibid.

171 *"I'll only"*: Ibid.

171 *"the only"*: Ibid.

171 *"a good"*: Ibid.

171 *"a cross"*: Ibid.

171 *"You know"*: Ibid.

171 *"Listen"*: Ibid.

172 *"I was"*: Ibid.

172 *"What are"*: Ibid.

172 *"Yes, you"*: Ibid.

172 *"Who is"*: Ibid.

172 *"And in"*: Stone.

172 *"unless it"*: Ibid.

172 *"had people"*: Ibid.

172 *"Sonny became"*: Ibid.

173 *"There was"*: Ibid.

173 *"an $18,500"*: McDonough, *Shakey*.

173 *"Sonny was"*: Stone.

173 *"locked up"*: Ibid.

173 *"Ahmet was"*: Ibid.

173 *"Ahmet, I've"*: Ibid.

174 *"We went"*: Ibid.

174   *"to make"*: Ibid.

174   *"something like"*: Ibid.

175   *"in various"*: Hirschfield.

175   *"'I'm raising'"*: Stone.

## TWELVE: HEY, WHAT'S THAT SOUND

PAGE

176   *"When Ahmet"*: McDonough, *Shakey*.

176   *"We talked"*: Stone.

176   *"very special"*: AE, *"What'd I Say."*

177   *"A nice"*: McDonough, *Shakey*.

177   *"could sing"*: Ibid.

177   *"music business"*: Ibid.

177   *"best band"*: Goodman.

177   *"We were"*: Priore, *Riot on Sunset Strip*.

178   *"Overwhelmed by"*: McDonough, *Shakey*.

178   *"they quickly"*: Ibid.

178   *"outrageously stoned"*: Goodman.

178   *"They said"*: Stone.

179   *"I'll never"*: AE, Rock and Roll Hall of Fame Induction Speech for Neil Young, AE Archive.

179   *"Neil Young"*: Stone.

179   *a royalty statement*: Long, "A Brief History of Buffalo Springfield."

179   *"At one"*: AE, Rock and Roll Hall of Fame Induction Speech for Neil Young, AE Archives.

180   *"What they did"*: AE, Unidentified video interview, AE Archive.

180   *"When the"*: Stone.

180   *"Stephen's poetry"*: McDonough, *Shakey*.

180   *"a great musician"*: Ibid.

180   *"wanted to"*: Ibid.

180   *"You're ruining"*: Goodman.

180   *"full of"*: McDonough, *Shakey*.

181   *"They were"*: Stone.

181   *"a musician's"*: McDonough, *Shakey*.

181   *"knows music"*: Ibid.

181   *"Ahmet always"*: Ibid.

181   *"The Sunset"*: Priore, *Riot on Sunset Strip*.

182   *"ingesting hallucinogens"*: Ibid.

182   *"Hey, I just"*: Stone.

182   *"So we"*: Ibid.

182   *"Yes, you do"*: McDonough, *Shakey*.

182   *"The guys"*: Stone.

182   *"No, man"*: Ibid.

183 *"captured the"*: McDonough, *Shakey*.
183 *Jackie Kennedy:* Reeves, http://streetsyoucrossed.blogspot.com/2007/10/lets
-swim-to-moon-uh-huh.html.
183 *bikers who:* Ibid.
183 *"When they"*: McDonough, *Shakey*.
184 *"Dewey Martin"*: Stone.
184 *"Otis was so"*: Medious.
184 *"Nescafe"*: Rebennack.
184 *"that he liked"*: Werbin, "The Big M Is Taking Care of Business."
184 *"kinda like"*: McDonough, *Shakey*.
184 *"Otis Redding"*: Stone.
185 *"I never"*: McDonough, *Shakey*.
185 *"Ahmet used"*: Stone.
185 *"They were"*: Ibid.
185 *"Greene and Stone"*: McDonough, *Shakey*.
185 *"called Wexler"*: Stone.
185 *" 'Listen, I'll' "*: Ibid.
186 *"Charlie and I"*: Ibid.
186 *"didn't want"*: Ibid.
186 *"It was"*: Flom.
186 *" 'This record' "*: Ibid.
186 *"Ahmet had"*: Stone.
186 *"You will"*: McDonough, *Shakey*.
187 *"They had"*: AE, Unidentified video interview, AE Archive.
187 *"Stephen and"*: Nash.
187 *"I had"*: McDonough, *Shakey*.

## THIRTEEN: SELLING OUT

PAGE
188 *"We were"*: AE, *"What'd I Say."*
188 *"something of"*: Wexler and Ritz, *Rhythm and the Blues*.
189 *"What the"*: AE, Columbia University Oral History Research Office, January 30, 2003, AE Archive.
189 *"It was"*: Wade and Picardie, *Music Man*.
190 *"I didn't"*: Bienstock.
190 *"between two"*: AE, Columbia University Oral History Research Office, March 14, 2003, AE Archive.
190 *"I represented"*: Marshall.
190 *"I had"*: Wade and Picardie, *Music Man*.
191 *"Wexler was"*: AE, Columbia University Oral History Research Office, May 1, 2003, AE Archive.
191 *"In the"*: Mica Ertegun.

191  *"could have"*: AE, Columbia University Oral History Research Office, May 1, 2003, AE Archive.
191  *"whose wife"*: Hirschfield.
192  *"to meet"*: Ibid.
192  *"very anxious"*: Ibid.
192  *"mainly regarding"*: Ibid.
192  *"the white"*: Ibid.
192  *"It was"*: Ibid.
192  *"had every"*: Ibid.
192  *"Some of"*: Ibid.
193  *"been paying"*: Ibid.
193  *"who loved"*: Ibid.
193  *"the point"*: Ibid.
193  *"I said"*: Ibid.
193  *"I explained"*: Ibid.
194  *"there was"*: Ibid.
194  *"and literally"*: Ibid.
194  *"That was"*: Ibid.
194  *"the earnings"*: Ibid.
194  *"Jerry and"*: Ibid.
194  *"Ahmet"*: Ibid.
194  *"has its"*: Jerry Wexler, Author Interview.
195  *"I have"*: Ibid.
195  *"My end"*: Ibid.

## FOURTEEN: HELPLESSLY HOPING

PAGE
196  *"Jerry Wexler"*: AE, Columbia University Oral History Research Office, April 22, 2003, AE Archive.
196  *"Here's a"*: Nash.
196  *"It was"*: Ibid.
198  *"We all"*: Ibid.
198  *"In the"*: Goodman.
198  *"were morally"*: Zimmer and Diltz, *Crosby, Stills & Nash*.
198  *"was really"*: Ibid.
198  *"reached in"*: Nash.
198  *"Ahmet was"*: Stigwood.
199  *"was that"*: Zimmer and Diltz, *Crosby, Stills & Nash*.
199  *"because we"*: Ibid.
199  *"King David"*: Goodman.
200  *"the rudiments"*: King, *The Operator*.
200  *"rockoids"*: Jerry Wexler, *Author Interview*.
200  *"Get the"*: King, *The Operator*.

200   *"My God"*: Lewis, *Academy All the Way.*
200   *"love at first"*: Ibid.
200   *"Our relationship"*: Geffen, Author Interview.
201   *"he was"*: Lewis, *Academy All the Way.*
201   *"Clive said"*: Ibid.
201   *"Ahmet knew"*: Goodman.
201   *"They made"*: AE, Author Interview, 3/11/88.
202   *"Look, I"*: Clive Davis with Willwerth, *Clive.*
202   *"The group"*: Ibid.
202   *"Ahmet stole"*: Goodman.
202   *"That's pretty"*: Lewis, *Academy All the Way.*
202   *"Ahmet, you must"*: Ibid.
202   *"Ahmet, you gotta"*: Stills, *RS* staff interview.
203   *"Yessir, we're"*: Sander, *Trips.*
203   Music from: Ibid.
203   *"Guess they"*: Ibid.
203   *"This guy"*: Nash.
203   *"At that"*: Ibid.
204   *"Everybody is"*: Sander, *Trips.*
204   *"Did you"*: Nash.
204   *"They're going"*: King, *The Operator.*
204   *"Absolutely, there"*: Nash.
205   *"We ought"*: King, *The Operator.*
205   *"But, Ahmet"*: Ibid.
205   *"Neil and"*: Nash.
205   *"concert price"*: Sander, *Trips.*
205   *"and family"*: http://garyburdenforrtwerk.com/archives/51.
205   *"beautiful paper"*: Ibid.
205   *"a family-operated"*: Ibid.
205   *"Fucking artist"*: Burden.
206   *"That group"*: Sander, *Trips.*
206   *"Paul McCartney"*: Ibid.
206   *"That's a"*: Holzman, lefsetz.com/wordpress.
206   *"I wonder"*: Sander, *Trips.*
206   *"Who is"*: King, *The Operator.*
207   *"really drunk"*: McDonough, *Shakey.*
207   *"Neil"*: Ibid.
207   *"Ahmet's here?"*: Ibid.
207   *"All right!"*: Ibid.
207   *"CSN signed"*: Nash.
207   *"What's the"*: Author Interview (confidential).
208   *"loved him"*: Ibid.
208   *"always respected"*: Ibid.

208 *"complaining bitterly"*: Ibid.

208 *"You fucking"*: Ibid.

208 *"That was"*: Ibid.

209 *"the sound"*: Blackwell.

209 *"The key"*: Ibid.

209 *"popped"*: Ibid.

209 *"for no"*: Ibid.

209 *"because we"*: Ibid.

209 *"thought"*: Ibid.

210 *"this little"*: Stone.

210 *"Stevie Winwood"*: Ibid.

210 *"sounded like"*: AE, *The Charlie Rose Show*, 2/21/05, AE Archive.

210 *"there was"*: Ibid.

210 *"Wilson"*: Ibid.

210 *"My guitarist"*: Ibid.

210 *"this kid"*: Ibid.

210 *"You really"*: Smith and Fink, *Off the Record*.

210 *"He's fabulous"*: Ibid.

210 *"So Stigwood"*: Ibid.

210 *"I took"*: Stigwood.

210 *"He wanted"*: Ibid.

211 *"pretended he"*: Ibid.

211 *"Just coincidentally"*: Ibid.

211 *"and put"*: Ibid.

211 *"It was"*: Ibid.

212 *"utterly amazed"*: AE, *"What'd I Say."*

212 *"in terms"*: Ibid.

212 *"musicians"*: Ibid.

212 *"dropped a"*: Stigwood.

212 *"Basically"*: Ibid.

213 *"Cream was"*: Wenner, *"Rolling Stone* Interview with Phil Spector."

213 *"We were"*: Stigwood.

214 *"Look, I've"*: Bruck, *Master of the Game*.

214 *"You mean"*: Ibid.

215 *"Yeah, man"*: Ibid.

215 *"who or"*: Newsham, *Once in a Lifetime*.

215 *"Give us"*: Bruck, *Master of the Game*.

215 *"particularly knew"*: AE, *"What'd I Say."*

215 *"got a"*: Ibid.

215 *"he just"*: Ibid.

216 *"So they"*: Ibid.

216 *"hotheaded"*: Ibid.

216 *"I'm a"*: Ibid.

216 *"Well"*: Ibid.
216 *"Remember you"*: Ibid.
216 *"Sheldon"*: Holzman.
216 *"That's the"*: Ibid.
216 *"played his"*: Wexler and Ritz, *Rhythm and the Blues*.
216 *"a hell"*: Ibid.
217 *"thick Americans"*: Stephen Davis, *Hammer of the Gods*.
217 *"the exact"*: Atlantic Press Release, www.ledzeppelin.com.
217 *"shaken hands"*: Blackwell.
217 *"It was"*: Ibid.
218 *"I signed"*: Jerry Wexler, Author Interview.
218 *"I went"*: Carson.
218 *"the Ingram"*: Ibid.
219 *"Having worked"*: Curbishley.
219 *"Even though"*: Robinson, Author Interview.
219 *"in the"*: Curbishley.
219 *"Then gradually"*: Ibid.
219 *"Zeppelin was"*: Carson.
220 *"Zeppelin had"*: Medious.
220 *"the wickedest"*: en.wikipedia.org/wiki/Aleister_Crowley.
220 *"a misunderstood genius"*: en.wikipedia.org/wiki/Boleskine_House.
220 *"Ahmet and"*: Medious.
220 *"Ahmet had"*: Curbishley.
220 *"Ahmet was"*: Jerry Wexler, Author Interview.
221 *"throw out"*: Ibid.
221 *"It all"*: Curbishley.
221 *"Page was"*: Ibid.
222 *"When Grant"*: Ibid.
222 *"The lifestyle"*: Ibid.
222 *"Right in"*: Poole, "Lush Life."

## FIFTEEN: ROMANCING THE STONES

PAGE
223 *"It was"*: Smith and Fink, *Off the Record*.
224 *"the most"*: AE, Author Interview, 11/72.
224 *"We had"*: Ibid.
225 *"Ahmet got"*: Rudge.
226 *"Mick and"*: Krasnow.
226 *"was in"*: Chess.
226 *"We talked"*: Ibid.
227 *"I used"*: Greenberg.
227 *"marvelous relationship"*: AE, Author Interview, 11/72.
227 *"a terrific"*: Ibid.

227  *"all the color"*: Wade, "The Godfather of Rock and Roll."

227  *"Ahmet had"*: Holzman, Author Interview.

227  *"very deliberately"*: Holzman, *Follow the Music.*

227  *"Mick"*: Ibid.

228  *"I have"*: Holzman, Author Interview.

228  *"Ahmet was"*: Holzman, *Follow the Music.*

228  *"Columbia was"*: Clive Davis with Willwerth, *Clive.*

228  *"a staggering"*: Ibid.

228  *"I think"*: Richards, Author Interview.

229  *"Whenever I"*: Trow, "Profiles."

229  *"I felt"*: Chess.

229  *"I think"*: Trow, "Profiles."

230  *"a very"*: Johns.

230  *"was struggling"*: Ibid.

230  *"It was"*: Wade, "The Godfather of Rock and Roll."

231  *"During this"*: Rudge.

231  *"I don't"*: Trow, "Profiles."

231  *"It is"*: Ibid.

231  *"Ahmet said"*: Gefffen, Author Interview.

232  *"Wexler was"*: Cornyn with Scanlon, *Exploding.*

232  *"I was"*: Greenberg.

232  *"I'm signing"*: Ibid.

233  *"the odd"*: Trow, "Profiles."

233  *"France is"*: Ibid.

233  *"It didn't"*: Geffen, Author Interview.

234  *"You're not"*: Trow, "Profiles."

234  *"We have"*: Ibid.

234  *"If we"*: Ibid.

234  *"Ahmet is"*: Ibid.

234  *"That was"*: Ibid.

234  *"We are"*: Ibid.

236  *"I know"*: Faithfull with Dalton, *Faithfull.*

236  *"There's only"*: Ibid.

236  *"some guarantee"*: Ibid.

236  *"We brought"*: Mica Ertegun.

237  *"I was"*: AE, Author Interview, 11/72.

237  *"standing there"*: Pompili.

237  *"Keith was"*: Flom.

238  *"was keen"*: Wyman, *Rolling with the Stones.*

238  *"We had"*: Richards, RS staff interview.

238  *"I was with"*: AE, Columbia University Oral History Research Office, May 1, 2003, AE Archive.

239  *"It was"*: Rudge.

240 *"Mick and Keith"*: AE, Author Interview, 11/72.

240 *"a good"*: Ibid.

240 *"It's one"*: Ibid.

241 *"Mick Jagger?"*: Ibid.

241 *"Ahmet brought"*: Rudge.

242 *"There were"*: AE, Author Interview, 11/72.

242 *"Right now"*: Greenfield, *S.T.P.*

243 *"intuition told"*: Capote.

243 *"would not"*: Ibid.

243 *"they were"*: Ibid.

243 *"Ahmet and"*: Ibid.

243 *"lolled in"*: Trow, "Profiles."

244 *"She never"*: AE, Columbia University Oral History Research Office, March 14, 2003.

244 *"Oh well"*: Frears, "Gotham Satyricon."

244 *"Dollink, ven"*: Greenfield, *S.T.P.*

244 *"And when"*: Hughes.

244 *"It's encompassing"*: Lichtenstein, "Mick Jagger, 29."

244 *"a Felliniesque"*: Ibid.

244 *"like a"*: Ibid.

244 *"It was"*: Medious.

245 *"It's a"*: Lichtenstein, "Mick Jagger, 29."

245 *"Society finally"*: Greenfield, *S.T.P.*

245 *"Ahmet and"*: Rudge.

246 *"a very close"*: Trow, "Profiles."

246 *"And what"*: Ibid.

247 *"Because we"*: Sheffield, "How the Rolling Stones Got their Bitch Back."

247 *"I suppose"*: Wyman, *Rolling with the Stones.*

247 *"to please"*: AE, *"What'd I Say."*

247 *"a stupid"*: Ibid.

247 *"supposed to"*: Ibid.

247 *"I said"*: Ibid.

247 *"I thought"*: Ibid.

248 *"had no"*: Wade and Picardie, *Music Man.*

248 *"Ahmet"*: AE, *"What'd I Say."*

248 *"Ahmet, you're"*: Ibid.

248 *"vulgar and"*: Wyman, *Rolling with the Stones.*

248 *"an insult"*: Ibid.

248 *"We do"*: Ibid.

248 *"everybody you"*: Wade and Picardie, *Music Man.*

248 *"Ahmet was"*: Rudge.

249 *"He used"*: Jerry Wexler, Author Interview.

249 *"like my"*: AE, *"What'd I Say."*

249 *"a great"*: Ibid.

249 *"and say"*: Ibid.

249 *"just go"*: Ibid.

249 *"Scared to"*: Ibid.

249 *"a sea"*: Ibid.

249 *"I thought"*: Wade and Picardie, *Music Man*.

249 *"quite to"*: AE, *"What'd I Say."*

249 *"Oh man"*: Ibid.

249 *"started to"*: Ibid.

249 *"On the"*: Ibid.

250 *"And suddenly"*: Ibid.

250 *"we all"*: Ibid.

250 *"That man"*: Wade and Picardie, *Music Man*.

250 *"pushy"*: Ibid.

250 *"I shouted"*: Ibid.

250 *"big trouble"*: Ibid.

250 *"a thousand"*: Ibid.

250 *"Ahmet had"*: Jerry Wexler, Author Interview.

251 *"I don't"*: Cornyn with Scanlon, *Exploding*.

251 *"Familiarity breeds"*: Wade and Picardie, *Music Man*.

251 *"It always"*: Rudge.

251 *"Mick is"*: Ibid.

## SIXTEEN: THE BOY WONDER

PAGE

252 *"I was"*: Geffen, *RS* staff interview.

252 *"It's about"*: Morris.

253 *"He plays"*: Goodman.

253 *"I'm telling"*: Ibid.

254 *"Ahmet looked"*: Geffen, *RS* staff interview.

254 *"I thought"*: King.

254 *"kind of"*: Geffen, Author Interview.

254 *"We're going"*: King.

255 *"be number"*: Ibid.

255 *"Ahmet was involved"*: Geffen, *RS* staff interview.

255 *"Ahmet was unbelievably"*: Geffen, Author Interview.

256 *"very congenial"*: Holzman, Author Interview.

256 *"In many"*: Ibid.

256 *"We bought"*: AE, Columbia University Oral History Research Office, May 1, 2003, AE Archive.

257 *"regarded as"*: Smith, Author Interview.

258 *"They lined"*: Ibid.

258 *"OK, David"*: King.

258  *"Well, if"*: Ibid.

258  *"You stole"*: Ibid.

258  *"You're an"*: Ibid.

258  *"You agent!"*: Ibid.

258  *"enormous temper"*: Smith, Author Interview.

258  *"We can't"*: King.

258  *"I'm outta"*: Ibid.

258  *"I couldn't"*: Wexler and Ritz, *Rhythm and the Blues.*

259  *"I had"*: Smith, Author Interview.

259  *"What happened"*: Ibid.

259  *"Jerry was"*: Geffen, Author Interview.

259  *"I was"*: Horowitz, unidentified article, AE Archive.

259  *"David said"*: AE, Columbia University Oral History Research Office, May 1, 2003, AE Archive.

260  *"We have"*: King.

260  *"been frightened"*: Ibid.

260  *"Jerry Wexler"*: Ibid.

260  *"mutiny was"*: Ibid.

260  *"One day"*: Wexler and Ritz, *Rhythm and the Blues.*

260  *"How can"*: King.

260  *"Now come"*: Ibid.

260  *"This is"*: Ibid.

260  *"much more"*: Greenberg.

260  *"Mel goes"*: Ibid.

261  *"I don't"*: Ibid.

261  *"Steve, I've"*: Ibid.

261  *"The next"*: Ibid.

261  *"So then"*: Wade and Picardie, *Music Man.*

261  *"Ahmet never"*: Ibid.

262  *"By the"*: Ibid.

262  *"another lady"*: Ibid.

262  *"There's got"*: Ibid.

262  *"for a"*: Ibid.

262  *"beautiful in"*: Ibid.

262  *"Look at"*: Ibid.

262  *"David, what"*: Ibid.

262  *"Of course"*: Ibid.

263  *"We never"*: Ibid.

263  *"That was"*: Ibid.

263  *"one of"*: Stevenson, "Geffen Records Sold to MCA."

263  *"When I"*: Geffen, Author Interview.

263  *"Are you"*: King.

264  *"couldn't slip"*: Greenberg.

264  *"viewed as"*: Ibid.
265  *"For me"*: Wexler and Ritz, *Rhythm and the Blues*.
265  *"The problem"*: Smith, Author Interview.
265  *"Under no"*: Wexler and Ritz, *Rhythm and the Blues*.
265  *"Man, you"*: Ibid.
265  *"One of"*: Horowitz, unidentified article, AE Archive.
265  *"When I"*: Wexler, Author Interview.
265  *"Ahmet sees"*: Trow, "Profiles."
265  *"He Meant"*: Ibid.
265  *"There was"*: Wexler, Author Interview.
266  *"Jerry called"*: Hochberg.
266  *"they didn't"*: Paul Wexler.

## SEVENTEEN: THE YEARS WITH ROSS

PAGE
268  *"At the"*: Trow, "Profiles."
268  *"an extremely"*: Ian Frazier, Author Interview.
268  *"style was"*: Hertzberg, "Swift."
268  *"was the"*: Ibid.
269  *"jazzy, telegraphic"*: Ibid.
269  *"as a cultural"*: Ibid.
269  *"George went"*: Ian Frazier, Author Interview.
269  *"blue suit"*: Graham and Greenfield, *Bill Graham Presents*.
269  *"looked like"*: Ibid.
269  *"I knew"*: Ibid.
269  *"Ahmet, may"*: Ibid.
269  *"I would"*: Ibid.
270  *"beat the shit"*: Wexler, Author Interview.
270  *"five or six"*: AE, Author Interview, 3/11/88.
270  *"took one"*: Ibid.
270  *"minor record"*: Trow, "Profiles."
270  *"a striking"*: Ibid.
270  *"Yah. They"*: Ibid.
271  *"But I"*: Ibid.
271  *"one at"*: Trow, "Profiles."
271  *"looked ravaged"*: Ibid.
271  *"Such a"*: Ibid.
271  *"a burlesque"*: Ibid.
271  *"A lot"*: Ibid.
272  *"What do"*: Greenberg.
272  *"There was"*: Ian Frazier, Author Interview.
272  *"and closed"*: Ibid.
272  *"Ahmet had"*: Kincaid.

273 *"I wouldn't"*: Ibid.
273 *"When it"*: Ibid.
273 *"First and"*: Ian Frazier, Author Interview.
274 *"He must"*: Trow, "Profiles."
274 *"We'll give"*: Ibid.
274 *"sound business"*: Ibid.
274 *"If you're"*: Ibid.
274 *"chintzy"*: Ibid.
274 *"You know"*: Ibid.
274 *"There was"*: Ibid.
274 *"You're responsible"*: King.
274 *"Don't be"*: Ibid.
274 *"And he didn't"*: Geffen, Author Interview.
275 *"Oh, David"*: Wenner, Author Interview.
275 *"who liked"*: Ibid.
275 *"wound up"*: Ibid.
275 *"had a huge"*: Ibid.
275 *"He said"*: Geffen, Author Interview.
275 *"simply get"*: Ibid.
275 *"a metropolis"*: Wolcott, "Splendor in the Grit."
275 *"the tourists"*: Ibid.
275 *"getting back"*: Ibid.
276 *"I like"*: New York magazine, title and author unknown, January 15, 1988.
276 *"Ahmet was"*: Horowitz, unidentified article, AE Archive.
276 *"started lighting"*: Wexler and Ritz, *Rhythm and the Blues.*
276 *"I used"*: Morris.
276 *"a ten-course"*: Wexler and Ritz, *Rhythm and the Blues.*
277 *"an apparently"*: Tobias, "The Middle-Aged Turk of the Pop Music Business."
277 *"favorite artist"*: Ibid.
277 *"Where do"*: Bennetts, "Devil in a Bespoke Suit."
277 *"And he"*: Hughes.
277 *"He was"*: Howar.
278 *"For Ahmet"*: Ibid.
278 *"He is"*: Wade and Picardie, *Music Man.*
278 *"Clever as"*: Horowitz, unidentified article, AE Archive.
278 *"Steve had"*: Emmett, Author Interview.
278 *"So I"*: Ibid.
279 *"no shares"*: Ibid.
279 *"at a"*: Ibid.
279 *"made a"*: Ibid.
279 *"Talk to"*: Ibid.
279 *"Ahmet wanted"*: Horowitz, unidentified article, AE Archive.
279 *"Steve gave"*: Emmett, Author Interview.

279  *"Ahmet would"*: Greenberg.
280  *"I said"*: Ibid.
280  *"a major"*: Ibid.
280  *"He said"*: Ibid.
280  *"called Steve"*: Ibid.
280  *"Is Ahmet"*: Ibid.
280  *"I said"*: Ibid.
281  *"the record"*: Ibid.
281  *"Sheldon Vogel"*: Ibid.
281  *"It would"*: Ibid.
281  *"It wasn't"*: Grubman.
282  *"a brilliant"*: Geffen, Author Interview.
282  *"If you"*: Ibid.
282  *"I'm not"*: Emmett, Author Interview.
282  *"This is"*: Grubman.
282  *"Now, do"*: Ibid.
282  *"In those"*: Ibid.
283  *"What Steve"*: Author Interview.
283  *"I want"*: Crowder and Dower, *Once in a Lifetime*.
284  *" for anybody"*: Vecsey, "New Mission for Kissinger."
284  *"a big"*: Emmett, Author Interview.
284  *"Steve told"*: Ibid.
285  *"completely hands-on"*: Newsham, *Once in a Lifetime*.
285  *"My God"*: Ibid.
285  *"anticorporate"*: Ibid.
286  *"with the"*: Ibid.
286  *"Ahmet brought"*: Ibid.
286  *"and the"*: Ibid.

## EIGHTEEN: THE ROCK AND ROLL HALL OF FAME

PAGE
287  *"I knew"*: Marsh.
287  *"real job"*: Poole, "Lush Life."
287  *"to play"*: Ibid.
287  *"There's a"*: Ibid.
287  *"set the"*: Ibid.
288  *"slipped badly"*: Horowitz, unidentified article, AE Archive.
288  *"I listen"*: Poole, "Lush Life."
288  *"Why should"*: Evans, *Ray Charles*.
289  *"Noreen"*: Ibid.
289  *"I was"*: Grubman.
289  *"Atlantic Records"*: Evans, *Ray Charles*.
289  *"You couldn't really"*: Wenner, Author Interview.

289 *"When we"*: Evans, *Ray Charles.*

290 *"We were"*: Ibid.

290 *"A courtesy"*: Ibid.

290 *"approached"*: Ibid.

290 *"He said"*: Ibid.

290 *"if the"*: Ibid.

291 *"We want"*: Ibid.

291 *"But you're an old man"*: Suzan Hochberg Evans, Author Interview.

291 *"really didn't"*: Evans, *Ray Charles.*

291 *"Ahmet was so"*: Wenner, Author Interview.

291 *"I've got it"*: Evans, *Ray Charles.*

292 *"a lot of"*: Ibid.

292 *"the forms"*: Dr. Lori, "Masters of Architecture."

292 *"large walkways"*: Ibid.

292 *"travel from"*: Ibid.

292 *"off-centered"*: en.wikipedia.org/wiki/I._M._Pei.

292 *"a sense"*: Ibid.

292 *"Ahmet was delighted"*: Evans, *Ray Charles.*

292 *"Ahmet was the"*: Wenner, Author Interview.

292 *"deputized"*: Ibid.

292 *"Okay, I'll be"*: Ibid.

292 *"In the record"*: Ibid.

293 *"nonplussed"*: Ibid.

293 *"had changed"*: Evans, *Ray Charles.*

293 *"Some years"*: Wenner, Author Interview.

293 *"mightily resisted"*: Ibid.

293 *"it was wrong"*: Ibid.

294 *"Ahmet wanted"*: Krasnow.

294 *"I get"*: Ibid.

294 *"And Ross"*: Ibid.

295 *"Ahmet was"*: Begle.

295 *"A big"*: Begle.

295 *"laid herself"*: Ruth Brown with Yule, *Miss Rhythm.*

295 *"entitled to more"*: Ibid.

296 *"I truly"*: Begle.

296 *"So I"*: Ibid.

296 *"I was"*: Ibid.

297 *"the smoking"*: Ibid.

297 *"We did"*: Ibid.

297 *"What they"*: Ibid.

297 *"these people"*: Ibid.

297 *"awful, terrible"*: Ibid.

297 *"I'd spoken"*: Poole, "Lush Life."

298 *"Ahmet loved"*: Begle.
298 *"We went"*: Ibid.
299 *"It was"*: Ibid.
299 *"The gala"*: Ibid.
299 *"Ahmet could"*: Marsh.
300 *"pushing to"*: Begle
300 *"a really"*: Ibid.
300 *"In a"*: Ibid.
300 *"We were"*: Marsh.
301 *"The guys"*: Ruth Brown with Yule, *Miss Rhythm.*
301 *"Ahmet was"*: Ibid.
301 *"to what"*: Ibid.
301 *"No, they"*: Ibid.
301 *"Jerry claimed"*: Burke.
301 *"I showed"*: King.
301 *"Ahmet had"*: Ibid.
302 *"failed stock"*: Ruth Brown with Yule, *Miss Rhythm.*
302 *"Is it"*: Ibid.
302 *"vicious and"*: Ibid.
302 *"There is"*: Landau.
302 *"Ahmet was"*: Jon Landau e-mail, 6/30/09.
302 *"I really"*: Ruth Brown with Yule, *Miss Rhythm.*
302 *"The only"*: Ibid.
302 *"Many tried"*: Ibid.
303 *"good-natured"*: Ibid.
303 *"It was"*: Wexler, Author Interview.
303 *"Ruth was"*: Begle.
303 *"a little"*: Ruth Brown with Yule, *Miss Rhythm.*
303 *"It's Ahmet"*: Jeske, "Ruth Brown."
303 *"I just"*: Ibid.
303 *"You know, Ruth"*: Ibid.
304 *"You know that"*: Collins, *RS* staff interview.
304 *"Ahmet was"*: Ibid.
304 *"On more"*: Ibid.
305 *"who did"*: Pond, "Atlantic's Birthday Bash."
305 *"I got"*: Lydon, *Ray Charles.*
305 *"Tell Ray"*: Ibid.
305 *"I won't"*: Ibid.
305 *"Don't"*: Ibid.
306 *"Ahmet had"*: Kissinger, *RS* staff interview.
306 *"It was"*: Gross, "The Real Sultan of Swing."
306 *"I tried"*: Kissinger, *RS* staff interview.
306 *"I didn't"*: Wade and Picardie, *Music Man.*

306 *"had no"*: Kissinger, Author Interview.
306 *"Henry, this"*: Poole, "Lush Life."
307 *"Henry Kissinger"*: Ibid.
307 *"Mr. Pickett"*: Ibid.
307 *"How do"*: Shelley Lazar e-mail, 7/27/10.
307 *"I luff"*: Ibid.
307 *"I'm a happy man"*: Pond, "Atlantic's Birthday Bash."
307 *"Dear Jerry"*: Document, AE Archive.
307 *"I declined"*: Wexler, Author Interview.
308 *"He went"*: Greenberg.

## NINETEEN: CLASH OF THE TITANS

PAGE
309 *"You get"*: AE, Columbia University Oral History Research Office, January 30, 2003, AE Archive.
309 *"all the"*: Moran.
309 *"let over"*: Ibid.
309 *"The music"*: Smith, Author Interview.
310 *"imperially"*: Cornyn with Scanlon, *Exploding*.
310 *"Ahmet stood"*: Ibid.
310 *"area of"*: Ibid.
310 *"a euphemism"*: Ibid.
310 *"Nesuhi put"*: Moran.
310 *"loose, undirected"*: Cornyn with Scanlon, *Exploding*.
310 *"With all"*: Ibid.
310 *"I don't"*: Ostin.
311 *"be fully"*: Letter from Nesuhi Ertegun to Jerry Wexler, 3/20/89.
311 *"some peace"*: Ibid.
311 *"Frankly"*: Ibid.
311 *"Elegant and"*: Anderson, "Nesuhi Ertegun."
311 *"mother's favorite"*: AE, Eulogy for Nesuhi Ertegun, www.youtube.com.
312 *"Nesuhi was"*: Ibid.
312 *"the most"*: Morris.
312 *"I'm the"*: Greenberg.
313 *"I learned"*: Morris.
313 *"amazing"*: Ibid.
313 *"Wow, what"*: Ibid.
313 *"Ahmet then"*: Ibid.
313 *"They had"*: Ibid.
313 *"I said"*: Ibid.
313 *"So help"*: Ibid.
314 *"Oh, here's"*: Ibid.
314 *"Doug and"*: Ibid.

314 *"There was"*: Ibid.

314 *"If you"*: Cornyn with Scanlon, *Exploding*.

314 *"Like all"*: Ibid.

314 *"genius for"*: Ibid.

314 *"Atlantic isn't"*: Ibid.

314 *"I felt"*: Ibid.

314 *"Ahmet worked"*: Moran.

315 *$600,000:* Official Memorandum, Time Warner, September 13, 1991, AE Archive.

316 *"Okay"*: Morris.

316 *"the junior"*: Ibid.

316 *"not at"*: Ibid.

316 *"Tell them"*: Ibid.

316 *"What do"*: Ibid.

316 *"Well"*: Ibid.

316 *"In the"*: Ibid.

316 *"George Bailey"*: Bruck, *Master of the Game*.

316 *"his full"*: Dannen, "Showdown at the Hit Factory."

316 *"appeared to"*: Ibid.

317 *"questioned it"*: Morris.

317 *"actually made"*: Horowitz.

317 *"the label heads"*: Ibid.

317 *"The Clash"*: Phillips and Hilburn, "Clash of the Titans."

317 *"The Showdown"*: Dannen, "Showdown at the Hit Factory."

317 *"an unprecedented"*: Phillips and Hilburn, "Clash of the Titans."

318 *"We have"*: Mica Ertegun.

318 *"was then"*: Ibid.

318 *"a reputation"*: Dannen, "Showdown at the Hit Factory."

319 *"blown way"*: Ibid.

319 *"merely speculation"*: Ibid.

319 *"without merit"*: Ibid.

319 *"chairman and CEO"*: Ibid.

319 *"Morgado had"*: Ibid.

319 *"This isn't"*: Phillips and Hilburn, "Clash of the Titans."

319 *"We're coming"*: Smith, Author Interview.

320 *"Us bandits"*: Ibid.

320 *"DOUG MORRIS"*: Cornyn with Scanlon, *Exploding*.

320 *"I was"*: Morris.

320 *"Of all"*: Dannen, "Showdown at the Hit Factory."

321 *"When Morgado"*: Holzman, Author Interview.

321 *"Doug wanted"*: Moran.

321 *"bumping into"*: Morris.

321 *"I talked"*: Ibid.

321 *"the most"*: Ibid.

## TWENTY: BAWITDABA IN BODRUM

PAGE

322 *"I'm not"*: AE, Columbia University Oral History Research Office, January 30, 2003, AE Archive.

322 *"Ahmet was"*: Hughes.

322 *"before the"*: Berman, Naples Museum of Art.

322 *"Ahmet had"*: Ibid.

323 *"When Ahmet"*: Mica Ertegun.

323 *"corporate in"*: Berman, Naples Museum of Art.

323 *"reflect his"*: Ibid.

323 *"If Ertegun"*: Ibid.

323 *"to assemble"*: Ibid.

323 *"he enjoyed"*: Ibid.

324 *"with strong"*: Ibid.

324 *"compatible"*: Ibid.

324 *"the hottest"*: "Turkey Trot," *Vanity Fair.*

325 *"bread, honey"*: Ibid.

325 *"one of"*: Ibid.

325 *"later in"*: Ibid.

325 *"After dinner"*: Ibid.

325 *"Ahmet was"*: Simon.

325 *"Cher loved"*: Geffen, Author Interview.

326 *"He was"*: Joseph.

326 *"His thing"*: Carvello.

326 *"the local mayor"*: Jenni Trent Hughes, Author Interview.

326 *"cleaner"*: Confidential Author Interview.

326 *"The only person"*: AE, Columbia University Oral History Research Office, November 13, 2002, AE Archive.

327 *"I don't think"*: Geffen, Author Interview.

327 *"Ahmet had"*: Mica Ertegun.

327 *"young Elvis"*: Flom.

327 *"that white"*: en.wikipedia.org/wiki/Kid_Rock.

328 *"When Twisted"*: Flom.

328 *"It was"*: Ibid.

328 *"I dragged"*: Ibid.

328 *"all sat"*: Ibid.

329 *"We did"*: Kid Rock.

329 *"proceeded to"*: en.wikipedia.org/wiki/Kid_Rock.

329 *"he fell"*: Ibid.

329 *"I'll never"*: Ibid.

330 *" 'I don't' "*: Ibid.

330 *"I had"*: Ibid.

330 *"I arrived"*: Mica Ertegun.

330 *"Ahmet sort"*: Landeau.

331 *"They wanted"*: Fine.
331 *"running back"*: Ibid.
331 *"It was"*: Ibid.
331 *"an incredible"*: Ibid.
331 *"There was"*: Ibid.
331 *"Kid was"*: Ibid.
332 *"Ya boys"*: Ibid.
332 *"Hot dogs"*: Ibid.
332 *"wiped out"*: Ibid.
332 *"another"*: Ibid.
332 *"I never"*: Kid Rock.
332 *"We're by"*: Ibid.
333 *"The villa"*: Simon.
333 *"Ahmet hung"*: Kid Rock.
333 *"Winston"*: Ibid.
333 *"Bette Midler"*: Ibid.
333 *"a convention of"*: Bennets, "Devil in a Bespoke Suit."
334 *"I've never been"*: Bette Midler, Author Interview.
334 *"It was"*: Ibid.
334 *"Ahmet always"*: Robinson, Author Interview, McCormick, "The Gold Lamé Dream of Bette Midler."
334 *"at this"*: Kid Rock.
334 *"and everybody"*: Ibid.
334 *"a pretty"*: Mica Ertegun.
334 *"to puncture"*: Ibid.
335 *"It's my"*: Marsh.
335 *"Ahmet wanted"*: Mica Ertegun.
335 *"brilliant and"*: Ibid.
335 *"Up to"*: AE, Columbia University Oral History Research Office, March 14, 2003, AE Archive.
335 *"I know"*: Ibid.
335 *"no withdrawal"*: Ibid.
335 *"He must"*: "The Man From Atlantic," *The Tatler*.
336 *"wisteria"*: Mica Ertegun.
336 *"It was"*: Ibid.
336 *"He said"*: Chantly.
336 *"To me"*: Kallman.
336 *"We're going"*: Ibid.
337 *"nappy haircut"*: Evangelista, "How Napster Made an Industry Change Its Tune."
337 *"It was"*: Curbishley.
337 *"The Titanic"*: Sisario, "Retailing Era Closes with Music Megastore."
337 *"What made"*: Geffen, Author Interview.
338 *"There's a"*: Sisario, "Retail Era Closes with Music Megastore."

338 *"The basic"*: Lyor Cohen, Author Interview.
338 *"Little Lansky"*: Rich Cohen, "Little Lansky and the Big Check."
339 *"because I"*: Lyor Cohen, Author Interview.
339 *"to right-size"*: Ibid.
339 *"many, many"*: Ibid.
339 *"no one"*: Ibid.
339 *"the previous"*: Ibid.
339 *"What Ahmet"*: Ibid.
339 *"made me"*: Ibid.
340 *"not getting"*: Flom.
340 *"When Edgar"*: Kallman.
340 *"It's a"*: AE, *The Charlie Rose Show*, 2/21/05, AE Archive.
341 *"made a"*: Bardach, "Interrogating Ahmet Ertegun."
341 *"absolutely crazed"*: Howar.
341 *"Mica said"*: Ibid.
341 *"Ray was"*: Wexler, Author Interview.
341 *"The best"*: Hackford, Author Interview.
341 *"Eventually"*: Ibid.
342 *"Ahmet Ertegun"*: 200 Motels.

## TWENTY-ONE: "THE ENCORE WAS HEAVEN"

PAGE
343 *"When Ahmet"*: Bennetts, "Devil in a Bespoke Suit."
343 *"He was"*: Joseph.
343 *"It was"*: Kid Rock.
343 *"in this"*: Ibid.
344 *"I've never"*: Ibid.
344 *"the last"*: Kaus.
344 *"Ahmet didn't"*: Ibid.
344 *"at that"*: Ibid.
345 *"Ahmet, we"*: Ibid.
345 *"They put"*: Ibid.
345 *"I knew"*: Mica Ertegun.
345 *"Ahmet was"*: Pigozzi.
345 *"We spent"*: Simon.
345 *"Ahmet came"*: Kaus.
346 *"Ahmet was"*: Kallman.
346 *"we were"*: Landeau.
346 *"I said"*: Ibid.
346 *"hometown wedding"*: Kid Rock.
346 *"I'm so"*: Ibid.
347 *"a well-done"*: Kallman.
347 *"sex, drugs"*: Ibid.

347  *"could get"*: Ibid.

347  *"a full-blown"*: Ibid.

347  *"Make sure"*: Ibid.

347  *" 'Listen' "*: Ibid.

347  *"The chosen"*: www.woodlawncemetery.org.

348  *"made this"*: Chantly.

348  *"talk about"*: Morris.

348  *"Well, we"*: Mica Ertegun.

348  *"Because we"*: Ibid.

348  *"Ahmet was"*: The Charlie Rose Show.

348  *"I was"*: Ibid.

349  *"Feel the"*: Richards, Author Interview.

349  *"He asked"*: Richards, *RS* staff interview.

349  *"Ahmet said"*: Mica Ertegun.

349  *"Ahmet was"*: Dunn.

349  *"Alan Dunn"*: Shelley Lazar e-mail, June 19, 2010.

350  *"When I"*: The Charlie Rose Show.

350  *"A few"*: Mica Ertegun.

350  *"The doctors"*: Wenner, Author Interview.

350  *"Mica came"*: Ibid.

350  *"We tried"*: Landeau.

351  *"The way"*: Ibid.

351  *"Dear Ahmet"*: Photo, AE Archive.

351  *"ghostly"*: Richards, Author Interview.

351  *"Ahmet, never"*: Photo, AE Archive.

351  *"beloved boss"*: Frances Chantly e-mail, 5/11/10.

351  *"was alone"*: Chantly, Author Interview.

351  *"a kind"*: Wenner, Author Interview.

351  *"I did"*: Bardach, "Interrogating Ahmet Ertegun."

352  *"It's suitable"*: Young, *RS* staff interview.

352  *"described some"*: Lyor Cohen, Author Interview.

352  *"What I"*: Ibid.

352  *"We stopped"*: Ibid.

353  *"The Islamic tradition"*: Wenner, Author Interview.

353  *"Muslims believe"*: Lyor Cohen, Author Interview.

353  *"It was the"*: Wenner, Author Interview.

353  *"The chauffeur missed"*: Mica Ertegun.

353  *"Mica was incredibly"*: Wenner, Author Interview.

354  *"When Ahmet"*: Landeau.

# Bibliography

## BOOKS

Akcam, Taner. *A Shameful Act.* New York: Metropolitan, 2006.

Balakian, Peter. *Black Dog of Fate.* New York: Basic Books, 1997.

——. *The Burning Tigris.* New York: HarperCollins, 2003.

Barlow, William. *Voice Over: The Making of Black Radio.* Philadelphia: Temple University Press, 1998.

Brendon, Piers. *The Decline and Fall of the British Empire, 1781–1997.* New York: Alfred A. Knopf, 2008.

Brown, Mick. *Tearing Down the Wall of Sound: The Rise and Fall of Phil Spector.* New York: Alfred A. Knopf, 2007.

Brown, Ruth, with Andrew Yule. *Miss Rhythm: The Autobiography of Ruth Brown, Rhythm & Blues Legend.* New York: Donald I. Fine, 1996.

Bruck, Connie. *Master of the Game: Steve Ross and the Creation of Time Warner.* New York: Simon & Schuster, 1994.

Charles, Ray, and David Ritz. *Brother Ray: Ray Charles' Own Story.* New York: Da Capo, 2004.

Clapton, Eric. *Clapton: The Autobiography.* New York: Broadway, 2007.

Clark, Dick, and Richard Robinson. *Rock, Roll and Remember.* New York: Popular Library, 1976.

Cohen, Rich. *Machers and Rockers.* New York: W. W. Norton, 2004.

Cohodas, Nadine. *Spinning Blues into Gold.* New York: St. Martin's, 2000.

Conant, Jennet. *The Irregulars.* New York: Simon & Schuster, 2008.

Cornyn, Stan, with Paul Scanlon. *Exploding.* New York: Rolling Stone Press/ HarperCollins, 2002.

Crosby, David, and Carl Gottlieb. *Long Time Gone: The Autobiography of David Crosby.* New York: Doubleday, 1998.

Dannen, Fredric. *Hit Men: Power Brokers and Fast Money Inside the Music Business.* New York: Times Books, 1990.

Darin, Dodd, and Maxine Paetro. *Dream Lovers: The Magnificent Shattered Lives of Bobby Darin and Sandra Dee*. New York: Warner, 1994.

Davis, Clive, with James Willwerth. *Clive: Inside the Record Business*. New York: William Morrow, 1975.

Davis, Stephen. *Hammer of the Gods: The Led Zeppelin Saga*. New York: William Morrow, 1985.

Deffaa, Chip. *Blue Rhythms: Six Lives in Rhythm and Blues*. Urbana: University of Illinois Press, 1996.

Ertegun, Ahmet. *"What'd I Say": The Atlantic Story*. New York: Welcome Rain, 2001.

Evans, Mike. *Ray Charles: The Birth of Soul*. London: Omnibus, 2005.

Faithfull, Marianne, with David Dalton. *Faithfull: An Autobiography*. New York: Little, Brown, 1994.

Federal Writers Project. *The WPA Guide to Washington, D.C.* New York: Pantheon, 1983.

Gelardi, Julia P. *Born to Rule: Five Reigning Consorts, Granddaughters of Queen Victoria*. New York: St. Martin's, 2005.

Gillett, Charlie. *Making Tracks: Atlantic Records and the Growth of a Multi-Billion-Dollar Industry*. New York: Dutton-Sunrise, 1974.

Goodman, Fred. *Fortune's Fool: Edgar Bronfman, Jr., Warner Music, and an Industry in Crisis*. New York: Simon & Schuster, 2010.

———. *The Mansion on the Hill: Dylan, Young, Geffen, Springsteen, and the Head-on Collision of Rock and Commerce*. New York: Times Books, 1997.

Graham, Bill, and Robert Greenfield. *Bill Graham Presents: My Life Inside Rock and Out*. New York: Doubleday, 1992.

Greenfield, Robert. *Exile on Main St.: A Season in Hell with the Rolling Stones*. New York: Da Capo, 2006.

———. *S.T.P.: A Journey Through America with the Rolling Stones*. New York: Saturday Review Press, 1974.

Holzman, Jac, and Gavan Daws. *Follow the Music: The Life and High Times of Elektra Records in the Great Years of American Pop Culture*. Santa Monica, Calif.: FirstMedia Books, 1998.

Jackson, John A. *American Bandstand*. New York: Oxford University Press, 1997.

———. *Big Beat Heat*. New York: Schirmer, 1991.

King, Tom. *The Operator: David Geffen Builds, Buys, and Sells the New Hollywood*. New York: Random House, 2000.

Kinross, Lord. *The Ottoman Centuries: The Rise and Fall of the Turkish Empire*. New York: William Morrow, 1977.

Kinzer, Stephen. *Crescent and Star: Turkey Between Two Worlds.* New York: Farrar, Straus & Giroux, 2001.

Lawrence, A. H. *Duke Ellington and His World.* London: Routledge, 2003.

Leiber, Jerry, and Mike Stoller, with David Ritz. *Hound Dog: The Leiber and Stoller Autobiography.* New York: Simon & Schuster, 2009.

Lewis, Grover. *Academy All the Way.* San Francisco: Straight Arrow, 1974.

Lydon, Michael. *Ray Charles: Man and Music.* New York: Riverhead, 1998.

Mango, Andrew. *Ataturk.* Woodstock, N.Y.: Overlook, 2000.

McDonough, Jimmy. *Shakey: Neil Young's Biography.* New York: Random House, 2002.

Metz, Helen Chapin, ed. *Turkey: A Country Study.* Latham, Md.: Federal Research Division, Library of Congress, 1996.

Mezzrow, Mezz, and Bernard Wolfe. *Really the Blues.* Garden City, N.Y.: Anchor, 1972.

Minassian, Edward. *Musa Dagh.* Nashville: Cold Tree, 2007.

Motion, Andrew. *The Lamberts: George, Constant, and Kit.* New York: Farrar, Straus & Giroux, 1986.

Newsham, Gavin. *Once in a Lifetime: The Incredible Story of the New York Cosmos.* New York: Grove, 2006.

Priore, Domenic. *Riot on Sunset Strip: Rock 'n' Roll's Last Stand in Hollywood.* London: Jawbone, 2007.

Salewicz, Chris. *Mick and Keith.* London: Orion, 2002.

Sander, Ellen. *Trips: Rock Life in the 60's.* New York: Charles Scribner's Sons, 1973.

Shaw, Stanford J., and Ezel Jural Shaw. *History of the Ottoman Empire and Modern Turkey.* Vol. 2. *Reform, Revolution, and Republic, 1808–1975.* London: Cambridge University Press, 1977.

Shepherd, John. *Continuum Encyclopedia of Popular Music of the World: Performance and Production,* Vol. 11. London: Continuum, 2003.

Shore, Michael, with Dick Clark. *The History of American Bandstand.* New York: Ballantine, 1985.

Smith, Joe, ed. by Mitchell Fink. *Off the Record: An Oral History of Popular Music.* New York: Warner, 1988.

Storey, John. *Cultural History and Popular Culture: An Introduction.* New Jersey: Prentice Hall, 2000.

Tosches, Nick. *Unsung Heroes of Rock 'n' Roll: The Birth of Rock in the Wild Years Before Elvis.* New York: Da Capo, 1999.

Wade, Dorothy, and Justine Picardie. *Music Man: Ahmet Ertegun, Atlantic Records, and the Triumph of Rock 'n' Roll.* New York: W. W. Norton, 1990.

Wexler, Jerry, and David Ritz. *Rhythm and the Blues: A Life in American Music.* New York: Alfred A. Knopf, 1993.

Wilentz, Sean. *Bob Dylan In America.* New York: Doubleday, 2010.

Wolfe, Tom. *The Kandy-Kolored Tangerine-Flake Streamline Baby.* New York: Farrar, Straus & Giroux, 1965.

Wyman, Bill. *Rolling with the Stones.* London: DK Adult, 2002.

Wyman, Bill, with Ray Coleman. *Stone Alone: The Story of a Rock 'n' Roll Band.* New York: Viking, 1990.

Zimmer, Dave, and Henry Diltz. *Crosby, Stills, & Nash: The Authorized Biography.* New York: St. Martin's, 1984.

## ARTICLES

Abramson, Herb. "Rock 'n' Roll—Seen in Perspective." *Cash Box*, July 28, 1956.

Altham, Keith. "Sonny and Cher Get Even." *New Musical Express*, October 22, 1965.

Anderson, Susan Heller. "Nesuhi Ertegun, a Top Record Producer, Dies at 71." *New York Times*, July 16, 1989.

Arsu, Sebnem. "Armenians and Turks Agree on Ties." *New York Times*, September 1, 2009.

"The Atlantic Records Story (1948–1958)." *Billboard*, January 13, 1958.

Bardach, A. J. "Interrogating Ahmet Ertegun." www.Slate.com, February 25, 2005.

Baumgold, Julie. "The Winning of Cher." *Esquire*, February 1975.

Bennetts, Leslie. "Devil in a Bespoke Suit." *Vanity Fair*, January 1998.

"The Bones Have Names." *Time*, December 22, 1961.

Bordowitz, Hank. "Ahmet Ertegun, Sage of Atlantic." *Spectrum*, Winter 1991–92.

"Calloway Assoc. Formed." *The Billboard*, July 30, 1949.

"Check the Angles!" *The Billboard*, December 20, 1947.

Cohen, Harvey G. "Dawn of the Jazz Age: Sir Duke Ellington's Adventures in Britain." *The Independent*, November 13, 2008.

Cohen, Rich. "Little Lansky and the Big Check." *Rolling Stone*, June 21, 2001.

Dannen, Fredric. "Showdown at the Hit Factory." *The New Yorker*, November 21, 1994.

"Disc Jockeys: The Big Payola." *Time*, June 8, 1959.

Egoyan, Atom. "Response to NPR Review of Movie *Ararat* by a Canadian of Armenian Descent." September 5, 2002.

Evangelista, Benny. "How Napster Made an Industry Change Its Tune." *San Francisco Chronicle*, June 12, 2009.

Frazier, George. "The Art of Wearing Clothes." *Esquire*, September 1960.

Frears, Timothy. " 'Gotham Satyricon': Chocolate Mousse at the End of the Road." *Rolling Stone*, August 31, 1972.

Gelb, Arthur. "Habitues of Meyer Davis Land Dance the Twist." *New York Times,* October 19, 1961.

Greenfield, Robert. "The Greatest Record Man of All Time." *Rolling Stone*, January 25, 2007.

Gross, Michael. "The Real Sultan of Swing." *Sunday Correspondent Magazine*, October 14, 1990.

Hertzberg, Hendrik. "Swift." *The New Yorker,* December 11, 2006.

Hiatt, Brian. "Because Atlantic Records Has Entered the 21st Century." *Rolling Stone*, April 29, 2010.

Holland, Bill. "I Met Everybody in the Business . . . All Sorts of Characters." *Billboard,* November 27, 2004.

Horowitz, Craig. Unidentified Article, source unknown, February 1985, AE Archive.

Jeske, Lee. "Ruth Brown." *Rolling Stone,* April 19, 1990.

Katz, Jamie. "Lester Young Turns 100." Smithsonian.com, August 25, 2009.

Kelton, Jim. " 'Farther on Up the Road.' " *Arkansas Times,* January 26, 2006.

Kornbluth, Jesse. "Ahmet Ertegun: The Pasha of Pop." Source Unknown, March 1984.

Kramer, Gary. "Atlantic and R&B Trend Developed Side by Side." *The Billboard*, January 13, 1958.

"Landon's Rock and Roll Legend." *Landon Magazine,* Winter 2006.

Lichtenstein, Grace. "Mick Jagger, 29, Gets a Put On, Turned On Sendoff." *New York Times*, July 28, 1972.

Lori, Dr. "Masters of Architecture: Wright and Pei." http://www.drloriv.com/lectures/rrhallfame.htm.

"Malcolm X Scores U.S. and Kennedy." *New York Times*, December 21, 1963.

"The Man from Atlantic." *The Tatler,* December 2002.

Marcus, Greil. "Atlantic Records 1947–54." *"What'd I Say."*

McCormick, Ed. "The Gold Lamé Dream of Bette Midler: 'Please Honey,' " *Rolling Stone,* February 15, 1973.

Newsham, Gavin. "When Pele and Cosmos Were Kings." *The Guardian,* June 10, 2005.

*New York,* January 15, 1988, title and author unknown.

Palmer, Robert. "Etta James: The Comeback of a Fifties Star." *Rolling Stone,* October 14, 1973.

Pareles, Jon. "A Tribute That Is Both Rocking and Soulful." *New York Times,* April 18, 2007.

Phillips, Chuck, and Robert Hilburn. "Clash of the Titans: Ten Days in the Music Wars." *Los Angeles Times,* November 14, 1994.

Pond, Steve. "Atlantic's Birthday Bash." *Rolling Stone,* June 30, 1988.

Poole, Eric. "Lush Life: The Hot and Cool World of the Erteguns." *New York* June 20, 1988.

Robinson, Lisa. "Boogie Nights: An Oral History of Disco." *Vanity Fair,* February 2010.

Ross, Alex. "Voice of the Century." *The New Yorker,* April 13, 2009.

Sassounian, Harut. "Ahmet Ertegun Knew What's Good for Turkey: Genocide Recognition." *California Courier,* December 2006.

Scaggs, Austin. "Remembering Ahmet." *Rolling Stone,* May 31, 2007.

Schmidt, Michael. "Cher's Fashion History: I Got Clothes Babe." *Details,* August 1989.

Scott, Gail. "Turkish Delight." *Washington Life,* May 1, 2007.

Sheffield, Rob. "How the Rolling Stones Got Their Bitch Back." *Rolling Stone,* June 25, 2009.

Sisario, Ben. "Retailing Era Closes with Music Megastore." *New York Times,* June 15, 2009.

Sobol, Louis. "New York Cavalcade." *New York Journal-American,* November 20, 1957.

Stevenson, Richard W. "Geffen Records Sold to MCA for Stock Worth $550 Million." *New York Times,* March 15, 1990.

Tobias, Andrew. "The Middle-Aged Turk of the Pop Music Business." *New York,* July 16, 1973.

Trow, George W. S., Jr. "Profiles—Eclectic, Reminiscent, Amused, Fickle, Perverse." *The New Yorker,* May 29, 1978, June 5, 1978.

"Turkey Trot." *Vanity Fair,* July 1986.

Vecsey, George. "New Mission for Kissinger." *New York Times,* March 31, 2009.

Veiga, Alex. "Death of the Record Label." Associated Press, *Monterey Herald,* October 16, 2007.

Wade, Dorothy. "The Godfather of Rock and Roll." *London Sunday Telegraph Magazine,* April 1994.

Weiner, Tim. "Ahmet Ertegun, Music Executive Who Championed Soul and Rock, Dies at 83." *New York Times,* December 15, 2006.

Wenner, Jann S. "Rolling Stone Interview with Phil Spector." *Rolling Stone,* November 1, 1969.

Werbin, Stu. "The Big M Is Taking Care of Business." *Rolling Stone,* October 12, 1972.

White, Adam. "Herb Abramson, Atlantic's 1st President, Dies at 82." *Billboard,* November 27, 1999.

Wolcott, James. "Splendor in the Grit." *Vanity Fair,* June 2009.

———. "A Twist in Time." *Vanity Fair,* November 2007.

The World of Soul: Documenting the Impact of Blues and R&B Upon Our Musical Culture." *Billboard,* June 24, 1967, Section II.

## AUTHOR INTERVIEWS

Barbara Abramson—6/18/07, 6/23/07, 6/28/07, 7/16/07, 10/29/08, 2/10/09, 8/15/09, 12/21/09

George Avakian—2/16/09

Eve Babitz—10/27/09

Peter Balakian—2/16/09

Howell Begle—6/16/09

Miriam (Abramson) Bienstock—5/8/07, 5/14/07, 12/12/08, 6/2/09, 5/25/10

Chris Blackwell—7/20/09

David Brendel—2/15/10

Gary Burden—2/6/10

Solomon Burke—11/13/09

Truman Capote—11/72

Phil Carson—6/15/09

Dorothy Carvello—6/3/09, 6/4/09

Frances Chantly—6/30/09

Marshall Chess—4/11/05, 12/23/06

Lyor Cohen—9/25/09

Bill Curbishley—6/10/09

Jimmy Douglass—5/14/09

Alan Dunn—1/4/07, 6/1/09

Jay Emmett—7/29/09

Ahmet Ertegun—11/72, 3/11/88

Belkis Ertegun—5/7/09

Mica Ertegun—4/11/09, 4/25/09, 4/28/09, 6/19/09, 8/26/09

Suzan Hochberg Evans—10/21/09

Jason Fine—12/22/06

Jason Flom—9/17/09

Ian Frazier—6/11/09

David Geffen—7/17/08, 6/10/09

Charlie Gillett—9/19/09

Selma Goksel—12/29/08

Harvey Goldsmith—7/10/09

Delia Gottlieb—5/24/2007

Jerry Greenberg—5/29/09

Allen Grubman—7/29/09

Taylor Hackford—11/7/09

M. Sukuru Hanioglu—4/6/09

Alan Hirschfield—6/1/09, 6/24/09

Jac Holzman—4/13/09

David Horowitz—9/15/09

Barbara Howar—1/7/09

Jenni Trent Hughes—6/29/09

Andy Johns—12/20/06

Susan Joseph—6/11/09

Craig Kallman—10/7/09

Bob Kaus—9/11/09

Jamaica Kincaid—10/27/09

Ben E. King—12/14/09

Henry Kissinger—12/2/09

Bob Krasnow—7/6/09

Jon Landau—6/25/09

Erith Landeau—8/27/09

Fran Lebowitz—5/21/09

Dave Marsh—6/17/09

Paul Marshall—4/2/09, 4/30/09, 7/21/09

Mario Medious—7/27/09

Ina Meibach—11/2/09

Bette Midler—9/30/09

Linda Moran—9/18/09

Doug Morris—5/19/09

Graham Nash—7/21/09

Mo Ostin—4/22/09

Jean Pigozzi—7/13/09

Jerry Pompili—2/11/05

Mac Rebennack (Dr. John)—7/18/08

Keith Richards—12/72, 7/30/09

Lisa Robinson—5/18/09

Kid Rock—6/4/09

Peter Rudge—11/18/05, 6/24/09

Ellen Sander—4/20/09

Alejandro Santo Domingo—5/18/09

Julio Mario Santo Domingo—5/18/09

Dr. Veronique Simon—6/23/09

Joe Smith—6/23/09

Seymour Stein—7/24/09

Robert Stigwood—5/28/09

Brian Stone—6/15/09, 6/16/09

Francine Wakschal—5/31/07

Jann Wenner—12/24/06, 12/26/06, 8/31/10

Jerry Wexler—5/25/07, 5/30/07, 6/19/07, 6/30/07, 8/18/07

Paul Wexler—4/10/09

Bill Wyman—12/72

## ROLLING STONE MAGAZINE INTERVIEWS

*(These interviews were conducted by the staff of* Rolling Stone
*magazine in conjunction with the tribute to Ahmet Ertegun*
*published in their January 25, 2007, issue.)*

Chris Blackwell

Solomon Burke

Phil Collins

Joel Dorn

David Geffen

Jimmy Iovine

Mick Jagger

Mick Jones

Craig Kallman

Henry Kissinger

David "Fathead" Newman

Robert Plant

Keith Richards

Stephen Stills

Mike Stoller

Neil Young

## OTHER SOURCES

Atlantic Records Discography and Session Index—www.jazzdisco.org/atlantic-records.

"A Brief History of Buffalo Springfield." Booklet, *Buffalo Springfield, Box Set*, Adapted from *Ghosts on the Road—Neil Young in Concert*, Pete Long, Old Homestead Press, 1996, revised 2000.

*The Charlie Rose Show,* Ahmet Ertegun Interview, 2/21/05, AE Archive.

Ertegun, Ahmet. Interviews by Steve Rowland and Leila Ertegun, November 13, 2002, January 23, 2003, January 30, 2003, March 14, 2003, April 22, 2003, May 1, 2003. Columbia University Oral History Research Office, Ahmet Ertegun Archive, Rock and Roll Hall of Fame and Museum.

Ertegun, Ahmet, Tribute Video.

Gottlieb, Bill. Photos. American Memory Digital Display Web site.

Naples Museum of Art, 1913–1954, New York: Hollis Taggart Galleries, 2008, Essay by Avis Berman—works originally from the Ahmet Ertegun Collection.

Reeves, Jim, blog quote. http://streetsyoucrossed.blogspot.com/2007/10/lets-swim-to-moon-uh-huh.html.

www.rocksbackpages.com.

Turda, Dr. Marius. "To End the Degeneration of a Nation: Debates on Eugenic Sterilization in Interwar Romania," http://www.pubmedcentral.nih.gov/.

Weeks, Todd Bryant. Interview. www.allaboutjazz.com.

Wexler, Jerry. Interview by Dave McFarland, associate professor at KKSU, and Ralph Titus, assistant manager of KKSU, October 29, 1986.

http://www.thewoodlawncemetery.org/africanamerican.html.

## FILMS

*Atlantic: Hip to the Tip.* Fragile Films. Directed by Uri Fruchtmann, 1993.

*Atlantic Records: The House That Ahmet Built.* Directed by Susan Steinberg, 2006.

*Beyond the Sea.* Lionsgate Entertainment. Written by Lewis Colick and Kevin Spacey; directed by Kevin Spacey, 2004.

*Cadillac Records.* Tristar Pictures. Written and directed by Darnell Martin, 2008.

*Once in a Lifetime: The Extraordinary Story of the New York Cosmos.* Written by John Dower and Mark Monroe; codirected by Paul Crowder and John Dower, 2006.

*Ray.* Universal Pictures. Written by James L. White; directed by Taylor Hackford, 2004.

*Tom Dowd and the Language of Music.* Directed by Mark Moorman, 2003.

*200 Motels.* Directed by Tony Palmer and Frank Zappa, 1971.

## FILMS

Brazil. *Hypoxia: The Fragile Thing.* Directed by Eli Productions, 1977.

Jumbo. Redshift: *The Nova ? The plasma Zone.* Directed by ... Seth Shostak, 2006

Beyond the Sea: *Titanic ... Exploration.* Written by Larry Childs and the ...
Spaceflight and the Sea in Space, 2004

Godzilla. Return: *Future ? written.* Written and directed by David McAlvie, 2008

Rock of Ages. *The Rocky Horror Show of the New York Comet.* Written by
John Carter and Mark Cooper, produced by Paul Crooks and John Dower,
2005

Against the Grain. *Written by France Law.* Written, directed by Richard Jackson,
2004

Tom Jones at the Anthony of Africa. Directed by Mark McGordon, 2003

200 Motels. Directed by Tony Palmer and Frank Zappa, 1971.

# Index